THE UNKNOWN LOVECRAFT

THE HIPPOCAMPUS PRESS LIBRARY OF CRITICISM

S. T. Joshi, *Primal Sources: Essays on H. P. Lovecraft* (2003)
S. T. Joshi, *The Evolution of the Weird Tale* (2004)
Robert W. Waugh, *The Monster in the Mirror: Looking for H. P. Lovecraft* (2006)
Scott Connors, ed., *The Freedom of Fantastic Things: Selected Criticism on
    Clark Ashton Smith* (2006)
Ben Szumskyj, ed., *Two-Gun Bob: A Centennial Study of Robert E. Howard* (2006)
S. T. Joshi and Rosemary Pardoe, ed.,*Warnings to the Curious: A Sheaf of
    Criticism on M. R. James* (2007)
S. T. Joshi, *Classics and Contemporaries* (2009)
Lovecraft Annual (2007–)
Dead Reckonings (2007–)

THE UNKNOWN LOVECRAFT

Kenneth W. Faig, Jr.

Hippocampus Press

New York

FOR CAROL

Published by Hippocampus Press
P.O. Box 641, New York, NY 10156.
http://www.hippocampuspress.com

Cover photograph of H. P. Lovecraft taken by Wilfred B. Talman, 1936.
Cover design by Barbara Briggs Silbert. Hippocampus Press logo
designed by Anastasia Damianakos.

First Edition
1 3 5 7 9 8 6 4 2

ISBN 978-0-9814888-7-5

Contents

Abbreviations

AB	*Accent on Barlow: A Commemorative Anthology*
AT	*The Ancient Track*
D	*Dagon*
DH	*The Dunwich Horror*
EG	R. H. Barlow, *Eyes of the God*
IO	*Ideas of Order in Experimental Poetry*
MM	*At the Mountains of Madness*
SL	*Selected Letters*
VH	*A View from a Hill*
WG	"The Wind That Is in the Grass" (R. H. Barlow)

THE UNKNOWN LOVECRAFT

Lovecraft: Artist or Poseur?

Howard Phillips Lovecraft has often been perceived as a bundle of contradictions. To cite only a few examples:

From the age of eight onward, he rejected orthodox religious belief in favor of a materialist philosophy which accepted only scientifically proven phenomena as truth. Yet, when he married Sonia H. Greene in 1924, he chose to be married in an Episcopalian ceremony at Manhattan's historic St. Paul's Chapel (1766).

He professed a deep love for the architecture, scenery, and traditions of his native New England and a particular admiration for Rhode Island pioneers like William Blackstone and Roger Williams who fled the Massachusetts Puritan oligarchy in the quest for personal freedom. Yet he regarded the representative form of government developed in the New England town meetings as impractical for a complex modern society and leaned toward technocratic totalitarian regimes. (He was an early enthusiast for Mussolini and Hitler.) He regarded the Puritan oligarchy not as founding fathers but as the final attempt to graft Old Testament morality onto Western civilization by governmental decree. The dark, harsh environment of seventeenth-century Massachusetts (closed by the Salem witch persecutions) provided ample inspiration for the stories set in his mythical "Arkham" country. History has supported Lovecraft's rejection of the Puritan fathers as paradigms of the American experience. Yet he also rejected the honor paid to the Revolutionary War patriots who led our country to independence and always maintained that they were traitors to King George and their own English heritage.

He was a generous man who fed and clothed himself on an extremely parsimonious budget so that he could regale his correspondents across the continent with extraordinary letters and closely inscribed postcards depicting the antiquarian places he visited all over the eastern half of the continent, from Quebec City to Key West. After rent, ink, paper, and postage were probably his largest expenses. In the depths of the Depression, when he himself was earning barely enough from writing and revision to get by, he donated food and clothing to his Providence friends Clifford and Muriel Eddy to help them support their young family. Yet, when his mother was admitted to Butler Hospital in 1919 after a long period of mental decline, he visited her only in warm weather, when they could meet outside on the hospital grounds. (In fairness both to Sarah Susan Lovecraft and her son, it should be noted that her institutionalization in 1919 was a blessing for both. Lovecraft's attempted enlistment in the Rhode Island National Guard in 1917 had helped push his

mother to the brink. He, in turn, barely escaped permanent damage from living for thirty years in close quarters with a mother whose attitude toward
him, he once acknowledged to his wife, had been "devastating.") Almost immediately upon his mother's institutionalization, Lovecraft's ill health disappeared and he began to travel and to make the personal acquaintances in
amateur journalism which led to his marriage to Sonia H. Greene in 1924.
Yet, during two years' residence in New York City in 1924–26, he neglected
his wife for the more congenial all-night meetings of his literary acquaintances. After he and his two surviving aunts, Lillian D. Clark and Annie E.
Gamwell, rejected Sonia's idea of supporting them in Providence with her
millinery business, he initiated divorce proceedings on the grounds of abandonment at his wife's urging in the spring of 1929. While he gave Sonia to
understand that she was a free woman, he revealed to his intimate friends
that he did not obtain a final decree because he lacked a "gentlemanly" reason to divorce his wife. Sonia remarried during Lovecraft's lifetime and lived
on until 1972; it bespeaks her generous nature that she recalled her husband
as an "adequately excellent lover" despite all she suffered.

During his youth he was a staunch conservative politically. He modelled
his views on those of his maternal grandfather Whipple V. Phillips, who had
been a successful entrepreneur and had built the handsome home on the
corner of Angell Street and Elmgrove Avenue on the East Side of Providence
where his grandson was born in 1890. Lovecraft's own economic decline and
the worldwide depression that began in 1929 converted him to a firm believer
in governmental restraints on capitalistic enterprise, and by 1936 he ridiculed
the fears of his younger aunt Mrs. Gamwell and her friends, who held out for
the presidential candidacy of Alfred M. Landon. Yet, as his biographer
L. Sprague de Camp has pointed out, he consistently undermined every opportunity that arose to better his own economic condition. Offered the editorship of a *Weird Tales*-type magazine by owner J. C. Henneberger in 1924,
Lovecraft declined, because acceptance would have forced him to leave the
Eastern seaboard for crass, modern Chicago. During the same period, he was
fruitlessly seeking a first salaried position as a married man in New York City.
Brown University professor Robert Kenny recalled that Lovecraft was reduced
to working as a ticket-taker at an all-night theatre to make ends meet after his
return to Providence. Yet, throughout his life, Lovecraft often chose to donate his literary labors (e.g., by participation in amateur journalism) or to accept poorly paid revision work from clients like popular psychology lecturer
David Van Bush. The early death of magician Harry Houdini in 1926 deprived him of his potentially most lucrative revision client.

As a materialist who saw all human history as an insignificant event in the
history of the universe, Lovecraft nevertheless insisted that the books, furniture, and type of people among whom he had grown up on the old East Side

of Providence were vital to his existence. He wrote to young correspondents that he had seriously considered suicide following the death of his grandfather and the loss of his birthplace in 1904 and suggested that he would do so again when and if economic circumstances forced him to part with the books and furnishings that were so vital to him. While he himself married a Jewess, he told his wife Sonia that he wanted Anglo-Saxon Protestants to predominate whenever they entertained in their home. (This home was in fact Sonia's own Brooklyn apartment.) Living in close proximity to Eastern European Jews and other immigrants who struggled to preserve their own cultures in America amidst economic difficulties made Lovecraft almost livid with rage for the loss of the familiar culture and faces of his youth. While he was willing to acknowledge Jewish friends like poet Samuel Loveman as intellectual equals, he maintained a lifelong prejudice against Jews in business and intellectual life. He considered blacks an inferior race unfit for assimilation and believed that the Southern segregationist model was the only feasible solution to black-white racial problems. While he acknowledged the social benefit of organized religion, he railed against Catholicism as an unfit faith for an Englishman when his protégé Frank Belknap Long, Jr., threatened to follow in the footsteps of G. K. Chesterton and Hilaire Belloc.

He eschewed all artificialities in prose style and urged his correspondents to write in the most direct and natural way. Yet he loved nothing better in his correspondence than to lapse into the mannerisms of his beloved eighteenth century.

He bemoaned the lack of intellectual friends in Providence and had only three or four social friends during the last decade of his life in Providence. Yet, when his younger aunt Mrs. Gamwell let it be known to him that Bertrand K. Hart, then literary editor of the *Providence Journal*, wished for a meeting, he avoided the occasion. After his mother's insidious combination of overprotection and rejection had so handicapped him that he could neither complete high school nor attend college, Lovecraft chose to live in isolation in Providence. After the death of his mother in 1921, his two surviving aunts were his only close companions. His father, a "pompous Englishman" who was a travelling salesman for Gorham & Company of Providence, had died of paresis in 1898 after five years of confinement at Butler Hospital, too early to influence his son, except perhaps to instill through his tragic end a hatred for Victorian sentimentality and hypocrisy. Lovecraft's closest boyhood friends were the brothers Chester and Harold Monroe, the sons of Providence politician Addison P. Munroe, who remembered Lovecraft's intellectual gifts as sadly wasted.

Surely, the greatest obstacle to Lovecraft's literary recognition—which has been slow in coming—has always been the specialized field of weird fiction and poetry in which he worked by necessity of artistic inclination. However, the second greatest barrier to Lovecraft's recognition has undoubtedly centered around the seriousness of his artistic endeavors, an issue intimately related to the apparent contradictions in his personality and beliefs. While his weird fiction was appreciated during his lifetime by the likes of Stephen Vincent Benét, Vincent Starrett, and Bertrand K. Hart, the posthumous "boom" in Lovecraftiana during the forties was harshly criticized by *New Yorker* literary critic Edmund Wilson, who maintained that Lovecraft's fiction ought to have remained in the pulp magazines where it was originally published. Wilson expressed especial irritation at the perceived attempt of Lovecraft's publishers to nourish a personality cult around the writer, a cult that he regarded as even more juvenile than the Baker Street Irregulars. (Late in his life Wilson sought out and read with interest the first volume of Lovecraft's *Selected Letters*, but he is not known to have recorded any revisions to his 1945 *New Yorker* evaluation of Lovecraft's work.) Even a writer as profoundly sympathetic to weird fiction as Vincent Starrett, who was so instrumental in introducing the weird fiction of Arthur Machen to American readers, was forced to conclude that Lovecraft was a literary poseur, albeit a gifted one. Winfield Townley Scott, the poet who succeeded Bertrand K. Hart as literary editor of the *Providence Journal*, concluded that Lovecraft was "his own most fantastic creation." While Lovecraft's work has gained a European reputation nearly equal to Poe's, many academic critics still complain that Lovecraft's proponents refuse to evaluate his work except as entertainment in a popular culture mode.

The real "balance" of the man and his work still eludes the best efforts of proponents and critics despite the incredible paper record left by the author, most of it preserved in the John Hay Library at Brown University. Lovecraft was likely not more idiosyncratic than the average man—he simply articulated his inconsistencies better than the average man in his incredibly frank and lucid correspondence. (Whether the movement to honor Lovecraft with a commemorative United States postage stamp can survive the social and racial views expressed in his correspondence is open to question.) While his wife Sonia H. Greene was probably correct in her estimation that his love for the arcane and otherworldly probably derived largely from his loneliness and isolation—indeed, the loneliness and rejection of the narrator of Lovecraft's famous story "The Outsider" is probably at least partially autobiographical—Lovecraft nevertheless experienced a genuine and unique aesthetic sense of wonder and expectancy in the scenes of his native city and of rural New England, a sense he struggled all his life to express on paper. "To me there is nothing more fraught with mystery & terror than a remote Massachusetts farmhouse against a lonely hill," he wrote to his correspondent Elizabeth Toldridge in 1931, and the manner in which he used his extensive knowledge of New England antiquities to ground his fiction in his native soil is absolutely unique in the field of weird literature. Works like "The Picture in the

House," "The Colour out of Space," and "The Dunwich Horror" will likely never be exceeded as evocations of the darkness of backwoods New England. Latter-day interpreters like filmmaker Stuart Gordon have mixed sex and sadism into their interpretations of Lovecraft, but few if any have been able to equal the artistic thrill of a first reading of one of Lovecraft's great New England stories. While Lovecraft's early poetry was in the eighteenth-century mode, he adopted a more naturalistic style in verse later in life. Some of the later poetry, in which he attempted to evoke the sense of wonder and expectancy he experienced in familiar surroundings bathed with late afternoon sunlight and contrasting shadow, was first published in the literary pages of the *Providence Journal* in 1929–30. Perhaps the final stanza of the sonnet cycle *Fungi from Yuggoth*, which he wrote during this period, best summarizes his fundamental artistic motivations:

> It moves me most when slanting sunbeams glow
> On old farm buildings set against a hill,
> And paint with life the shapes which linger still
> From centuries less a dream than this we know.
> In that strange light I feel I am not far
> From the fixt mass whose sides the ages are.

In the wake of the centennial observation of his birth, Lovecraft seems assured of a small niche in the fields of weird fiction and American regional literature. By now, his friends and associates have largely passed from among us; even the teenaged fans of the pulp magazines in which his fiction appeared are now men in their seventies. Within another century, the record that will survive for Lovecraft's appraisal will likely be completed, and it is likely to be a rich one indeed. We are, however, still a long way removed from the richness and depth of assessment that his work deserves. Only a person with a very deep and abiding love for Providence and New England could ever hope to approach a definitive assessment of the man and his work. Perhaps there is such a person among the readers of this brief article. I envy you your task.

Quae Amamus Tuemur:
Ancestors in Lovecraft's Life and Fiction

In Memory of Violet E. Kettelle
February 21, 1905–June 4, 2004

Quae Amamus Tuemur ("We Defend the Things We Love")
—Lovecraft Family Motto [Translation by S. T. Joshi]
(Lovecraft to Richard F. Searight, November 14, 1934 [Searight 36])

References to family history and genealogical investigations abound in H. P. Lovecraft's fiction. In "The Picture in the House" (1920), a traveler "in quest of certain genealogical data" (*DH* 117) is driven by rain into a weather-beaten farmhouse in the Miskatonic Valley, where he discovers an isolated, ancient resident who delights over the illustrations of a cannibal butcher shop in an old book and who apparently practices cannibalism in his own right. "The bare statistics of my ancestors I had always known, together with the fact that my first American forbear had come to the colonies under a strange cloud," relates the narrator (*DH* 27) in an even more famous story, "The Rats in the Walls" (1923). In "Facts concerning the Late Arthur Jermyn and His Family" (1920), Arthur Jermyn, "great-great-great grandson of Sir Wade Jermyn and an unknown wife" (*D* 82), makes a discovery concerning his ancestress that makes his life unbearable. In "The Lurking Fear" (1922), the narrator encounters a living brood of horror that more than justifies the evil reputation of the deserted Martense Mansion on Tempest Mountain. An emphasis on "ancestral taint" persisted in Lovecraft's fiction even after he moved from horror tales to science fiction. Relates the narrator of "The Shadow over Innsmouth" (*DH* 305): "I was celebrating my coming of age by a tour of New England—sightseeing, antiquarian and genealogical—and had planned to go directly from ancient Newburyport to Arkham, whence my mother's family was derived." Ultimately, he discovers he is linked by his own ancestry with the horrors he discovers in Innsmouth. Many more citations from Lovecraft's fiction bearing upon family history and genealogical investigations could be made.

Lovecraft was very interested in his own family history, and references to his ancestry abound in his correspondence. We are fortunate that S. T. Joshi's *An Index to the Selected Letters of H. P. Lovecraft* contains excellent coverage of Lovecraft's ancestry (Joshi-1:25); there are even citations for individual ances-

tral lines (Allgood, Carter, Casey, Hazard, Morris, Place, and Tyler) and citations for Lovecraft's discussions of the claimed Lovecraft family coat of arms
(under "heraldry," Joshi-1:21). In fact, most researchers of Lovecraft's ancestry, like the present writer, have begun their investigations with Lovecraft's
own accounts in *Selected Letters*. Lovecraft was never a serious genealogist in
his own right, but from adolescence onward he was interested in his own family history. As early as 1905, when he was fifteen, he borrowed and copied
charts of his paternal family history from his father's maternal aunt Sarah Allgood (1824–1908) (*SL* 2.179). As a young man, he came under the tutelage of
Dr. Franklin C. Clark (1847–1915), M.D., who had married his elder aunt
Lillian D. Phillips (1856–1932) in 1902. Dr. Clark was a writer on many local
and family history topics[1] and was the model for Dr. Elihu Whipple in Lovecraft's famous story "The Shunned House" (1924). James N. Arnold (1844–
1927), the editor of *Vital Record of Rhode Island*, acknowledged the help of Dr.
Clark in the introduction of his first volume: "To Dr. F. C. Clark of Providence, we have been indebted for many valuable suggestions which we have
carried out in this compilation" (Arnold-1:I:vii). Lovecraft's early accounts of
his family history are plain and simple. Writing to Maurice W. Moe on January 1, 1915, he stated:

> Turning to my maternal ancestors, from whom my middle name is de-
> rived, we find a typical line of New-England Yankees. The first Phillips of this
> branch came to Rhode Island from Lincolnshire in the latter part of the sev-
> enteenth century, and established himself in the western part of the colony,
> afterward the town of Foster. (*SL* 1.5)

Of his paternal ancestors, he recorded in the same letter (*SL* 1.5): "The Lovecrafts were a family of small country gentry in Devonshire." Writing to
Rheinhart Kleiner on November 16, 1916, he stated (*SL* 1.31): "My father was
the son of an Englishman who came from Devonshire to the state of New York
in 1847[2] on account of a loss of fortune . . . On my mother's side, I am a complete New-England Yankee, coming from Phillipses, Places & Rathbones . . ."

The references to family history in Lovecraft's fiction from the period 1920–
23—several of them cited above—show that the subject remained on his mind
during this period even if references to family history in surviving correspondence from this period are sparse. The death of Lovecraft's mother in May
1921 freed the author for a tremendous burst of activity in the amateur journalism hobby and for his 1921-24 romance with Sonia Greene (1883-1972),
culminating with his marriage in 1924. "The Shunned House," written after his
marriage in 1924, shows a lively continuing interest in local and family history.
But it was his return to Providence in 1926 that saw the second great awaken-
ing of Lovecraft's interest in family history. Lovecraft's correspondent Wilfred
B. Talman was an avid family historian and reawakened Lovecraft's interest in

the subject. *The Case of Charles Dexter Ward* (1927) shows Lovecraft's deep and abiding interest in the history of Providence and its families and even features a cameo appearance by Lovecraft's remote kinsman Commodore Abraham Whipple (1733–1819).[3] On the other hand, "The Silver Key" (1926) contains many echoes of Lovecraft's fascination with the scenery and families of Foster, Rhode Island, where Whipple Phillips's and Robie Place's forbears resided for several generations.[4] I suspect that Lovecraft's genealogical investigations during the twenty-year period 1905–24 were largely conducted using his own family papers and the resources of the Providence Public Library on Empire Street, which surely owned basic references like Arnold's *Vital Record*.[5] However, encouraged by Talman, Lovecraft after his return to Providence in 1926 learned to use the more ample genealogical resources at the library of the Rhode Island Historical Society. Talman was a specialist in Dutch ancestry, but also deeply interested in heraldry and royal and noble lineages.

Lovecraft's introduction to reference works like Burke's *Peerage and Baronetage* and *Landed Gentry* and to an ample library of published family histories at the Rhode Island Historical Society Library was a mixed blessing. On the one hand, we have an abundance of accounts of his family history in his letters from this period. On the other hand, like many other beginners in genealogy, Lovecraft succumbed to temptation to link his own family with the lines he found in these published reference works and family genealogies. Somewhat diffidently, he wrote to Frank Belknap Long on September 24, 1927:[6]

> When I get other genealogical tables from my aunt I shall look up all the arms at the library—if my enthusiasm for the subject lasts that long. It is an admirably gentlemanly pastime—but takes too much research, I fear, for a feeble and increasingly childish old man. As soon as my visitor is gone I shall probably lapse back into my customary state of incurious quiescence. But Talman is indefatigable in this species of quest. Whilst I was digging up my various hereditary shields and paraphernalia, he was beside me and exhuming about ten of his ancestral escutcheons to every one of mine. (*SL* 2.171)

However, Lovecraft's interest did persist—at least temporarily—as reflected in the extended genealogical discussion in his letter of "Thursday November 1927" to Long (*SL* 2.179–85). Therein, Lovecraft linked his Allgood and Morris lines directly with the lines he had found in Burke's *Landed Gentry* at the Rhode Island Historical Society. We also find this account of the contents of the Lovecraft charts he borrowed from great-aunt Sarah Allgood and copied:

> The line of *Lovecraft* is not traceable back to the Conquest, but it is pure Anglo-Saxon until a marriage in 1766, of which more anon. Lovecrafts, saith a note on the back of the main chart, are found in Devonshire near the Teign about 1450. God, the parvenus! ... In 1500, continues the note, a Thomas Lovecroft (note the spelling) bore as arms a chevron *or* between three towers *or* on

a field *vert*. But stop! This is not the *main* line, although it very soon marries into us. Not—don't tell Mack[7] this—till 1560 do we strike the *direct line* of your poor plebeian Grandpa Theobald! . . . In 1560 we find John Lovecroft (note spelling) bearing the present arms of a chevron *or* between three foxes' heads *or* on a field *vert*, with a tower *or* on a wreath as crest. Well—*John* begat *Richard* who begat *William* who begat *George* who begat *Joseph* who begat *John* who begat *Thomas* who begat *Joseph* who begat *George* who begat *Winfield* who begat your ancient Grandpa. The seat at Minster Hall was sold in 1823 by Thomas Lovecraft, poor devil, (he died in 1826) and in 1827 his second surviving son Joseph removed with his own wife and children to northern New York state. . . . In 1766 Thomas Lovecraft . . . espoused Letitia Edgecombe of the Cornwall line. . . . Thomas's son Joseph followed the favourite family pastime of cousin-marrying and espoused Mary Fulford, daughter of his mother's sister Ellen Edgecombe and of her husband the Reverend (again—the woods are full of 'em!) Francis Fulford, Vicar of Dunsford. (*SL* 2.182–83)

While Lovecraft did learn to use the then-standard books of a good genealogical library while working at the Rhode Island Historical Society, including difficult-to-use references like John Osborne Austin's *Genealogical Dictionary of Rhode Island* (*SL* 2.323), for the long run his uncritical adoption of lines that he found in published resources into his own ancestry did not enhance the credibility of the genealogical data he inherited from his great-aunt Sarah Allgood on the paternal side and from his aunts Lillian Clark and Annie Gamwell on the maternal side.[8] A case in point concerns Michael Phillips, 1668 freeman of Newport, R.I., the progenitor of Lovecraft's Phillips line on the North American continent. As early as February 3, 1924—less than a decade after writing the sober account of his maternal ancestry in his letter to Maurice W. Moe dated January 1, 1915—Lovecraft claimed descent from Rev. George Phillips (d. 1644) of Watertown, Mass., in a letter to Edwin Baird of *Weird Tales*:

> His [Lovecraft's] ancestry was that of unmixed English gentry . . . in a Yankeefied way maternally, his emigrant ancestor being the Reverend George Phillips, who came from Norfolk in 1630 with Mr. Winthrop's colony, buried his wife in Salem in the same year, and finally settled in Watertown, rearing a numerous posterity and earning from Cotton Mather the not unfulsome epitaph: "Hic Jacet GEORGIVS PHILLIPPI, Vir Incomparabilis, nisi SAMVELVM genuisset."[9] It is the cankering sorrow of my life, that I am descended through another son than the incomparable Samuel! (*SL* 1.296)

Writing to Maurice W. Moe on April 5, 1931, Lovecraft made specific his claim that Michael Phillips was a son of Rev. George Phillips of Watertown:

> The Phillips line here begins with the Rev. George Phillips, son of Christopher Phillips, Gent. of Rainham St. Martin's in Norfolk, who came on the *Arbella* in 1630 and settled in Watertown, Mass. From his eldest son Samuel comes the founder of the Exeter and Andover academies; but I come from his youngest

son Michael who emigrated to Newport in 1668. Michael's son (from two of whom I am descended) crossed the bay and settled in the Narragansett Country. . . . The younger children of Narragansett planters generally moved north to smaller farms in the exquisitely idyllick Scituate-Foster country—and there we find my Phillipses after 1750. (SL 3.363)

The fact is that Lovecraft must have at some point encountered Albert M. Phillips's *Phillips Genealogies* (1885)—perhaps his grandfather Whipple V. Phillips or another relative owned a copy[10] or he consulted the copy at the Rhode Island Historical Society. The principal line followed in this book was that of the Rev. George Phillips of Watertown, Mass. It is my belief that Lovecraft (or perhaps one of his relatives) simply determined to assert a claim that Michael Phillips of Newport, R.I., was a son of Rev. George Phillips, despite his absence from the list of George's children in *Phillips Genealogies* (Phillips 11). Family history in Lovecraft's day was only just beginning to be developed as an exacting discipline by Donald Lines Jacobus and his peers, and "adopting" illustrious lines from published genealogies was one of the favorite pastimes of genealogical hobbyists. To have failed to be descended from Rev. George Phillips at all—let alone to have failed to be descended from his illustrious son Rev. Samuel Phillips (1625–1696)—was apparently a "cankering sorrow" that the mature Lovecraft was unwilling to accept. Even after decades of development as an exacting discipline, family history still suffers from disinformation. It is still possible today to find unsubstantiated claims concerning the origin of Michael Phillips on the Internet.[11]

Beginning about twenty years ago, I decided to learn as much as I could about Lovecraft's ancestry and family background. My primary starting point was Lovecraft own accounts as published in *Selected Letters*, but there was other literature available as well. R. Alain Everts [Everts] had published a pioneering article on the Lovecraft family in 1975. Richard D. Squires [Squires] followed with a fuller account of the Lovecraft family in America from Necronomicon Press in 1995. Henry L. P. Beckwith [Beckwith-2] contributed an article on the Lovecraft family arms to my own *Moshassuck Review* in 1998. (He had written about the Lovecraft family arms earlier in *Lovecraft's Providence and Adjacent Parts* [Beckwith-1].) Steve Sneyd [Sneyd] followed in 1999 with an article pointing out for the first time in print the frequent occurrence of the Lovecraft family name in Broadhempston parish in Devon, England. In 1988 I published a very early account of some of my work entitled "Lovecraft's Ancestors" in *Crypt of Cthulhu* (Faig-1); this article included a Phillips line of ascent for Lovecraft—based upon information I found in the Henry Byron Phillips Collection at the California State Genealogical Society—that differed from Lovecraft's own account. I published a fuller account of Lovecraft's ancestry—including family charts—in *Moshassuck Review*[12] for May 1992 (Faig-2). There were various follow-up articles in the same periodical over the next five years. From my Moshassuck Press I published a genealogy, *Some of the Descendants of Asaph Phillips and Esther Whipple of Foster, Rhode Island* (Faig-4)—including some 210 descendants of this couple—in 1993, with a volume of corrections and additions in 1994. In 1996 I published "The Impact of the Fulford Will on Lovecraft's Claims of Fulford Ancestry" in *Moshassuck Review* (Faig-5). Finally, my collaborators Chris J. Docherty and A. Langley Searles and I published *Devonshire Ancestry of Howard Phillips Lovecraft* [DSF] in 2003. All these references may be consulted in the Lovecraft Collection at Brown University; my Phillips genealogy [Faig-4] and the Docherty-Searles-Faig monograph [DSF] are also available on microfilm at LDS Branch Libraries and may also be found in some genealogical libraries.

My objective in this article for the general reader is twofold. First, I wish to provide an account of some of the major progress that I and my collaborators have been able to make in this subject area. Second, I wish to provide some record of the fruits of part of that research in the ancestor table for Howard Phillips Lovecraft, which is appended to the article. An ancestor table is very easy even for a non-specialist to use. The individual whose ancestry is developed is listed as number 1 in the table—hence, Howard Phillips Lovecraft himself is number 1 in my table. The father of that individual—in this case Winfield Scott Lovecraft—is listed as number 2 and the mother—in this case Sarah Susan Phillips—as number 3. And so it goes. The parents of individual N in the ancestor table are individuals $2 \times N$ (father) and $2 \times N + 1$ (mother). Thus, the parents of Winfield Lovecraft (2) are George Lovecraft (4) and Helen Allgood (5), and the parents of Sarah Susan Phillips (3) are Whipple V. Phillips (6) and Robie A. Place (7). The parents of the subject of the ancestor table (individual 1) are individuals 2 and 3. The grandparents of the subject are individuals 4, 5, 6, 7. Each generation of ancestors begins with an individual numbered 2^N (N = 0 for subject of table, N = 1 for parents, N = 2 for grandparents, N = 3 for great-grandparents), etc., and contains 2^N persons numbered 2^N through $[2^{(N+1)}] - 1$. Among the 2^N individuals belonging to each generation, the first $2^{(N-1)}$ individuals are ancestors of the principal's father (paternal ancestors) and the second $2^{(N-1)}$ individuals are ancestors of the principal's mother (maternal ancestors). Where an individual is missing in the table, the compiler of the table lacks information. For example, Dorcas Ellis is individual 109 in the ancestor table. Ordinarily, her father would appear as individual 218 (2×109) and her mother as individual 219 ($2 \times 109 + 1$).[13] However, these individuals are both missing from the ancestor table. I did search for ancestors for Dorcas Ellis but failed to find any. Aside from any errors it may contain, the gaps in an ancestor table provide ample field for future researchers to make progress.

The other point to make is that there are many overlaps (persons bearing multiple numbers) in any ancestor table extended for a significant number of generations. In the case of Lovecraft's ancestor table, the earliest duplicate numbers are interjected when Roby Rathbun (13) married Jeremiah Phillips (12) and Sarah Rathbun (15) married Stephen Place Jr. (14)—the reason being that Roby Rathbun and Sarah Rathbun were full sisters having common parents John Rathbun (1750-1810) and Sarah Casey (1755-1813). Thus, John Rathbun bears numbers 26 *and* 30 in Lovecraft's ancestor table and Sarah Casey bears numbers 27 *and* 31 in the same table. Without duplication, Lovecraft would have sixteen 2xgreat grandparents numbered 16 through 31 in the ancestor table. However, he actually has only fourteen distinct 2xgreat grandparents because John Rathbun (26, 30) and Sarah Casey (27, 31) are both represented twice. The occurrence of a duplication like this produces further duplications in the remoter generations. The thing to remember is that duplications are inevitable. Without duplications, the laws of exponentiation tell us that the ancestors of any single individual would within a certain number of generations exceed the known historical human population of this planet. Generally speaking, for persons of English ancestry, it is not possible to get back of 1450-1500 unless the line touches nobility or royalty. While I believe that Lovecraft had at least one *bona fide* royal line of descent, I have not chosen to include it his ancestor table, but will discuss it separately below.

On the maternal side, with a limited number of exceptions, I believe the ancestor table as presented below is very similar to Lovecraft's own records. Lovecraft included lists of his most important maternal surnames in letters to James F. Morton dated January 26, 1933 (*SL* 4.143) and to Robert H. Barlow dated December 17, 1933 (*SL* 4.337). The two lists are essentially identical except that the surname "Millard" is printed as "Willard" in the letter to Morton. The only maternal surname listed by Lovecraft not included in the appended ancestor table is Dyer—and that omission occurs because, as explained below, I have rejected Mercy Dyer as Lovecraft's ancestor 55 (and 63) in favor of Mercy Babcock. The maternal surnames listed by Lovecraft along with the lowest corresponding individual number in the appended ancestor table are as follows: Phillips (3); Place (7); Rathbone[14] (13 & 15); Whipple (25); Casey (27, 31); Perkins (29); Matthewson (51); Dyer [Babcock], (55, 63); Wilcox (57); Godfrey (59); Millard (101); Fish (105, 121); Ellis (109, 125); Hazard (115); Safford (107, 117, 123); Clemence (205); Malavery (193, 207); Dodge (209, 241); Brownell (231); West (213, 233, 245); Newman (215, 235); Field (403, 409, 413); and Gater (849).

Of Lovecraft's paternal ancestry, as reported by him based on the charts he copied from his great-aunt Sarah Allgood in 1905, the most charitable thing that can be said is that it appears to be largely the invention of the creator. I presented this ancestry largely as described by Lovecraft himself in Faig-2. However, a more critical examination indicates that Lovecraft probably did not descend from any of the "great" lines claimed by his charts—Fulford,

Edgecombe, Chichester, Carew, Musgrave, and Reed are just a few of the lines probably not actually in Lovecraft's ancestry. Lovecraft's claimed Allgood and Morris ancestors beyond his great-grandparents William Allgood (10) and Rachel Morris (11) represent unsubstantiated links to the Allgood and Morris lines shown in Burke's *Landed Gentry*. I have included in the ancestor table only an Allgood "cadet" line from the LDS church records that appears to me to have some credibility. It may be noted that this line of ascent ends in Northumberland, the same home county claimed by the Allgoods of the *Landed Gentry*, but in any case Lovecraft is far removed from the main line. Lovecraft's Allgood and Morris ancestry certainly deserve to be the subjects of future genealogical research.

The greater tragedy is the claim of Fulford ancestry that was made by the anonymous Lovecraft family historian in the charts copied by Lovecraft in 1905. With the help of the Devon Record Office (DRO) and the Devon Family History Society (DFHS), my colleagues Chris J. Docherty, A. Langley Searles, and I found that the September 26, 1805, bride of the emigrant Joseph Lovecraft (8) in Woodland Parish (Devon) was not Mary Fulford, but Mary Full, spinster, of Denbury Parish (Devon), the daughter of Richard and Elizabeth (Brusey) Full of that parish (DSF 12–13). Of their eight children, seven were baptized in Woodland Parish: John Full, September 7, 1806; William, February 23, 1808; Joseph, November 22, 1810; Mary, February 12, 1813[15]; George, February 9, 1815; Aaron, November 6, 1817; and Eliza, August 11, 1820.[16] Joseph was a carpenter by profession and between 1813 and 1820 resided in the hamlet of Pulsford in Woodland Parish, no doubt serving the surrounding farms. By 1828, however, Joseph and his family had relocated to Bickington Parish, where he operated a worsted-spinning business. In this business, he was apparently unsuccessful, for my co-author Chris Docherty found record of bankruptcy proceedings in October 1831, some six months after Joseph and his family had departed for America (DSF 14–16). Readers interested in the lives of Joseph Lovecraft and his children in America should consult Squires.

The fact that Joseph and Mary Lovecraft named their first son John Full Lovecraft ought to have been a strong clue that the claim of Fulford ancestry was false. More definitive proof, however, came from the records of the Prerogative Court of Canterbury, where the last will and testament of Rev. Francis Fulford (1734–1772), vicar of Dunsford, was admitted to probate on December 24, 1772. Rev. Fulford was a bachelor and never married Ellen Edgecombe, as claimed by Lovecraft's charts. Mary (Full) Lovecraft's tombstone in Mt. Hope Cemetery in Rochester, N.Y., records her death, aged eighty-two years, on August 14, 1864; hence, she was born between August 15, 1781, and August 14, 1782, and could not have been the child of Rev. Francis Fulford (DSF 11–12, Faig-5:1–3).[17] The Allgood chart claimed for Lovecraft a direct paternal line of ascent as follows: Howard(4) Winfield(3) George(2) Joseph(1) Thomas (A) John(B) Joseph(C) George(D) William(E) Richard(F) John(G) (SL 2.182). With the help of DRO and DFHS, Chris Docherty, Langley Searles, and I were unable to verify any of the claimed Lovecraft ancestry beyond Joseph(1). Our sketch of Lovecraft's direct paternal line—as far as we were able to trace it back— appeared in DSF (42). The emigrant Joseph Lovecraft (1774–1850) appears to have been the son of John Lovecraft (1742–1780), a mariner, and his wife Mary Tapper, married January 2, 1768, in Woodland Parish (Devon).[18] In turn, it appears likely that John Lovecraft was the son of Joseph Lovecraft (1703–1781) and Mary Pitts, married December 22, 1728, in Woodland Parish (Devon). We believe that Joseph may be identified with the Joseph Lovecraft, baptized at Broadhempston Parish (Devon) on June 13, 1703. This Joseph Lovecraft was the son of Will Lovecraft and his wife George (Merifeild) Lovecraft, both weavers by trade, who had been married at Broadhempston on December 27, 1699. And that is as far back as Docherty, Searles, and I have been able to trace Lovecraft's direct paternal ancestors.

We have not been able to find any Thomas Lovecraft (1745–1826) who married Letitia Edgecombe in 1766 and was proprietor of Minster Hall near Newton Abbot.[19] Devon has no record of any estate called Minster Hall.[20] As for the claimed Lovecraft family arms, Henry L. P. Beckwith believes them to be a "punning coat" based on louve (French for wolf-bitch) and "croft" (meaning place, farm field, lair cave, den). The Norroy and Ulster King of Arms (R. P. Graham-Vivian) wrote Mr. Beckwith in 1969 that the arms "vert a chevron between three towers or" occur under different tinctures in the 1620 Visitation of Cornwall, but only as quartering to Elliott and to Boscawen. Graham-Vivian wrote to Mr. Beckwith: "The fact that it appears only as an ancient Quartering by the time of the Visitations means that whatever it was, and it was unnamed, was extinct in the male line, and even the name lost sight of."[21] The Lovecraft family arms were enrolled in the New England Historic Genealogical Society's roll of arms as number 645 and have been blazoned by Henry L. P. Beckwith (Beckwith-1, DSF). Most of the royal lines of descent published for H. P. Lovecraft depend upon dubiously claimed paternal ancestors. The line descending from King Edward III (d. 1377) in Roberts (136–38) depended upon the identification of Joseph Lovecraft's 1805 bride as Mary Fulford and has been removed from subsequent editions. However, the same reference work [Roberts (233–35)] contains a line of descent from King Edward I (d. 1307) that includes in the descent Ann Marbury (1591–1643), the wife of William Hutchinson. The reader need only glance at number 455 of the appended ancestor table to note that Ann (Marbury) Hutchinson was Lovecraft's ancestor through his Place line. So, Lovecraft does have at least one bona fide royal line of descent, albeit through his maternal rather than his paternal line.[22]

Curiously, I am not aware of any Lovecraft letter that claims Ann (Marbury) Hutchinson (who was killed by Indians in New York in 1643 after her exile from New England) as an ancestor. Lovecraft is known to have used John Osborne Austin's *The Genealogical Dictionary of Rhode Island* at the Rhode Island Historical Society (SL 2.323), and Austin's entry for Enoch Place (1631–1695) (Austin 154) clearly shows that his son Thomas married Hannah Cole, daughter of John and Susannah (Hutchinson) Cole. John Cole is number 226 and Susannah Hutchinson number 227 in the appended ancestor table. From Susannah Hutchinson (number 227) it is only one step to William Hutchinson (number 454) and Ann Marbury (number 455) in the ancestor table. But it is a discovery that Lovecraft apparently never made—unless he made the discovery but chose to remain silent. It is fortunate that Ann (Marbury) Hutchinson is a *bona fide* ancestor of H. P. Lovecraft, since another notable religious figure—the Quaker martyr Mary (Barrett) Dyer, hanged on Boston Common on June 1, 1660—whom he claimed as an ancestor (SL 3.359) is probably not in fact his ancestor.

Lovecraft enjoyed telling the story of his Casey ancestry. John Rathbun (1750–1810) of Exeter, R.I., had married Sarah Casey (1755–1813) in 1776. They had daughters Sarah (Sally) Rathbun (1787–1868) and Roby Rathbun (1797–1848), who both became great-grandmothers of H. P. Lovecraft by marrying, respectively, Stephen Place, Jr. (1783–1849) and Jeremiah Phillips (1800–1848).[23] Lovecraft's great-great-grandmother Sarah (Casey) Rathbun was the daughter of John Casey (1723–1794)[24] and his wife Mercy. Mercy is numbers 55 and 63 in the ancestor table and by her surname hangs the entire disputed question of whether the Quaker martyr Mary (Barrett) Dyer was Lovecraft's ancestor or not. In April 1893, Gen. Thomas Lincoln Casey published an article "Early Families of Casey in Rhode Island," in the *Magazine of New England History*, which identified the wife of John Casey as Mercy Dyer (Casey 27). Family historians have struggled for decades over the ancestry of this Mercy Dyer. The late Gladys Palmer of Hope Valley R.I. gave these Williams and Dyer family lines of descent to Violet E. Kettelle:

WILLIAMS
Roger(1) Williams (c. 1603–1683), married Mary Barnard;
Joseph(2) Williams, married 1669 Lydia(2) Olney (of Thomas(1) and Mary Small);
Joseph(3) Williams (b. 1673), married Lydia Herenden;
Mercy(4) Williams, married 1720 William(4) Randall [William(3-1)];
Mercy(5) Randall m. William(4) Dyer;
Mercy(6) Dyer m. 1744 John Casey (1723–1794), son of Samuel and Dorcas (Ellis) Casey.

DYER

William(1) Dyer (b. 1609), married Mary Barrett, executed June 1, 1660, Boston Common;

Charles(2) Dyer (1650–1709) of Newport, R.I., married Mary Lippitt;

Charles(3) Dyer (d. 1727) married 1709 Mary Lapham (1686–1710+);

William(4) Dyer, married Mercy Randall;

Mercy(5) Dyer, married 1744 John Casey.

If these lines could be trusted, H. P. Lovecraft could claim descent not only from the Quaker martyr Mary (Barrett) Dyer but also from the founder of Providence, Roger Williams, and many other illustrious early Rhode Island families including Randall, Olney, Herenden, Lapham, Lippitt, Small, Mann, and White.[25] There are, however, serious problems with the identification of the Mercy Dyer of these two lines of descent as the wife of John Casey. The most serious is posed by the Richmond, R.I., will of one Elizabeth Dye as abstracted by Alden G. Beaman (RIGR 5:335):

> DYE, ELIZABETH, of Richmond. Will dated 2 Sept. 1764, proved 15 Sept. 1783, pgs. 346-348 [Richmond R.I. Probate Court V. 2]. Mentions: Sons Elisha Babcock & Jonathan Babcock. Daughters Mercy Casey & Elizabeth Babcock. Grandson Benjamin Babcock son of Elisha. Ganddaughter Mercy Babcock. 3 granddaughters Mercy Casey, Sarah Casey, & Mary Casey. Cozen [cousin] Elizabeth Phillips. Cozen Elizabeth Dye, Daniel Dye's daughter.

In recent years, Mabry Benson has done new research on John Casey's wife Mercy, and her conclusion is that Mercy's maiden name was Babcock, not Dyer or Dye. Her mother Elizabeth married first Jonathan Babcock of Westerly, R.I., and second (in 1752 in Charlestown, R.I.) Richard Dye. Her second husband Richard Dye died of smallpox in 1760. Since Mercy's mother Elizabeth bore the surname Dye when she died in Richmond, R.I., in 1783, Gen. Thomas Lincoln Casey apparently concluded erroneously that her daughter Mercy Casey had been born a Dye or Dyer.[26] I have included the Babcock ancestry provided by Ms. Benson for the wife of John Casey in the appended ancestor table; I have rejected the Dyer ancestry as provided by Gladys Palmer.

One would think that of all Lovecraft's maternal ancestry, the direct Phillips family line of ascent from his mother Sarah Susan Phillips (1857-1921) would be the simplest of all. In actuality, the Phillips line presents some of the most challenging problems the Lovecraft family history researcher is likely to encounter. We have already discussed Lovecraft's claim that Michael (1) Phillips, 1668 freeman of Newport, R.I., was a youngest son of Rev. George Phillips (d. 1644) of Watertown, Mass., and can probably safely set that claim aside. I discussed Lovecraft's views concerning his Phillips ancestry at some length in the chapter "Howard Phillips Lovecraft's Beliefs Concerning His

Phillips Ancestry" in Faig-4 (241–59) and so will include only a capsule discussion of the most important facts here. Lovecraft gave his Phillips line as:
Howard(9) Sarah Susan (8) Whipple(7) Jeremiah(6) Asaph(5) James (4-3) Mi-
chael(2) George(1) and there is no dispute up through Asaph(5) (number 24
in the ancestor table). There are several immediate problems with Lovecraft's
version of his Phillips line. First of all, Austin (152) shows no son James(3) for
Michael(1) Phillips's son James(2). James(2) Phillips died in Smithfield, R.I.,
on December 12, 1746, aged about eighty. Second, Cooley (132)[27] appears to
suggest that Whipple's male line of ascent is Jeremiah (father), Asaph (grandfather), James (great-grandfather), and Jeremiah (great-great-grandfather):
"Jeremiah Phillips settled in the Town of Foster, then a part of Scituate,
about 1750." In support of the thesis that a Jeremiah Phillips belongs in the
direct Phillips line of ascent, we have the recurrence of the name in the family: not only did Asaph Phillips (24) name his youngest son Jeremiah (12), but
the name also recurs in succeeding generations (e.g., Jeremiah Wheaton Phillips [1863–1902] [son of James W. Phillips (1830–1901)] and Jeremiah Benoni Phillips (1828–1907) [son of Benoni Phillips (1788–1850)]) (Faig-4,
127–30 and 41–43).

In the late 1980s and early 1990s I had the opportunity to consult the
Henry Byron Phillips Collection at the California State Genealogical Society,
first by correspondence and then subsequently by visit. Henry Byron Phillips
(1850–1924) was himself of the line of Michael(1) Phillips of Newport, R.I.,
but had as his goal tracing all the Phillips lines that came to America.[28] One
of Mr. Phillips's correspondents was Pardon Tillinghast Howard (1839–1925)
of Windsor, Conn.,[29] whose grandfather Daniel Howard (1787–1879) of Foster, R.I., had married Asaph Phillips's eldest daughter Betsey Phillips (1788–
1849). In any case, Pardon T. Howard's version of Lovecraft's Phillips ancestry was Howard(9) Sarah Susan(8) Whipple(7) Jeremiah(6) Asaph(5) James(4)
Jeremiah(3) Joseph(2) Michael(1) and that is the version of the direct Phillips
line that I have used in the ancestor table.

Very little is known of Michael(1) Phillips except that he became a freeman of Newport, R.I., on October 28, 1668, and was deceased by August 13,
1676. He and his wife Barbara —— (m.(2) Edward Inman) had sons John,
William, James, Richard, and Joseph and a daughter Alice (Austin 152, Sowa
269). Writing to James N. Arnold in 1900, Henry Byron Phillips stated:

> There is a tradition in my family that two brothers came over & that they
> were Welch[30] [sic], but no names or dates. I have a theory that they might have
> been of Sir Fernando Georges [sic] colony & came to Smithfield from the
> North. Sir Fernando was a native of Ashton Phillips, Somersetshire, Eng., in
> that part of England [where] there were PHILLIPS in plenty. Another straw I
> find is that I find the names Fernando Georges [sic] as a given name in a
> branch of my family about 100 years back. I have heard an aunt talk of her

uncle Georges or Gorges[31] and she tells me his full name was as stated, but did not know how or why he bore it. The Smithfield Phillips seems to be the next for me to crack now.

Next up in Pardon T. Howard's account of Lovecraft's direct Phillips line is Joseph(2) Phillips, born perhaps 1669 in Newport, R.I., died September 3, 1719, in Providence, R.I. He married Elizabeth Malavery and had by her, among other children, a son Jeremiah(3) Phillips, born perhaps 1695 in Providence, R.I. Jeremiah(3) Phillips died January 23, 1779, in Glocester, R.I. He appears to have farmed in Smithfield, R.I., until he acquired property in Glocester, R.I., in the 1750s (freeman, 1759). Jeremiah(3)'s wife was his first cousin —— (3) Phillips [James(2) Michael(1)].[32] Jeremiah(3) Phillips was often called "Great Jeremiah" Phillips to distinguish him from his son Jeremiah(4) Phillips.[33] The most shadowy figure in the entire paternal line of descent is undoubtedly Jeremiah(3) Phillips's son James(4) Phillips. Born about 1740, probably in Smithfield, R.I., James(4) Phillips married about 1760 his second cousin Anna(4) Phillips [John(3) Richard(2) Michael(1)].[34] James and Anna Phillips had a son Asaph, born July 4, 1764, and daughters Alice, Nancy, and Freelove. In 1767, Jeremiah(3) Phillips deeded land in Glocester, R.I., to his son James, but in the following year, James deeded this land to his brother William(4) Phillips. James and his family may have removed to Scituate, R.I. (the part of the town that later became Foster) about this time. In 1794 James and Anne Phillips deeded eight acres in Foster to Daniel Howard, Sr. I do not know the whereabouts of James and his wife in the 1800 U.S. census. H. P. Lovecraft (SL 3.25) gives 1807 as the year of James(4) Phillips's death. It seems to me that the shadowy figure of James(4) Phillips is the crucial link between Michael(1) Phillips and Asaph(5) Phillips. Perhaps future genealogical research will reveal more about him.

Michael(1) Phillips was of Newport, R.I., and Lovecraft had a persistent belief that some of his Phillips ancestors had remained in southern Rhode Island. After viewing the grave of Asaph Phillips in the Cole-Phillips cemetery in Foster in 1929, he told correspondents that he intended to seek the graves of Asaph's father James (d. 1807) and grandfather James (d. 1746) far to the south of Foster (SL 3.16, 25).[35] He even expressed the intention to seek the grave of Michael(1) Phillips in Newport, although he was probably two hundred years too late to find what was probably the simple burial place of Michael(1) Phillips.[36] Some families bearing the Phillips surname did remain in the South Country in the eighteenth century. Volume 4 of Arnold's *Vital Record of Rhode Island*, devoted to Newport County (Arnold-1:IV:Middletown Births & Deaths 37) the following two Phillips names:

PHILLIPS, James, of James and Hope, born November 14, 1727
PHILLIPS, James, of James and Alice, born August 14, 1753

Fiske (221–33) identifies both of these James Phillipses as descendants of William(2) [Michael(1)] Phillips. The first is a son of James(3) [William(2) Michael(1)] Phillips; the second is the son of the first and his wife Alice Brown. According to Fiske, James(3) Phillips was born about 1695, probably in Newport, and died between December 28, 1754, and July 5, 1755 in Middletown. He was admitted as a freeman of Newport on May 1, 1722, and lived in that portion of the town set off as Middletown in 1746. His wife was Hope Fish, daughter of John and Joan[na] Fish. Yet another Phillips line in the south country was that of Samuel Phillips (1656–1736) of Kingstown, R.I.[37] Samuel Phillips and his family were reputed to have originated in Exeter, England, and have no known connection with Michael(1) Phillips of Newport. For many years the descendants of Samuel Phillips of Kingstown occupied the house known as "Mowbra" or "Phillips Castle" in North Kingstown (demolished 1960). Some writers, including Norman M. Isham and Albert F. Brown,[38] even associated this house, dated to 1695, with Michael(1) Phillips of Newport, even though Michael(1) Phillips had been deceased for nearly twenty years by the time of its construction. So it is not surprising that Lovecraft retained a belief that some of his Phillips ancestors after Michael(1) Phillips had lived in southern Rhode Island. If Elizabeth (——) Dye (nos. 111 and 127 in the ancestor table) was actually a Phillips by birth, there may be something more to be said for the belief retained by Lovecraft.

In trying to write a paper on Lovecraft's ancestry for the general reader, I have struggled to impart a generally accurate picture and to touch upon open research questions without becoming lost amidst a welter of details. My colleagues and I have certainly caught the Lovecraft family genealogist—be it great-aunt Sarah Allgood or some other person—in a number of apparently deliberate falsehoods, but we realize at the same time that what Lovecraft believed is important, whether it is true or not. Nevertheless, we take much greater pride in Will Lovecraft and George Merifeild, weavers, married in Broadhempston Parish (Devon) in December 1699, than we do in highly questionable noble or royal descents.[39] If Lovecraft has a *bona fide* royal descent—and my colleagues and I believe he does—it derives from his ancestor Ann (Marbury) Hutchinson (1591–1643). In Ann Hutchinson Lovecraft and Presidents George H. W. and George W. Bush share a most noble ancestor whom anyone could be proud of. Lovecraft is also related to the poet John Dryden in this line. If research has deprived Lovecraft of his claimed descent from Mary Dyer and possible descent from Roger Williams as well, it confirms his descent from two Brown family pioneers in Rhode Island: Chad Browne of Providence, who succeeded Roger Williams as minister of the First Baptist Church and was the progenitor of the illustrious Brown merchant family, and Nicholas Brown of Portsmouth, R.I.

Another maternal surname that would probably have pleased Lovecraft is that of Hawthorne, which we find in his Millard line (see individuals 407 and 814 in the ancestor table). In fact, Lovecraft was the fifth cousin (at four removes) of Nathaniel Hawthorne (1804-1864) through their common ancestor William Hathorne (c. 1576-1650) in Binfield Berks, England (number 1628 in the ancestor table):

> Nathaniel Hawthorne (1804-1864) Salem, Mass.
> Capt. Nathaniel Hawthorne (1775/6-1808) Salem, Mass.
> Daniel Hawthorne (1731-1796) Salem, Mass.
> Capt. Joseph Hawthorne (1692-1762) Salem, Mass.
> Justice John Hawthorne (1641-1717) Salem, Mass.
> Maj. William Hawthorne (1606/7-1681) Salem, Mass.
> William Hathorne (c. 1576-1650) Binfield Berks, England (no. 1628)
> John Hawthorne (1621-1677) Salem, Mass., Lynn, Mass. (no. 814)
> Priscilla Hawthorne (b. 1649) (no. 407) m. Jonathan Shores (no. 406)
> Phoebe Shores (1674-1715) (no. 203) m. Nehemiah Millard (no. 202)
> Esther Millard (d. 1777+) (no. 101) m. Benjamin Whipple (no. 100)
> Benedict Whipple (1739-1819) (no. 50) m. Elizabeth Mathewson (no. 51)
> Esther Whipple (1767-1842) (no. 25) m. Asaph Phillips (no. 24)
> Jeremiah Phillips (1800-1848) (no. 12) m. Roby Rathbun (no. 13)
> Whipple V. Phillips (1833-1904) (no. 6) m. Roby A. Place (no. 7)
> Sarah S. Phillips (1857-1921) (no. 3) m. W. S. Lovecraft (no. 2)
> Howard P. Lovecraft (1890-1937) (no. 1)

A revolution in genealogy is transpiring as records migrate to more accessible digital format. I am convinced that new discoveries await researchers who may become interested in the ancestry of H. P. Lovecraft in the future. There are undoubtedly errors in my ancestor table that need to be corrected. There are certainly all too many gaps that need to be filled. I do not offer the ancestor table as a fully documented ancestry but only as a reasonable starting point that hopefully avoids some of the worst pitfalls while pointing the way to future discoveries. I am certainly aware that many readers may find this account of the highlights and lowlights of Lovecraft's ancestry wearying. I can only plead that he himself found it of significant interest from two perspectives. One perspective is the ordinary pride which many persons from long-established New England families take in their ancestry. Lovecraft was thrilled to find that he had friends—James F. Morton and Robert H. Barlow—with whom he shared common ancestors, Morton through his Perkins line and Barlow through his Rathbun line.[40] He undoubtedly discussed genealogical matters with his aunts and family friends as well. From time to time he made additions and amendments to his charts—for example, the Gater ancestry derived from the Dawes-

Gates genealogy.[41] He searched for intellectuals among his ancestors, and rejoiced over his late discovery of the English astronomer John Field (c. 1525-1587) in his Field line.[42] He was less enthusiastic about another dubious ancestor—the Quaker martyr Mary Dyer—and I am not sure how he would have felt about his *bona fide* ancestor Ann (Marbury) Hutchinson. Where he sought for intellectuals, he generally found sturdy yeomen and their wives, earning a hard living from the soil. His spurious English ancestry may have been ridden with clergymen, but his real English ancestry included carpenters, mariners, farmers, weavers. Lovecraft's ancestors prove that ordinary seed may produce from time to time an extraordinary flowering.

However, Lovecraft's preoccupation with family history also filters into his work. No one without a background in these endeavors could have written a story like "The Shunned House," with its elaborate history of a horror enduring generation after generation. The usual motivation in constructing an ancestor table is pride in one's ancestors—the numerous tribe of successful progenitors whose genes have collectively resulted in the individual who is the principal of the table. We may even try to imagine their joy in the making and in the rearing of their numerous offspring. But there is certainly a darker perspective from which one may view an ancestor table—that of the principal surrounded by legions of the dead, increasing twofold with each succeeding generation. The haunting of Roderick Usher in Poe's famous tale, according to Lovecraft, was not only by the ancestors entombed in the vaults below (including Usher's sister Madeline), but by the entire melancholy house itself—the idea of one's collective ancestry pressing down upon the feeble spark of life. In the succeeding generations there are surely hidden secrets we would be better off not knowing. Perhaps, just as in Lovecraft's story "The Tomb," trying to commune too closely with one's ancestors can be dangerous for the living. As Charles Dexter Ward discovers, they might not all have been as exemplary as we would like to imagine. The early New England records are full of dark moments—not just the everyday harshness of warnings-out and indentures but deeper hatreds and rivalries that resulted in the witchcraft executions in Danvers, Mass., in 1692. Of Lovecraft's ancestors as of our own ancestors, the truest thing we can say is that they were likely as human as we. Of course we take pride in illustrious ancestors like GEORGIVS and SAMVELVS, but the old Latin tombstone inscription warns us more generally:

QVISQVIS ERIS QVI TRANSIERIS STA PERLEGE PLORA
SVM QVOD ERIS FVERAM QVOD ES PRO ME PRECOR ORA[43]

We may be sure that busy yeomen like Asaph Phillips of Foster and yeomen's wives like Mercy Casey of Kingstown would have little use for shades from the future in quest for genealogical information. Much as we might wish to interview Barbara Inman of Providence in 1706 concerning her parentage and her first husband Michael Phillips, we are forever denied the opportunity. Most individuals like Lovecraft will adopt a balanced view of their ancestry: grateful for the cultural enrichment provided by such knowledge, but well aware of potential pitfalls, and resolved that ancestry shall not become obsession. For others like Charles Dexter Ward and the genealogical researchers of various Lovecraft stories, the past is a dangerous place. Only a heartbeat separates us from ancestors whose lives were once as real as our own. If we allow ourselves to become obsessed by the past, the verdict of Lovecraft's stories is that our ancestors and other figures from the past may break through and take possession of our lives. We need only consider such fearful invaders from the past as Joseph Curwen (*The Case of Charles Dexter Ward*), Etienne Roulet ("The Shunned House"), and Ephraim Waite ("The Thing on the Doorstep") to realize that the past is dangerous territory for the living.

Was Lovecraft then an anti-genealogist? Clearly not. As a member of one of the old families of Providence's East Side, he shared pride in his ancestry with many of his neighbors. The family historian naturally seeks a cultural identity with his or her ancestors through the consultation of surviving records. But there is a distinction between seeking a cultural identity and experiencing the past as reality. Perhaps Lovecraft is suggesting that explorations of the latter type are best undertaken when we too are part of eternity—the "fixt mass whose sides the ages are."[44]

Howard Phillips Lovecraft: An Ancestor Table
Corrections and Additions to: carolfaig@comcast.net

Principal (1)
1. Howard P. Lovecraft b. 1890 Prov. RI d. 1937 Prov. RI

Parents (2–3)
2. Winfield S. Lovecraft b. 1853 Rochester NY d. 1898 Prov. RI m. 1889 Boston MA
3. Sarah S. Phillips b. 1857 Foster RI d. 1921 Prov. RI

Grandparents (4–7)
4. George Lovecraft b. 1815 Woodland Devon UK d. 1895 Mt. Vernon NY m. 1839 Rochester NY
5. Helen Allgood b. 1821 UK d. 1881 Mt. Vernon NY
6. Whipple V. Phillips b. 1833 Foster RI d. 1904 Prov. RI m. 1856
7. Robie A. Place b. 1827 Foster RI d. 1896 Prov. RI

1× Great-Grandparents (8–15)

8. Joseph Lovecraft b. 1774 Woodland Devon UK d. 1850 Rochester NY
   m. 1805 Woodland Devon UK
9. Mary Full b. 1782 Denbury Devon UK d. 1864 Rochester NY
10. William Allgood b. 1786 Trevethin Monmouth UK m. 1817 Trevethin
    Monmouth UK
11. Rachel Morris b. ca. 1790 Pontypool Monmouth UK
12. Jeremiah Phillips b. 1800 Foster RI d. 1848 Foster RI m. 1823
13. Roby Rathbun (sister of 15) b. 1797 Exeter RI d. 1848 Foster RI
14. Stephen Place Jr. b. 1783 Foster RI d. 1849 Foster RI
15. Sarah Rathbun (sister of 13) b. 1787 Exeter RI d. 1868 Foster RI

2× Great-Grandparents (16–31)

16. John Lovecraft b. 1742 Woodland Devon UK d. 1780 m. 1768 Wood-
    land Devon UK
17. Mary Tapper d. 1815 Woodland Devon UK (m.(2) 1782 Henry Priston)
18. Richard Full [Denbury Devon UK] b. 1758 Woodland Devon UK
    m. 1782 Torbryan   Devon UK
19. Elizabeth Brusey [Torbryan Devon UK]
20. William Allgood b. ca. 1754 Trevethin Monmouth UK d. 1810 London
    Middlesex UK m. ca. 1784 Monmouth UK
21. Mary —— b. 1760 Trevethin Monmouth UK d. 1822 Pontypool Mon-
    mouth UK
24. Asaph Phillips b. 1764 d. 1829 Foster RI m. 1787
25. Esther Whipple b. 1767 Scituate RI d. 1842 Foster RI
26. John Rathbun (also 30) b. 1750 d. 1810 Exeter RI m. 1776
27. Sarah Casey (also 31) b. 1755 d. 1813
28. Stephen Place Sr. b. 1736 d. 1817 Foster RI
29. Martha Perkins b. 1747 d. 1822 Foster RI
30. John Rathbun (also 26) b. 1750 d. 1810 Exeter RI
31. Sarah Casey (also 27) b. 1755 d. 1813

3× Great-Grandparents (32–63)

32. Joseph Lovecraft b. 1703 Broadhempston Devon UK d. 1781 Woodland
    Devon UK m. 1728 Woodland Devon UK
33. Mary Pitts d. 1771 Woodland Devon UK
36. Richard Full m. 1756 Woodland Devon UK
37. Mary Tapper
40. Thomas Allgood b. 1727 Trevethin Monmouth UK d. 1779 Trevethin
    Monmouth UK m. 1753 Trevethin Monmouth UK
41. Mary Hughes b. ca. 1731 Trevethin Monmouth UK

48. James Phillips b. ca. 1740 Smithfield RI? d. 1807? Scituate RI? m. ca. 1768 Scituate RI 49. Ann Phillips
50. Benedict Whipple b. 1739 Prov. RI d. 1819 Scituate RI
51. Elizabeth Mathewson b. 1736 d. 1802
52. John Rathbun (also 60) b. 1723 New Shoreham RI d. 1810 Escoheag, Exeter RI m. 1744/45
53. Olive Perkins[45] (also 61)
54. John Casey[46] (also 62) b. 1723 d. 1794 [Kingstown RI]
55. Mercy Babcock[47] (also 63) d. 1792+
56. Enoch Place b. 1704 North Kingstown RI d. 1789 Foster RI m. 1743 Exeter RI
57. Hannah Wilcox b. ca. 1710 North Kingstown RI d. 1802 Foster RI
58. Newman Perkins b. 1711 d. 1796 m. 1732 East Greenwich RI
59. Mehitable Godfrey[48] b. ca. 1707
60. John Rathbun (also 52) b. 1723 d. 1810 Exeter RI m. 1744/45
61. Olive Perkins (also 53)
62. John Casey (also 54) b. 1723 d. 1794 [Kingstown RI]
63. Mercy Babcock (also 55) d. 1792+

4× Great-Grandparents (64–127)

64. Will Lovecraft (weaver) m. 1699 Broadhempston Devon UK
65. George Merifeild (weaver)
72. Richard Full [Paignton Devon UK] m. 1733 Denbury Devon UK
73. Joanna Earle [Paignton Devon UK]
80. John Allgood b. ca. 1678 Trevethin Monmouth UK d. 1753 m. ca. 1721 Trevethin Monmouth
96. Jeremiah Phillips b. ca. 1695 Prov. RI d. 1779 Glocester RI [Providence, Smithfield, Glocester (freeman 1759)]
97. —— Phillips
98. John Phillips
99. Sarah Brown b. 1709
100. Benjamin Whipple[49] b. 1688 Prov. RI d. 1788 Prov. RI
101. Esther Millard[50] d. 1777+
102. James Mathewson b. 1702 Prov. RI d. 1735 Scituate RI m. 1729
103. Elizabeth Mathewson b. 1706
104. John Rathbun (also 120) b. 1693 New Shoreham RI d. 1752 Escoheag, Exeter RI [freeman (New Shoreham) 1732, (Exeter) 1744] m. 1720
105. Patience Fish (also 121) d. 1737-
106. Ebenezer Perkins (also 116,122) b. 1681 Ipswich MA d. 1743 Coventry RI m. 1710
107. Hannah Safford (also 117,123) b. ca. 1690

108. Samuel Casey (also 124) b. ca. 1675 d. 1752 Exeter RI [Newport RI, Kingstown RI,   Exeter RI]
109. Dorcas Ellis[51] (also 125) b. ca. 1680 d. 1752+
110. Jonathan Babcock (also 126) b. 1702/3 Westerly RI d. 1752- m. 1723/4-
111. Elizabeth ——[52] (also 127) d. 1783 Richmond RI m.(2) 1752 (Charlestown RI) Richard Dye (b. 1709 Little Compton RI d. 1760)
112. Thomas Place b. 1663 d. 1727 North Kingstown RI
113. Hannah Cole b. 1668 d. 1721+
114. Thomas Wilcox b. 1664 Westerly RI d. 1728 North Kingstown RI m. 1687
115. Martha Hazard b. ca. 1668 Portsmouth RI d. 1753 Exeter RI
116. Ebenezer Perkins (also 106,122) b. 1681 Ipswich MA d. 1743 Coventry RI m. 1710
117. Hannah Safford (also 107,123) b. ca. 1690
118. John Godfrey d. 1735 Yarmouth MA
119. Martha Joyce b. ca. 1667 d. before 10 March 1741/42
120. John Rathbun (also 104) b. 1693 New Shoreham RI d. 1752 Escoheag Exeter RI [freeman (New Shoreham) 1732, (Exeter) 1744] m. 1720
121. Patience Fish (also 105) d. 1737-
122. Ebenezer Perkins (also 106,116) b. 1681 Ipswich MA d. 1743 Coventry RI m. 1710
123. Hannah Safford (also 107,117) b. ca. 1690
124. Samuel Casey (also 108) b. ca. 1675 d. 1752 Exeter RI [Newport RI, Kingstown RI,   Exeter RI]
125. Dorcas Ellis (also 109) b. ca. 1680 d. 1752+
126. Jonathan Babcock (also 110) b. 1702/3 Westerly RI d. 1752- m. 1723/4-
127. Elizabeth —— (also 111) d. 1783 Richmond RI m.(2) 1752 (Charlestown RI) Richard Dye (b. 1709 Little Compton RI d. 1760)

5× Great-Grandparents (128–255)

160. Thomas Allgood b. ca. 1640 Kettering Northampton UK d. 1716 Pontypool Monmouth UK m. ca. 1677 Trevethin Monmouth UK
161. Ann — b. ca. 1644 Trevethin Monmouth UK
192. Joseph Phillips (brother of 194 & 196) b. ca. 1669 Newport RI d. 1719 Prov. RI
193. Elizabeth Malavery (sister of 207) d. 1719+
194. James Phillips (brother of 192 & 196) b. ca. 1666 Newport RI d. 1746 Smithfield RI
195. Mary Mowry
196. Richard Phillips (brother of 192 & 194) b. 1667 Newport RI d. 1747 Smithfield RI

197. Sarah Mowry
198. Capt. [or Lieut.] Joseph Brown53 b. 1684 Newport RI d. 1764 Glocester RI [Newport RI, Westerly RI, Kingstown RI, Attleboro MA, Glocester RI]
199. Sarah Pray d. 1728-
200. Benjamin Whipple b. 1654 Dorchester MA d. 1704 Prov. RI
201. Ruth Mathewson54 d. 1704+
202. Nehemiah Millard b. 1668 Rehoboth MA d. 1751 Rehoboth MA m. 1696/97 Rehoboth MA
203. Phoebe Shores b. 1674 Lynn MA d. 1715 Rehoboth MA
204. James Mathewson b. 1666 Prov. RI d. 1737 Scituate RI m. 1696
205. Elizabeth Clemence b. 1673 d. 1736+
206. John Mathewson d. 1716 Prov. RI m. 1698
207. Deliverance Malavery (sister of 193) d. 1716+
208. John Rathbun (also 240) b. 1658 d. 1723 New Shoreham RI m. 1688
209. Ann Dodge (also 241) b. 1723+
210. John Fish (also 242) d. 1742 [Portsmouth RI/Dartmouth MA]
211. Joanna —— (also 243) d. 1744
212. Samuel Perkins (also 232,244) b. 1655 Ipswich MA d. 1700 Ipswich MA
213. Hannah West (also 233,245)
214. John Safford (also 234) b. 1662 Ipswich MA d. 1736 Preston CT m. 1685? Ipswich MA
215. Hannah Newman (also 235) b. ca. 1665
216. Thomas Casey (also 248) b. ca. 1636 d. ca. 1719 [Newport RI]
217. Sarah Elliott (also 249) d. 1706+
220. James Babcock (also 252) d. 1721- Westerly RI [blacksmith]
221. Mercy —— (also 253) d. 1725/6+ m. (2) 1725/6- Charles Oherrow
224. Enoch Place b. 1631 d. 1695 [Dorchester MA, Kingstown RI]
225. Sarah Mumford
226. John Cole b. Sandwich Kent UK d. 1707 Kingstown RI
227. Susanna Hutchinson d. 1713-
228. Stephen Wilcox b. ca. 1633 d. 1690 [Portsmouth RI, Westerly RI]
229. Hannah Hazard (sister of 230) b. 1637 Boston MA d. 1690
230. Robert Hazard (brother of 229) b. 1635 d. 1710+ [Portsmouth RI, Kingstown RI]
231. Mary Brownell55 b. 1639 d. 1739
232. Samuel Perkins (also 212,244) b. 1655 Ipswich MA d. 1700 Ipswich MA
233. Hannah West (also 213,245)
234. John Safford (also 214) b. 1662 Ipswich MA d. 1736 Preston CT m. 1685? Ipswich MA
235. Hannah Newman (also 215) b. ca. 1665
236. Richard Godfrey b. ca. 1631 England d. 1691 Taunton MA [Taunton MA 1651,1652]
237. Jane Turner d. before 9 March 1670/71 [Taunton MA]

238. Hosea Joyce [Yarmouth MA]
239. Martha —— d. 1670 Yarmouth MA
240. John Rathbun (also 208) b. 1658 d. 1723 New Shoreham RI m. 1688
241. Ann Dodge (also 209) d. 1723+
242. John Fish (also 210) d. 1742
243. Joanna —— (also 211) d. 1744
244. Samuel Perkins (also 212,232) b. 1655 Ipswich MA d. 1700 Ipswich MA
245. Hannah West (also 213,233)
248. Thomas Casey (also 216) b. ca. 1636 d. ca. 1719 [Newport RI]
249. Sarah Elliott (also 217) d. 1706+
252. James Babcock (also 220) d. 1721- Westerly RI [blacksmith]
253. Mercy —— (also 221) d. 1725/6+ m.(2) 1725/6- Charles Oherrow

6× Great-Grandparents (256–511)

384. Michael Phillips (also 388,392) b. ca. 1630 Wales? d. 1676- Newport RI
385. Barbara —— [56] (also 389,393) d. 1706+ Prov. RI m.(2) Edward Inman
    (d. 1706 Prov. RI)
386. John Malavery (also 414) d. 1712 Prov. RI
387. Elizabeth —— (also 415) d. 1718+ Prov. RI
388. Michael Phillips (also 384,392) b. ca. 1630 Wales? d. 1676- Newport RI
389. Barbara —— (also 385,393) d. 1706+ Prov. RI m.(2) Edward Inman
    (d. 1706 Prov. RI)
390. John Mowry (brother of 394) d. 1690 Prov. RI
391. Mary —— d. ca. 1690 Prov. RI
392. Michael Phillips (also 384,388) b. ca. 1630 Wales? d. 1676- Newport RI
393. Barbara —— (also 385,389) d. 1706+ Prov. RI m.(2) Edward Inman
    (d. 1706 Prov. RI)
394. Nathaniel Mowry (brother of 390) b. 1644 Prov. RI d. 1718 Prov. RI
395. Joanna Inman d. 1718+
396. Jeremiah Brown b. 1634 High Wycombe Buckinghamshire UK d. 1690
    Newport RI [arrived in Boston MA on ship *Martin* with parents in
    1638] m. 1680-
397. Mary Sherman[?][57] (widow of Thomas Cook)
398. John Pray d. 1733 [Prov. RI, Smithfield RI]
399. Sarah Brown d. 1733+ [Prov. RI, Smithfield RI]
400. John Whipple b. 1618 d. 1685 Prov. RI
401. Sarah —— b. 1624 Dorchester MA d. 1666 Prov. RI
402. James Mathewson (also 408,412) d. 1682 Prov. RI
403. Hannah Field (also 409,413) d. 1703+ m.(2) Henry Brown
404. Robert Millard b. 1632 d. 1699 Rehoboth MA m. 1662 Rehoboth MA
405. Elizabeth Sabin b. 1643 d. 1717/18 Rehoboth MA

406. Jonathan Shores b. 1643 m. 1669 Lynn MA [Charlestown MA/Lynn MA/Woodbury CT]
407. Priscilla Hawthorne b. 1649 Salem MA
408. James Mathewson (also 402,412) d. 1682 Prov. RI
409. Hannah Field (also 403,413) d. 1703+ m.(2) Henry Brown
410. Thomas Clemence d. 1688 Prov. RI
411. Elizabeth —— d. 1721+
412. James Mathewson (also 402,408) d. 1682 Prov. RI
413. Hannah Field (also 403,409) d. 1703+ m.(2) Henry Brown
414. John Malavery (also 386) d. 1712 Prov. RI
415. Elizabeth (also 387) —— d. 1719+
416. John Rathbun (also 480) b. 1634 Roxbury MA d. 1702 New Shoreham RI [purchaser (New Shoreham), 1660, freeman (New Shoreham), 1664]
417. Margaret Dodge (also 481) d. 1702+
418. Tristram Dodge b. 1628? d. 1720 [Newfoundland, resident (New Shoreham RI), 1662, freeman (New Shoreham RI), 1664]
420. Thomas Fish (also 484) d. 1687 Portsmouth RI
421. Mary —— (also 485) d. 1699
424. John Perkins (also 464,488) b. 1609 Hillmorton Warwickshire UK d. 1686 Ipswich   MA
425. Elizabeth —— (also 465,489) d. 1684
426. Twifford West (also 466,490) [emigrated 1635, Marshfield MA 1643, Rowley MA 1667, Salem MA 1677, Ipswich MA 1678]
427. Hannah —— (also 467,491)
428. John Safford (also 468) [Ipswich MA] b. 1633 m. ca. 1661
429. Sarah Lowe (also 469) b. ca. 1637 d. 1708+
432. Thomas Casey (also 496) d. 1641
440. James Babcock (also 504) b. 1641 Portsmouth RI d. 1698 Westerly RI [blacksmith]
441. Jane Brown (also 505) b. ca. 1645 Reading MA d. 1718/9 Westerly RI
452. Isaac Cole
453. Joan ——
454. William Hutchinson b. 1586 d. ca. 1642 RI [emigrated 1634] m. 1612 London Middlesex UK
455. Ann Marbury[58] b. 1591 d. 1643 Pelham Bay NY (killed by Indians)
456. Edward Wilcox [Portsmouth RI, Kingstown RI]
458. Thomas Hazard (also 460) b. 1610 d. 1680 [Boston MA, Newport RI, Portsmouth RI] m.(2) Martha Sheriff (d. 1691+) (widow of Thomas)
459. Martha —— (also 461) d. 1669
460. Thomas Hazard (also 458) b. 1610 d. 1680 [Boston MA, Newport RI, Portsmouth RI] m.(2) Martha Sheriff (d. 1691+) (widow of Thomas)
461. Martha —— (also 459) d. 1669

462. Thomas Brownell d. ca. 1665 Portsmouth RI
463. Anne —— d. 1665+
464. John Perkins (also 424, 488) b. 1609 Hillmorton Warwickshire UK d. 1686 Ipswich   MA
465. Elizabeth —— (also 425, 489) d. 1684
466. Twifford West (also 426, 490) [emigrated 1635, Marshfield MA 1643, Rowley MA 1667, Salem MA 1677, Ipswich MA 1678]
467. Hannah —— (also 427, 491)
468. John Safford (also 428) [Ipswich MA] b. 1633 m. c. 1661
469. Sarah Lowe (also 429) b. c. 1637 d. 1708+
474. John Turner (ironworker) b. ca. 1612 [Lynn MA 1653, Taunton MA 1654-1690]
475. Jane —— living 1679 Taunton MA
476. John Joyce d. 1666 Yarmouth MA [Sandwich MA 1637, Yarmouth MA 1643]
477. Dorothy —— d. 1680 Yarmouth MA
480. John Rathbun (also 416) b. 1634 Roxbury MA d. 1702 New Shoreham RI [purchaser (New Shoreham) 1660, freeman (New Shoreham) 1664]
481. Margaret Dodge (also 417) d. 1702+
482. Tristram Dodge (also 418) [Newfoundland Canada, resident (New Shoreham RI) 1662, freeman (New Shoreham RI) 1664]
484. Thomas Fish (also 420) d. 1687 Portsmouth RI
485. Mary —— (also 421) d. 1699
488. John Perkins (also 424, 464) b. 1609 Hillmorton Warwickshire UK d. 1686 Ipswich   MA
489. Elizabeth —— (also 425, 465) d. 1684
490. Twifford West (also 426, 466) [emigrated 1635, Marshfield MA 1643, Rowley MA 1667, Salem MA 1677, Ipswich MA 1678]
491. Hannah —— (also 427,467)
496. Thomas Casey (also 432) d. 1641
504. James Babcock (also 440) b. 1641 Portsmouth RI d. 1698 Westerly RI [blacksmith]
505. Jane Brown (also 441) b. c. 1645 Reading MA d. 1718/9 Westerly RI

7× Great-Grandparents (512–1023)

780. Roger Mowry (also 788) d. 1666 Prov. RI [Plymouth MA, Salem MA, Prov. RI]
781. Mary Johnson (also 789) d. 1679 m.(2) 1674 John Kingsley
788. Roger Mowry (also 780) d. 1666 Prov. RI [Plymouth MA, Salem MA, Prov. RI]
789. Mary Johnson (also 781) d. 1679 m.(2) 1674 John Kingsley

790. Edward Inman d. 1706 Prov. RI [Warwick RI 1648, Prov. RI 1651] m.(2) Barbara Phillips (d. 1706+) (widow of Michael)

792. Chad Brown b. ca. 1600 High Wycombe Buckinghamshire UK d. 1650- Prov. RI m. 1626 High Wycombe Bukcinghamshire UK

793. Elizabeth Sharparowe b. ca. 1604 Melchbourne Bedfordshire UK d. 1672+ Prov. RI

806. John Field (also 818, 826) d. 1686 Prov. RI

808. John Millard (miller) d. 1688/89 Rehoboth MA

814. John Hawthorne b. 1621 Binfield Berks. UK d. 1677 Lynn MA [Salem MA 1635, Lynn MA 1650]

815. Sarah ——

818. John Field (also 806, 826) d. 1686 Prov. RI

826. John Field (also 806, 818) d. 1686 Prov. RI

848. John Perkins[59] (also 928) b. 1583 Hillmorton Warwickshire UK d. 1654 Ipswich MA m. 1608 Hillmorton Warwickshire UK

849. Judith Gater (also 929) b. 1588 Hillmorton Warwickshire UK d. 1654+

880. James Babcock (also 1008) b. ca. 1612 Wivenhoe Essex UK d. 1679 Westerly RI or Stonington CT [Portsmouth RI 1642, freeman 1655; Westerly RI 1664, freeman 1669]

881. Sarah —— (also 1009) d. 1665+

882. Nicholas Brown (also 1010) b. UK d. 1694 Portsmouth RI [Aquidneck RI 1638]

908. Edward Hutchinson b. ca. 1564 St. Mary Le Wigford, Lincoln, Lincolnshire UK d. 1631/2 Alford, Lincolnshire UK

909. Susanna —— d. 1645/6 Wells, York County, ME

910. Rev. Francis Marbury [Lincolnshire UK] b. ca. 1555 d. 1610/1-

911. Bridget Dryden b. ca. 1563 Northamptonshire UK d. 1645- Hartfordshire UK

928. John Perkins (also 848) b. 1583 Hillmorton Warwickshire UK d. 1654 Ipswich MA m. 1608 Hillmorton Warwickshire UK

929. Judith Gater (also 849) b. 1588 Hillmorton Warwickshire UK d. 1654+

948. John Turner (ironworker) [Lynn MA 1643-1654]

1008. James Babcock (also 880) b. ca. 1612 Wivenhoe Essex UK d. 1679 Westerly RI or Stonington CT [Portsmouth RI 1642, freeman 1655; Westerly RI 1664, freeman 1669]

1009. Sarah —— (also 881) d. 1665+

1010. Nicholas Brown (also 882) b. UK d. 1694 Portsmouth RI [Aquidneck RI 1638]

8× Great-Grandparents (1024–2047)

1578. John Johnson [Roxbury MA]

1579. Margery ——

1628. William Hathorne b. ca. 1576 d. 1650 Binfield Berks. UK [Bray & Binfield Berks. UK]

1629. Sarah —— d. 1655 Binfield Berks. UK

1696. Henry Perkins (also 1856) d. 1609

1698. Michael Gater (also 1858)

1699. Elizabeth —— (also 1859)

1760. James Babcock (also 2016) b. 1580 Wivenhoe Essex UK d. 1660 Westerly RI

1761. Mary —— (also 2017) b. c. 1584 Wivenhoe Essex UK

1816. John Hutchinson b. ca. 1515 UK d. 1565 Lincoln, Lincolnshire UK m. (1) Margaret ——

1817. Anne —— d. 1586- UK

1820. William Marbury b. 1524 Grigsby, Burgh-upon-Bain, Lincolnshire UK d. 1581 UK

1821. Agnes Lenton [UK]

1822. John Dryden[60] b. Canons Ashby, Northamptonshire UK d. 1584 Canons Ashby, Northampstonshire UK

1823. Elizabeth Cope [UK]

1856. Henry Perkins (also 1696) d. 1609

1858. Michael Gater (also 1698)

1859. Elizabeth —— (also 1699)

2016. James Babcock (also 1760) b. 1580 Wivenhoe Essex UK d. 1660 Westerly RI

2017. Mary —— (also 1761) b. c. 1584 Wivenhoe Essex UK

9× Great-Grandparents (2048–4095)

3256. William Hathorne b. c. 1545 d. 1626- [Bray & Binfield Berks. UK]

3257. Agnes [Ann] Perkins d. 1626/7-

3392. Thomas Perkins (also 3712) d. 1592 [Hillmorton Warwickshire UK]

3393. Alice Kebble (also 3713)

3554. Richard Carver (also 4066) b. c. 1587 m. 1614 Filby Norfolk UK

3555. Margaret Skurrie (also 4067) d. 1618 Filby Norfolk UK

3640. Robert Marbury b. ca. 1490 d. 1545 [UK]

3641. Katherine Williamson[61] b. c. 1508 d. 1525 (died age seventeen) [UK]

3642. John Lenton [UK]

3644. David Dryden [Staff Hill, Cumberlandshire UK]

3645. Isabel Nicholson [UK]

3646. Sir John Cope b. 1498? d. 1559 [UK]

3647. Bridget Raleigh [UK]

3712. Thomas Perkins (also 3392) d. 1592 [Hillmorton Warwickshire UK]

3713. Alice Kebble (also 3393)
4066. Richard Carver (also 3554) b. ca. 1587 m. 1614 Filby Norfolk UK
4067. Margaret Skurrie (also 3555) d. 1618 Filby Norfolk UK

10× Great-Grandparents (4096–8191)

6512. Thomas Hathorne b. ca. 1520 d. 1565/6 [East Ockley or Oakley, Bray,
      Berks. UK] 6513. Jone —— (m. (1) —— Powney)
6784. Henry Perkins (also 7424) d. 1547 [Hillmorton Warwickshire UK]
7280. William Marbury b. c. 1445 d. 1508- [UK]
7281. Anne Blount b. c. 1453 d. 1537 [UK]
7282. John Williamson [UK]
7283. Jane Angevine [UK]
7288. William Dryden [Walton, Cumberlandshire UK]
7292. Sir John Cope d. 1513 [Banbury UK]
7293. Jane Spencer d. 1525 [UK]
7294. Sir Edward Raleigh b. 1470? d. 1517? [UK]
7295. Anne Chamberlayne [UK]
7424. Henry Perkins (also 6784) d. 1547 [Hillmorton Warwickshire UK]

11× Great-Grandparents (8192–16383)

13024. Thomas Hathorne b. c. 1490 d. 1557? [Bray Berks. UK]
13568. Thomas Perkins (also 14848) d. 1528 [Hillmorton Warwickshire UK]
13569. Alys —— (also 14849) d. 1538 [Hillmorton Warwickshire UK]
14560. John Marbury d. 1460 [UK]
14561. Eleanor —— [UK]
14562. Sir Thomas Blount [UK]
14563. Agnes Hawley [UK]
14586. Sir John Spencer [Hodnell UK]
14587. Ann Empson [UK]
14588. Sir Edward Raleigh [UK]
14589. Margaret Verney [UK]
14590. Sir Richard Chamberlayne [UK]
14591. Sybel Fowler [UK]
14848. Thomas Perkins (also 13568) d. 1528 [Hillmorton Warwickshire UK]
14849. Alys —— (also 13569) d. 1538 [Hillmorton Warwickshire UK]

Notes

1. A bibliography of Dr. Clark's writings may be found in Clark (168–87).

2. So printed in *Selected Letters*. Writing again to Maurice W. Moe on 5 April 1931 (*SL* 3.361), Lovecraft claimed that the emigrant Joseph Lovecraft (1774–1850) arrived

in Canada in 1827 and soon thereafter died in New York. In fact, family records un-covered by Richard D. Squires (Squires 21, 24) reveal that the Lovecraft family emi-grated in May 1831. The emigrant Joseph Lovecraft did not in fact die until 1850.

3. Many persons commented upon Lovecraft's own resemblance to the painting of Commodore Abraham Whipple at the Rhode Island Historical Society (*SL* 3.366).

4. For a detailed development of Foster and Place-Phillips family references in this story, see "'The Silver Key' and Lovecraft's Childhood" (p. 148).

5. Arnold had a dispute with the Rhode Island Historical Society (RIHS) before his death in 1927, and as a result his papers are divided between RIHS and the Rhode Island Collection at the Elmwood Branch of the Providence Public Library.

6. Actually dated 1727 in Lovecraft's letter. The "old man" had celebrated his thirty-seventh birthday only a few weeks before he wrote to Long.

7. The reference is to Kalem Club member Everett McNeil.

8. Lovecraft's mother Sarah Susan (Phillips) Lovecraft was also interested in family history, witness the long section devoted to Place family relatives in her commonplace book preserved at the John Hay Library. It is possible that her mother Robie Alzada (Place) Phillips (1827–1896) or her maternal aunt Olive Lucinda (Place) Valentine (1816–1908) may also have been interested in family history.

9. "Here Lies George Phillips, an Incomparable Man, had he not begat [his son] Samuel."—my translation.

10. The catalogue of Lovecraft's library compiled by S. T. Joshi [Joshi-2] does not con-tain many volumes of family or local history. The only Phillips title is Sir Richard Phillips's *A Geographical View of the World* (1826) [Joshi-2:112 (item 690)]. One book with a genealogical connection that is listed is John Osborne Austin's novel *The Jour-nal of William Jefferay* (1899) [Joshi-2:26 (item 53)]. Lovecraft's surviving genealogical papers and notes are today owned by the descendants of Annie E. P. Gamwell's lega-tee Ethel M. Phillips Morrish (1888–1987). Perhaps Mrs. Gamwell gave these materi-als (and any associated books) to Mrs. Morrish before Miss Mary Spink compiled a list of the remainder of Lovecraft's library in 1940.

11. One Internet genealogist claims that Michael Phillips was the cousin, not the son, of Rev. George Phillips. Based on circumstantial evidence, this genealogist identifies Michael Phillips, 1668 freeman of Newport, R.I., with Michael Phillips, son of John Phillips and Mary Street, born September 1623 in Duncton, Sussex, England. Six generations back, he finds Sir Thomas Phillips (d. 1520) of Picton Castle, Castle-blythe, Haverfordwest, Pembrokeshire, Wales in Michael's ancestry. Having linked Michael with the Welsh gentry, he proceeds to trace his ancestry deep into the Mid-dle Ages. In 2008, some of this research could be found on the Phillips-Weber-Kirk-Staggs family space on Rootsweb.

12, *Moshassuck Review* was printed in tiny editions and circulated primarily to mem-bers of the E.O.D. (Esoteric Order of Dagon) amateur press association. A complete file of the mailings of this amateur press association is available for consultation in the Lovecraft Collection at Brown University.

13. Dorcas Ellis is also individual 125 in the ancestor table, so individuals 250 (father) and 251 (mother) are also missing from the table. See the discussion of duplicate numbers in the following paragraph.

14. Rathbone and Rathbun are used interchangeably from colonial times into the nineteenth century. I have chosen to use the older form of the surname (Rathbun) throughout this paper.

15. This Mary Lovecraft, aged two months, was buried in Woodland Parish on 7 April 1813. The eighth and final child of Joseph and Mary (Full) Lovecraft was another daughter Mary, baptized in Bickington Parish (Devon) on 4 November 1828.

16. The fate of Eliza Lovecraft is not known. All the other surviving children accompanied their parents when they emigrated to New York in 1831.

17. She was in fact baptized privately in Denbury Parish (Devon) on 10 September 1782.

18. Joseph had an elder brother John Lovecraft (baptized 1768) and a younger brother Joshua (baptized 1776). Both of these brothers remained in England, Joshua dying in Combeinteignhead Parish (Devon) in 1850. Two of Joshua's daughters—Elizabeth and Mary—married and emigrated to the United States. In fact, Elizabeth Lovecraft married her first cousin Joseph Lovecraft, son of the emigrant (DSF 19). It is possible that Joseph's elder brother John may be the John Lovecraft, stated age 71, buried in Woodland Parish (Devon) on 4 December 1844. John Lovecraft was the last person bearing the Lovecraft surname to be buried in Woodland Parish (DSF 32).

19. Joseph Lovecraft (1703-1781) had a brother Jonah (1705-1780). Among the children of Jonah Lovecraft and his wife Elizabeth Ludgar was a Thomas Lovecraft, baptized at Woodland Parish (Devon) on 22 November 1736. A Thomas Lovecraft married Martha Hollock (or Hollett) at Torbryan Parish (Devon) on 4 August 1772 (DSF 26-28). Whether these individuals had any connection with the Thomas(A) Lovecraft in Lovecraft's charts my colleagues and I cannot say.

20. Another brother of Joseph Lovecraft (1703-1781) was Joshua Lovecraft (b. 1706). Joshua married Elizabeth Willinge in 1731. They had a son, Joshua Lovecraft (1739-1811), who married Sarah Ashweek and was keeper of the Church House in Broadhempston between 1774 and 1810. He was succeeded as proprietor by his son-in-law William Hooper (1762-1841) between 1810 and 1832. The Church House Inn (now operated as The Monk's Retreat) was housed in the former Broadhempston parish house and may possibly have been a source for "Minster Hall." There is also a parish of Minster on the north coast of Cornwall which was formerly the site of Talkarne priory (DSF 8-11).

21. For a fuller discussion of the arms, see Beckwith-1, Beckwith-2, and DSF 3-7. The fact that the given name "Elliott" persisted in the Lovecraft family in America in the nineteenth century (e.g., Joshua Elliott Lovecraft [1844-1898] and George Elliott Lovecraft [1868-1910+]) may indicate that the family was aware of the quartering in the Elliott arms reported by Graham-Vivian.

22. I published a number of royal descents for Lovecraft in *Moshassuck Review* for May

1993, of which I believe only that through Ann (Marbury) Hutchinson (Faig-3:16-18) is likely valid. An interesting feature of this line of descent is that it establishes Lovecraft as a second cousin (at seven removes) of the poet John Dryden (1631-1700), a relationship he might have valued more than his royal ancestry. From Edward I one can trace twenty-seven generations further back to Cerdic King of Wessex (reigned 519-534 C.E.). By the way, the line of descent from King Edward I in Roberts (233-35) establishes President George H. W. Bush (and his son President George W. Bush) as descendants of King Edward I through Ann (Marbury) Hutchinson. So Ann (Marbury) Hutchinson is a common ancestor of H. P. Lovecraft and the two Presidents Bush. The two Presidents Bush are seventh cousins of H. P. Lovecraft at three [George H. W.] and four [George W.] removes.

23. A third sister, Nabby Rathbun (1794-1854), married Abraham Place (1800-1852) of Foster, who built the home where Whipple V. Phillips's brother James W. Phillips (1830-1901) later lived (burned in 2004). The three sisters were close, and during their lifetimes their three homes in Moosup Valley (Foster, R.I.) were linked by footpaths which they had worn by their frequent visits (Faig-4:Additions & Corrections:vii).

24. John was the brother of the famous Rhode Island silversmith Samuel Casey, who was sentenced to death for counterfeiting in 1770 but was freed from jail by a mob of friends and disappeared from history. Lovecraft loved to tell the story of his relative Samuel Casey, who was indeed a fine silversmith. Miller (1-9) was the primary source for Lovecraft's accounts (SL 2.322-24).

25. I published charts including this ancestry in *Moshassuck Review* for February 1993, based on the lines of descent provided by Gladys Palmer.

26. The surnames Dyer and Dye were often used interchangeably in colonial times, but it does not appear that the second husband Richard Dye (1709-1760) of the 1783 decedent Elizabeth Dye was descended from William(1) Dyer of Newport and his wife Mary (Barrett) Dyer (the Quaker martyr). Richard Dye was the son of John Dye (1684-1715/6) and his wife Remember (Potter) Dye of Little Compton, R.I. John Dye was in turn the son of William Dye (1654-1729 South Kingstown, R.I.), who married Sarah Hayward (d. 1720). They had another son Daniel Dye (b. 1713 Little Compton, R.I.), who married Mary Merithew, and is mentioned in the 1783 Richmond, R.I., will of Elizabeth Dye. The maiden name of the 1783 decedent remains an open question. The fact that she left another cousin Elizabeth Phillips may provide a clue. Lovecraft is believed to descend from three sons of Michael(1) Phillips: Joseph (192), James (194), and Richard (196). However, Michael(1) Phillips and his wife Barbara had another son William, who left descent in southern R.I. (see Fiske). It would certainly be a surprise to find that Lovecraft descends from four of the five sons of Michael(1) and Barbara Phillips.

27. Cooley's Rathbone genealogy is certainly no unimpeachable authority on this line of the family, witness the many known errors in his listings for Rhobie Rathbone and Whipple Vaughn [sic] Phillips (Cooley 132). Nevertheless, it is noteworthy that Cooley mentions an ancestor Jeremiah Phillips. Lovecraft was familiar with Cooley's Rathbone genealogy (SL 5.168).

28. For a further discussion of Henry Byron Phillips and his collection, see Faig-4:234-40.

29. Mr. Howard's son Daniel Howard (1864-1967) became superintendent of schools in Windsor Locks CT and was the author of *A History of Isaac Howard of Foster, Rhode Island and His Descendants Who Have Borne the Name of Howard* (Windsor Locks, CT: privately published, 1901).

30. Another small piece of circumstantial evidence for the possible Welsh origin of Michael(1) Phillips is the occurrence of the given name Asaph—in honor of the Welsh saint Asaph (d. ca. A.D. 600)—among his descent. Lovecraft's great-great-grandfather was Asaph Phillips (1764-1829) of Foster RI and Asaph's son Benoni Phillips (1788-1850) named one of his sons Asaph (doubtless in honor of his grandfather). However, Henry Byron Phillips did receive other accounts of the origins of Michael(1) Phillips. Charles Reuben Phillips of Youngstown OH wrote him "the three brothers owned their ship and sailed from Ireland, one was Michael born in 1629." In research distributed on the Internet in 2001 and later, Richard Ripley of Canada has proposed new theories concerning the origins of Michael(1) Phillips.

31. The usual spelling of Sir Fernando's surname.

32. Thus Lovecraft descends from James(2) [Michael(1)] Phillips, but not in the *direct* paternal line.

33. Henry B. Phillips identified Jeremiah(4) Phillips with Jeremy Phillips of Glocester, R.I. (Phillips 174-75).

34. Thus, Lovecraft descends from Michael(1) Phillips's son Richard(2) Phillips, but not in the *direct* paternal line.

35. The major problem with Lovecraft's account of his direct paternal ancestry was not the lack of Phillips families in the South Country (see below) but the facts that (1) James(2) Phillips [Michael(1)] (c. 1666-1746) was of Smithfield and (2) had no recorded son James(3). Also, the period from the birth of James(2) Phillips (ca. 1666) to the death of Asaph Phillips's father James (d. 1807?) is nearly one hundred forty years—almost too long to be covered by only two generations. A family historian is naturally led to suspect that Lovecraft's account of his direct paternal ancestry might have been missing a generation.

36. Michael(1) Phillips lived in that part of Newport which was later set off as the town of Middletown. Mike O'Shea's *Death Comes Once, But a Cemetery Is Forever: The Search for Middletown's Lost Graveyards* (Norfolk, VA: Privately printed, 1997) does not contain the Phillips surname in its index.

37. See Alden G. Beaman, "A Line of Descent from Samuel Phillips of Kingstowne" (RIGR 7:324-33).

38. Norman M. Isham and Albert F. Brown, *Early Rhode Island Houses* (Providence, RI: Preston & Rounds, 1895), p. 65. A colorful sketch of "Mowbra Castle and the Phillips Family" by Mary Kenyon Huling appears in *Facts and Fancies Concerning North Kingstown, Rhode Island* (North Kingstown, RI: Pettaquamscutt Chapter, Daughters of the American Revolution, 1941), pp. 86-89. I wrote on the subject in "A Very Ancient Home-

stead Now Falling to Ruin" in *MR* (November 1991, 9-13). The same issue (20-37) contained my "fugitive" David Parkes Boynton story "A Pair of Old Shears" (not included in *Tales of the Lovecraft Collectors* [Necronomicon Press, 1995]), which provided an alternative, fictional ancestry for a James Phillips (c. 1740-1807?) who left the South Country to seek a brighter future in Scituate-Foster, R.I. This story was subsequently published electronically by Peter Worthy.

39. Lovecraft himself was well aware of the insignificance of remote royal and noble lines. He wrote to Maurice W. Moe on 5 April 1931 (SL 3:359): ". . . the three or four really great lines that I touch—Musgrave of Edenhall, Cumberland; Chichester; Carew of Haccombe; Legge, Lord Dartmouth; etc., etc.—are so far back that no trait from them could conceivably have any perceptible share in moulding me." There does not seem to be good evidence for any of these claimed lines in Lovecraft's ancestry.

40. Lovecraft provided charts of his own Rathbone line (SL 5.167) and of his relationship with R. H. Barlow through his Rathbone line (SL 5.301). He provided a sketch of his relationship with James F. Morton in his letter to R. H. Barlow dated 17 December 1933 (SL 4.339). Lovecraft's and Morton's common ancestor was John Perkins (1609-1686) of Ipswich, Mass. (individual 424, 464, 488 in the ancestor table). Lovecraft descended from John Perkins's son Samuel Perkins while Morton descended from his son Isaac. See Perkins for this family.

41. Mary Walton Ferris, *Dawes-Gates Ancestral Lines* v. 2 (*Gates & Allied Families*) (Boston: Privately printed, 1931), pp. 483-91.

42. Lovecraft recounted this late genealogical discovery in his letter to Richard F. Searight dated 12 June 1936 (Searight 77): "The other day I ran into a caller of my aunt's—an old lady related to us in the Field & Wilcox lines—& she mentioned how proud I ought to be of our common forbear, *the astronomer John Field or Felde*. That rather floored me, since our charts carried the Field line back only to the original Providence settler John Field, who died in 1686, & I knew *he* was no moon-starer! Well—it soon turned out that the ancestry of this settler has been known for ages among genealogists, though I had no inkling of it. The 16th century astronomer (whose 1557 Ephemeris contained the first English account of the Copernican system, & who has been called 'the proto-Copernican of England') was the Providence colonist's *own grandfather*—hence *my* nine-times-great-grandfather. It certainly gave me a kick to get a real man of science in my pedigree—which as a general thing is lousy with clergyman but short on straight thinkers." Lovecraft proceeded to consult Frederick Clifton Pierce's *Field Genealogy* (Chicago: W. B. Conkey Co., 1901), which carried the ancestry of John Field of Providence all the way back to a companion of William the Conqueror. However, this claimed ancestry for John Field of Providence has been controversial since the nineteenth century. I discussed Lovecraft's claiming of the astronomer John Field as an ancestor in *MR* (May 1993:2-3). Gary Boyd Roberts reprinted the NEHGR articles discussing this claim in his collection *English Origins of New England Families from The New England Historical and Genealogical Register* (Baltimore: Genealogical Publishing Company, 1985, v. 1, pp. 824-48). The Providence town records contain a manuscript iden-

tifying John Field of Providence as the brother of James Field of St. Albans in Hertford-shire, which militates against the identification of the astronomer John Field of York-shire as grandfather of the Providence settler.

43. "Whoever you will be who has crossed, stand, read, weep. I am what you will be, I had been what you are. I beg you, pray for me." Translation by Nicholas Oster, *Ad Infini-tum: A Biography of Latin* (New York: Walker & Co., 2007), p. 183. Quoted from Denis Stuart, *Latin for Local and Family Historians* (Chichester, UK: Phillimore, 1995), p. 54.

44. "Continuity," *Fungi from Yuggoth* XXXVI.

45. I am indebted to the late Violet E. Kettelle for identifying the ancestry of Olive Perkins. See *MR* (February 1993) 14–16.

46. Brother of the noted Rhode Island silversmith Samuel Casey (c. 1724-1770+), who was freed by a mob from the Kingstown jail under sentence of death for counter-feiting. For Samuel Casey, see Casey (30) and Miller (1–9). Lovecraft loved to tell the story of Samuel Casey (*SL* 2.322–24 *et al.*).

47. Probably misidentified as Mercy Dyer in Casey (27). I am grateful to genealogist Mabry Benson for sharing her identification of John Casey's bride with me.

48. I am indebted to the late Violet E. Kettelle for identifying the ancestors of Mehi-table Godfrey. See *MR* (February 1993) 16–17.

49. Benjamin Whipple married (1) 1722 Sarah Bernon, daughter of Gabriel Bernon. Lovecraft, however, descended from Benjamin Whipple's second wife Esther Millard. His comment: "No curst French in Grandpa" (*SL* 3.364). Benjamin Whipple lived into his one hundredth year and was one of Lovecraft's longest-lived ancestors; for another, see Mary Brownell (number 231).

50. For the ancestry of Esther Millard, see Francis Davis McTeer & Frederick C. Weaver, "The Millards of Rehboth, Massachhusetts," *Detroit Society for Genealogical Research Magazine*, Fall 1959–1962 (95–97). The authors acknowledge not proving the parentage of Esther Millard, but they believe their identification of her parents is the most probable barring the presence of a completely unknown Millard line. A discus-sion of Lovecraft's Millard ancestry appeared in *MR* (August 1995) 8–9. I am in-debted to Roberta (Mrs. Dean) Smith, Judith J. Ray, and Joseph B. Comstock for answering my *Rhode Island Roots* inquiry concerning Esther Millard.

51. Casey (24) notes the 1715 Exeter, R.I., marriage of Dorcas Ellis and Samuel Casey but provides no additional information concerning her. Her ancestry is also unidenti-fied in several other family genealogies which mention her. One Internet genealogist cites contemporary Gideon and Jeremiah Ellises in West Greenwich, R.I., records and comments that Dorcas Ellis and her husband Samuel Casey similarly named sons (I find Gideon but not Jeremiah among the sons of John and Mercy Casey in Casey 25). The same genealogist also recollects (but does not cite) a source identifying Dor-cas's father as William Ellis of Connecticut. It is possible that Dorcas Ellis was a widow and had a different maiden name. Gladys Palmer noted that her husband Samuel(2) Casey was ordered in 1726 by North Kingstown to take the inventory of the estate of Elizabeth Sweet and wondered whether there was any relationship.

52. Elizabeth's 1764 will (proved in Richmond, R.I., in 1783) is abstracted in RIGR (5:335). It mentions a cousin Elizabeth Phillips, which may possibly provide a clue for the identity of the testator. Michael Phillips's son William had descent in southern Rhode Island (q.v. Fiske). It would certainly be amazing if Lovecraft had a fourth line of descent from Michael and Barbara Phillips of Newport, R.I.

53. I will follow the parentage for Joseph Brown given by Boyer (65–68) [Jeremiah(396), Chad (792)] and by William B. Browne, "Chad Browne of Providence, Rhode Island and Four Generations of His Descendants," NEHGR, v. 80, January, April 1926 (reprinted GRF-NEHGR, 64–94). Note that Austin (260) gives no children for Jeremiah Brown (396). Austin (28) lists Joseph Brown (198) as the son of Henry Brown (1625–1708) and Waite (Waterman) Brown of Providence, R.I.

54. I am indebted to Jean Phillips (Henry) Peckham for providing me with ancestry for Ruth Mathewson. See MR (May 1993) 1–2, for a discussion of this ancestry.

55. Mary Brownell was one of Lovecraft's longest-lived ancestors; for another see Benjamin Whipple (number 100). Mary came from a long-lived family: her sister Martha Brownell (born May 1643, died 15 February 1744) was also a centenarian (Austin 29).

56. One Internet genealogist identifies the wife of Michael Phillips as Barbara Pierce, born about 1624 in Tewkesbury, Gloucestershire, England, based solely on selection from a list of three available Barbaras who arrived in the colony in the correct period. In one posting, this Internet genealogist suggests that Barbara (Pierce) Phillips died in 1662 and that Michael Phillips married as his second wife Alice Inman, an assertion which flies in the face of the 1689 deed of Edward and Barbara Inman in favor of her Phillips sons. This assertion has been corrected in the information found on the Phillips-Weber-Kirk-Staggs space on Rootsweb in 2008.

57. For Mary's possible identification as the daughter of Philip Sherman, see Fiske, NEHGR, v. 128, October 1974, pp. 306–8 (reprinted GRF-NEHGR 95–99). Fiske provides evidence against Mary's identification as Mary Slocum, daughter of Giles.

58. For royal lines of descent from King Edward I for Ann Marbury, see Roberts (233–35) and Faig-3 (16–18).

59. The standard Perkins family genealogy gives the birthplace of John Perkins as Newent Gloucestershire UK and the birth year as 1590 (Perkins 1). A different account of John Perkins's origin is given in Mary Walton Ferris, *Dawes-Gates Ancestral Lines* v. 2. (*Gates & Allied Families*) (Boston: Privately printed, 1931), pp. 483–91. I have followed the account given in the Dawes-Gates genealogy in the ancestor table. Lovecraft was somewhat inconsistent, citing family origin from the Perkins genealogy but claiming the Gater line from the Dawes-Gates genealogy. See Faig-2 (55–56) for a discussion of Lovecraft's Perkins-Gater ancestry.

60. This John Dryden was the great-grandfather of the poet John Dryden (1631–1700), through his son Sir Erasmus Dryden, 1st Baronet and his grandson, Erasmus Dryden. The grandson Erasmus Dryden was the third son of Sir Erasmus, married —— Pickering, and became the father of the poet John Dryden. See MR (May 1993) 18–19.

61. Katherine Williamson was probably the youngest of Lovecraft's known progenitors at death. See Benjamin Whipple (100) and Mary Brownell (231) for the oldest.

Works Cited

Arnold, James N. *Vital Record of Rhode Island.* Providence, RI: Narragansett Historical Publishing Company, 21 vols., 1891–1912. [Arnold-1.]

——, ed. *The Narrangansett Historical Register.* Providence, RI: Narragansett Historical Publishing Company, 9 vols., 1882/3–91. Reprinted Bowie, MD: Heritage Books, 1994–96. [Arnold-2.]

Austin, John Osborne. *The Genealogical Dictionary of Rhode Island.* Albany NY: Joel Munsell's Sons, 1887. Rpt. Baltimore: Genealogical Publishing Co., 1968f.

Beckwith, Henry L. P. *Lovecraft's Providence and Adjacent Parts.* West Kingston, RI: Donald M. Grant, 1986. [Beckwith-1.]

——. "The Lovecraft Family Arms." *Moshassuck Review* (February 1998): 2–3. [Beckwith-2.]

Boyer, Carl, III. *New England Colonial Families: Volume I.* Newhall, CA: Carl Boyer III, 1981.

Casey, Gen. Thomas Lincoln. "Early Families of Casey in Rhode Island." *Magazine of New England History* 3, No. 2 (April 1893). Rpt. Higginson Genealogical Books (pagination follows reprint).

Clark, Franklin C. *Susan's Obituary.* Glenview, IL: Moshassuck Press, 1996.

Cooley, John C. *Rathbone Genealogy.* Syracuse, NY: Courier Job Print [for the author], 1898.

Docherty, Chris J., A. Langley Searles, and Kenneth W. Faig, Jr. *Devonshire Ancestry of Howard Phillips Lovecraft.* Glenview, IL: Moshassuck Press, 2003. [DSF]

Everts, R. Alain. "The Lovecraft Family in America." *Xenophile* 2, No. 6 (October 1975): 7, 16.

Faig, Kenneth W., Jr. "Lovecraft's Ancestors." *Crypt of Cthulhu* No. 57 (St. John's Eve 1988): 19–25. [Faig-1.]

——. "The Ancestors of Howard Phillips Lovecraft: Working Towards an Ahnentafel." *Moshassuck Review* (May 1992): 7–71. [Faig-2.]

——. "Howard Phillips Lovecraft: Some Royal Lines of Descent." *Moshassuck Review* (May 1993): 7–23. [Faig-3.]

——. *Some of the Descendants of Asaph Phillips and Esther Whipple of Foster, Rhode Island.* Glenview, IL: Moshassuck Press, 1993. With supplemental addenda and corrigenda issued in 1994. [Faig-5.]

——. "The Impact of the Fulford Will on Lovecraft's Claims of Fulford Ancestry." *Moshassuck Review* (August 1996): 1–3. [Faig-6.]

Fiske, Jane Fletcher. "A Family Discovered for William and Christiana (Barker) Phillips of Newport, Rhode Island." *NEHGR* no. 571 (July 1989): 221–33. [Fiske]

Genealogies of Rhode Island Families from Rhode Island Periodicals. Baltimore: Genealogical Publishing Company, 1983. 2 vols. Indexed by Carol Lee Ford. [GRF-RIP.]

Genealogies of Rhode Island Families from The New England Historic and Genealogical Register. Ed. Gary Boyd Roberts. Baltimore: Genealogical Publishing Co., 1989. 2 vols. [GRF-NEHGR.]

Joshi, S. T. *An Index to the Selected Letters of H. P. Lovecraft.* West Warwick, RI: Necronomicon Press, second revised edition, 1991. [Joshi-1.]

———. *Lovecraft's Library.* New York: Hippocampus Press, 2002. First edition published by Necronomicon Press, 1980. [Joshi-2.]

Lovecraft, H. P. *Letters to Richard F. Searight.* Ed. David E. Schultz, S. T. Joshi, and Franklyn Searight. West Warwick, RI: Necronomicon Press, 1992. [Searight.]

———. *Selected Letters.* 5 vols. Sauk City, WI: Arkham House, 1965–76. [SL.]

Miller, William Davis. *The Silversmiths of Little Rest.* Kingston RI, 1928. Rpt. Concord, MA: Joslin Hall Publishing, 1992.

Moshassuck Review. Ed. Kenneth W. Faig, Jr. Published approximately quarterly for the Esoteric Order of Dagon Amateur Press Association, 1973–98. [MR.]

Perkins, George A. *The Family of John Perkins of Ipswich, Massachusetts.* Salem, MA: [the author], 1889.

Phillips, Albert M. *Phillips Genealogies.* Auburn MA: [the author], 1885. Rpt. Higginson Genealogical Books.

Rhode Island Genealogical Register. Ed. Alden G. Beaman and Nellie M. C. Beaman. Princeton, MA, & Ashburn, VA: 1978–96. Vols. 1–20. [RIGR.]

Roberts, Gary Boyd. *The Royal Descents of 500 Immigrants to the American Colonies or the United States.* Baltimore: Genealogical Publishing Co., 1993.

Savage, James. *A Genealogical Dictionary of the First Settlers of New England.* 4 vols. Boston, 1860–62. Rpt. Baltimore: Genealogical Publishing Co., 1986f.

Sneyd, Steven. "Hunting for Lovecraft's Ancestors." *Ibid* (Teaneck, NJ: Benjamin F. Indick) No. 106 (January–March 1999).

Sowa, Iona Ingram. *The Phillips and Associated Families of Early New England.* Santa Clara, CA: Published by the author, 1988.

Squires, Richard D. *Stern Fathers 'neath the Mould.* West Warwick, RI: Necronomicon Press, 1995.

Torrey, Clarence Almon. *New England Marriages Prior to 1700.* Baltimore: Genealogical Publishing Co., 1985.

Whipple, Henry E. *A Brief Genealogy of the Whipple Families Who Settled in Rhode Island.* Providence, RI: A. Crawford Greene Job Printer [for the author], 1873.

Whipple V. Phillips and the
Owyhee Land and Irrigation Company

In 1933-34, Howard Phillips Lovecraft acquired several young correspondents in the far Northwest. On January 13, 1934, Lovecraft wrote to F. Lee Baldwin, then of Lewiston, Idaho:

> What you say of the weather & physiography of your locality interests me greatly, since my maternal grandfather—the late Whipple V. Phillips—spent a great deal of time in the same general region (in Idaho) in the 1890's. He was president of the Owhyee Land & Irrigation Co., which had for its object the damming of the Snake River & the irrigation of the surrounding farming & fruit-growing region. I was a small boy then; but his trips out there & his descriptions of the country, interested me prodigiously. In his offices downtown [in Providence, Rhode Island] he had all sorts of samples of Idaho minerals and produce, & his occasional letters postmarked "Boise City", "Mountain Home", and "Grand View" (the latter place named by him, & occupying land owned by the company) lent a sense of reality to these exotic specimens. There was considerable trouble about building the dam, & it was twice washed away by floods. When my grandfather died in 1904 his estate was in considerable confusion, so that we were all left poor. His Idaho holdings were closed out—but I have always wondered what became of the Snake River project, & whether his enthusiastic dreams for the future of the region were ever realized. . . .

Writing further to Baldwin on January 31, 1934, he continued:

> Thanks immensely for the Idaho views, & for the verbal sidelights on a region my grandfather knew so well. So the old dam wasn't finished until two years ago! The last I knew of the project was in 1904—the year of my grandfather's death. The dam was then washed away, & no one knew when it could be replaced. So much of the enterprise depended on my grandfather personally, that the Owyhee Company eventually went out of existence—at least, as a Rhode Island institution—without attempting to rebuild. Probably the thing was ultimately carried through by a whole new generation of men. The engineer of the original project—in my grandfather's time—was a Mr. Wylie. My uncle Edwin E. Phillips—who died in 1918—was also in the company, & made several trips to Idaho. The beginning of my grandfather's business interest in Idaho was about 1887, & in 1888 he organized (together with his nephew Jeremiah W. Phillips & a group of other Providence men) the Snake River Co.,[1] which dealt in land and cattle. Very soon, however, he saw that irrigation was the big thing—hence in Oct. 1889 the company was reorganized and reincorporated as a Maine corporation (heaven knows why—the offices & officials

were all in Providence!) under the name Owyhee Land & Irrigation Co.[2] My grandfather was General Manager as well as President. It was a tremendous responsibility, & the two successive burstings of the dam virtually wiped the Phillips family out financially & hastened my grandfather's death—age 70, of apoplexy [March 28, 1904]. But he had a great idea of the future of the Snake River Valley under irrigation, & I always take pleasure in learning of the gradual justification of his hopes. In a way, I think he was rather ahead of his time. He thought of agriculture, fruit-raising, land development, irrigation &c. on a large scale not very common in the 1890's—& yet nowadays similar projects of the vastest magnitude are springing into existence all over the West . . .

Lovecraft's 1934 accounts of the Owyhee Land and Irrigation Company (OLIC) as provided to Baldwin are largely accurate and probably based at least in part upon advertisements for the Company which appeared in the *Providence Directory* for every year from 1888 through 1898. An earlier, poignant account of his grandfather's financial difficulties, written to Rheinhart Kleiner on November 16, 1916, had mistakenly labelled OLIC an Idaho corporation. Lovecraft's major error in his 1934 accounts was, of course, in the location of the dams erected by OLIC, which were not erected on the Snake River itself, but about one and one-half miles above the mouth of the Bruneau River, a tributary of the Snake. [The Snake River was not dammed until 1900-01 at Swan Falls, by the same engineer, A. J. Wylie, who also worked for OLIC.] The primary intention of the Company, as stated in its 1888 advertisement in the *Providence Directory*, was as follows:

> The Company owns the Bruneau Canal System. Its Canals will supply Fifty Thousand Cubic Inches of Water, to be utilized for the irregation [sic] of Sixty Thousand Acres of excellent land, propelling Machinery, Mining, and furnishing water to the Town of Grand View.

The first local reference to Whipple V. Phillips is a claim for a water right filed by Phillips, Eugene Howard, and H. S. Cheasbro for 30,000 cubic inches of water on the Bruneau River dated January 4, 1884, and filed with the Owyhee County Recorder one week later. A subsequent claim for a water right on the Bruneau was filed on behalf of OLIC by Charles L. Wing, its western manager (c. 1890–93), in July 1892. The primary source for information about the activities of OLIC is the famous *Owyhee Avalanche*, published in the mining boom town of Silver City from 1865 until some time after the county seat was lost to Murphy in 1935.

Accounts of the mining activities of Phillips's co-filer, H. S. Cheasbro, during the period from 1884 to 1886 and the settling up of the Bruneau Valley by ranchers may be found in the *Avalanche*. On July 9, 1887, the *Avalanche* reported that the Bruneau Ditch Company (common early local label for

OLIC) was at work on a dam to be 27 feet high upon completion; and on October 1, 1887, the *Avalanche* further reported that Mr. Phillips of the Bruneau Ditch Company had purchased the Henry Dorsey Ferry, located near the mouth of the Bruneau River. The really important notices concerning OLIC's activities were found in the *Avalanche* for November 12, 1887—the first a brief notice of the construction of the Grand View hotel (40 feet by 60 feet deep, 22 hard-finished rooms, kitchen, large dining room, etc.), initially, along with the ferry, to be managed by Phillips's son, Edwin E. Phillips.[3] The second important notice is an extended account of the construction of the dam based upon an interview granted by Whipple Phillips to the editor of the *Avalanche*. Providing contemporary evidence for the primary intention of the builders, the interview concludes:

> As soon as the dam is completed work will begin on the canal, which has already been partially dug for a mile or more. This enterprise is one of the grandest every undertaken in Owyhee county, and will add greatly to the wealth of Owyhee, by inducing emigration here, where thousands of farms can be had for filing on them. The scheme was doubtless well considered, before the Snake River company ever invested a dollar, and the stockholders know well that they will receive dollars, for every dollar invested. Besides the mere selling of water a woolen factory can be established, which could supply all the demands of Idaho and adjoining territories. The company can also raise hay enough to feed thousands of head of cattle stock, and as the stock business pays well, where feed can be raised, as it can along the banks of the Snake river, in the course of a short time, this company may engage in that business also.

In the issue of the *Avalanche* for November 26, 1887, is a brief contemporary account of the origin of the name Grand View:

> Grand View is to be the name of the town situated at Dorsey's ferry on Snake river in this county. We suppose it is so named by reason of the view that can be had from that point of old War Eagle mountain and Quicksilver mountain in this county and the Saw Tooth range of mountains in Alturas county, to say nothing of the serpentine Snake flowing near the hotel now being built.

Whether Lovecraft's claim that his grandfather was personally responsible for the naming of the town can be substantiated, I do not know.

The *Avalanche* for January 25, 1890, reported completion of repairs on the dam by OLIC, creating a lake of 20 acres available, according to the newspaper account, for romantic adventure by local youth. A further report, on February 22, 1890, predicted that the region, placed under irrigation, would be fully settled by ranchers within five years. Disaster was not long in striking, however. On March 15, 1890, the *Avalanche* reported that the dam had been completely washed out by high waters on March 5, 1890. The article, recording that OLIC had expended something like $70,000 on the construction of the dam, predicted that "Mr. Phillips, the manager, is not the man to be disheartened by an accident of kind above mentioned, and he will no doubt have a better dam than the one destroyed in the same place in less than two years." Later issues provided further details of the wash-out, and on May 10, 1890, gloomily reported that OLIC had discharged all but two or three of its hands as of April 26, 1890.

Nevertheless, the *Avalanche* was not mistaken in its initial prediction that OLIC and Mr. Phillips would persevere. On May 24, 1890, it was first reported that the dam would be reconstructed as soon as the recession of the waters permitted, and the *Avalanche* of July 26, 1890, reiterated this report with further details. The *Avalanche* of May 23, 1891, reported that the company was expecting a visit by President Whipple Phillips about the first of June, at which time it would be decided whether to rebuild the dam or extend the canal system. A dam it was to be, and superintendent Charles L. Wing provided extensive details of the construction plans to the *Avalanche* in an interview on July 11, 1891. The dam was to be built of timbers, placed on an incline for strength. The interview predicted that 375 farms of 160 acres each would be opened up by the irrigation permitted by the dam. The *Avalanche* for October 10, 1891, reported the visit of Phillips and progress on the construction of the new dam.

During the course of 1892, the *Avalanche* reported further progress on the dam. President Phillips visited the construction personally in July of 1892 and an item picked up from the Lewiston *Teller* on July 9, 1892, first mentions engineer A. J. Wiley in connection with OLIC. Under "Bruneau Notes" for February 4, 1893, the *Avalanche* reported that the dam had been completed, and that work on the canal would soon commence. An extensive description of the new dam was picked up by the *Avalanche* from the Mountain Home *Range and Valley* on March 11, 1893, and a similar report is quoted as having appeared in the De Lamar *Nugget* for March 4, 1893.

The *Avalanche* reported placer mining activity in the Grand View area in 1898 and 1899; what, if anything, was the involvement of the OLIC, this author does not know. The recollections of Sam Mullenix, an early resident, as published in the *Owyhee Outpost* #6, record that the "Boston company" (OLIC) was interested in placer mining. The Owyhee County "Blue Book" (1898) records A. J. Wiley as being superintendent, chief engineer, and postmaster for OLIC at Grand View, with manager George A. Snook assisting with the post office, hotel and store. Of 42 Grand View residents in 1898, 24 listed their occupation as "miner".

The reminiscences of Thams, Mullenix, and Bailey as printed in *Owyhee Outpost* #6 tell most of the rest of what is known about the fate of OLIC. The last published delinquent tax list in which the author found OLIC was for

1899, published in the Avalanche on May 25, 1900, showing OLIC assessed for total property as follows: 160 acres of land on Snake River, $880; improvements on the same, $1,850; 40 acres of land on Bruneau River, $55; improvements on the same, $500; mining ditch, $5,000; personal property, $1,145. The amount of the delinquent taxes and costs for 1899 was $249.45. Further, OLIC is last found listed in the Providence City Directory for 1900. Owyhee County records do show that OLIC was in financial difficulty in 1900-01. On March 12, 1901, the company was sold at a sheriff's sale in Silver City. Purchasers were Dexter Potter, Whipple Phillips, Aaron McCrillis, Abraham Gray, and Charles Shillaber. So, although OLIC was probably dissolved as a corporation in 1900–01, Whipple Phillips (as his grandson recalled) retained a financial interest in the company's former property.

In the spring of 1904, the canal, not the dam, was washed out, and this is probably the second and final disaster mentioned by Lovecraft. In 1904, Russ Massey, James Garbutt, and Benjamin Code bought out the interests of the Phillipses/Phillips estate and formed the Grand View Irrigation Company, Limited, purportedly at a price of $10 per acre of land; which, if the total acreage held by the Phillipses was still in the neighborhood of 200, would mean a total land-only price of $2,000. This company became bankrupt after the 1893 dam itself was washed out in the spring floods. The total estate of Whipple Phillips as settled by his friend and executor Clarke H. Johnston in 1904 amounted to approximately $10,000; and from this daughters Lillian, Sarah Susan, and Annie and his grandchildren Howard Phillips Lovecraft (Sarah Susan) and Phillips Gamwell (Annie) had to draw their allowances for life. Son Edwin E. Phillips was left a lesser share of the estate. From the figures quoted in the Avalanche between 1887 and 1893 on the total expenditures of OLIC, it must certainly be concluded that Whipple Phillips invested far more in the enterprise than he ever recovered. Lovecraft wrote on to his friend Rheinhart Kleiner on November 16, 1916:

> As President of the Owyhee Land & Irrigation Co., an Idaho corporation with Providence offices, he struggled hard to achieve vast success in the reclamation of Western land. He had weathered many calamities such as the bursting of his immense dam on the Snake River; but now that he was gone, the company was without its brains. He had been a more vital & important figure than even he himself had realized; & with his passing, the rest of the board lost their initiative & courage. The corporation was unwisely dissolved at a time when my grandfather would have persevered—with the result that others reaped the wealth which should have gone to its stockholders. My mother & I were forced to vacate the beautiful estate at 454 Angell Street [in Providence], & to enter the less spacious abode at 598, three squares eastward. The combined loss of grandfather & birthplace made me the most miserable of mortals. My grandfather was a cheerful man, whose conversation always

brightened me; but it was to be heard no more. My home had been my ideal of Paradise & my source of inspiration—but it was to be profaned & altered by other hands. Life from that day has held for me but one ambition, to regain the old place & reestablish its glory—a thing I fear I can never accomplish. For twelve years I have felt like an exile.

Lovecraft was accurate in his prediction that he would never regain his paternal estate; the closest he came was the reassembling of some of the original furnishings in the quarters which he shared with his aunt Annie Gamwell at 66 College Street in Providence in 1933-37. Number 454 Angell Street, the commodious mansion erected by Whipple Phillips in 1880-81, eventually became a warren of doctors' offices and was finally pulled down about 1961. However, while the vision of Whipple Phillips failed to achieve financial success for himself and his family, Lovecraft properly assessed its importance in the historical framework. Whipple Phillips, OLIC, and other for-profit pioneers like them, helped establish irrigated agriculture in the West. Productive capacity worth many, many millions, if not billions, of dollars, remains their most fitting memorial. The affection and interest with which Whipple's grandson, Howard Phillips Lovecraft, regarded the Owyhee territory is a fascinating sidelight on this achievement.

Sources of Information

H. P. Lovecraft, *Selected Letters*, Volumes 1, 4
Providence Directory, 1888-1900
Owyhee Outpost, Number 6, April 1975
Owyhee Avalanche (Silver City, Idaho, newspaper)
An *Historical, Descriptive, and Commercial Directory of Owyhee County, Idaho*, January, 1898 (commonly referred to as the "Blue Book")

Acknowledgments

The author gratefully acknowledges the assistance of Linda Morton, Director (in 1988) of the Owyhee County Museum in Murphy, Idaho.

Notes

1. Records from the State of Rhode Island show that "an Act to Incorporate the Snake River Company" was passed in May 1884.

2. The Owyhee Land and Irrigation Company was again reorganized in 1892, this time as a Rhode Island corporation.

3. Edwin E. Phillips (1864-1918) apparently returned to Providence in 1889.

Lovecraft's Parental Heritage

In Memory of My Friend
George Townsend Wetzel
1921–1983

It is easy to wonder why one should spend much time or trouble over the parents of Howard Phillips Lovecraft. Surely, no artist has ever been more conscious of his aesthetic isolation than Lovecraft. In "Waste Paper," his famous parody of T. S. Eliot's *The Waste Land,* he wrote:

> My great-great-grandfather was born in a white house
> Under green trees in the country
> And he used to believe in religion & the weather. (AT 253)[1]

Because of improved intercity bus schedules, he and his aunt Annie Phillips Gamwell even had the opportunity to visit the homesite and burial place of his great-great-grandfather Asa (Asaph) Phillips (1764–1829) in 1929. His letters from the time are replete with praises of the beautiful western Rhode Island countryside and still-preserved family connections from the time of his grandfather Whipple V. Phillips, in whose home in Providence he had been born in 1890 (SL 3.15-20, 25). Yet what a profound separation exists between the aesthete Lovecraft and Asa Phillips, yeoman farmer of Foster, Rhode Island, who, with his wife Esther Whipple (1767–1842), sired a family of four boys and four girls. The Phillipses were, first of all, yeomen farmers; second of all, Baptists; and third of all, Democrats. Despite Lovecraft's justifiable pride in his ancestry, it seems he might have had little to say to them; perhaps his inveterate hatred of wintertime cold would have been his only common ground with men like his great-great-grandfather Asa and his great-grandfather Jeremiah.

What is known concerning Lovecraft's parents can be summarized very briefly. If it were not for their son, the record left by Sarah Susan Phillips (1857–1921), the second daughter of Whipple V. Phillips and his wife Robie A. Place (1827–1896), and Winfield Scott Lovecraft (1853–1898), the Rochester, New York–born son of English emigrants (c. 1831) from the vicinity of Newton-Abbot in Devonshire, would likely consist wholly of the slender trace of vital records and directory listings which most of us leave behind during our lifetimes. Winfield Lovecraft, then a travelling salesman for Gorham & Company of Providence, and a resident of New York City, married Sarah Susan Phillips at St. Paul's Church (Episcopal) on Tremont Street in Boston on June 12, 1889. Their only child Howard Phillips Lovecraft was born at the home of his maternal grandparents in Providence on August 20, 1890. On April 25, 1893, Winfield Lovecraft was admitted to Butler Hospital in Providence, where he died of general paresis on July 19, 1898. Attorney Albert A Baker (1862–1959) was appointed his guardian by the probate court on June 6, 1893, because of his insanity. Baker was a also to serve as guardian of H. P. Lovecraft, following the death of Winfield Scott Lovecraft, from 1899 to 1911.

Shortly after the death of his grandfather on March 28, 1904, Lovecraft and his mother Sarah Susan removed several blocks eastward to a flat at 598 Angell Street in Providence, where Lovecraft lived until he eloped to New York City to marry Sonia Haft Greene on March 3, 1924. Since her son found no gainful employment other than freelance writing and revision, which produced only a trickle of income, Sarah Susan continued to live on the diminishing principal of her father's and her husband's estates; her financial worries seem to have been the principal cause of her increasing anxiety and eccentricity. Finally, on March 13, 1919, she was herself hospitalized at Butler Hospital. Her son visited her only on the grounds of the hospital and then only in fair weather. Indeed, his attempted enlistment in the Rhode Island National Guard, in 1917, had represented a major crisis point in the uneasy relationship between mother and son, and it is likely that Sarah Susan's doctors suggested that her exposure to her son be limited for her own good. She died in Butler Hospital on May 24, 1921, of cholecystitis cholangitis.

Providence newspaperman, poet, and essayist Winfield Townley Scott (1910–1968) painted the first significant portrait of Lovecraft's father in his ground-breaking essay "His Own Most Fantastic Creation." Enriched with the succinct recollections of family attorney Albert A. Baker and of friends and neighbors like Addison P. Munroe, Scott's portraits of Lovecraft's parents have remained largely unaltered, even with the publication of Lovecraft's *Selected Letters* and the work of a whole new generation of researchers. Scott was, of course, the first to reveal the cause of death of Lovecraft's father, and the weight of the evidence points toward the conclusion that Winfield Scott Lovecraft died of the ravages of tertiary neurosyphilis after five years as a paretic. The Butler Hospital medical records for Lovecraft's father, recently discovered by Professor John McInnis, should help add to the portrait of Winfield Lovecraft, the immaculately dressed travelling salesman who was so proud of his British accent and mannerisms. The image we possess is of a man proud of his family, friends, and business connections, stripped of all that he valued as a result of his increasing mental disorder.

By way of contrast, the fundamental portrait of Lovecraft's mother was painted not by Scott but by a family friend and neighbor, Clara Hess, in an extended recollection printed by August Derleth in his essay on "Lovecraft's Sensitivity" in *Something about Cats and Other Pieces*. Scott's essay provides a basic picture of Sarah Susan's mental disintegration (her own Butler Hospital re-

cords have apparently been destroyed since his time) and Lovecraft's old amateur friends W. Paul Cook and Rheinhart Kleiner both left brief recollections
emphasizing Mrs. Lovecraft's over-protection of her son (Cook 7-9; Kleiner
218-19). However, only Mrs. Hess left a recollection of twenty-five years of acquaintance with Sarah Susan Lovecraft, ranging from social calls at the home
of Whipple V. Phillips's cousin, Theodore W. Phillips, on Angell Street in the
mid-1890s to Sarah Susan's final dark days of confusion and distress at 598
Angell Street. Perhaps it is most notable that Mrs. Hess never saw mother and
son together in twenty-five years as a close neighbor. Mrs. Lovecraft bemoaned
her handsome son's appearance in conversation with Mrs. Hess; in an intimate
moment, Lovecraft himself revealed to his wife that his mother's attitude had
been "devastating" (Davis, "Memories" 116-17). Sarah Susan's hospitalization
in 1919 was in fact a liberation for her son; within months, under the more
liberal regime of his aunts Lillie and Annie, he became an active social member of Boston amateur journalism, which he had never become while he lived
with his mother, despite having been active in the hobby since his recruitment
in 1914. He had romances with amateurs Winifred Virginia Jackson (1876-
1959) and Sonia Haft Greene (1883-1972), the second of which resulted in
his marriage and removal to New York City in 1924.

Acknowledging the tragedy that marked their lives, ought we then to leave
these parents to the famous family photograph (c. 1892), in which their
young son appears in dress and curls, according to the custom of the day?
This photograph[2] is surely the most precious relic we have of Lovecraft's immediate family and worth more than many, many thousands of words of idle
speculation. It tells us more of Lovecraft's parents than any writer could. It is
apparently the only surviving photograph of his father, and the only known
later photographs of his mother are snapshots that show her only as a tiny
figure (c. 1895 at 454 Angell Street and c. 1908 at the James Wheaton Phillips farm in Foster, Rhode Island). (A. Langley Searles and R. Alain Everts
have both published earlier photographs of Sarah Susan as a young woman.)[3]
Nevertheless, the importance of Lovecraft's parents transcends the obvious
influences and deserves some comment.

Let us first dispose of some of the obvious influences. Heredity. The negative Wassermann test result obtained from the moribund Lovecraft in 1937,
discovered by M. Eileen McNamara, M.D., and first published by Robert M.
Price, pretty much disposes of David H. Keller's speculation that Lovecraft
may have suffered from hereditary syphilis. What Lovecraft did acknowledge
was the inheritance of a high-strung temperament from both sides of his family. While he described his father's illness as an apoplectic stroke that left his
father paralyzed and comatose, Lovecraft mentions insomnia and nervous
strain as among its antecedent symptoms (SL 1.6, 33). Dr. McInnis believes
that Lovecraft was intimately exposed to his father's illness at 454 Angell

Street, where he was treated before his removal to Butler Hospital. When Lovecraft writes of wearing his father's clothing, "left all too immaculate" (*SL* 3.362)[4] by his early death, we are led to believe that he was defending an "honorable turf" that he knew in fact to be blemished. The immaculate Englishman of a father is in fact the origin of Lovecraft's lifelong affection for and allegiance to all things English, which astounded his grandfather and aunts when he denounced the American Revolution as early as 1896. (His Anglophilism would have constituted another dividing line between Lovecraft and his maternal forebears; certainly his loyalist views would have been very unpopular in western Rhode Island in the 1770s.) In combination with his mother's insidious blend of over-protectiveness and denial of ordinary affection,[5] Lovecraft's high-strung temperament left him a virtual invalid until his liberation in 1919. Even in later years, we find him voicing suicidal ideation in letters to young correspondents, ideation largely revolving around the same financial anxieties that deprived his mother of her mental balance (*SL* 2.21, 4.357–59, 5.189–92). Although its episodes were increasingly well-modulated with the author's age and life-experience, Lovecraft undoubtedly suffered from a recurrent unipolar affective disorder. In many ways his illness molded his life and career.

The idea of an "ancestral taint" flows into Lovecraft's fiction and undoubtedly derives, at least in part, from the tragedy of his father's illness. The young scholar Charles Dexter Ward is destroyed by the dark portion of his ancestry represented by Joseph Curwen. Evidence of a heritage of evil dating from prehistoric times undoes the narrator Delapore, after he restores the English residence from which his ancestors fled, in the classic story "The Rats in the Walls." The fear of ape descent leads the protagonist of "Facts concerning the Late Arthur Jermyn and His Family" to suicide. Familial decay and inbreeding run riot in the early potboiler "The Lurking Fear" and return again in a more sophisticated form in "The Dunwich Horror." In his paper given at the Centennial Conference, Dr. John McInnis interpreted "The Colour out of Space"—now often acknowledged as Lovecraft's finest story –in the light of early childhood trauma resulting from exposure to the circumstances surrounding his father's illness. We see the tragedy of Winfield Lovecraft's illness and death reflected over and over again in his son's writing. Winfield Lovecraft's early illness and death deprived both mother and son of the financial stability that might otherwise have moderated the hardship of their lives. Sarah Susan and her son were left dependent upon Whipple V. Phillips, whose health and fortunes were already declining by the mid-1890s. A sensitive youth, Lovecraft was devastated by losses in his immediate family; the death of his maternal grandmother Robie A. Place Phillips in 1896 brought him terrifying nightmares of rubbery night-gaunts (*SL* 1.34–35) and the loss of his home following the death of his maternal grandfather Whipple V. Phillips in 1904 brought him to the edge of suicide on the banks of the Barrington River (*SL* 4.357-59).[6] Indeed, Lovecraft's fiction can only partially reflect the traumas he endured during the difficult years of his adolescence and young manhood, when his possessive mother effectively prevented him from forming normal associations and making a normal transition to adult life and responsibilities.

Yet, beyond the undeniable influences of his genes upon his life and of his childhood experience upon his writing, Lovecraft's relationship with his parents has a transcendent importance in defining his relationship with his native environment both past and present—the former being a purely mental relationship, the latter a living relationship with real persons and places. This transcendent importance lies precisely in the realization that his parents in fact defined for Lovecraft his relationship, not only with the ancestry and tradition he valued so highly but also with the living city in which he spent all but two years of his adult life. While her husband was yet alive, confined in Butler Hospital, Sarah Susan listed herself as "Miss Susie Lovecraft" in the Providence directories (1896-99), but after his death she seems to have decided to instill in her son Howard a sense of pride in his paternal as well as his maternal ancestry. In 1905, he corresponded with his paternal great-aunt Sarah Allgood (*SL* 2.178-79),[7] from whom he copied the genealogical notes relating to the Lovecraft family that embellish many of his letters from the 1920s and later, after his enthusiasm for genealogy was reawakened by his friend Wilfred B. Talman. Lovecraft's paternal ancestry, his descriptions of which have sent researchers like A. Langley Searles (see his research in *Fantasy Commentator*) on a fascinating chase after the facts, like all good genealogical problems has the potential to provide occupation for generations of researchers to come as well.

Lovecraft could "reach" when he waxed enthusiastic about his ancestry. Not content with his Rhode Island Phillipses, he claimed (*SL* 3.25, 250-51, 363) that the first of them, Michael Phillips, a freeman of Newport in 1668, was the son of Rev. George Phillips (d. 1644) of Watertown, Massachusetts, an emigrant aboard the *Arbella* in 1630—a claim not supported by any genealogical authority.[8] (Lovecraft's descent from Michael Phillips is not proven, although Henry Byron Phillips listed his great-great-grandfather Asa Phillips as Asa (5) James (4) Jeremiah (3) Joseph (2) Michael (1) in the Phillips family card catalog held at the California Genealogical Society in San Francisco. Henry Byron Phillips's information concerning Asa Phillips and his family derived largely from Pardon T. Howard of Windsor, Connecticut.) Despite his love for the simple colonial architecture and the beautiful settings of the western Rhode Island farmhouses where his ancestors lived—he treasured a crayon drawing that his mother made of the Place-Battey farmhouse where she and her own mother were born—Lovecraft would have been wholly out of place in their world, and he himself knew it well.

As a nominal "high church" Anglican,[9] he would have found no places of worship closer than Providence. As an English loyalist when it came to the American Revolution, he would have been lucky not to have been tarred and feathered. The harshness of the economic demands of eighteenth and nineteenth century farm life would have left little time for school, let alone literature. Before the nineteenth century, the majority of Lovecraft's maternal ancestors were probably illiterate. Had his unusual aptitude and intelligence somehow shone through, perhaps the best he might have hoped for would have been a career as a rural schoolmaster, which was in fact how his grandfather Whipple V. Phillips started in adult life, after he and his siblings were left orphans by the death of both mother and father in 1848. Jeremiah Phillips, tragically crushed to death in his Moosup River grist mill in November of that year, left insufficient assets to satisfy his creditors, and his executor Raymond G. Place had to sell his farm and mill to pay his debts in 1849. If the Lovecrafts had ceased to be gentlemen with the forced sale of Minster Hall near Newton-Abbot in Devonshire by the unfortunate Thomas Lovecraft in 1823 (*SL* 3.360–61), mid-century marks the dividing point by which time economic forces had forced most of the Phillipses off the Rhode Island farms where they were born.

Most of Asa Phillips's and Esther Whipple's sons went to the city. Benoni Phillips (1788–1850) spent his adult life in Providence as a blacksmith; he and his wife Lucy Fry (1794–1878) had a family of eleven children, all still living at home at the time of the 1850 U.S. Census. The next oldest brother, James Phillips (1794–1878), was both grocer and gunsmith and ended his life as a wealthy cattle and land dealer in Delavan, Tazewell County, Illinois. (Lovecraft's grandfather went to Illinois to live on James's farm in 1852–53.) Whipple Phillips (1797–1856), the third brother, from whom Lovecraft's grandfather took his name, spent most of his adult life as a mason in Providence. Only the fourth and youngest brother, Jeremiah Phillips (1800–1848), spent the major portion of his life as a farmer, although even he had a side business as a miller.

James Phillips was the only outstanding economic success in the generation of Asa's and Esther's children, but the situation changed with the generation of their grandchildren. Both Whipple V. Phillips (1833–1904) and his cousin Theodore W. Phillips (1836–1904) (the son of Whipple Phillips (1797–1856) and his wife Eliza Gardiner) were outstanding entrepreneurs, the former in the land, lumber, and Western irrigation businesses and the latter in the steam engine industry. In 1876, Theodore Phillips built his home at 612 Angell Street and, in 1881, Whipple V. Phillips erected his own at 454 Angell Street, only a few blocks westward. It was in the home of Theodore W. Phillips that Clara Hess first met her neighbor Sarah Susan Lovecraft. (Theodore W. Phillips and his wife Sarah Lawton had no children; his heir was his nephew and namesake Theodore W. Phillips II who may be found listed in Providence directories through 1916.) Open fields stretched from these spacious homes to the steep, wooded banks of the Seekonk River and the child Lovecraft in truth never knew what it was to play in crowded city streets (*SL* 3.317).

By the mid-1890s, however, the specter of economic decline was already hanging over the young Lovecraft. A dam bursting in the spring floods of 1890 cost Whipple V. Phillips, and his fellow investors in the Owyhee Land and Irrigation Company, a considerable sum. Although that dam was rebuilt by 1893, the company never recovered its prosperity, and was sold to Whipple Phillips and his fellow investors for back taxes, at an Owyhee County, Idaho, sheriff's sale in Silver City in 1901. The Phillips household felt the pinch of reduced economic circumstances and declined from five servants in 1890 to only one by the time of the 1900 U.S. Census. The early spring rains of 1904 washed out the investors' remaining irrigation ditch in Idaho and Whipple Phillips was dead of a cerebral hemorrhage within days of receiving this gloomy news.

Whipple's executor, his old friend Clarke H. Johnson (1830–1917), later Chief Justice of the Rhode Island Supreme Court, was forced to liquidate virtually all of the deceased's real estate to fulfill the terms of his will, which left $5,000 to each of his surviving daughters (Lillie, Susie, and Annie) and $1,500 to each of his grandchildren (Susie's son Howard Phillips Lovecraft and Annie's son Phillips Gamwell). Whipple's only son Edwin E. Phillips (1864–1918), with whom he had quarreled throughout his lifetime, was left only a residual share of the estate. On this modest inheritance, by and large, Lovecraft's mother and aunts had to make do for the rest of their lives. [Susie had been left about $10,000 by her husband Winfield Lovecraft. Lillie married Dr. Franklin C. Clark (1847–1915; A.B., Brown University, 1869; M.D., College of Physicians and Surgeons, New York City, 1872) late in life (1902); any additional inheritance following his death must have been modest, since she spent most of the rest of her life in rented housekeeping rooms. Annie and her husband Edward F. Gamwell (1869–1936; A.B., Brown, 1894), a Cambridge, Massachusetts, newspaper editor and proprietor, separated early in their marriage.] Simply because Lovecraft is so reticent about his uncle Edwin E. Phillips, we may speculate that the uncle was a larger figure in the lives of his surviving sisters than we may today realize. Lovecraft blamed him for a considerable diminution of his own, and his mother's, principal through a bad investment made c. 1911 (*SL* 3.367). Edwin's death of tuberculosis in the Providence City Hospital on November 18, 1918, at the age of fifty-four may well have been the trigger that pushed the insecurities of his sister Sarah Susan beyond her limit and necessitated her hospitalization the following March.

Lovecraft wrote plaintively of this decline in "Waste Paper":

> I used to sit on the stairs of the house where I was born
> After we left it but before it was sold. (*AT* 252–53)[10]

Here the young Lovecraft makes his last, mournful farewell to better days. His future, along with that of his mother and of his aunts, lay in modest rented rooms and flats, and only a rigid attention to budget made possible even this modest standard of living. The young hopes of Winfield Lovecraft and his family—which had extended to the purchase of a homesite in Auburndale, Massachusetts—had been dashed by his illness; and now the death of Whipple V. Phillips, in reduced circumstances, removed the family's last pretenses of belonging to the economic "gentry" of Providence. (Lovecraft nevertheless delighted in showing his friends the small Providence quarry operated by the De Magistris family on which he held a small mortgage; his friend James E Morton, Jr. took many specimens from this quarry for the Paterson, New Jersey, museum where he served as curator. This small mortgage, valued at $500, was the only substantial property in Lovecraft's 1937 estate.) Amidst the rented rooms and parsimonious budgets there remained pride—pride in the spare colonial farmhouses in which the family's ancestors had lived, pride in the Baptist religion shared with their ancestors (all three Phillips sisters remained on the rolls of the First Baptist Church of Providence until their deaths), pride in the cultural and physical acquisitions that Whipple Phillips's prosperity had made possible. One need only read the housekeeping letters that Lovecraft sent to his aunt Lillie after his removal to New York City in 1924 to judge how important the very furnishings of 454 Angell Street were to the sisters and Susie's son (SL 1.323–24, 335–36). These familiar objects were, in fact, all that remained to a gentleman of better times, and Lovecraft did not lie to his correspondents when he wrote that his life was at stake in his ability to retain such objects in his surroundings.

Lovecraft's only close friend in 1930s Providence was Harry K. Brobst, whose moving reminiscences of Lovecraft were first offered at the Centennial Conference. While Lovecraft's letters are replete with references to "family" friends, when it comes to his own friends in Providence the list cannot extend much beyond Clifford M. Eddy, Jr., his wife Muriel, and Harry K. Brobst. With the Eddys Lovecraft shared mostly an interest in writing, both amateur and professional, but with Brobst, training as a psychiatric nurse, he shared many diverse intellectual interests. (His avid interest in abnormal psychology, remembered by Brobst, surely derived in part from his consciousness of mental illness in his parents' background.) The "family" friends were largely acquaintances maintained by Lovecraft's aunt Annie, since both Lillie and Susie, because of illness, lived very secluded lives in their later years. Lovecraft purposely avoided the occasion of meeting persons from the social and literary "mainstream" of Providence, not because he did not have the aptitude for personal friendships, but because he perceived himself as an "outsider" in the milieu of the social and literary world of Providence.

In the world of amateur journalism Lovecraft moved socially among people with extraordinarily diverse backgrounds—from a policeman like Albert A. Sandusky to business executives like Ernest A. Edkins and Herman C. Koenig. In the literary world of the pulps and supernatural fiction he moved among equals and is still revered as the mentor of a whole generation of writers of fantastic fiction. But in Providence—"where but in Providence," in his own favorite phraseology—he could not be other than Whipple V. Phillips's grandson, who had never fulfilled the early promise he had shown before the family entered upon darker days. Where but in Providence would it have been impossible for Sonia Lovecraft, struggling to save her marriage, to attempt the grand experiment of supporting Lovecraft and his aunts with her millinery business? Where but in Providence might not a man of Lovecraft's background and culture have passed as a university graduate without question? (In fact, he had not even been able to obtain his high school diploma because of a nervous breakdown in 1908-1909.) But in Providence—at least in Lovecraft's perception—the only possibility that remained was an obscure and retired life, restricted to intimate family and the necessary tradespeople, which could at least preserve some memory of the old blood that flowed in his veins and the better times his family had seen.

Popular psychologists might opine that H. P. Lovecraft needed to "reach out and touch somebody." He did this, of course, through his letters, which represented for him an egalitarian form of social intercourse without the constraints of social acquaintance. Many have bemoaned the hours he spent corresponding with persons of far lesser intellectual endowments than himself, but in truth his correspondence represented for him the social intercourse that he found impossible with all but a few persons in his native city. Increasingly incapacitated by ill health and the harsh Providence winters of the 1930s, Lovecraft nevertheless chose to remain in his native city, although summertime respites in the South probably bought him several extra years of life. For the Providence in which he was in some respects so isolated was also home—a home where the possibility of regaining the spacious residence of his grandfather Whipple V. Phillips[11] had long since become negligible but where the ties of pride and blood and place still bound tight.

The parents in that priceless photograph of 1892 were largely unremarkable people. But in capturing them the lens of the photographer also captured the focal point between past and present for their son, Howard Phillips Lovecraft. The blood that flowed in their veins defined his past. The place that they and their ancestors held in society defined his expectations for his own life. His marriage, which might have held the key to escaping this prison of expectations, failed after only six months of living together; it is ironic to note that Lovecraft and his wife proceeded to the identical benchmark attained by Lovecraft's parents—the acquisition of a homesite in Yonkers, New York. His marriage a failure, he returned to Providence and the ties that bound, after two years of increasing hopelessness in New York City. "I AM PROVI-DENCE" he wrote, and these words are inscribed on his grave marker in Swan Point Cemetery in his native city. But if he was Providence, it was an identification that he made on terms that were largely ingrained by his perception of his parents' and his grandparents' place in the milieu of the city.

We must regret, at this remove, that Winfield Townley Scott did not undertake the biography of Lovecraft that he at one time contemplated. The potential sources for such work in the 1940s, when Scott was pursuing his interest in Lovecraft, included many living persons, whereas today even the youngest of Lovecraft's teenaged correspondents are now men in their seventies. The saving grace is the wonderful paper record that Lovecraft left of his activities, a record that will endure and become richer with time. Yet, even in the 1940s, a hypothetical Lovecraft biographer would undoubtedly have found that the people among whom Lovecraft moved from day to day had a reserve as deep as the author himself. Albert A. Baker continued to practice law in Providence until the age of ninety-seven. He served on the board of Butler Hospital and attended meetings in his nineties. It is impossible that he did not know the details of Winfield Scott Lovecraft's illness. Yet Winfield Townley Scott had to glean the information that he published about the illness of the elder Lovecraft from Winfield Scott Lovecraft's death certificate. The recorded portraits of Lovecraft's parents from the lips of Albert A. Baker are a characterization of the father as a "pompous Englishman" and of the mother as "weak sister."[12] Providence and Judge Baker maintained their habitual New England reserve. This reserve was a frustrating aspect of Lovecraft's personality for some friends and correspondents who preferred to give more direct voice to their feelings. But reserve was the very mechanism of Lovecraft's day-to-day existence in the city that knew him better than any other.

Without the reserve, without the isolation, one wonders if he would have had the same freedom to imagine. Could other than a lonely child have found a whole world of wonder in the byways of Providence's ancient hill, and the glint of late afternoon sunlight reflected in the windows of the colonial homes still found there? Lovecraft's detailed discussions of the minutest detail of the arrangement of his household furnishings, and of every regretted change made to the house at 454 Angell Street after his family's departure, may seem at times almost childish—until we realize the importance these things assumed in the constrained life he led in his native city. Yet we see his tremendous intellectual strength and physical endurance in the face of adversity—his lengthy bicycle journeys in his teens and his social "blooming" in amateur journalism in his late twenties. Surely the bicycle journeys had as their object not only the charm of the countryside but also respite from the narrow world of 598 Angell Street. The foray into amateur journalism had as its result not only lifelong friends, such as Maurice W. Moe, James F. Morton, Jr., Rheinhart Kleiner, W. Paul Cook, and Edward H. Cole, but also marriage and a New York City adventure that, despite its misery, gave birth to the wiser, broader-minded Lovecraft of the author's last decade.

Many ghosts walk Providence's scenic Benefit Street, especially during the late afternoon hours that produce the magical interplay of waning sunlight and contrasting shadow that so delighted the city's native author H. P. Lovecraft. Certainly Lovecraft and his predecessor Edgar Allan Poe are among them, but some early autumn visitors to the city also report seeing the shades of a man and a woman, dressed in the attire of the upper middle class of the 1890s, walking side by side in the fading sunlight of late afternoon. The man, with curly brown hair and a formidable moustache, is immaculately attired in afternoon dress with wing collar, ascot tie, and a golden watch chain dangling from his vest pocket. The woman, of pale complexion but distinctive features, is dressed conservatively in a dark dress and wears a shawl about her shoulders despite the warmth of the early autumn afternoon. These two shades appear only rarely, but when they do they are most often seen walking northward along Benefit Street in the vicinity of the Athenaeum. Some visitors report another haunting when these shades infrequently appear; for just as the two shades approach the corner of College Street there is the faintest whirr of a bicycle and a ghostly cyclist, apparently a teenaged boy, passes just in front of them, descending the precipitous College Street hill at high speed. Some visitors report experiencing only the faintest sensation of a tail-wind in the cyclist's wake. The other two shades hardly seem to notice the cyclist at all; in fact, most often they disappear as quickly as the cyclist himself. Some reports place the ghostly cyclist on the busy streets of downtown Providence as well; yet others place him on the Plainfield Pike, headed out for the open country. Perhaps, one might speculate, he is looking for a simple white house where the residents still believe in religion and the weather.

What anniversary these shades mark is unknown, although one learned scholar has persisted in attempts to record sightings on October 17 and October 26.[13] We may, however, wish them well, whether they continue their hauntings or not. For the man and the woman define between them the relationship of their son, the ghostly cyclist, to his native city. Perhaps the quest of the cyclist is for that deeper sense of identification with place and time that H. P. Lovecraft strove to express in his literary work. Whether these shades will appear during this, the year marking the centenary of the birth of H. P. Lovecraft, is not yet known. Let us hope, however, that the ghostly cyclist has long ago reached that white house in the country which is the goal of his journey. Perhaps he has relaxed his lifelong strictures against alcoholic beverages to enjoy a glass of pear brandy made from the fruit of old Asa Phillips's roadside tree.[14] One of his friends once recorded how the author became more than usually voluble at a meeting of the Kalem Klub after Samuel Loveman surreptitiously "spiked" the punch. Perhaps he has time to admire the handiwork of Asa's daughters Betsey, Waite, Ann, and Esther; or to meet their husbands Daniel Howard, Jr., Richard Fry, Gardner Lyon, and Israel Cole. When the fire burns low and bucolic thoughts turn to the comforts of the bedstead, however, we may rest assured that some extraordinary story of the dark woods and meadows surrounding their home awaits the family from the lips of their distinguished visitor. Let us leave the illustrious shade in this ancestral bower and ponder his words in the final stanza of his great sonnet cycle:

> It moves me most when slanting sunbeams glow
> On old farm buildings set against a hill,
> And paint with life the shapes which linger still
> From centuries less a dream than this we know.
> In that strange light I feel I am not far
> From the fixt mass whose sides the ages are. (AT 79)

Works Cited

Cook, W. Paul. *In Memoriam: Howard Phillips Lovecraft.* Montpelier, VT: Driftwind Press, 1941; facsimile reprint, West Warwick, RI: Necronomicon Press, 1977.

Davis, Sonia H. "Memories of Lovecraft." *Arkham Collector* No. 4 (Winter 1969): 116–17.

——. *The Private Life of H. P. Lovecraft.* Ed. S. T. Joshi. West Warwick, RI: Necronomicon Press, 1985.

Derleth, August. "Lovecraft's Sensitivity." In Lovecraft's *Something about Cats and Other Pieces.* Sauk City, WI: Arkham House, 1949. 247–52.

Keller, David H., D.D. "Shadows over Lovecraft." *Fantasy Commentator* 2, No. 7 (Summer 1948): 237–46. Rpt. *Fresco* 8, No. 3 (Spring 1958): 12–27.

Kleiner, Rheinhart. "A Memoir of Lovecraft." In Lovecraft's Something about Cats and Other Pieces. Sauk City, WI: Arkham House, 1949). 218–28.

McInnis, John. "'The Colour out of Space' as the History of H. P. Lovecraft's Immediate Family." In *The H. P. Lovecraft Centennial Conference: Proceedings.* West Warwick, RI: Necronomicon Press, 1991. 35–37.

Price, Robert M. "Did Lovecraft Have Syphilis?" *Crypt of Cthulhu* No. 53 (Candlemas 1988): 25–26.

St. Armand, Barton L., and John H. Stanley. "H. P. Lovecraft's 'Waste Paper': A Facsimile and Transcript of the Original Draft." *Books at Brown* 26 (1978): 31–52.

Scott, Winfield Townley. "His Own Most Fantastic Creation." In Lovecraft's *Marginalia.* Sauk City, WI: Arkham House, 1944. Rpt. in Winfield Townley Scott. *Exiles and Fabrications*. Garden City, NY: Doubleday & Co., 1961. 50–72.

Notes

1. See St. Armand and Stanley for an extensive discussion of this important poem.

2. It served as the frontispiece for H. P. Lovecraftt, *The Shuttered Room and Other Pieces* (Sauk City, WI: Arkham House, 1959) and for Kenneth W. Faig, Jr., *The Parents of Howard Phillips Lovecraft* (West Warwick, RI: Necronomicon Press, 1990), and has also been reproduced elsewhere. The original photograph, from the collection of Philip Jack Grill (1903–1970), was first catalogued (item 523) in Mark S. Owing and Irving Binkin, *A Catalog of Lovecraftiana* (Baltimore, MD: Mirage Press, 1975), and offered again (item 423) in Bruce Francis, ed., *The Undead* (Orange, CA: The Book Sail, 1984). At an offering price of $150.00 in 1984, this photograph was surely one of the infrequent "sleepers" in offerings of Lovecraftiana by the antiquarian book trade in recent decades.

3. The c. 1895 photograph of the Phillips residence at 454 Angell Street, originally in the collection of Philip Jack Grill, may be found reproduced in H. P. Lovecraft, *The Shuttered Room and Other Pieces*, opposite p. 48, and in *SL* 3, opposite p. 390. The 1908 photograph of the James Wheaton Phillips farmhouse may be found in *Nyctalops* 2, No. 11 (April 1973): 11. A. Langley Searles reproduced a photograph of Sarah Susan Phillips dating to c. 1882–85 in *Fantasy Commentator* 2, No. 6 (Spring 1948). R. Alain Everts reproduced photographs of Sarah Susan Phillips that he dated to 1870 and 1880 in *Arkham Sampler: Special Photograph Issue–II* 2, No. 4 (Madison, WI: Strange Company, 1985). A snapshot that Lovecraft took of his mother on the grounds of Butler Hospital in the fall of 1919 (perhaps on the occasion of her sixty-second birthday, on 17 October of that year; see *SL* 1.138) is not known to survive.

4. See *SL* 4.355 for another description of Lovecraft's father's as "an immaculate figure." It seems clear that most of Lovecraft's "memory" of his father's appearance derived from the c. 1892 photograph (see note 2 above).

5. For a recollection of her over-protectiveness of her son as an infant, see Scott 313–14. For Sarah Susan's withholding of expressions of normal affection from her son, see the recollections of Mrs. Clara Hess as cited in Derleth, "Lovecraft's Sensitivity," and Sonia Davis's candid recollection of a visit that she and Lovecraft paid to Marblehead, Mass., during their romance in Sonia H. Davis, *The Private Life of H. P. Lovecraft*, 14. The latter is worth quoting in detail: "His continued enthusiasm the next day was so genuine and sincere that in appreciation I surprised and shocked him right then and there by kissing him. He was so flustered that he blushed, then he turned pale. When I chaffed him about it he said he had not been kissed since he was a very small child and that he was never kissed by any woman, not even by his mother or aunts, since he grew to manhood, and that he would probably never be kissed again. (But I fooled him.)"

6. By way of contrast, Lovecraft never saw his paternal grandparents George Lovecraft (1815-1895) and Helen Allgood (1821-1881). He knew them only through photographs that one fears were likely destroyed when the contents of 66 College Street were sold following the death of Annie E. Phillips Gamwell in January 1941.

7. Sarah Allgood was the sister of Lovecraft's paternal grandmother Helen Allgood.

8. Contrast these statements regarding Lovecraft's Phillips ancestry (all dating to 1924 and later) with his early (1915) statement in *SL* 1.5 that the Phillipses emigrated from Lincolnshire, England, "in the latter part of the seventeenth century." Lovecraft may have been nearer the truth regarding his maternal ancestry in 1915 than he was at the end of his life.

9. When Lovecraft himself married in 1924, he insisted upon being married in an Episcopal ceremony conducted by Rev. George Benson Cox at St. Paul's Church (1766) in Manhattan (see Sonia H. Davis, *The Private Life of H. P. Lovecraft*, 13).

10. That returning to the steps of his former home at 454 Angell Street was an important emotional breaking point for Lovecraft may be seen in his wife's citation of the same incident in Sonia H. Davis, *The Private Life of H. P. Lovecraft*, 1. The original place of publication of "Waste Paper" in a newspaper is still unknown as of this writing.

11. Subdivided for doctors' offices in Lovecraft's own lifetime, the home that Whipple V. Phillips erected at 454 Angell Street (corner, Elmgrove Avenue) c. 1881 was finally demolished around 1960.

12. In "His Own Most Fantastic Creation," Scott attributes these descriptions of Lovecraft's father and mother to, respectively, "a friend of the family" (312) and "the family lawyer" (319). Since Whipple V. Phillips's own attorney, Clarke H. Johnson, was long deceased at the time Scott conducted his research, "the family lawyer" can refer only to Albert A. Baker, and I suspect that "a friend of the family" may also refer to him. Because of the nature of Winfield Scott Lovecraft's illness and his fiduciary relationship as guardian, the attorney would naturally have been more circumspect in his recollections of the father than of the mother, despite the fact that the father had been dead for forty-five years, and the mother for less than half of that period, at the time Scott was doing his research (1943). It is also notable that Scott was given access to Sarah Susan Lovecraft's medical records at Butler Hospital (apparently destroyed since that time), but not to Winfield Scott Lovecraft's records, which were released to Dr. John McInnis only in 1990.

13. The birthdays of, respectively, Sarah Susan Lovecraft and Winfield Scott Lovecraft.

14. Asa Phillips and his wife Esther Whipple and several of their children (Benoni, Jeremiah, Esther, and their spouses) are buried in the Phillips-Cole Cemetery off Briggs Road in Foster, R.I.; a photograph of this cemetery, by Richard Hurley, appeared in Barton L. St. Armand, *The Roots of Horror in the Fiction of H. P. Lovecraft* (Elizabethtown, NY: Dragon Press, 1977). See *SL* 3.15-20, 25, for Lovecraft's accounts of his visit to this region.

The Friendship of Louise Imogen Guiney and Sarah Susan Phillips

H. P. Lovecraft wrote to many of his correspondents about the friendship of his mother Sarah Susan (Phillips) Lovecraft (1857-1921) and the poet Louise Imogen Guiney (1861-1920).[1] He claimed that their friendship began in the 1870s when Miss Guiney attended Elmhurst Academy, the convent school run by the sisters of the Society of the Sacred Heart in Providence, Rhode Island (SL 1.33). Sarah Susan Phillips married Winfield Scott Lovecraft at St. Paul's Church (Episcopal) on Tremont Street in Boston, Massachusetts, on June 12, 1889, and the couple spent their early married life in Boston and its suburbs. Sarah Susan did return to her parents' home at 454 Angell Street on the East Side of Providence to give birth to her son on August 20, 1890. Lovecraft claimed that he and his parents spent the entire winter of 1892-93 at the home of Miss Guiney and her mother on Vista Avenue in Auburndale, Massachusetts, after they had bought a house lot in Auburndale to construct their own home (SL 2.107; 4.354). During this period, Lovecraft claimed that he recited verses from Mother Goose for Miss Guiney and her mother and was dubbed by them "Little Sunshine" because of the golden curls which his mother could not bear to cut (SL 1.32-33). While he claimed to have no active recollection of the event, his mother told him that he once rode on the knee of the aged Oliver Wendell Holmes, Sr., when Holmes came to visit his friend Miss Guiney in Auburndale (SL 1.296). The illness and hospitalization of Winfield Scott Lovecraft in April 1893 disrupted the family's homebuilding plans, and Lovecraft and his mother returned to the home of her parents Whipple V. and Robie A. (Place) Phillips in Providence, Rhode Island (SL 1.296).

Other than this, Lovecraft does not provide us with much concrete information concerning the relationship of his mother and Miss Guiney.[2] Some months after the death of Miss Guiney at her home in Chipping Campden, Gloucestershire, England, on November 2, 1920, Lovecraft reminded his mother that his fellow amateur journalist Winifred Virginia Jackson (1876-1959) had for years sent him copies of every newspaper or magazine reference to Miss Guiney which she found for the benefit of Mrs. Lovecraft (SL 1.126-27). Writing to his friend J. Vernon Shea in 1934, he recalled that he had revisited Auburndale in 1908 and walked directly to the Guiney home based upon his childhood memories of the locale (SL 4.355). He does not state whether he was accompanied by his mother or whether they visited Miss Guiney's mother, then still living at the home in Auburndale. Miss Guiney herself had lived in England since 1901, to be close to Oxford's Bodleian Library and other libraries that she used in her literary and historical researches. She returned to the United States only for a six-week visit in 1906 and for a more extended visit during her mother's final illness in 1909–10 (Fairbanks 187, 223–24).

While her son professed no very high regard for Miss Guiney's poetry (*SL* 1.20, 127), it seems quite clear that Sarah Susan Lovecraft was very proud of her relationship with the poet. Lovecraft scholars, however, have always been skeptical about the claims for this relationship. It seemed highly unlikely to many that Sarah Susan Phillips, who was received into the First Baptist Church in Providence along with her mother and two surviving sisters in April–May 1883 (King 110), would have attended the academy operated by the Sacred Heart sisters in Providence. In addition, no books by Miss Guiney are to be found in the catalogue of Lovecraft's library compiled by Miss Mary Spink in 1940 (see Joshi, *Lovecraft's Library*). Even more damagingly, when librarians examined Miss Guiney's letters to her friend and publisher Frederick Holland Day (1864–1933) owned by the Library of Congress at the behest of Lovecraft's biographer L. Sprague de Camp, they found references not to valued friends and house guests who stayed over the entire winter of 1892–93 but to unnamed boarders with a small child who stayed only a few weeks in June–July 1892. In her letters to Day, Miss Guiney called their unwelcome boarders "heathens," "atrocious Philistines," "cussed inmates," and "unmentionables" (de Camp 13–14). However, when I consulted this letter file in person at the Library of Congress during the summer of 1996, I found references in Miss Guiney's letter of June 4, 1892, which made it apparent that the unwelcome boarders in the Guiney household in June–July 1892 could not have been the Lovecrafts:

> What do you think we have here? Not fleas! but worse bugs; boarders, 2 of them, and half of another. Germans, great gabbers, and likely to break my temper with everlasting approaches, and endearments, and general curiosity about the Muse. I retire to the cellar to swear several times a day.

The aspiring businessman and Anglophile Winfield Scott Lovecraft would surely have been horrified to be mistaken for a German immigrant. I reviewed all of Miss Guiney's letters to Day from the period 1889–93 and found no further references to boarders or extended visits by house guests. It seemed clear from Miss Guiney's comments that the Guineys took in boarders in June–July 1892 only because of financial necessity and that they quickly resolved not to repeat the experience. Clearly, the Lovecrafts were not with the Guineys in Auburndale for the entire winter of 1892–93, as Lovecraft claimed. Indeed, Prof. John McInnis, who obtained copies of Winfield Scott Lovecraft's medical records from Butler Hospital in Providence,[3] believes that the Lovecrafts took up residence with Whipple V. and Robie A. Phillips in Providence after Winfield's grandiose behavior began to interfere with his business activities as a salesman for the Gorham Company of Providence.[4] Indeed, Lovecraft does write that his father was under considerable stress before his final collapse in April 1893 (*SL* 1.33). Perhaps the vacation that the family took in Dudley, Massachusetts, during the summer of 1892 was an attempt to relieve the stress that Winfield Scott Lovecraft felt as his illness began to overtake him (*SL* 4.354). He attempted a final business trip to Chicago in the early spring of 1893, but became delusional and had to be returned to Providence under restraint (Koki 9–10).[5] Lovecraft always stated in correspondence that his father had suffered an apoplectic stroke that left him speechless and paralyzed (*SL* 1.33), but the Butler Hospital medical records that were released to Prof. McInnis make it apparent that the truth was otherwise. The likelihood is that Winfield Scott Lovecraft died of tertiary syphilis.[6]

The reader may justifiably wonder how much fact underlies Lovecraft's vivid accounts of the friendship of his mother and Miss Guiney. Essentially a modest man, Lovecraft was not prone to lying or exaggerating in his correspondence. How much he knew of his father's actual condition will likely always remain a mystery, but his lifelong interest in abnormal psychology, well attested by his friend Harry Kern Brobst, makes it likely that he knew or surmised more than he revealed in correspondence. He was also reticent about the exact status of his marriage and of his high school record. In fact, he failed to obtain a final decree of divorce from his wife in 1929, although judgment had been granted in favor of his petition,[7] and he was never graduated from Hope Street High School in Providence.[8] Apart from these understandable mental reservations, however, Lovecraft was usually quite frank in his correspondence. He did not fawn upon or seek the attention of famous persons, declining, for example, to introduce himself and his companions to Lord Dunsany when the latter lectured in Boston in 1919 (*SL* 1.91–93). Unlike some of his younger correspondents, he did not seek to correspond with master writers of supernatural fiction like Algernon Blackwood, Montague Rhodes James, or Arthur Machen. The magician Harry Houdini was undoubtedly the most famous person with whom he was personally acquainted; among writers and editors, he met Hart Crane, Robert Davis, A. Merritt, and numerous pulp fiction writers. He felt a natural pride in the many generations of his maternal Phillips ancestry, but made no exaggerated claims for his maternal ancestors, who were mostly farmers and farmers' wives. That he claimed for his paternal ancestry descent from many illustrious lines was probably more due to the defective records which he copied from his great-aunt Sarah Allgood in 1905 than to any "reaching" on his own behalf (*SL* 2.179). He wrote modestly of catching glimpses of Theodore Roosevelt and Franklin D. Roosevelt during the presidential campaigns of 1912 and 1936 (*SL* 5.426), respectively, and noted that during one 1935 lecture that he attended at Brown University, he sat directly in front of Governor Theodore Francis Green (*SL* 5.212). Some of his Phillips line had gone westward to settle in the temperance town of Delavan, Illinois, and James Phillips (1794–1878), the pioneer, was a very successful man who early in his career served for two years as a gunsmith under Simon Bolivar and who knew Abraham Lincoln well from the days when the latter was still a circuit-riding lawyer. (One might justifiably say that James Phillips knew personally both the Great Liberator of South America and the Great Emancipator of North America!) As a young boy, Lovecraft's maternal grandfather Whipple V. Phillips, born in 1833, met Abraham Lincoln during a visit with his uncle James in the 1840s.[9]

Given Lovecraft's customary truthfulness and modesty, we may speculate that any exaggerated claims for the relationship of Susan Susan Lovecraft and Miss Guiney may have more likely originated with the author's mother than with the author himself. While he claimed in correspondence to have quite concrete memories from the period when he was two and a half years old (*SL* 1.32, 4.354–55), it may be that Sarah Susan Lovecraft helped to embellish her son's recollections. If she felt shame over her husband's illness, which had deprived her of the family life she hoped for, she would naturally have sought to reinforce in her son's memory everything that was positive about their early family life, including her husband's business successes and her own relationship with Miss Guiney. We may note that Lovecraft himself acknowledged that he had no personal memory of riding on the knee of the aged Oliver Wendell Holmes. Given the diversity of their religions and backgrounds, we may justifiably ask what if any facts support the statements in Lovecraft's letters regarding the relationship of his mother and Miss Guiney.

Miss Guiney was born in Roxbury, Massachusetts, on January 7, 1861, the daughter of Patrick Robert Guiney (1835–1877) and his wife Janet Margaret (Doyle) Guiney. Her father, a native of County Tipperary, Ireland, served heroically in the Civil War and was gravely wounded in the Battle of Wilderness on May 5, 1864, after which he was commissioned Brigadier General on March 13, 1865. His health was ruined by the grave injuries that he received during the war, and he died at the young age of forty-two. He spent his final years in Boston, Massachusetts, where he served as an assistant district attorney (1866–70) and as registrar of the probate court of Suffolk County (1869–77).

The Society of the Sacred Heart was founded in France as a teaching order by St. Madeline Louise Sophie Barat (1779–1865) (canonized in 1925) and her companions on November 21, 1800. Mother Philippine Duchesne (1769–1852) and four companions made the first foundations of the Society in the New World in the Missouri Territory in 1818.[10] The Society's primary mission was the education and preparation of young women both for lay and religious life. Created the first bishop of Providence, Rhode Island, in April 1872,

Thomas F. Hendricken promoted the establishment of religious schools in his diocese despite resistance from the community. The Sacred Heart sisters were among the first he invited to the Providence diocese. When in 1872, "Elmhurst," the North Providence estate of Dr. William Grosvenor, came up for sale, Bishop Hendricken and Mother Aloysia Hardey, the North American superior of the Sacred Heart sisters, promptly examined the property. Dr. Grosvenor had erected his capacious brick and brownstone country villa in the gothic style on twenty-three forested acres in what was then North Providence about the year 1855, from plans drawn by the noted Rhode Island architect Thomas Alexander Tefft (1826-1859). After studying chemistry and philosophy at Yale University, Grosvenor graduated as a medical doctor in Philadelphia in 1830. However, he did not practice medicine for long, but made his fortune as owner of one of the largest cotton mills in the country, the Grosvenor Dale Co., in Grosvenor, Connecticut. Like other members of Providence's commercial aristocracy in the years prior to the Civil War, he sought refuge from the crowded conditions of College Hill in the then-open expanses of Smith Hill, where he built the mansion that Tefft designed for him. Like Elmhurst, the other homes that the wealthy built on Smith Hill—with names like Pinehurst, Lyndhurst, Oakland, Roslyn, Hilltop, and Wyndham—are today recalled only by street names in the vicinity, which was annexed to Providence itself in 1874. By 1871, however, Dr. Grosvenor found that the pressures of business dictated that he resume residence on College Hill, where he purchased the Seth Adams house on the corner of Prospect and Angell Streets. Here his family continued to reside until the residence was demolished in 1942.[11] His initial asking price for his erstwhile suburban retreat at Elmhurst and its twenty-three acres was $100,000.[12]

The sisters purchased the Grosvenor property on November 19, 1872, for the sum of $75,000 and took possession the same month. The school began operation in March 1873 with only a handful of pupils. By 1875, the sisters had also taken charge of the parochial school of St. Mary's Parish on Broadway in the City of Providence. Additions to Elmhurst itself were built in 1881 and 1888, and in 1891 a chapel of the Sacred Heart was dedicated.[13] Elmhurst Academy (736 Smith Street, Providence 8, Rhode Island) continued in operation as a boarding and day school for young women from the elementary grades through high school through 1961. The enrollment had reached 153 young women by 1923, and a gymnasium-auditorium was added later in the twentieth century. In the 1950s the tuition (including luncheon) for day students was $300-$400 per annum; tuition and board for weekly students (who returned to their homes for weekends) was $800 per annum and for permanent students $1000 per annum.[14] Elmhurst Academy closed its Providence campus in 1962 and removed to Portsmouth, Rhode Island. This institution in turn closed in 1972 and the records were sent to the archives of the

Society of the Sacred Heart in North America in St. Louis, Missouri.[15] The fate of Dr. Grosvenor's "Elmhurst" was told to me by architectural historian William McKenzie Woodward in a letter dated March 6, 1998:

> The Grosvenor House was destroyed by fire in the late spring of 1967. The property remained untouched until the late 1970s, when the main drive into the property was developed with new housing; at the southern end of the property a residential retirement facility was erected in the early 'nineties. Only the original stone and wrought-iron fencing and gates remain along the Smith Street side of the property.

The Providence campus with its buildings had been sold by the Society of the Sacred Heart to Providence College after the removal of the Academy to Portsmouth, Rhode Island, in 1962. About 1973 Providence College traded the property, now vacant as a result of the destruction of the buildings by fire by 1967, to the City of Providence for the former Chapin Memorial Hospital and its grounds. The City of Providence subsequently partitioned the property and sold it for development.[16]

We are fortunate that Louise Imogen Guiney left us a memoir of her own association with Elmhurst Academy, "Memories of an Old Girl," which she wrote for a reunion sponsored by the Elmhurst Alumnae Association in 1907.[17] Let her tell the story of her first acquaintance with the school where she spent so many of her youthful years:

> *Moi qui vous parle* was the twelfth applicant on the new foundation at Elmhurst, which had already started on its second year. They gave me the number 12, which I didn't like. I said it was "too Judas-y." On the hot August day [1873] when I first saw the place, I made the journey from Boston rather unwillingly, in the wake of my mother. I had made up my mind that I had no use for Convents anyhow; so to comfort and fortify myself, I carried my best blue gun and a collection of agate marbles in my pocket. Very often since I have been reminded of that gun—coming thus armed to the spot where I was to spend six very contented years! What quite decided me to agree to being sent to that school the next September was nothing less than Madame, not Mother, Samuella Shaw. The temporary Superior, Mother Major, had kissed me; Madame Lizzie Lake had shown me a picture-book; Madame Marie Ange (in whose particular charge her friend, my dear father, afterwards put me) had betrayed quite a lively interest in the unloading of the gun; but such blandishments did not go far. What did go far was my being taken into the old garden, where there were high and overgrown box hedges: just Madame Shaw and I alone. There the demon of mischief got into her worship, bless her!—she was a young nun, and as full of life as she is now—and leading a chase into one of the orchards to get me some early apples, she twice took the wide box hedge in a graceful leap, with my long thin legs enthusiastically following. (Gymnastics are still nearer my heart than most things are.) I was but eleven,

and I judged everything, male and female, by its capacity to jump, run and swim. She didn't know that, but she broke down, by that one flight in air, all my objections to a contemplative life. When we got back to the drawing-room I announced to my parents, giving no reason for my conversion, and stacking the gun in the corner: "I'm comin' back here to stay. I like nuns, like 'em awfully!" So in September in duly settled down in the Fourth Class.

Later in her essay, the athletic Louise wrote: "Mention of games reminds me to record with pride that I was President of Games from the day I entered Elmhurst until the day I left, and that I held no other office whatever!" The sisters must have been gentle spirits indeed to put up with Louise's pranks. She was notoriously absent from classes, like arithmetic and sewing, which she disliked, and was famous for taking solitary refuge in high places like the Academy roof and the top of an ancient pine tree, finally cut down to make way for the new chapel constructed in 1891. Of Louise's passion for heights (physical and spiritual) her friend Katherine C. E. Macdonald wrote in Miss Guiney's obituary in *Signet* for April 1921:

Elmhurst holds dear memories of the child whose perch was always on the steepest roof, the highest tree. That is typical, as, in its passion for perfection, is that first Confession which she herself loved to describe. On that occasion, it seems, finding no one in the confessional (for the slide was closed), this determined aspirant for grace proceeded to climb up and over the top, declaring, when discovered, that she was "looking for God," and could with difficulty be restrained. But on the second occasion, she returned to her confessor with bitter tears: "Oh, I've made a bad confession! I've done the same things over again!"

The gentle Sacred Heart sisters of Elmhurst nourished the soul, but did not dampen the spirit of young Louise. The young woman who graced literature with her elegant poems and essays and commanded her own menage of St. Bernard dogs surely owed much to her school days at Elmhurst. Until her first sojourn in Europe in 1889-91, she was a frequent visitor to her alma mater, delighting especially in the wintertime sport of "coasting," facilitated by Elmhurst's ample grounds. She was sentimental about the place itself as well:

Yes, I loved the old Grosvenor house with its corona of long-vanished elms; and its long corridors; and the three great orchards; and the jolly Playroom, a two-decker, for rainy days; and the deep Frog Pond, rather foolishly filled up after four or five of us fell in through the ice one December afternoon; and the dear dog "Lion," a thirty-year-old ghost by now [1907]; and the wonderful sled "Glorioso," made out of a rubber-shoe case, which would accommodate eight daring spirits on a mad cruise down the frozen hill; and the first little Chapel, with the windows always open, and the fragrance of a thousand flowers within it and without, where so many of us have made our First Communions, and got our grip on life on supernatural things, "the things that are more excellent." The memory of it all is precious. The only circumstance we resent, we ancients, is change not for the better. Architecturally, the old gray house, with its half-Gothic gables, porches, and piazzas, was beautiful; the additions, from first to last, are intensely ugly, incongruous, and lamentable.

Nor was social life absent at Elmhurst Academy. Wrote Louise of her exploits into the wider community:

> Most of the girls (then about 20 in all) were big, or biggish, but there were four or five younger than I, and there was of course at that time, a great deal of liberty allowed, especially to the little ones. When the remembered Xavier first came as Convent factotum, he used to take some of us rather often in "the Black Maria" to spend the day at Hope Carroll's in the city. The party consisted of Lota and Nelly Root, Hattie Wadsworth, Hope, and me. We had all sorts of superstitions about Smith Street, then a rather remote and uninhabited highway, and we used to crowd up against Xavier as he drove homewards after dark, extracting from him the most bloodthirsty and incredible tales known to Alsatians. The four companions just named were very dear to me then, particularly Lota, the closest friend of all my life, who became a Visitation nun and died young. Her photograph is yet on my desk over here in England, and her gay, wild, resolute, saintly little face, "loved long since," is not even "lost awhile" to me.

In response to my inquiries, the Sacred Heart sisters promptly verified that neither Sarah Susan Phillips nor either of her surviving sisters had attended Elmhurst Academy. This did not surprise me, since I knew that both Lillie and Susie Phillips had attended the Wheaton Seminary in Norton, Massachusetts, early in the 1870s and that their younger sister Annie later attended Miss Wheeler's School in Providence. I had never thought it likely that the Phillips sisters had themselves attended Elmhurst Academy. But it was the Index to the School Register for 1873-1914, which the sisters copied for me, that finally provided the clue which I believe explains the friendship of Sarah Susan Phillips and Miss Guiney. I had thought that I might find a Phillips relative—a Place, a Thomas, a Valentine, a Rathbun—enrolled at Elmhurst Academy, but instead what I found were two names which immediately struck me: Mary Banigan, enrolled in 1874-80, and Alice Banigan, enrolled in 1878-84.[18] These names sent me scurrying to Lovecraft's long letter to Robert E. Howard dated October 4, 1930, from which I quote the relevant portion:

> Very early in life I had an opportunity to see the Celtic poetic imagination at its very best, for my mother was a friend of the late Louise Imogen Guiney, a poet of pure Irish blood who now ranks among the really major figures of American literature. When I was three years old we spent a whole winter at the Guiney home in Auburndale, Mass., and I can still recall how the poetess used to teach me simple rhymes which I would recite standing on a table! Another Celtic sidelight of my youth was still nearer home [Whipple V. Phillips's

house at 454 Angell Street]—my next-door neighbours and best playmates being three brothers whose relation to the Irish stream might be said to be our
own, reversed—that is, they were descended from a line of Irishmen given to
marrying Rhode Island Yankees, so that although they were about 80% Anglo-Saxon, they considered themselves heirs to the Irish tradition through descent in the male line and the possession of the name of Banigan. Their
family always made a point to travel to Ireland as often as possible, and were
great collectors of Celtic antiquities. Their grandfather had a veritable museum of prehistoric Irish artifacts—indeed, I wish I knew what has become of
that collection now that the family has left Providence and the brothers are all
dispersed. (SL 3.184)

I will allow the reader his or her own enjoyment of Lovecraft's account of two
of these relics that the Banigan brothers presented to him. But a prosperous
Irish family named Banigan were next-door neighbors to Sarah Susan Phillips
family from 1880 or so, when Whipple V. Phillips built his home on the
northwest corner of Angell Street and Elmgrove Avenue.

This reference in turn sent me to Richard M. Bayles's still useful *History of
Providence County, Rhode Island* (New York: W. W. Preston & Co., 1891),
whose first volume (pp. 682–84) contains both a portrait and a sketch of the
prosperous manufacturer Joseph Banigan, the "grandfather" of Lovecraft's
account, born in County Monaghan, Ireland, on June 7, 1839, the son of
Bernard and Alice (Banigan) Banigan. They left Ireland in the midst of the
potato famine of the 1840s and sojourned in Dundee, Scotland, for two years
before coming to Providence. Young Joseph spent but one year in the public
school, and then went to work at age of nine years for the New England
Screw Company. After serving as an apprentice and journeyman in the jewelry trade, the entrepreneurial Joseph Banigan at the age of twenty-one years
joined forces with John Haskins in what was later organized as the Goodyear
India Rubber Bottle Stopper Company. In 1866 he helped organize the
Woonsocket Rubber Company, which had by time of the publication of
Bayles's history become the leading manufacturer of rubber products in the
world, with factories both in Woonsocket and Millville, Massachusetts. Joseph Banigan travelled to Brazil to organize his sources of supply of crude
rubber and established a commercial office in Para. By the time of the publication of Bayles's history, the Woonsocket Rubber Company had become the
largest importer of crude rubber in the United States. Its new factory, then
under construction in Woonsocket, was to be the largest rubber shoe factory
in the world. (Perhaps the rubber shoe packing crate which supplied the
frame for Miss Guiney's beloved coaster "Glorioso" had originally contained
rubber shoes given to Elmhurst Academy for its young ladies by Mr. Banigan.)
Mr. Banigan became expert not only in rubber manufacture, but also in the

worldwide currency markets that affected the supply and demand for raw rubber.

Joseph Banigan was a director on many corporate boards and in addition a philanthropist. He built the home for aged poor in Pawtucket, Rhode Island, completed in May 1884 and placed in charge of the Little Sisters of the Poor. In honor of his many services, Pope Leo XIII created him a Knight of the Order of St. Gregory the Great. Joseph Banigan died at his home at 510 Angell Street in Providence on July 23, 1898, just four days after the death of Lovecraft's father at Butler Hospital.[19] Perhaps most significantly, Bayles provided a short summary of Joseph Banigan's family history:

> In 1860 Mr. Banigan was married to Margaret, daughter of John F. Holt of Woonsocket, by whom he had four children: Mary A., wife of W. B. McElroy; John J., William B., and Alice, wife of Doctor James E. Sullivan. He was a second time married November 4, 1873, to Maria T. Conway of New York City.

Surely, the Mary Banigan enrolled at Elmhurst in 1874–80 and the Alice Banigan enrolled in 1878–84 must have been the daughters of Joseph and Margaret (Holt) Bannigan recorded by Bayles. If they entered Elmhurst at about the same ages as Miss Guiney, they were probably born about 1862 and 1866, respectively;[20] Mary, nearly the contemporary of Louise, and Alice, some years younger. Since Louise by her own account continued to visit Elmhurst frequently after her graduation in 1879, it seems quite likely that she may have been invited to visit the home of the Banigan sisters. There, in 1880 and after, the next-door neighbors would have been Whipple V. and Robie A. (Place) Phillips and their three surviving daughters: Lillian Delora (1856–1932), Sarah Susan (1857–1921), and Annie Emeline (1866–1941). [There was also a son Edwin Everett (1864–1918) and a daughter Emeline Estella (1859–1865) who died in childhood.] It seems likely that Louise got to meet all three Phillips sisters when she visited Mary and Alice Banigan. The connection between the Phillips and Banigan families remained close so that when Howard Phillips Lovecraft was growing up at 454 Angell Street during the period 1893–1904 three of Joseph Banigan's grandsons were his closest friends.[21] Mary (Banigan) McElroy did not die in Rhode Island between 1890 and 1920, but her younger sister Alice (Banigan) Sullivan died at her home at 254 Wayland Avenue in Providence on Sept. 28, 1909, just after her forty-third birthday. She was survived by her husband Dr. James E. Sullivan.[22]

So we have a plausible connection between Louise Imogen Guiney and Sarah Susan Phillips Lovecraft by way of the daughters of Joseph Banigan, who were schoolmates of Miss Guiney at Elmhurst Academy. To my way of thinking this circumstantial evidence tips the balance in favor of the supposition that Sarah Susan Phillips and Louise Imogen Guiney were actually acquainted. Both Lovecraft and Miss Guiney were copious correspondents, so that it is possible that newly discovered correspondence of one or of both of them may eventually provide more information about the relationship of Sarah Susan Phillips and Louise Imogen Guiney.[23] Absent the discovery of new correspondence that enriches our knowledge, we can only say that the presence of the Banigan sisters on the rolls of Elmhurst Academy during and after Miss Guiney's 1873-79 term at that institution makes it at least likely that Miss Guiney did make the acquaintance of Sarah Susan Phillips. Whether their relationship extended to anything like the closeness described in Lovecraft's letters must be severely doubted. Miss Guiney's copious correspondence with Frederick Holland Day from the 1889-93 period does not describe any extended visits by house guests such as Lovecraft claimed his parents paid Miss Guiney and her mother in Auburndale during the winter of 1892-93.

In addition to being partner in the publishing firm of Copeland & Day, Frederick Holland Day was also a photographer of note; and much of the renewed interest in Miss Guiney derives from a renewed interest in his photographic work. At one time, I dreamed I might find a photograph of the aged Oliver Wendell Holmes with an infant on his knee, with Miss Guiney and her mother and an unidentified couple sitting nearby. But librarians at the Library of Congress told me that many of Day's photographs were destroyed by a fire in his studio and that it is his art photographs that have survived and are studied. I certainly believe it is entirely possible that Sarah Susan Lovecraft and her husband did visit Miss Guiney and her mother while Winfield Scott Lovecraft was engaged in business in the Boston area in 1889-92. It may also be that Lovecraft's assertion that his parents acquired a house lot in Auburndale, Massachusetts, is still capable of verification, since records of real estate transactions are generally among the best-preserved of public records. But there is no primary evidence whatever to indicate that the Lovecrafts spent the entire winter of 1892-93 in the Guiney household in Auburndale; and the silence of Miss Guiney's correspondence about any such extended visits during this period is a very strong counterindication.

As John McInnis has suggested, I believe it is likely that the Lovecrafts, or at least Sarah Susan and her son, retreated to the Phillips home in Providence as Winfield Scott Lovecraft's difficulties escalated in 1892-93. The summer vacation of 1892 did not resolve Winfield Scott Lovecraft's problems, and by the time he was hospitalized at Butler Hospital in April 1893 he was suffering from grandiose delusions. It is entirely possible that Sarah Susan Lovecraft and Louise Imogen Guiney exchanged visits in Auburndale and Providence during this period—and not beyond the realm of possibility that the aged Oliver Wendell Holmes did indeed give the young Howard Phillips Lovecraft a ride on his knee during a visit to the Guiney home in Auburndale. Perhaps a Holmes scholar will one day have something to contribute with respect to the assertion that the aged Holmes met the infant Lovecraft.

What seems certain is that Sarah Susan Lovecraft, faced with the disintegration of all her plans for a happy family life on account of her husband's illness, focused all her attention on her young son, to an almost suffocating degree. Miss Ella Sweeney, a diminutive schoolteacher who met the Lovecrafts during their vacation in Dudley, Massachusetts, in 1892, remembered that Sarah Susan would not allow her young son out of her sight (Scott 313). The facts concerning Winfield Scott Lovecraft were transfigured into an account of an elegant, cultured Englishman felled by business cares and an apoplectic stroke. Probably the photograph of the couple with their son which has been reproduced so often was the only image which Lovecraft retained of his father, despite his protestation that he could "just remember" Winfield Scott Lovecraft (SL 4.355).

Similarly, it seems likely that Sarah Susan embellished for her son her relationship with the famed poet Louise Imogen Guiney. What was perhaps at best a friendly acquaintance was transformed into an intimate relationship involving an extended coresidency over the winter of 1892-93—actually likely the most desperate period of Sarah Susan Lovecraft's life, when her husband was clearly failing because of the personality aberrations caused by his illness. Perhaps in her mind the Guiney household in Auburndale became a refuge from what was doubtless the havoc of the final months of her life together with Winfield Scott Lovecraft, wherever they spent it. If Winfield did indeed buy a house lot in Auburndale at Susie's urging, the expenditure could have become yet another cause of stress as Winfield's health disintegrated. Perhaps a quiet coresidency with the Guineys in sylvan Auburndale represented the best substitute her mind could conjure for the final tortuous disintegration of her family life. We shall probably never know. But I believe that the presence of the Phillips's neighbors Mary and Alice Banigan on the rolls of Elmhurst Academy during the period Louise Imogen Guiney was also a student makes it quite likely that Sarah Susan Phillips and her sisters did know Louise Imogen Guiney.[24] We may hope that far from finding her a nuisance and an "atrocious Philistine," Miss Guiney may have extended her care and sympathy to a friend. For a single act of kindness the troubled soul may pour forth rivers of thanks. Perhaps that is what Sarah Susan Lovecraft did, when she talked about Miss Guiney to her son Howard. How she must have treasured notes and cards from Miss Guiney in the wake of her own tragedy. Given Howard's general distaste for Miss Guiney's work, perhaps Sarah Susan saw to it that a more congenial soul succeeded to any collection of Miss Guiney's books and letters that she may have possessed. As it was, Sarah Susan did not long survive her friend; she died on May 24, 1921, only six months after Miss Guiney expired in England. That Sarah Susan Lovecraft treasured the memory of even a casual friendship with the poet Louise Imogen Guiney should not surprise us at all. But perhaps in this world there is not much more of their history which we can hope to write.

Notes

1. See letters to Rheinhart Kleiner, 2 February 1916 (SL 1.20); Rheinhart Kleiner, 16 November 1916 (SL 1.31-33); Sarah Susan Lovecraft, Mar. 17, 1921 (SL 1.126-27); Edwin F. Baird, 3 February 1924 (SL 1.296); Bernard Austin Dwyer, 3 March 1927 (SL 2.107); Robert E. Howard, 4 October 1930 (SL 3.184); J. Vernon Shea, 4 February 1934 (SL 4.354-55). Since the letters published in *Selected Letters* represent only a minority of Lovecraft's epistolary output, it seems quite likely that he wrote about the friendship of his mother and Miss Guiney to other correspondents as well.

2. The published letter to Kleiner dated 16 November 1916 (SL 1.31-33) has an ellipsis at the end of its extended account of the relationship of Lovecraft's mother and Miss Guiney. It is possible that further information will become available when the full Arkham House transcriptions of the Lovecraft letters become available for scholarly use. (The full Arkham House Transcript of this letter as published in Lovecraft (62-80) contains only a little more information about the claimed relationship of the Lovecrafts with Miss Guiney. On pp. 65-66 Lovecraft recollects that he would respond "Louise Imogen Guiney!" when asked "Who do you love?" He also recollected slapping his father on the knees and exclaiming, "Papa, you look just like a young man!")

3. Winfield Scott Lovecraft's Butler Hospital records were published in full in *Lovecraft Studies* No. 24 (Spring 1991): 15-17, with commentary by M. Eileen McNamara, M.D.

4. The only known reference to Winfield Scott Lovecraft's employment by Gorham & Co. occurs in Sonia H. Davis [S. T. Joshi, ed.], *The Private Life of H. P. Lovecraft* (West Warwick, RI: Necronomicon Press, rev. ed. 1992), p. 7.

5. Koki misdates Winfield Scott Lovecraft's hospitalization to 1898. See also de Camp 14.

6 M. Eileen McNamara, commentary on Butler Hospital medical records of Winfield Scott Lovecraft (note 3). See also Kenneth W. Faig, Jr., "Some Thoughts Concerning Winfield Scott Lovecraft," *Moshassuck Review* (Esoteric Order of Dagon Amateur Press Association), April 1991, pp. 1-21.

7. For an example of Lovecraft's infrequent statements concerning his marriage, see August Derleth, *H.P.L.: A Memoir* (New York: Ben Abramson, 1945), pp. 15-16. Koki 208-11 was the first to reveal the fact that Lovecraft did not take the steps necessary to finalize his divorce.

8. For Lovecraft's high school record, see S. T. Joshi, *H. P. Lovecraft: A Life*, pp. 62-63 and de Camp 42, 50-51. For a letter wherein Lovecraft claims to have graduated from Hope Street High School, see SL 2.110.

9. Lovecraft to Maurice W. Moe, 1 September 1929; ALS, JHL.

10. Louise Callan, RSCJ, *The Society of the Sacred Heart in North America* (London: Longmans, Green & Co., 1937) provides an extensive history of the Society in North America. Pages 604-11 of this work are devoted to the Society's Elmhurst Academy in Providence, Rhode Island.

11. His son William Grosvenor, Jr., born in Providence on 4 August 1838, died at this home at 51 Prospect Street on 20 June 1906, and was buried in the family lot at Swan Point Cemetery. William Grosvenor, Jr., had married Rose Dinnard Phinney , the daughter of Theodore W. and Rose (Dinnard) Phinney, in Newport, Rhode Island. The bride was twenty-five years of age at the time of her marriage. Thomas M. Clark, Episcopal Bishop of Rhode Island, officiated at the wedding. Mr. Grosvenor had continued in his father's business as a cotton manufacturer and was survived by his wife. Information courtesy Kenneth S. Carlson, Reference Archivist, Rhode Island State Archives.

12. I am indebted to William McKenzie Woodward, Architectural Historian, Rhode Island Historical Preservation and Heritage Commission, for information about Dr. William Grosvenor's home Elmhurst. For published material, see Ruth Little Stokes and William H. Jordy, "William Grosvenor House (Elmhurst)" in William H. Jordy and Christopher P. Monkhouse, *Buildings on Paper: Rhode Island Architectural Drawings 1825-1945*, pp. 165-66. See also Monkhouse's essay on the "Seth Adams, Jr., House" in the same work, pp. 182-83, and William McKenzie Woodward's *Thomas Alexander Tefft: American Architecture in Transition, 1845-1860*, pp. 234-35. Tefft's original architectural drawings for Elmhurst form part of the collections of the John Hay Library at Brown University.

13. Details concerning the early history of Elmhurst Academy may be found not only in Callan (pp. 604-11) but also in Robert W. Hayman, *Catholicism in Rhode Island and the Diocese of Providence 1780-1886*, pp. 256-57.

14. Brochure, *Convent of the Sacred Heart: Elmhurst*, c. 1952. The brochure contains photographs of Elmhurst, its Sacred Heart chapel, outdoor shrine to Our Lady, classroom, and gymnasium scenes.

15. Information courtesy National Archives, Society of the Sacred Heart, St. Louis, Missouri.

16. Information concerning the Elmhurst property courtesy Margaret (Mrs. John G.) McMahon, Pawtucket, Rhode Island.

17. I am grateful to James Mahoney, Curator, Rare Books and Special Collections, Dinand Library, College of the Holy Cross, Worcester, Massachusetts, for a copy of a typescript of this memoir, corrected in Miss Guiney's hand. I have not been able to ascertain whether this memoir was actually published in 1907 or not. A generous extract does appear under the title "Elmhurst in the Seventies" in the program for the Tenth Biennial Conference of the Associated Alumnae of the Sacred Heart dated 12 May 1955. In addition, Margaret A. O'Reiley's memoir of Miss Guiney, which appeared in *Signet* for October 1921, contains generous quotations from "Memoirs of an Old Girl." Ms. O'Reiley's memoir appeared together with memoirs by Kittie Kinney

Macdonald, Mabel Fuller Blodgett, and Grace Phalan Tracy under the general title "Louise Imogen Guiney, Sacred Heart Girl" in this issue of *Signet*, which was the magazine of the Sacred Heart Alumnae Association. In addition, an obituary of Miss Guiney by Katherine C. E. Macdonald appeared in *Signet* for April 1921, and "A Study of Louise Imogen Guiney" by Regina Twibill Clark in *Signet* for November 1927. I am indebted to the National Archives of the Society of the Sacred Heart in St. Louis, Missouri, for copies of all these Sacred Heart Alumnae Association materials.

18. In the school register their names are spelled "Bannigan."

19. Information courtesy Kenneth S. Carlson, Reference Archivist, Rhode Island State Archives, Providence, Rhode Island.

20. Mary Ann Banigan was born in Boston, Massachusetts. She was twenty years of age when she married William Bartholomew McElroy in Providence on 7 November 1882. Mr. McElroy, a grocer, was twenty-six years of age at the time of their marriage. He was born in Providence, the son of William and Mary McElroy. Rev. William B. Cleary, a Roman Catholic pastor, officiated at their wedding. Alice Margaret Banigan was born in Smithfield, Rhode Island, on 14 September 1866. (Her marriage and death records state that Alice Margaret Banigan was born in Woonsocket, Rhode Island, but her birth record takes precedence as a record contemporary with the vital statistic it records.) She married James Edmund Sullivan, M.D., in Providence on 4 November 1885. Dr. Sullivan was thirty-five years of age at the time of his marriage. He was born in Fall River, Massachusetts, the son of Edmund and Ellen Sullivan, both Irish-born. Rev. Robert J. Sullivan, a Roman Catholic pastor, officiated at their wedding. Information courtesy Kenneth S. Carlson, Reference Archivist, Rhode Island State Archives, Providence, Rhode Island.

21. One may question Lovecraft's assertion in his letter to Robert E. Howard dated 4 October 1930 (*SL* 3.184) that the Banigans were "next-door" neighbors to Whipple V. and Roble A. Phillips. After the 1895 renumbering of Angell Street, the residences of Whipple V. Phillips and of Joseph Banigan were located at 454 and 510 Angell Street, respectively. But that the Phillipses and Banigans were close neighbors on Angell Street on Providence's East Side there can be no doubt.

22. Information courtesy Kenneth S. Carlson, Reference Archivist, Rhode Island State Archives, Providence, Rhode Island.

23. James Mahoney, Curator, Rare Books and Special Collections, Dinand Library, College of the Holy Cross, Worcester, Massachusetts, informs me that the letters of Miss Guiney to George and Rachel Norton, written during the period Miss Guiney attended Elmhurst Academy, do not mention Sarah Susan ("Susie") Phillips.

24. Sarah Susan (Phillips) Lovecraft was survived by her sisters Lillian Delora (Phillips) Clark and Annie Emeline (Phillips) Gamwell. Perhaps Lovecraft made one of his aunts the custodian of any Guiney relics he may have inherited from his mother. Any Guiney books and letters that were owned by Mrs. Gamwell would likely have fallen into the hands of Providence bookseller H. Douglass Dana when he bought the re-

maining books and papers at 66 College Street following the death of Mrs. Gamwell on 30 January 1941.

Works Cited or Consulted

[Anonymous]. *Convent of the Sacred Heart, Elmhurst.* Providence, RI: Elmhurst Academy, c. 1952. Promotional brochure with photographs.

[Anonymous]. Index to School Register 1873-1914 [Elmhurst Academy]. A.Ms., National Archives, Society of the Sacred Heart, St. Louis, Missouri.

Bayles, Richard M. *History of Providence County, Rhode Island.* New York: W. W. Preston & Co., 1891. 2 vols.

Cady, John Hutchins. *The Civic and Architectural Development of Providence.* Providence, RI: The Book Shop, 1957.

Callan, Louise, RSCJ. *The Society of the Sacred Heart in North America.* London: Longmans, Green & Co., 1937.

Clark, Regina Twibill. "A Study of Louise Imogen Guiney." *Signet* 8, No. 1 (November 1927): 51-54.

de Camp, L. Sprague. *Lovecraft: A Biography.* Garden City, NY: Doubleday & Co., 1975.

Faig, Kenneth W., Jr. "The Lovecrafts and the Guineys." *Moshassuck Review* (Esoteric Order of Dagon Amateur Press Association), November 1996, pp. 1-5.

——. "Some Thoughts on Louise Imogen Guiney." *Moshassuck Review* (Esoteric Order of Dagon Amateur Press Association), May 1994, pp. 1-15.

Fairbanks, Henry G. *Louise Imogen Guiney: Laureate of the Lost.* Albany, NY: Magi Books, 1972. An abridged version of this work was published in the Twayne's English Authors Series in 1973.

Guiney, Louise Imogen. Letters to Frederick Holland Day. Library of Congress, Washington, DC.

——. "Memories of an Old Girl." T.Ms. with holograph corrections, Special Collections, Dinand Library, College of the Holy Cross, Worcester, Massachusetts. Reprinted in part as "Elmhurst of the Seventies," Convent of the Sacred Heart, Elmhurst: Tenth Biennial Conference of The Associated Alumnae of the Sacred Heart. Providence, RI: Elmhurst Academy, May 12, 1955, pp. 12-13 and in Margaret A. O'Reiley, "Louise Imogen Guiney, Sacred Heart Girl," q.v.

Hayman, Robert W. *Catholicism in Rhode Island and the Diocese of Providence 1780-1886.* Providence, RI: Diocese of Providence, 1982.

Jordy, William H., and Christopher P. Monkhouse. *Buildings on Paper: Rhode Island Architectural Drawings 1825-1945.* Providence, RI: Brown University, Rhode Island Historical Society, Rhode Island School of Design, 1982.

Joshi, S. T. H. P. *Lovecraft: A Life*. West Warwick, RI: Necronomicon Press, 1996.

——. *An Index to the Selected Letters of H. P. Lovecraft*. West Warwick, RI: Necronomicon Press, 1980, 1991.

——. *Lovecraft's Library: A Catalogue*. Rev. ed. New York: Hippocampus Press, 2002.

King, Henry Melville. *Historical Catalogue of the Members of the First Baptist Church in Providence, Rhode Island*. Providence, RI: F. H. Townsend, Printer, 1908.

Koki, Arthur S. "H. P. Lovecraft: An Introduction to his Life and Writings." M. A. thesis: Columbia University, 1962.

Lovecraft, H. P., *Letters to Rheinhart Kleiner*. New York, NY: Hippocampus Press, 2005. Edited by S. T. Joshi and David E. Schultz.

Macdonald, Katherine C. E. "Louise Imogen Guiney." *Signet* 2, No. 1 (April 1921): 36–39.

McInnis, John L., III. "An Autobiographical Study of 'The Colour Out of Space.'" *Books at Brown* 38–39 (1991–92): 67–100.

——. "Father Images in Lovecraft's 'Hypnos.'" *Fantasy Commentator* 7, No. 1 (Fall 1990): 41–48.

O'Reiley, Margaret A.; Macdonald, Kittie Kinney; Blodgett, Mabel Fuller; and Tracy, Grace Phalan. "Louise Imogen Guiney, Sacred Heart Girl." *Signet* 2, No. 1 (October 1921): 3–15.

Scott, Winfield Townley. "His Own Most Fantastic Creation." In Lovecraft's *Marginalia*. Sauk City, WI: Arkham House, 1944.

Tenison, Eva Mabel. *Louise Imogen Guiney*. London: Macmillan, 1923.

Woodward, William McKenzie. *Thomas Alexander Tefft: American Architecture in Transition, 1845–1860*. Providence, RI: Brown University, 1988.

The author wishes to thank for their invaluable assistance: the sisters of the National Archives, Society of the Sacred Heart, St. Louis, Missouri; Kenneth S. Carlson, Reference Archivist, Rhode Island State Archives, Providence, Rhode Island; James Mahoney, Curator, Rare Books and Special Collections, Dinand Library, College of the Holy Cross, Worcester, Massachusetts; Margaret (Mrs. John G.) McMahon, Pawtucket, Rhode Island, a 1946 graduate of Elmhurst Academy and former president of the Elmhurst Alumnae Association; and William McKenzie Woodward, Architectural Historian, Rhode Island Historical and Heritage Commission, Providence, Rhode Island.

The Unknown Lovecraft I: Political Operative

When browsing through Michael White's article "Fond Memories That Linger On" in the *Fossil* for January 1948,[1] I unexpectedly encountered this passage concerning H. P. Lovecraft (p. 102):

> Let us now skip fifteen years during which I heard nothing of amateur journalism. On a night of 1917 while attending a meeting of a small literary club in Boston, a tall sallow faced, grimly serious individual, dressed in black, asked and obtained permission, to give us a talk. He spoke of the United Amateur Press Association. His sincerity was obvious, and although he was not a magnetic speaker, or one to make converts, he was never lost for a suitable expression. It was Howard Lovecraft. At that time Howard took a little part in international politics. His pet aversion was that little band of radical intellectuals trying to push the noble British lion into Dublin's Liffey. His opinions crept into *The Conservative*, which he published at the time. He was associated in his endeavors with DeMarest Lloyd, a paid British agent, whose headquarters was in Boston. Lloyd, dressed in the inevitable tweeds, knickers, cane, and spats, was the theatregoer's conception of an Englishman. He worked among the Back Bay Brahmins while Howard did the literary persuading. Lovecraft did for conviction what DeMarest did for hire. Howard made one exception: he was an outspoken admirer of Lord Dunsany. He did not know at the time, and probably never knew, that the Dublin playwright was a trusted fellow rebel of the Irish. Dunsany "castle" is outside Dublin. Its architecture is, as a local wag would have it, half Gothic and half Sears Roebuck. Through Lovecraft I became acquainted with the Hub Club.

One would give much to know more details of the events that Michael White recounts. What was the identity of the "small literary club" that Lovecraft addressed on behalf of the United Amateur Press Association in Boston in 1917? When, exactly, did the meeting addressed by Lovecraft occur? And what was his relationship with the paid British agent DeMarest Lloyd?

Regrettably, I can answer none of these tantalizing questions. DeMarest Lloyd is not mentioned in either de Camp's or Joshi's biographies of Lovecraft, nor is his name indexed in Joshi's *An Index to the Selected Letters of H. P. Lovecraft*. Both de Camp and Joshi discuss Lovecraft's strong pro-British sympathies during World War I and his defense of England's suppression of the Easter Rising in Ireland in 1916. But neither hint of his association with paid British agents. Lovecraft discussed Anglo-Irish relations extensively in his correspondence with fellow Providence amateur John T. Dunn (1889–1983) in 1915–17, but neither this published correspondence nor the editors' notes make any reference to his association with DeMarest Lloyd. It's interesting to note that in Dunn and White Lovecraft had friends of strong pro-Irish feelings.

Who are the *dramatis personae* of the January 1948 *Fossil* account? The *Fossil* for April 1960 contains a brief obituary of amateur journalist Michael White (p. 155), contributed by Edward H. Cole (1892-1966). Born in Ireland on September 7, 1884, White was working for an uncle in Torrington, Connecticut, when he first became acquainted with amateur journalism in 1902. He published six issues of *Nutmeg Review* before the tumultuous New York City convention of the National Amateur Press Association in July 1902 scared him off. Eventually, he moved to Boston, where he served as chief clerk for the Quartermaster Corps in South Boston in 1917-20. The major part of his working life in Boston was spent as special clerk in the main post office, from which position he retired in October 1947 after thirty years of service.

While White contributed to the newspaper press in Boston and its suburbs, he remained primarily an amateur journalist. A very dear friend of Edith Miniter (1867-1934), whom he first met through H. P. Lovecraft, White joined W. Paul Cook in publishing *In Memoriam: Jennie E. T. Dowe* in 1921. Mrs. Dowe (1840-1919) was Mrs. Miniter's mother and shared in most of her daughter's career in amateur journalism. An able poet in her own right, Mrs. Dowe found her metier in Irish verse and a welcome home for her poems in the *Century Magazine* under the editorship of Richard Watson Gilder. White's own appreciative article "The Poetry of Jennie Dowe" appeared in the *National Amateur* for November [1922]-January 1923. He was present with Mrs. Miniter at one of the very last Hub Club dinners, held in a Chinese restaurant in Boston on April 23, 1924, to celebrate the one hundredth anniversary of Byron's death. Shortly thereafter, after only partially successful attempts to share housekeeping with Charles and Laura Sawyer in Allston, Massachusetts, and with Charles and Augusta Parker in Malden, Massachusetts, Mrs. Miniter retreated back to her birthplace of North Wilbraham, Massachusetts, where she resided until her death with her distant cousin Evanore Olds Beebe (1858-1935) in a rambling old farmhouse filled with antiques. For more than thirty years (1893-1924), Mrs. Miniter had been the mainstay of the Hub Amateur Journalists' Club (founded by Ella Maud Frye and other Boston amateurs on March 10, 1890), and the Club disintegrated soon after her final departure from Boston. White continued to be associated with amateur magazines through the 1940s and published a slender collection of verse entitled *Verses in a Lighter Vein* three years before his death, which occurred on September 11, 1959. He married Caroline Edmunds in 1909 (his wife died in 1958), and was survived by a daughter and a sister.

But what of the principal figure of Mr. White's account, the British agent DeMarest Lloyd? I think he is probably the DeMarest Lloyd who appears in

Marquis's *Who Was Who in America 1897-1942* (vol. 1) (1943; reprinted 1981) and I will probably do well to cite his entry in the 1981 edition in full:

> LLOYD, Demarest, journalist, publicist, b. Chicago, Ill., Feb. 19, 1883; s. Henry Demarest and Jessie (Bross) L.; A. B., Harvard, 1904; Harvard Law Sch., 1906-07; m. Katharine Nordell, Dec. 6, 1916; children—Angelica, Demarest, Karen Gallup. Joined F. A. Central Officers Training Sch., Camp Zachary Taylor, Ky., Oct. 1918. Pres. Loyal Coalition, Mar. 1920-Jan. 1922[2]; diplomatic corr. of *The Christian Science Monitor*, 1922-24; European cable editor, at London, 1924-25; editorial representative *Christian Science Monitor*, at Washington, D.C., 1925-26; dir. *Chicago Tribune*, 1926-31; chmn. National Immigration Legislative Committee of Patriotic Societies, 1928-29; editor and publisher "Affairs," Dec. 1931-. Vice chmn. bd. Am. Coalition of Patriotic Socs., mem. Nat. Council of Nat. Economic League; exec. sec. Taxpayers Union; mem. bd. Nat. Rep. Builders, Advisory Council Am. Liberty League. Home: Washington, D. C. Died June 24, 1937.

Demarest Lloyd also has a citation in the *National Cyclopedia of American Biography* (J. T. White & Co., 1892-1977, 57 vols., v. 1, 1897-1940), but I have not been able to consult this reference at the time of this writing. He was the son of the noted journalist and reformer Henry Demarest Lloyd (b. May 1, 1847, New York, NY; d. Sept. 28, 1903, Chicago, IL) who merits more than a page in the *Dictionary of American Biography* (Scribners, 1933). Using the Internet, I learned that there is a Demarest Lloyd State Park in South Dartmouth, Mass. An Internet search for Demarest Lloyd also produced several university archives that have holdings of his correspondence.

So do I have the right man? I believe so, despite the fact that White gives the name of his British agent as DeMarest Lloyd rather than Demarest Lloyd. Note that White does not say that Lloyd was a British citizen, only that he was a paid British agent. As a graduate of Harvard University and a sometime student in its law school, he is located in Boston until the next citation for him in his *Who Was Who*'s entry at Camp Zachary Taylor in Kentucky in 1918. Like Lovecraft, Lloyd was probably eager to join the battle against Germany once America declared war in 1917. Lovecraft, of course, was frustrated in his own attempt to serve in the military; but White's account reveals that he may have aided the cause of his beloved England on the intellectual front, in a more organized fashion than polemics in amateur journals. One is led to wonder if there is an entire anonymous or signed literature by Lovecraft in political publications of which we have as yet no knowledge. While Lloyd's participation in patriotic associations is cited by *Who Was Who* to the 1920s and later, it is certainly believable that he was involved with predecessor organizations in the Boston area in the prior decade.

The unsubstantiated (as far as I know) story that Lovecraft sought military service on behalf of England has been rattling around Lovecraft studies for many decades. Perhaps, however, his endeavor was on the intellectual rather than on the military front. Convincing the American public to go to war has never been an easy job. Perhaps Lovecraft did his part, in an intellectual sense, in a more organized fashion than has hitherto been realized. Perhaps there is an entire new chapter of his life waiting to be written by a diligent and thorough researcher.

Notes

1. I wish to thank Hyman Bradofsky for making the texts of all the amateur publications cited in this article available to me.

2. Lovecraft's essay "Lucubrations Lovecraftian" (originally published in the *United Co-operative* 1, no. 3 for April 1921) had a section entitled "The Loyal Coalition" dealing with this organization which Lloyd chaired in 1920-22. (See *Collected Essays 1* (pp. 277-80) for the text. In his essay, Lovecraft urged members of the United Amateur Press Association to join the Loyal Coalition (then headquartered at 24 Mount Vernon St., Boston 9, Massachusetts), which opposed foreign (particularly Irish) intervention in American affairs. I am indebted to S. T. Joshi for the citation of this essay. It is probable that Lloyd and Lovecraft were involved in predecessor organizations during the period before the formation of the Loyal Coalition.

Works Cited

de Camp, L. Sprague. *Lovecraft: A Biography*. Garden City, NY: Doubleday, 1975.

Joshi, S. T. *H. P. Lovecraft: A Life*. West Warwick, RI: Necronomicon Press, 1996.

Joshi, S. T., David E. Schultz, and John H. Stanley. "H. P. Lovecraft: Letters to John T. Dunn." *Books at Brown* 38-39 (1991-1992 [published 1995]): 157-223.

The Unknown Lovecraft II: Reluctant Laureate

*Lovecraft and the Politics of NAPA's
E. Dorothy Houtain Administration (1921–22)*

Collected Essays 1: Amateur Journalism contains the following, seemingly benign letter from the *National Amateur* for January 1922:[1]

[c. November 1921]

My dear Mr. Heins:—

Permit me to thank you most sincerely for the attractive silver medal which your Association has been so kind to award me. The honourable mention is as gratifying as any ordinary laureateship, since my superior is no less a person than James F. Morton, Jr. The idea of the medals, for which I believe your Association is indebted to you alone, is certainly a most desirable one; since it stimulates in the contests a keen interest otherwise lacking. I regret that my prime allegiance to the United Association forbade me to contribute to your medal fund in these lean times, but am sure you can appreciate the principle involved. If you ever join the United and start such a fund, you may depend upon my fullest coöperation!

It was not without a qualm of conscience that I accepted the medal when informed of it by Mr. Houtain—it seemed to some degree unethical to step into another Association grab a valuable prize, and then step out again[2] with only a brief word of thanks. My qualms were overruled, however, and I now tender the thanks with as much contribution as the occasion demands.

Thanking you again—both you and your association, in fact—and assuring you to have any part of this letter published if you so choose.

Believe me,

Most sincerely yours,
H. P. Lovecraft.[3]

The guarded phraseology of Lovecraft's letter to John Milton Heins[4] is understandable in view of Lovecraft's primary allegiance to the Hoffman-Daas faction of the United Amateur Press Association, into which he was recruited by Edward F. Daas in April 1914. Lovecraft retained his primary allegiance to this UAPA faction until its demise in the 1925–26 official year, serving in many offices including president in 1917–18 and official editor under Alfred Galpin (1920–21), Ida C. Haughton (1921–22), Sonia H. Greene (1923–24), and Sonia H. Lovecraft (1924–25). He did yeoman's work for UAPA's department of public criticism over many years as reflected in *Collected Essays 1*.

While his long stay in the United was generally happy, there was always some resistance to his emphasis on the literary aspect of the hobby. During the 1921-22 official year, his friends Paul J. Campbell, Frank B. Long, and Alice Hamlet all served with him on the official board under president Ida C. Haughton. Lovecraft's relationship with president Haughton was strained; he was responsible for administration of the official organ fund, which Haughton accused him of mismanaging.[5] William J. Dowdell and Leo Fritter charged Lovecraft with filling the official organ (*The United Amateur*) with material written by his friends. As a result of the controversy, Lovecraft was defeated by Leo Fritter for the office of official editor for the 1922-23 term by a vote of 44-29.[6] Lovecraft was voted back into office as official editor for the 1923-24 term and Sonia H. Greene was elected president; but they were left helpless by the refusal of outgoing secretary-treasurer Alma B. Sanger to release funds and only published one issue of the official organ (dated May 1924) for the 1923-24 official year. Before the conclusion of the official year, Lovecraft and Greene married on March 3, 1924. Re-elected to the same offices for the 1924-25 term, they produced just one more issue of the official organ (dated July 1925), dominated by contributions by members of Lovecraft's circle of literary friends. For the 1925-26 term, Edgar J. Davis was elected president and Victor E. Bacon official editor. Bacon produced a few thin issues of the *United Amateur*, but UAPA Hoffman-Daas faction lapsed into inactivity during the 1925-26 term. No officials were elected for 1926-27 and subsequent years.[7]

Lovecraft never joined the rival faction of the United, dominated for many years by J. F. Roy Erford and Clyde F. Noel of Seattle, Washington. For the first three and one half years of his participation in the amateur journalism hobby, he was exclusively a "United" man; in fact, his mentor Edward F. Daas strongly advocated exclusive allegiance to the Hoffman-Daas United faction. The National Amateur Press Association was the oldest of the associations, having been founded in Philadelphia in 1876. As he wrote to his friend Rheinhart Kleiner on November 8, 1917, Lovecraft finally succumbed to pressure from friends to join NAPA:[8]

At the repeated solicitation of many persons who declared that my aloofness from the National was a barrier to inter-associational harmony, I sent in an application for membership about a week ago. My connexion, however, will be purely nominal; as I gave the Nationalites very clearly to understand. I have time & strength only for my own association, yet was willing to have my name on the National's list if it would help any. I bear no ill will toward the present Martin administration,[9] which is quite different from the former conditions which so strongly repelled me. There was an unscholarly & blustering character about certain political rings which I could not help loathing. Daas will be furious at my recognition of the National, but personally, I deemed it best to respond to what seem to be genuinely friendly overtures on the part of the older association. Should the National presume to treat the United with disrespect again, I shall be the first to resent the act. My exhibition of good will is based upon Edward H. Cole's statement that he has induced Graeme Davis[10] to abandon his anti-United campaign. If Davis will be so good, so will I!

It should be remembered that Lovecraft was serving as president of the Hoffman-Daas United faction when he acted to join NAPA. His application was probably intended primarily as a gesture of inter-associational goodwill. He says as much in the above-referenced letter to his friend Rheinhart Kleiner.

My file of the *National Amateur* for these years is only partial, but it does not appear that Lovecraft renewed his membership in NAPA in 1918. He had ceased to serve as UAPA president, and perhaps he no longer saw the need to maintain his "nominal" NAPA membership for the sake of goodwill–this despite the election of his close friend W. Paul Cook (1880-1948) as NAPA's official editor for the 1918-19 term and as NAPA's president for the 1919-20 term. Indeed, it was not until after NAPA's Cleveland convention in July 1920, which elected Anthony F. Moitoret (1892-1979) as president and Boston's Marjorie H. Outwater as official editor, that Lovecraft resumed his formal association with NAPA. The March 1921 issue of the *National Amateur* notes Lovecraft as a member admitted since the July 1920 convention. As far as I am able to tell, Lovecraft maintained his membership in NAPA from that point forward until his death.

It is not too difficult to understand Lovecraft's decision to re-join NAPA. He was beginning to emerge from the hermitry at 598 Angell Street in Providence that marked the early years of his participation in amateur journalism. W. Paul Cook and Rheinhart Kleiner both visited him in Providence in 1917 and in 1918. (Before that time, William B. Stoddard and Edward H. Cole, both of whom came to visit him in Providence in 1914, were the only amateur journalists who had met Lovecraft in person.) The admission of Lovecraft's mother to Butler Hospital in March 1919 (where she died in May 1921) left her son freer to travel. In October 1919, Lovecraft traveled to Boston to attend a lecture by Lord Dunsany at the Copley Plaza Hotel; his UAPA friend Alice Hamlet and her aunt accompanied him. Lovecraft's old UAPA mentor Edward F. Daas came to Providence for a two-day visit on June 21-23, 1920. The Boston amateurs who were not traveling to Cleveland to support the candidacy of Marjorie H. Outwater for NAPA official editor held an extended gathering over the 4th of July holiday in 1920. Lovecraft arrived on July 4, 1920, and stayed overnight at the home of Alice Hamlet at 109 Greenbriar Street in Dorchester.[11] The doyenne of Boston amateurdom at the time of Lovecraft's visits was Edith (Dowe) Miniter (1867-1934).[12] While UAPA had its own adherents in Boston like Alice Hamlet and S. Lillian McMullen, Miniter's Hub Club (whose members were primarily affiliated with NAPA) was the center of activity. (The primary affiliation of the Boston amateurs probably explains Lovecraft's decision to re-join NAPA after the July 1920 convention.) Lovecraft returned once more for the Hub Club annual picnic on August 7, 1920, and yet again on September 5, 1920. On the latter visit, he met for the first time James F. Morton, Jr. Lovecraft made a day trip to Boston on February 22, 1921, to attend the amateur journalists' conference sponsored by the Hub Club held at the Quincy House. Then, on March 10, 1921, Lovecraft returned once again, to attend a St. Patrick's Day party at the Sawyer household in Allston. On this occasion, he read his weird story "The Moon-Bog." It was the second time he stayed overnight in Boston. On this occasion he slept on the famous well-worn sofa "Epgephi" where so many other weary amateur journalists had rested their bones. Both Sawyer and Miniter were a generation older than Lovecraft, so presumably there was no need of a chaperon. Lovecraft's mother passed away on May 24, 1921. This did not stop him from completing his plans to visit Myrta A. Little in Hampstead, New Hampshire, on June 8, 1921,[13] and to attend a Hub Club meeting in Boston on June 9, 1921. The stage was set for Lovecraft to attend NAPA's Boston convention in July 1921, where he met his future wife Sonia H. Greene for the first time.

One observer of the emergence of Lovecraft was George Julian Houtain (1884-1945). Houtain, the *bête noir* of NAPA politics in the first quarter of the twentieth century, first entered the hobby in 1898. He earned the enmity of the Boston amateurs (and especially of Edith Miniter) for his role in the 1902 NAPA convention in New York City, which notoriously refused to "count the proxies" and elected Anthony F. Wills president over John L. Peltret. (Miniter would struggle unsuccessfully for years to have Peltret's name added to the NAPA presidential roster for the official year 1902-03; Wills took the position that he would ask for the removal of his own name if this action were taken.) When Mrs. Miniter was elected president for the 1909-10 term at NAPA's New York convention in July 1909, Houtain was elected her official editor. He and others of the official board did all they could to ruin Mrs. Miniter's administration, and she finally removed him as official editor (in favor of C. A. A. Parker of the famous "Parker Principles") at the beginning of October 1909 after he failed to produce any issue of the *National Amateur*. Houtain responded with several "rump" issues of the purported official organ, one of which contained a lengthy legal complaint against Mrs. Miniter. A relentless self-promoter and organization-promoter, Houtain probably ranks with David V. Bush (1882-1959) and Harry Houdini (1874-1926) as among the strongest "Type A" personalities encountered by Lovecraft. Nevertheless, it is notable how well Lovecraft got along with all three of these men. For many years, he cultivated David V. Bush as a profitable revision client. His association with Houdini, which began with his ghost-writing of "Under the Pyramids" (published as "Imprisoned with the Pharaohs") in 1924, was only ended by Houdini's premature death in 1926. Houtain wrote extensively of his encounter with Lovecraft in Boston in July 1920 in his *Zenith* for January 1921.

Lovecraft's own impression of Houtain from the same meeting is recorded in his letter to Rheinhart Kleiner dated September 10, 1920:[14]

> Fancy my surprise when I encountered, as I crossed the portal, none other than George Julian Houtain, your genial & exuberant fellow-Brooklynite, whose presence I had not even remotely anticipated. I was really much pleased, for I cannot help liking the rascal! He is such a battery of animal spirits that he electrifies all the atmosphere about him, shedding & diffusing a goodly share of the overflowing vitality with which Nature has endowed him.

Writing in the *National Tribune* for August 1921, Houtain described Lovecraft at the time of his attendance at the NAPA convention in Boston in July 1921 (p. 18):

> The time will never be when I will the less enjoy the splendidness of Howard Lovecraft. He is a big man in every way. Much to my delight he has proven himself to be the most human of documents. He possesses a sense of humor that is astounding, because one would doubt he possessed the gift. He is also a man with a deep sense of honor and can always be trusted. He is a modest man and great was my joy when I arranged with our official vamp, Sonia Greene, to steal up on him suddenly, get a half-Nelson clutch on his august form so that I could Brownie No. 2A him—which I did. Then the fun that followed with Lovecraft burlesquing himself as a victim of a blackmailing gang and accusing Sonia and me of being in cohorts—which we were.
>
> Finally a deal was patched up that the negative of the said picture is to be placed under a certain rock on the corner of Broadway and 42nd Street, New York City, July 4, 1922 [i.e., one year hence]. If Lovecraft is there at ten o'clock P.M. it is to be his—otherwise (and this is the dire threat) it is to be published immediately following the New York convention. Woe be unto him if he doesn't appear.

Knowing of Houtain as a long-time political opponent of Mrs. Miniter, Lovecraft was surely surprised to meet him in her home in September 1920. But there was in fact another agenda in progress: Houtain's romance with Mrs. Miniter's friend Elsie Dorothy (Grant) MacLaughlin. Both the *Zenith* for January 1921 and the *National Tribune* for August 1921 are full of photographs of Houtain and MacLaughlin together. By May 1921, Mrs. MacLaughlin had removed from Boston to 208 Quincy Street in Brooklyn; before marrying Houtain in August 1921, she was divorced from her husband, David S. MacLaughlin. Well before her removal from Boston to Brooklyn—in fact, at the very beginning of 1921—MacLaughlin had accepted the Hub

Club's endorsement for the NAPA presidency for the 1921–22 official year. Traditionally, the prior year's official editor often moved up to the president's post the following year, but Marjorie Outwater, who was engaged to be married, decided after some wavering that she did not want the position. So Houtain's sweetheart Mrs. MacLaughlin became Boston's candidate. One cannot help noticing Houtain's comments in the *National Tribune* for August 1921 that Howard Lovecraft also had a developing relationship with Sonia H. Greene. Houtain was right. Lovecraft would marry Sonia Greene less than three years after first meeting her in Boston in July 1921. In the meantime, she would produce two luxurious issues of the *Rainbow* featuring writing by Lovecraft and his friends. As early as September 1921, she would visit Lovecraft and his aunt Lillian D. Clark in Providence, hosting them for luncheon at the Crown Hotel. In April 1922 she would turn over her Brooklyn apartment to Lovecraft and his Cleveland friend, poet Samuel Loveman (1887–1976). It was Lovecraft's own first trip to New York City, and he delighted in the company of Loveman and Frank Belknap Long (1901–1994). In May 1922, Lovecraft visited Myrta A. Little again in New Hampshire and then in June 1922 he traveled to Cambridge, Massachusetts, to hear his revision client David V. Bush lecture. Sonia was in Boston on business that summer, and she came down to Providence on June 16 and met both of Lovecraft's aunts. Lovecraft himself joined her in Magnolia, Massachusetts, from June 26 to July 5. According to her own account, Sonia first kissed Lovecraft on this visit. As Houtain had written in the *National Tribune* for August 1921, the members of NAPA assembled in New York City for their July 1922 convention. It does not appear that Lovecraft attended any part of the 1922 convention; over all his years of participation in amateur journalism, he is believed to have attended only the 1921 and 1930 Boston NAPA conventions. Perhaps Lovecraft and Greene chose deliberately to absent themselves from the 1922 New York City NAPA convention. Sonia's business trip to Boston's North Shore may have offered a convenient excuse a convenient excuse for both to skip the convention and an opportunity to spend some private time together.

The candidates for the NAPA presidency at the 1921 Boston convention were E. Dorothy MacLaughlin and Edna Hyde (1893–1962). Edna Hyde was originally Edna von der Heide, but like many Americans of German descent, she Anglicized her name toward the end of the First World War. Nevertheless, she remained known to her friends as "Vondy," from the "von der" portion of her original surname. Later she married Philip B. McDonald (1888–1959) and was known as Edna Hyde McDonald. Edna first attended a NAPA convention in Bridgeport, Connecticut, in 1914, and found herself somewhat intimidated by that formidable trio of female amateurs, Edith Miniter, Laurie Sawyer, and Ethel Johnston-Myers. (Miniter and Sawyer were in their later forties and Johnston-Myers in her early thirties, while Hyde was a mere twenty-one years old.) A year later, Edna attended the UAPA convention in Rocky Mount, North Carolina, and had more fun among the younger crowd there.[15] Edna had been appointed NAPA official editor in 1914 by president Leston M. Ayres, after the resignation of Hubert A. Reading. In 1915, she was a candidate for the NAPA presidency, but she was defeated by George Julian Houtain on the first ballot with 45 votes for Houtain, 28 for Hyde, 15 for Kilpatrick, and 1 for Haggerty. Houtain offered her the office of official editor, to which she was duly elected by the convention, but she resigned on August 13, 1915. Houtain appointed Brooklynite Ernest A. Dench in her stead.[16] So opposed were some of the Boston amateurs to Houtain's election that they dropped their NAPA memberships during his presidency; Edith Miniter was among them. Now in 1921 the tables were turned. Houtain and his New Yorkers were supporting Boston's own E. Dorothy MacLaughlin. A significant number of amateurs felt that Vondy would be a better president. By and large, Boston amateurs remained committed to their MacLaughlin despite substantial support for Hyde from the Midwest and respected amateurs like "Tryout" Smith, Julian Baber, and former NAPA President Leston M. Ayres. In a letter published in John Milton Heins's *American Amateur* for April 1921, Lovecraft wrote as follows:[17]

> I shall vote for E. Dorothy MacLaughlin for President of the National because of her individual fitness for he post, as well as her representation of the elements devoted to honest literary endeavour. The encroachment of factions dealing only in personal malice and debased and scurrilous journalism should be resisted at the polls for the good of the whole amateur cause.

Regrettably, the NAPA presidential campaign of 1921 began early and was marred some of the worst personal mudslinging in the history of the association. Most of the mudslinging directed at the Houtains concerned their romantic relationship and the divorces of their respective spouses prior to their marriage on August 30, 1921. Solidly in the MacLaughlin camp, young John Milton Heins played a regrettable roll in the mudslinging of the 1921 campaign—particularly the character assassinations leveled at MacLaughlin's opponent Edna Hyde and her fiancé Philip B. McDonald, an assistant professor of English at New York University. John Milton Heins was actually responsible for Edna's meeting Professor McDonald. In April 1920, radical poet Elsa Gidlow (1898–1986), one of the star contributors to the *American Amateur*, moved from Montreal to New York City, and editor Heins decided that she should meet Hyde and McDonald. So he invited them to meet him at the New York Public Library Art Gallery at 2 P.M., on May 1, 1920, to be followed by a stroll in Central Park, dinner at an Italian restaurant, and then a Blue Pencil Club meeting at the home of the Denches at Sheepshead Bay. Charles W. Heins joined the party for dinner and for the subsequent Blue

Pencil Club meeting. Both Heinses and Professor McDonald wrote up the "May party" at which Hyde and McDonald first met in the *American Amateur* for July 1920. Gidlow and her fellow Montreal club member Roswell George Mills (1896–1966) had set amateurdom a-twitter with their radical, avant-garde amateur journal *Les Mouches Fantastiques*, which they had begun to publish from Montreal in 1918. The first volume of *Les Mouches* was produced using a mimeograph, but Gidlow and Mills had the first number of a projected second volume professionally printed in April 1920, just before Gidlow's removal to New York City. Within a few months, Mills joined Gidlow in New York City, and Joe Thalheimer and John Milton Heins visited them on September 25, 1920. Heins was publishing quite a bit of work by Mills and Gidlow in the *American Amateur*, including notably Gidlow's attack on the deficiency of literary merit in amateurdom in the July 1920 issue.

On October 17, 1920, the Heinses hosted a meeting of the Blue Pencil Club at their home in Ridgefield Park, New Jersey. Joe Thalheimer escorted young Miss Hyde to the meeting, and newcomers Mills and Gidlow attended as well. To say the least, the Heinses were offended by Miss Hyde's conduct at the club meeting. She and others of the young people spent their time smoking and flirting on the stairwell and in the grape arbor, rather than attending the meeting itself. Edna wanted Heins's support for her presidential campaign, but he was already committed to MacLaughlin. Whether with encouragement from Dorothy MacLaughlin (as he later claimed) or not, Heins published a lurid article "Why I Consider Edna Hyde Unfit to Be President of the N.A.P.A." in the *American Amateur* for May 1921. Young John Milton was not the only culprit—his sister Gladys E. Heins had published a scurrilous poem attacking Hyde in the issue for April 1921. Gladys's poem was entitled "Inspiration"— the title of Hyde's own amateur magazine—and contained lines like:

> Breathes my mother to my father:
> "Listen 'Hon' go in and cheer up lonesome Joe,—
> Vondy's very busy kissing in our arbor,
> He's her escort, and she treats him so!"

Heins proceeded to elaborate on the conduct that had given offense to the Heinses at the Blue Pencil Club meeting at their home on October 17, 1920:

> My sister's poem in my April number is absolutely the truth, which I glossed over in the November account. Not only did Miss Hyde prefer to sit outside and "carry-on" during the meeting of the Blue Pencil Club at our house, but actually came in and said those very amateurs whom she had staid [sic] had told her "the members of the Blue Pencil Club were impossible!"—a tattle-tale that got her an instant and open reprimand from Della Knack who is now the local president.

That "Vondy" as the "boys" familiarly call her prefers to "carry-on" at the rare amateur gatherings she condescends to attend, is of course her own business, but when she becomes a candidate for our highest office, we have to make it ours. How else can the fittest be selected?

Perhaps to console her "neglected" escort Joe Thalheimer, Miss Hyde apparently shared with him some intimate details of her relationship with Professor McDonald, which John Milton reported in print as follows: "I have Joe Thalheimer tell me, that he is looking for McDonald near a brick yard, so he can sprinkle him with 'Irish confetti' for what the 'fickle Edna' was telling him about the same McDonald." Heins further printed the names of Hyde's alleged partners in the flirting on the staircase and the kissing in the grape arbor. Amateur journalism was scandalized by Heins's indiscretions in his May 1921 number. He responded to criticism from Hyde's supporters Leston M. Ayres and Mrs. Brown in his June 1921 number (just before the presidential election):

> [Responding to Mrs. Brown:] Furthermore,—your promiscuous letters and wild statements show me you have a peculiar code of morality. Apparently it is all right for Miss Hyde to give a kissing episode, and a Sappho scene with legs dangling over the banister, and hob-nob with smoking ladies, in a home where all this is offensive,—but to refer to it! My! What a crime! My sister's "Vondy's Kissing in Our Arbor" poem shocked your dainty sensibilities and you fear your niece who is to qualify and vote for this "Vondy" might see such a contaminating thing in print. I wonder what you and your niece would have done—had all this happened in your home. Remember we once attended it, and no one there inflicted such disgusting conduct on your hospitality.

What young John Milton Heins appears to have forgotten in all these heated exchanges was the obligation that a host bears to a guest—howsoever the guest may conduct himself or herself—and the obligation of an editor to assure the decency of the material he places into print regardless of its truth or falsity.

Edna Hyde did not deign to respond to the abuse from the Heins household. But her fiancé Professor McDonald did, resigning from NAPA to protest the publication of such material. In his June 1921 number, John Milton Heins had only this response:

> That "dearest of all friends" has flown the coop,—when "angels" were most in demand. The bald statement that P. B. McDonald has resigned from the National,[18] not even stopping to vote for Edna Hyde, whom he blared to the skies, should prove food for thought to intelligent voters. Rats are only known to desert when the ship is sinking. But that an "angel" with a perfectly good vote leaves his candidate in the lurch (not church) is sad indeed.

John Milton's youthfulness provided some excuse for his offensive aggressiveness in print. His participation in the gutter politics of the 1921 NAPA presidential campaign—whether with or without the approval of Dorothy Mac-

Laughlin—should surely make us weigh with care his accusations after he subsequently fell out with MacLaughlin. That Charles W. Heins did nothing to attempt to rein in his son's offensive aggressiveness until the final Heins-Houtain
"peace treaty" of June 15, 1922, is a sad commentary—perhaps supporting his
son's "fights" was more important to Charles W. Heins than assuring the main-
tenance of common decency in his son's publications. According to William
Groveman, the senior Heinses called each other "muddah" and "faddah," and
there was undoubtedly a strong streak of puritanism in the rules by which they
conducted their lives; but John Milton's and Gladys's attacks on Edna Hyde
and Philip B. McDonald went well beyond the bounds of common decency.
Participating in "press wars" of this kind surely did nothing to help form the
Heins children's moral values. Some of the guests and many amateurs at large
must have been left wondering what kind of juvenile spies were posted on the
staircase and in the grape arbor for the October 17, 1920, Blue Pencil Club
meeting. In fairness to John Milton Heins, it is worth noting that he had
printed Leston M. Ayres's article "A Deserving Candidate," supporting Hyde's
presidential bid, in the April 1921 number of the *American Amateur*. Therein
Ayres recalled a candid passage from the December 1920 number of Hyde's
own *Inspiration:*

> Petty jealousies in amateur journalism are sometimes with us. We confess it is
> hard to battle with the green-eyed monster when somebody else wins the lau-
> reateship you coveted, or married the fellow you vamped last convention. But
> isn't it all part of the game? You know you're not a real one after all unless
> you are a good sport.

Hyde's frankness speaks well for her. That she declined to respond to the personal attacks of the 1921 campaign was always held to her credit. Her 1921
opponent, by way of contrast, was so hurt by the tempestuous politics of her
campaign and of her subsequent administration that after the death of her
husband in 1945, she determinedly had nothing more to do with amateur
journalists and their hobby.

It must have been a relief in 1921 to get to the convention and have an
end of all the mudslinging. As always, in the wake of the 1902 New York convention, the report of the proxy committee occupied a good deal of the time
of the convention on July 4, 1921.[19] By tradition, Edith Miniter served on
this committee. At last, however, the convention moved on to the election of
the president. William J. Dowdell nominated Edna Hyde; Mrs. A. C. Ellis
seconded. James F. Morton, Jr. nominated E. Dorothy MacLaughlin; William
Lapoint seconded. Nominations were closed. MacLaughlin received 71 proxy
ballots and 27 convention ballots, a total of 98; Hyde received 40 proxy ballots and 7 convention ballots, a total of 47; there were two scattered ballots
and one blank ballot. Seventy-five votes were necessary to elect; Mrs.

MacLaughlin was declared elected. Note that only 34 ballots were actually cast by those in attendance at the convention.

Most of the other contests were routine. W. Alvin Cook was elected first vice president, Anita Kirksey second vice president, and T. Orvan Martin secretary, all on the first ballot. By way of contrast, it took three ballots to elect Horace L. Lawson (publisher of the *Wolverine*) as treasurer over William T. Harrington. Probably the closest contest was for official editor. Veteran Willard O. Wylie nominated John Milton Heins and E. Dorothy MacLaughlin seconded. C. A. A. Parker nominated William J. Dowdell and Orvan T. Martin seconded. On the third ballot, Heins was finally chosen over Dowdell: Heins, 57 proxy, 12 convention, 69 total; Dowdell, 46 proxy, 22 convention, 68 total. It was indeed a close battle. Retiring president Anthony F. Moitoret and George Julian Houtain were elected executive judges on the first ballot; two additional ballots were necessary to choose Laurie A. Sawyer over Marjorie (Outwater) Ellis (the retiring official editor) as the third executive judge. New York, Akron, and Cleveland were placed in nomination for the 1922 convention site; New York emerged victorious on the second ballot. Earlier in the day, the convention had wrestled with a motion to appropriate an additional $25 for each bimonthly issue of the *National Amateur*. The idea was finally referred to a committee. Another motion not adopted was that of George Julian Houtain to allow the sale of advertising in the *National Amateur*.

In her "President's Message" in the *National Amateur* for September 1921, Mrs. MacLaughlin announced:

> The only announcements forwarded to me by the retiring President [Anthony F. Moitoret] of the closing year's laureateship contests are:
>
> SHORT STORY. Laureate, Chas. W. Heins. Honorable Mention, Edna Hyde.
> ESSAY. Laureate, James F. Morton, Jr. Honorable Mention, Howard P. Lovecraft.
> EDITORIAL. Laureate, "The Wolverine," editor Horace Lawson. Honorable Mention, "The American Amateur," editor John Milton Heins.

The president concluded her report:

> Two very important events have happened in my life within the last two months, both of which were not dreamed of a year ago. The first was my election as your president, July 4th, at Boston. This great honor, coming as it did in such an overwhelming fashion, has made a deep impression upon me. I want to assure you, as a student of the history of the association and of the fine records made by some of the former presidents, that I know I have no easy task before me. My best efforts will be spent in trying to live up to the

finest traditions of our well-beloved organization. I thank you most heartily for this expression of your confidence in me. I sincerely hope to merit it.

The second important event happened August 30th when I changed my name from E. Dorothy MacLaughlin to Mrs. George Julian Houtain.

Sincerely and fraternally, E. DOROTHY HOUTAIN, President.

In January 1920, John Milton Heins had commenced publication of the *American Amateur,* which he published as a cooperative venture, with pages contributed by various other amateur journalists.[20] During the same period, E. Dorothy MacLaughlin continued the publication of her magazine, the *National Tribute.* I have based my account of the controversies surrounding E. Dorothy Houtain's administration on my incomplete files of the *American Amateur, the National Amateur,* and the *National Tribute* from this period. It should be realized that my perspective on these long-ago events is limited by my sources.[21] New evidence will undoubtedly emerge in the future.

In his "Face to Face with Amateur Journalists" column in the *American Amateur* for January 1921 (p. 126), editor Heins printed the letter that gave rise to much of the controversy:

Office of the First Vice President

Dear Fellow Amateur;—

The National Amateur Press Ass'n this year intends to award suitable medals in connection with our Annual Laureate Awards, if a fund can be raised to defray the cost, there being no money in the treasury for this purpose.

As a representative Amateur of known generosity towards Amateur Journalism and our Ass'n, I venture to ask you if possible, to contribute your "mite" towards such a fund, acknowledgement for which will be made in my next report in our official organ.

These medals which are intended to stimulate the contest in our literary endeavors, will be eagerly contested for and this added result [sic] in more entries, should compensate you for with [sic] whatever financial aid you may have helped to bring it about. Any suggestions, on designs, lettering and place to get them is invited. Any offer to furnish a medal for any entry, to be called by the giver's name, will also be gladly considered.

Trusting to hear favorably from you with the donation you may desire to subscribe, I remain

Yours truly,
John Milton Heins

P.S. This is not a general notice being sent to just 28 Amateurs, and the replies will be used in a "Face to Face with Amateur Journalists" article in the January issue of the "American Amateur."

He also narrated the reaction of his father Charles W. Heins to the proposed letter:

After writing the above notice I showed it to my father. Sadly shaking his head, he said, "Kid, don't send it!" Of course I wanted to know why not. "Well, you see," he stammered, "Some of those amateurs on that list will not like to be shaken down and will hate you for trying to get money out of them." Hate me for trying to get money out of them? "But this money isn't for me!" I said, "It's for Amateur Journalism. Most of these men's dollars are like pennies to me. They were Ex-Presidents or leaders in our movement and this will give them a chance to show where they stand when Amateur Journalism calls for a sacrifice. Anyhow how did you get those medals from the N.A.P.A. and why did the amateurs who saw them in our house say, "What an elegant idea, and why isn't it tried now?"

My father threw up his hands, looked at my list of names (which to be exact was 25, and three Press Clubs), took out three dollars, said "how much yourself?" and then I addressed my envelopes.

In the *American Amateur* for March 1921, Heins printed many of the responses he received to his appeal for pledges for the medal fund. Just about the only negative response—which nevertheless generated a donation—came from Harry C. Hochstadter:

Responding to your appeal, I am enclosing check for $5.00 *not* to be applied to the purchase of medals "intended to stimulate the contest in our literary endeavors." If the present day amateurs cannot be induced to compete for Laureate awards without a stimulus of a gew-gaw, jimcrack or bangle, such as you suggest, the Laureate competition department of the N.A.P.A. ought to go out of business.

Heins sent Hochstadter's donation along to the Official Organ Fund. On the other hand, Mary Lehr Guthrey recalled the medals which had been awarded during the presidency of Heins's father:

. . . For thirteen years I have worn almost constantly the Laureate Gold Medal awarded me when you father was President—about the time you were cutting your teeth, and he doubtless walking the floor with you, nights. I had the medal made into a breastpin, and people have always inquired about it and admired it. So I think I owe a "fiver" though you did not apply to me.

Heins reported further in this issue:

I have already negotiated with a prominent jewelry house to strike these medals with suitable engraving except the winner's name; which will be struck in the last and want to thank each and every subscriber to the fund for the uniform generosity and kindness which they have met my "touch" which I made in behalf of our beloved N.A.P.A., for the advancement of Amateur Journalism; and those serious amateurs who see in our hobby, a road to self improvement, with success for its goal.

The 1920–21 official year had been a difficult one politically. There had been friction between president Moitoret and official editor Outwater. Outwater had called publicly for the removal of president Moitoret because of his failure to meet constitutional activity requirements. The special committee appointed to consider ex-president Moitoret's recommendation concerning the laureate judges saw fit to include in its report the following sentiments:

> This committee heartily endorses the hope expressed by the retiring President that the political differences that have developed this year will resolve themselves into a sentiment of harmony throughout the membership of the association and in a determination on the part of each member to work solely for the best interests of the N.A.P.A.

A substantial portion of the discussion at the convention concerned the expense of issuing the *National Amateur* bimonthly in the required format.[22] President MacLaughlin's message reported pledges totalling $151.00, $94.50 for the official organ and $56.50 for publicity. (She herself at $25 total stood at the head of the list of pledges, while Mr. & Mrs. William J. Dowdell pledged $15, and George J. Houtain, William W. Lapoint, Michael O. White, Sonia H. Greene, and Willard O. Wylie each pledged $10.) President MacLaughlin reported regarding the finances for the official organ:

> Official Editor Heins has arranged to publish a twelve page official organ at an expenditure of $75 each issue, not including wrappers and mailing. As long as he remains official editor he will contribute personally $5 an issue and his father, ex-President Chas. W. Heins, $10 an issue. These two contributions, together with the twenty-five dollar associational allowance, leaves a bimonthly deficit of $35. The official organ fund, to grant realization, must be increased by donations totalling $115.50.

Further discussion of the official organ finances took place on the final day of the convention, July 5. The minutes as set down by recorder *pro tem* Edith Miniter recorded the following discussions ensuing after a brief recess taken to bid farewell to Sonia H. Greene:

> Mr. Houtain embodied his suggestions in a motion that the Official Editor be empowered to sell space in the official organ, and also to receive additions to the official organ fund, subject to approval of the Executive Judges, as the Treasury had nearly $200.
> Mr. Parker moved to amend that the Official Editor be empowered to receive an additional sum of One Hundred and Fifty Dollars above the constitutional allowance the same to be paid in sums of $25 each two months, to be expended under the direction of the President and Executive Judges. Question raised by Mr. Cole as to whether such a proceeding would be constitutional. Debate followed, Messrs. Cole, Heins, Dowdell, Morton and Mrs. Miniter taking part. Mr. Houtain then withdrew his motion and stated that

the Convention could be kept in session several days discussing the official organ problem and moved that the President appoint a committee of three to investigate and report, so that their recommendations could be acted upon at the next Convention. Carried.

President MacLaughlin announced the appointment of William Dowdell as secretary of publicity. She had earlier announced in her presidential message that Dowdell had already invested $250 of personal funds for recruiting and publicity and that monies contributed to the publicity fund would be used, not to reimburse him, but "for additional activities of the bureau." James F. Morton made the traditional motion to adjourn *sine die*.

The National was not alone in its factionalism. Writing to Rheinhart Kleiner on August 30, 1921, Lovecraft reported on reading proofs for the forthcoming first issue of Sonia Greene's *Rainbow* and on plans for Mrs. Greene's forthcoming visit to Providence on September 4–5, 1921. Lovecraft also reported on a trip he made to Boston on August 17, 1921, to meet Anne Tillery Renshaw for the first time.[23] He failed to make a connection with UAPA member Alice Hamlet to discuss the disposition of a fund intended to reimburse Lord Dunsany for the expense of a cable message.[24] Lovecraft reported to his friend that Miss Hamlet "hates all the other Massachusetts amateurs except her own recruits & proteges & refused to attend any convocation." Later in the day, Lovecraft was invited to the home of UAPA member S. Lillian McMullen (that year's poetry laureate), where he had dinner with the hostess Mrs. McMullen, Anne Tillery Renshaw, and Edith Miniter. Lovecraft wrote: "It amused me to see Mrs. Miniter at a McMullen gathering—because Mrs. McMullen & the Boston United folk are now far from partial to the Hub element." Winifred Virginia Jackson arrived later and ignored Mrs. Miniter (with whom she had been feuding) for the first hour. Mrs. McMullen had brought in a neighbor's kitten for Lovecraft. He wrote: "And whilst the human cats aired their coolness, I held in my lap the prettiest actual kitten that I had seen for many a day—a grey furry double handful with a belled collar around his neck, who was brought in by a neighbour at the express suggestion of Mrs. McMullen, who knows of my predilection for the feline species." Mrs. McMullen and Mrs. Renshaw both sang, but Lovecraft declined an invitation, since "there was no St. Julian [George Julian Houtain] to drown me out."[25] Boston amateur politics aside, the 1920–21 UAPA official year would be especially difficult for Lovecraft because of conflicts with president Ida C. Haughton over the official organ fund and the content of the *United Amateur*. In the 1922 UAPA election, Lovecraft and his faction would be ousted completely.

A professional opportunity was also beckoning for Lovecraft from within amateurdom. He reported to Rheinhart Kleiner on September 21, 1921:[26]

Another business opportunity recently appearing is that afforded by St. Julian's new magazine, *Home Brew*. He wants a series of six ghastly tales to order—apparently unaware that art cannot be created to order. I doubt if any story from my pen could please the clientele of an essentially popular magazine, & have so informed the jovial publisher. However—if he will be satisfied with some frankly artificial hack-work, in no way related to my normal output, I will do my best for him. He offers five bucks per story—on publication. Rotten remuneration, but perhaps a better proposition than Bush work. Damn poverty!

"Herbert West—Reanimator" was duly published in six installments (titled "Grewsome Tales") in *Home Brew* between February and July 1922. Houtain must have been satisfied with Lovecraft's "hack-work," for another serialized story, "The Lurking Fear," appeared in *Home Brew* in four installments between January and April 1923. *Home Brew* was primarily a popular humor magazine.

The stage was clearly set for potential conflict. We can only theorize that the Houtains brought pressure to bear on Lovecraft—the winner of NAPA's essay laureate and the beneficiary of a writing assignment for *Home Brew*—to do more for the National. Clearly, Mr. and Mrs. Houtain were intent upon doing everything they could to boost the politically and financially troubled organization. In contrast to Sonia Greene's generous $10 pledge (allocated $5 for the official organ and $5 for publicity/recruiting), Lovecraft, primarily a UAPA loyalist, had pledged nothing. Yet he was the winner of a prize to be accompanied by a valuable medal and the beneficiary of a professional writing assignment which would yield $30. (The essay for which Lovecraft received honorable mention has not been identified.) At one point or another, he probably told the Houtains that his primary loyalty remained with the United, that he could not afford to donate additional sums to the National, and that he would decline the laureate award and medal. Thus was set into motion the conflict that ultimately led to the resignation of John Milton Heins as official editor on December 19, 1921.

The relationship of official editor Heins and president Houtain had begun on a favorable note. Heins wrote in his "Editorials" in the *National Amateur* for September 1921:

> As the custodian last year of the laureate entries I early realized that something had to be done to uplift and stimulate the literary interest of our members. The co-operation of fellow amateurs helped me by generous donations to be able to give gold and silver medals in addition to the certificates and distinction the Association gives the winners. I believe all this helped to create spirited contests for the prizes awarded and trust the incumbent of that office [First Vice-President W. Alvin Cook], will this year inject some stimulus of his own to encourage or aid, to a still higher degree, this year's literary activity.
>
> [. . .]

As this paper goes to press we have received the notice that our elected President, E. Dorothy MacLaughlin has been married to our Executive Judge, George Julian Houtain. In extending our best wishes to the happy couple in which we know all members of the Association join, we cannot forbear in expressing our belief that this joining of forces of two of the best known names in our little world of letters, makes the prospect of what already seemed a bright year for the Association, even better. Theirs is to be a real Amateur Journalist's honeymoon, for it's on to Cleveland and the Ohio Reunion, where E. Dorothy MacLaughlin elected at Boston will be hailed as Mrs. George Julian Houtain President of the National Amateur Press Association.

Heins had four pages of the *National Amateur* for January 1922, including Lovecraft's honorable mention essay, in press at the time of his resignation. But we should allow him to tell the story in his article "Memoirs of an Ex-Official Editor"[27] in the *American Amateur* for February 1922:

> To be brief, the Lovecraft Essay Medal Award is an insignificant matter, brought forward by the Houtains to becloud and obscure the fact, that I caught them red-handed in the act of tampering with entries for the History Award, unexpectedly placed in their hands by the failure of Mary Lehr Guthrey, the judge appointed by President Moitoret, to make a decision. Mr. A. M. Adams who was arbitrarily appointed the judge, received three entries less than officially listed by me as custodian of these entries last year. On inquiring why the entry of Mr. Wylie had been slyly taken from the official entries, I was told, "Oh! He wouldn't have won it anyhow, and besides, what would he care for a medal." With the stage so cleverly set for George to win a gold medal, the plan fell down, and Georgie only drew down a silver one—and this, only because other competitors, whom he feared had been illegally kept from competition, and this despite the fact that the Houtain administration had no right to meddle in this matter at all.
>
> The suppression of the Poetry Awards which I forced into the open, is merely another example of how I uncovered what was wished to be kept a secret. Even at that, there was no venom with me, in these matters. I was the Official Editor, I wanted complete records. The suave, "Don't bother, John, it's all right," meant I was being used as a dummy, and it was my place to record things as they came to my knowledge. This same spirit, led me to tell Mrs. Houtain, at the November meeting of the Blue-Pencil Club, that in her November message she was in error "that Mr. Lovecraft repudiated the medal awarded him." Since he had written me in an entirely different strain, she replied, "Oh! allright, I thought he didn't want it." As local Amateurs received their medals at this meeting, I then sent Mr. Lovecraft his medal, receiving in reply his appreciation, which I set up and printed for the January *National Amateur*. Seventeen days after, I received a peremptory demand from Mrs. Houtain, that I destroy these four pages, since they contained Mr. Lovecraft's winning entry, also "did I want a ruling from the Executive Judges that she

had a right to order this?" I courteously replied telling her that it was impossible for me to destroy work already printed, that Mr. Lovecraft had been awarded this honor by the Judge of Mr. Moitoret's selection, this had been so announced at the Boston Convention, and printed in the September *National Amateur,* and that on her O.K. I had sent the medal, and in good faith had proceeded to print the awards and medal acknowledgements. Imagine my surprise when a few days later, George Houtain, as Executive Judge, craftily informed me, that my request for a ruling on this matter, would be decided upon in a few days, in the meantime, forbidding me to do anything further in getting out the official organ. Since I had not asked for any ruling, I informed the other Judges, Mrs. Sawyer and Jas. F. Morton, that if they based an opinion on any request supposed to have come from me, they were doing this on a forgery. Nevertheless a few days later I received a decision wherein G. Houtain over the typewritten signatures of the other Judges informed me, that as a great favor I would be allowed to retain the four printed pages—provided I "inked out" the words 'Honorable Mention' on the Lovecraft winning entry. I at once demanded on what such a ruling was made, since Houtain had "faked" that I had asked for this information. Mr. Morton then informed me, "It all did not really matter, since the question had only been treated informally, and as such would not receive official recognition." Advising me however to comply with the Executive's finding, since a trap had been set for me, and this was the easiest way out of it. In fact Mr. Morton tried his utmost, to hush and create peace in the official family, but was taken in by the same treachery practiced on me. For on his advise I proceeded on the interrupted January *National Amateur,* until December 15th, when not receiving the President's Message, I wrote for same, receiving in reply, a document distorted with lies and vituperation, anent the Lovecraft matter, with a personal letter, in which she threatened, "if my issue contained the four pages complained of," which she knew was printed, and on which the Executive Judges had ruled—I would be removed. Twist this matter as you will, with the tenth page of the January *National Amateur* running on the press there was only one thing to do—and I stopped the press and set up my resignation as official editor, for you can't do business with a liar, not with an Executive Committee that allows one of its members to perpetrate forgery, or lulled me into getting out the January official organ only to be defrauded for its payment, and is constituted solely to protect the incubus whom without this protection, would be instantly removed from office.

Heins appears to have printed and mailed his disputed January 1922 number of the *National Amateur* before sending in his resignation. He also got out a special large-size issue of the *American Amateur* to announce his resignation publicly. The pages of this issue are numbered 203 and 204, consecutive to the highest page number reached in the *American Amateur* for July 1921, but the larger format gives rise to speculation that he also set these two pages up for the January 1922 number of the *National Amateur.* Heins was roundly criticized by some amateurs for including the details of his side of the dispute with the Houtains in the January 1922 number of the *National Amateur*. Traditionally, the *National Amateur* has been considered an appropriate forum for official business, rather than personal opinion—at least as relates to associational matters.

Heins also culled extracts from his correspondence in support of his position. Probably the most important regarding the issues at hand was the letter from ex-president Moitoret that he printed in the *American Amateur* for February 1922:

Sacramento, Jan. 2, 1922

Dear John:

The January *National Amateur* received today. Congratulations on your resignation. Have not always agreed with you in the past and still believe you have made many mistakes, easily excusable by your youth, but you have taken the right step in cutting loose from the present maladministration of the National Amateur Press Association.

The cat is now out of the bag on the reason why the Poetry Laureate Award winners were not announced. You certainly caught Dot with the goods there and I am glad I retained a carbon copy of my letter to her last September. . . . Recalling your query about the Lovecraft award it was and is my opinion that anyone who cares to withdraw a laureate entry should do so when the list of laureate entries in each class is published, not after the awards are made. I suppose Mr. Lovecraft had the right to decline the honor, but that the judge should thereupon be called upon to make another choice is ridiculous. The declination of a member to accept laureate honors, in my opinion, does not require a substitute award. There have been years when no awards have been made at all and merely leaving an honorable mention blank for a year, if the recipient thereof doesn't want to accept, is no calamity. So when Madame President informed me that Lovecraft would not accept, I said "Fiddlesticks! He can take it or leave it. I should worry."

For your own information, since it is a point at issue, I might mention that Mrs. Guthrey, whom I appointed judge of history, has never written to me to decline. The appointment of the judges for last year's laureates was within my power. I know nothing of the substitute judge's power to act. Mrs. Ellis [Marjorie Outwater Ellis] wrote asking me for her certificate and I told her I did not recognize her claim to it. How can I put my signature to an award the honesty of which I have no means of insuring? Now that you infer that some of the entries were withdrawn before Adams received them, I might add that no history certificates will be issued. . . .

Very truly,
Anthony F. Moitoret
Ex-President, N.A.P.A.

Charles W. Heins wrote in strong language to defend his son's actions:

Hartford, Feb. 10, 1922

My Dear John;—
    Although I regret all this mess, I must commend your effort to expose the brazen attempt to betray the cause of Amateur Journalism, by these Houtains who seem to have lost all decency, and self-respect once in their official "twin"-saddle. Not satisfied to "welsh" and "fourflush" on all pre-convention promises, these Houtains now present the sickening spectacle of venting their venom on you, for my refusal to either write for, or endorse that illicit decoction *Home Brew* and my demand that money withheld from and claimed by them, as "not rotting in the bank" be paid you, as per the purposes of these contributions.
    The bluster behind his wife's skirts that only she prevented him "from leaping at your throat"—or did this biped mean me?—alas! are like his other unsigned threats, the yelping of a whipped renegade, who will very carefully stay out of reach. In the meantime the findings of the Grand Jury, clipping, from the public press and sworn affidavits, now in your possession you may serenely defend the institution Amateur Journalism, even should the final chapter have to be waged at the Bar Association.
                    Your father,
                    —Chas. W. Heins

The dispute between John Milton Heins and the Houtains did not end with his resignation as official editor on December 19, 1921. President Houtain proceeded to appoint William J. Dowdell as Heins's replacement. Dowdell had narrowly lost the election as official editor at the Boston convention in July 1921. Dowdell proceeded to issue what Heins labelled a "cat's paw" issue of the *National Amateur* for January 1922. Heins had earlier completed and mailed his own issue of the *National Amateur* for January 1922.[28] He proceeded to demand the constitutional payment of $25 in respect of the issuance of that issue and filed a complaint with the board of executive judges when the Houtain administration failed to honor his demand. John Milton Heins showed no spirit of forgiveness or of reconciliation in the lengthy article "The 'Cats-Paw' National Amateur," which he published in the *American Amateur* for February 1922:

When I resigned as Official Editor on December 19th, after getting out the Third Number of the 44th Volume,[29] I sounded a warning, as far as money contributions were concerned, that amateurs should beware of the "Catspaw" who was slated for the office I was vacating. Mr. Rheinhart Kleiner soon noised it around locally that Lapoint [William J. Lapoint] who has a desk in the Houtains' office was the anointed appointee. When however my issue reached them (two weeks after most of our members had their copy) the Houtains realized that with this exposure, this would be a colossal blunder and so

Bill Dowdell was quickly substituted. Now someone has of course to be Editor. But how Bill Dowdell can stifle his self respect and stoop to write "That no one will control the policy of his volume—that his is the final word, as to its contents,"—and not only deliberately steal my issue with most of my contributed matter of which he brazenly calls himself the editor, I fail to understand. In this he plainly shows that he is the creature of those who appointed him—because in every instant he has either eliminated or altered the matter abstracted from my January "The National Amateur."

The date of August 19, on the letter of Mary Carolyn Davies, the Poet Award is slyly omitted, for it would again prove my assertion that this belated award having been suppressed by the President, I finally forced her to disgorge its possession, on proof that it was in her possession which she had to admit in an official letter to me of December 3d. What Mr. Dowdell however does not know and what these wonderfully smart Houtains with this letter three months in their possession failed to realize, is that they have proven that they nothing know about the Constitution, of which they continually prate, and try to screen themselves. For Article XI, Sec. 5 distinctly says:

> "No person may be awarded the title 'Laureate' in any one department for two successive years."

Though I called attention to the President's message, they carefully avoided a reference to this important matter. You can tell your President Houtains whoever it may be, who ordered you to credit the Poet Laureate titles on your Editorial page that first the suppression of this award was rank treachery. The ignoring of the matter in the two messages, signed by the "Miss-uss," was cowardice; and not knowing her constitution she displays a beautiful ignorance, in which you share, by conferring the title to Edna Hyde,—who being the Poet Laureate of last year, cannot, by the Constitution, hold the title again this year, and will also not get the gold medal from the Association. Miss Hyde, of course knowing this, must share with me, the laugh at this ridiculous blunder you and your Presidents have fallen into. While amateurs will watch with interest how these Constitution ignoramuses will have to swallow this little lesson I am imparting to them.

I will skip the wilful mistake of purposely using another name in place of mine in the editorial announcement, since of course this will be claimed a typographical blunder. Having beaten you at Boston, you of course as a chivalrous gentleman wouldn't do a thing like that on purpose. Or was it a natural sense of shame after stealing my contributed matter, thereby trying to supplant my issue, so that at the Houtains' command you could get *paid my money*, both constitutional and collected of which I have been defrauded—that you made a very convenient conscience stifling error. Also why Mr. Dowdell with this "blunder" against me, did you relegate my entire family to wrong addresses in the membership list?[30] Even the most disinterested amateur can understand such tactics and carrying out of "orders" by cowards who made you a welcome present of the office.

You of course had to leave out the medal award acknowledgements on account of the Lovecraft letter (a matter discussed elsewhere). But I am curious to learn why, since you cribbed everything else, did you leave out the "Ten Best Papers" of which three ex-Presidents were the judges? Was it because the winning issue was by one to whom your new "chiefs" did not want to give credit to, as they had the nerve to tell me, when I acknowledged editorially a book given me by Mrs. Miniter? Or was the rating their papers obtained the real cause?

I also noticed that you gave "Home Brew" your approval by a notice. Even the sly editorial reference of admiration in "New Ideas" anent the Amateur Grafters and Bootleggers of Home Brew Amateur Journalism, who only tried it to club our membership into lining their own pockets, reveals how completely you have swallowed the glittering bait of the Houtains, to make you President, if you obey orders. But now with their tag—hm! We'll see.

Dowdell to cover his eagerness and pride swallowing haste, to serve the Houtains, says, "that among other things, the fact that several of the members disqualified from voting at Boston, had been entitled to suffrage, added to his desire to be the Official Editor. Does he mean that their votes would have been for him? My father who was custodian of these ballots, says they gave me a majority of six votes, when finally they were opened.

Of course Mr. Dowdell I do not hold you to account or responsible for the context of the various Presidents messages you so kindly printed for them, this politeness from my experience I know they deeply appreciate. Of course for the third message I hold an entirely different document than you print, but that was to be expected after my exposure of them; that at once this would be rewritten to cover the blundering mess belatedly sent to me. However Mr. Dowdell if the issue you are fathering is really the third number of the 44th volume, why therein a President's Fourth Message? All our members know yours is the fourth issue, a steal on mine, and a convenient cloak, to try and protect the people to whom you owe your office. Even your Presidents admit this by their blundering Fourth Message. That dramatic shout "I repudiate it, and strike it from the files," won't make amateurs either forget or discard my "exit" issue but only emphasizes its existence. The false statement that I have been "removed" from office of course all amateurs know to be a falsehood, since I publicly resigned in "The National Amateur" sent out three weeks before I sent copies to the "rule or ruin gang." When the Presidents finally got their copy they grew so frantic they rushed off a registered letter and telegram addressed to me at Brooklyn, N.Y. The letter after the Post Office enquired of these smart Houtains for a better address, finally reached me ten days after it was originally sent, or to be exact January 16. The telegram was never delivered, for the advice from the Western Union that delayed wire, owing to wrong address, awaited us, failed to arouse our curiosity. This is only another example of these Presidents who addressed her last message to Ridgefield, N.Y., instead of Ridgefield Park, N.J. and early in the term one even to Boston, Mass. Also losing her Foxie fur set when she came to visit me at my home, and thereafter had me enquiring at the lost and found window of the West Shore Railroad daily, for the "cat-fur off Nellie's hat" that never came back.

My exposure of how only Kroywen members were to be appointed on the Convention Committee worked wonder, actually Blue Pencil members received some consideration. Though it is significant that Mrs. Sonia Green the largest money contributor to the deplorable Houtain mis-administration, who offered to double any amount raised by local Amateurs towards the Convention Fund, is strangely absent from that Committee. Let a little bird whisper the reason: Our "clever and diplomatic (?)" President picked a quarrel with the Editress of the *Rainbow*, at one of the Kroywen dinners (another professional venture—where a poor dinner at high cost leaves room for much thought). Mrs. Green is of course too superior a lady to even notice the affront, until she received a letter from our dear President that so grossly insulted her that it was everything local Amateurs could do to prevent this gifted lady from leaving our ranks forever. To show that everybody can't be wrong and "Dotty" right, it is only necessary to point back just a year to the Hub Club, where around and about her these same things occurred.

The reader's attention is called to the soothing words allegedly written by Madame President, how deeply she regrets she was forced to request the resignation of Orvan T. G. Martin.[31] Don't forget fellow members that this regret means that your elected Secretary was "fired" by those who meddled with his reports, which he resented, and not on the flimsy excuse they did not dare to voice on his rapid dismissal. While a little further on, Rowan R. White "received the air" and the office of Boy Scout Representative abolished, because of failure to get any other Boy Scout to risk the treatment given one of their members. The loss of Mr. White's services to our cause may be judged in the Treasurer's report wherein he submits ten dollars for members he secured. Only to secure a stab in the back for his pains.

I take pleasure of welcoming you Messrs. Martin and White to the fast growing "Sick of the Houtain Administration Officials Circle" of which Ex-President Moitoret is our worthy head.

The Presidents in their message again emphasize the urgent need of money, also it has a list of those who allegedly came to time [sic—came through on time?] owing to the urgent plea in her paper. They fail to say that this money was driven in before I could put amateurs on their guard. Two amateurs wrote me they would not have contributed one cent had they known how matters really stood. Doesn't it strike amateurs as queer while this small collection is bravely mentioned, not a word or acknowledgement has been made of all money actually collected. The fraternity at large is politely asked to wait for this! Why? Last year at the Boston Convention, the Executive Judges had to thresh out a money transaction of Houtain six years ago. Thanks to friends some settlement was voted for the matter was obscured by age anyhow. Money collected for whatever purpose should be given proper acknowledgement when received. So that at a convention an accounting need not be railroaded through, without data or credit to all concerned. In reviewing the "birthday wishes" handed by the Missus to our members which in conversation I did not think belonged in a message, it may be amusing to quote the brilliant reason given therefor. "Why John, you don't understand," said the missus, "By doing this we get in personal touch with our members, and when we ask them for contributions they will be much easier to get." I see now in these "messages" this jolly has been fancied up with "smilemakers," "farmers," etc.—that means to get ready to contribute or subscribe, for another drive will soon get under way.

All the foregoing even the casual reader of the "Cats-Paw" National Amateur of Dowdell's January issue, can ascertain for himself. Having thus repaid his benefactors for the "gift" office now in his possession, it remains to be seen how he will measure up in future issues. As to the Houtains, their end is already in sight to judge by the many letters amateurs have sent me in commendation in my stand to not allow them to use me to betray the cause of amateur journalism for the benefit of their private pockets. Or the benefit of the National Amateur Press Association for the same end.

And this is just what Bill Dowdell is allowing them to do at our expense—but he won't be allowed to get away with it.

Dowdell printed the reply of the executive judges to Heins's demand for payment for his January 1922 issue in the *National Amateur* for May 1922:

REPORT OF EXECUTIVE JUDGES[32]

(Opinion written by James F. Morton, Jr., and concurred in by George J. Houtain and Laurie A. Sawyer, executive judges.)

Fellow Amateurs:

In response to a communication from John Milton Heins, the executive judges have unanimously adopted the following decision, a copy of which has been forwarded to Mr. Heins:

Feb. 23, 1922.

Mr. John Milton Heins,
16 Winant Ave.,
Ridgefield Park, N.J.

Dear Sir:

The executive judges, overlooking certain discourteous expressions in your request for a ruling on the refusal of the president to honor your voucher for twenty-five dollars in payment of the paper sent out by you as the January issue of the National Amateur, hereby find that the Constitution gives them no power to overrule the president in a decision as to the propriety of approving a given bill against the association. They have obvious authority to determine whether the president has acted within the constitutional powers of the office, but not to decide whether the action was right or the constitutional discretion wisely or properly exercised. The letter of the constitution being so plain as to the exclusive right of the president to approve or disapprove of bills, it is impossible for the judges to interfere with its exercise.

The above ruling, that the president has acted within the authority conferred upon her by the Constitution, renders it manifestly improper for the judges to express any opinion as to the correctness of her decision or as to any of the more or less relevant assertions and comments in your letter of inquiry. The present ruling is in precise harmony with the earlier one to which you refer, in that it merely affirms the legality of the exercise of constitutional authority by the president, without deciding as to the merit of her decision.

To your further inquiry as to the remedy available to you, in case the ruling of the President is unjust and inflicts a wrong on you, the judges would reply that the coming convention of the National Amateur Press Association, to which the president will render a report of her actions and decisions during the year, will have full authority to review any of her official acts, and to overrule any decisions found by the convention to be improper. If there is merit in your contention, you will have the full right to ask the convention for redress; and that body will have the power to grant it. The judges see no way of overcoming the ruling of the president before that time.

Sincerely yours,
> GEORGE JULIAN HOUTAIN,
> LAURIE A. SAWYER,
> JAMES F. MORTON, JR.,
> Executive Judges

In her "President's Message" in the *National Amateur* for May 1922, president Houtain replied to some of Heins's assertions regarding the 1921 laureates:

> It has been called to my attention that the constitution prohibits any one member from receiving the title Laureateship in any one department for two successive years. Where [sic] ex-President Anthony Moitoret sent me a decision of the Laureate judges I considered the matter closed and assumed that he was sufficiently informed in his presidential duties as to make no announcement that was not constitutional. It appears that Miss Edna Hyde won the poet Laureateship in 1920 and in error the First Vice President, John Milton Heins, accepted her entries in the poetry contest last year when he should not have done so. These entries the First Vice President sent to President Moitoret to give to the judge for his decision. The judge selected Miss Hyde's entry as being the best and President Moitoret, again in error, conferred the title Poet Laureate upon her. I hereby rectify the mistake as follows:
>
> I decree that the title Poet Laureate be given to Dora H. Moitoret and Honorable Mention to Minna B. Noyes, these two having been judged second and third best.
>
> I hereby appoint Harry Goodwin, Luella Belden and Dwight L. Anderson a committee of three to audit the medal fund account receipts and expendi-

tures voluntarily raised and spent by John Milton Heins and approved by the Boston Convention as being association matter. I hereby direct John Milton Heins to forward a complete statement of receipts and expenditures, together with vouchers, to Harry Goodwin, chairman of the committee, at 373 East 148th St., N.Y.C. I further direct John Milton Heins to deposit with the Recorder, Miss Adeline E. Leiser, 1530 Union St., Brooklyn, N.Y., all medals in his possession not distributed or awarded, for safe keeping, they being the property of the association.

President Houtain reported further that $215.50 pledges to the official organ fund and publicity bureau had been collected, and that $35.00 remained outstanding. She reported paying John Milton Heins $35 each for the September 1921 and November 1921 *National Amateurs* and William J. Dowdell $35.00 and $36.00, respectively, for the January and March *National Amateurs*. Dowdell, it seemed, was making an effort to keep controversy to a minimum in the *National Amateur*. He printed Lovecraft's "The Music of Erich Zann" in his March 1922 issue, along with a glowing review of the first issue of Sonia H. Greene's *Rainbow*. In its May 1922 issue, the *American Boy*—the best-known juvenile publication in the world—printed Dowdell's article on John Milton Heins, fourteen-year-old editor of the *National Amateur*, which Dowdell had submitted in the fall of 1921. Dowdell reproduced this article in facsimile on the first page of the May 1922 issue of the *National Amateur*.

Clearly, Dowdell, who had been so severely raked over the coals by Heins for his decision to accept the official editorship and for the content of his January 1922 issue, wanted to avoid controversy, at least in the pages of the *National Amateur*. In the March 1922 issue, Dowdell noted that he was unemployed and had recently spent a week in Toledo, Ohio, to explore employment possibilities. In the same issue, he also noted that Sonia H. Greene had recently visited Cleveland and entertained Samuel Loveman and the Dowdells at the Hotel Cleveland. One result of this trip was Sonia's invitations to Loveman and to Lovecraft to spend a week at her apartment in Brooklyn—an event that occurred on April 6-12, 1922. From July 30 to August 15, 1922, Lovecraft paid a return visit to Loveman in Cleveland, where he also met for the first time his young protégé Alfred Galpin. More changes were in store for William J. Dowdell as the turbulent year 1922 progressed.

In the February 1922 issue of the *American Amateur*, Heins continued to pour on the sarcasm in a short, uncredited piece entitled "How to Start a Professional Paper on Your Nerve":

First get yourself elected President of an Amateur Press Association. See that you are safely guarded, so that you yourself cannot be officially ousted. Be sure to wish all members a happy birthday and flatter all who will swallow this bait, then impress on all members the urgency to become professionals. Tell the sad story you don't pay much for their literary talent, but—as you need the money, all may send in the money, you need to pay printer's bills, and thus endorse the project. All of course on a mere "Full of Moonshine" promise. Of course, a few fall for anything,—but goodness aint you glad, they are few and far between,—and that you are not one of them, who are searching the lake for this kind of moonshine.

Despite her differences with the Houtains the previous fall, Sonia H. Greene weighed in with a criticism of the current disputes in "Heins versus Houtain" in the May 1922 of her journal, the *Rainbow*:

> The writer regrets inexpressibly that the honorable name of Amateur Journalism should be dragged in the mire by such disgraceful episodes of petty personal warfare and recrimination as those recently developing in the National Association. The condition, culminating in the public outburst of John Milton Heins in his supplement to The National Amateur has become such that amateurdom's standing is in jeopardy. No person now feels his reputation secure in the National, and that even the United Amateur Press Association suffers through reflected discredit is shown by the widely regretted resignation of Professor McDonald from both associations last spring. . . .
>
> The Heins-Houtain feud, leading up to the explosive muckraking in the supplementary American Amateur, is the last straw. Of the "inside" merits of the case the writer is wholly ignorant. Previous offences may or may not have been committed on either side. But as a neutral spectator the writer is surely justified in insisting upon two things; first, that both sides allowed a love of personal power and celebrity to obscure the literary welfare of their association and of amateurdom as a whole; and second, that no matter what the provocation, the foul exposé perpetrated by Heins forms a revelation of the very groundwork of good taste and common decency, which not even his extreme youth and overheated temper can excuse. . . .
>
> As a sincere lover of amateur journalism, the writer trusts that never again may the institution be so convulsed by the malfeasance and indifference of those who misconceive its serious purpose. The time is ripe for action, and we must all hope that our better elements, instead of retiring in disgust, will place their shoulders to the wheel in one new and gigantic effort to keep their society worthy of themselves and their aspirations.

Sonia's impassioned plea against personal attacks and gutter politics probably reflected the views of a large number of members exposed to the Houtain-Heins feud. The pressure had clearly begun to build toward the "peace treaty" that was eventually brokered in mid-June 1922.

The Houtains cut Heins and his father off from their own publication, the *National Tribune*. In its April 1922 number, they apparently disclosed plans to take legal action against the Heinses, father and son. Heins responded with his article "Calling a Bluff" in the *American Amateur* for June 1922:

I am told that the April *National Tribute* (the publishers are too cheap to send me a copy), carries a reproduction of what is supposed to be a summons for some kind of a suit for $10,000.00—maybe a million,—it's all the same to me; for what in the article appended thereto, they profess to be an invitation to thresh out at law the controversy which these Houtains by their "rule or ruin policy" set in motion.

Of course, the whole thing is a bluff to frighten me, and to be used as a club against other amateurs who have suffered from the despicable behavior, mean motives and trickery of these two ignoramuses who foisted themselves upon us to use our Association for their private ends. A suit such as they invite me to accept service to, couldn't be tried even if they wanted it, for fully two years to come. Pretty, isn't it? When the peacocks have become feather-dusters and they have passed into oblivion, to thresh out their case, that they are at liberty to drop when the Association being rid of them, wouldn't care whether the case was thrown out of court, as it could be, and suing a boy whom they wrong would make a laughing stock of them.

However, the supposed summons contains a statement that the defendants—meaning my father and myself—are liable to arrest in this action. I am not sucker enough, Dorothy McLaughlin Houtain or George Julian etc., to accept service which hypocritically you tried to affect at the Blue Pencil Club Meeting, because, as I have stated above, such a cause would all be to your advantage—but that threat of arrest is something different; at the instigation of some prominent Ex-Amateurs I have been offered the best legal talent that Amateur Journalism has ever produced, and around whose doorstep Houtain vainly tried to polish his shoes, and, under those circumstances, I am quite ready to accept an arrest from the blustering Houtains—*if they dare*.

For an arrest means that these Houtains, who are after other peoples' money, will have to put up a heavy bond for the event that such a proceeding from them will cause a suit for damages for false arrest, security for such a contingency they will have to deposit and which will give me a chance, since he is looking for ten thousand dollars ($10,000.00), to bring suit for whatever bond they may have put up, which they may know in advance will certainly not be overlooked.

Writing in the same issue of the *American Amateur* (June 1922) under the title "Birds of a Feather," Heins also made clear that he was not ready to make peace with his replacement William J. Dowdell, despite the moderate course Dowdell was attempting to pursue in his issues of the *National Amateur*:

William Dowdell, Catspaw editor of the "National Amateur" earned for himself a few extra pennies writing an article about me in the "American Boy." In it he waxed eloquent about the $25 press, in which I raised myself to fame and the editorship until he, at the instigation of his masters, now bow-wows the job himself. Since he received the money for copying my National Amateur it may be well to let amateurs know that the Houtains didn't get fresh with me, until by their wonderful promises I allowed myself to buy a 10 × 15 Chandler & Price press for which I laid down $150 cash and obligated myself with monthly payment notes for a like amount or in other words spent $300 on the press Dowdell wants everybody to believe I obtained for $25. Once this press at my home, the Houtains wanted me to do hundreds of dollars worth of printing for them which not being in sympathy with the purpose I refused. (Ask Mr. Cook who was kidded into taking this job for his firm from who, when and where he got the money and how?) There was only one way the Houtains thought they could get square on me and that was by threatening to take the official organ away from me. Thanks to Dowdell, they also made away with a payment justly due me, but I considered my self-respect and the lesson learned traveling with such ilk well worth any financial loss I may have sustained. You, too, Dowdell will yet learn the same little lesson, if you dare try to stand on your own feet and obey the honest impulses that yet may lay dormant in you. The true opinion held of you by your present superiors could be not better expressed as when I offered to withdraw in your favor as Official Editor, the Houtains said, "That — Mick will never get this office," but I see you did, and of course it's the same old story, "Birds of a Feather Flock together."

Heins also carried an article "Electing the Next President" by oldtime Harry M. Konwiser. Konwiser acknowledged participating in his own share of fights within the amateur journalism hobby, but called upon the Houtains to explain their actions. Konwiser concluded his article with these words:

If John Milton Heins "did something wrong" why didn't the president prefer charges and appoint a lot of neutral judges (like the writer!) to hold a hearing—if the Executive Board is assumed to be incapable of trying any officer for misconduct.

Tell me that, George Houtain.

Sure, I'm neutral. Good luck, John Heins—we'll make you president of the National if the good George Houtain and Jim Morton and a few other politicians are not careful. Or worse, I'll take the office myself!

Meanwhile, like a good member of the National, for amateur journalism's sake, please let us all know what it is all about and pending that let us keep our mouths closed. (Excepting myself—I'm immune, because I must put over a credential for the coming convention.)

And speaking about the July convention I want to warn all the active members and Jim Morton that I intend to elect a president, a secretary and an official editor and a few other officers to serve the National and not themselves.

Is that fair?

If you're a 100 per cent. member you'll write me that you stand for the association and against any small-time selfish politicians.

Heins made his own editorial position clear:

The Association must be in a bad way when the great Jimmy Morton says in the "Clevelander" that we must take Dowdell's election [as the next president] for granted. His election would prove a calamity and add to the general list-lessness by which only this could be brought about. If amateurs really wish the future and good [sic—future good?] of the Association, they will rewrite their ballots which by trickery were sent out nearly two months ago. Ask to have them withdrawn and the following ticket substituted:

President, A. M. Adams
First Vice-President, Rowan R. White
Second Vice-President, James J. Hennesy
Secretary, Orvan T. G. Martin
Treasurer, Ernest A. Dench
Official Editor, Wm. T. Harrington
Executive Judges, by courtesy only, the Ex-President [E. Dorothy Houtain]
          Julian T. Baber
          Harry M. Konwiser
          Convention Seat, Akron, Ohio

In the spring of 1922, John Milton Heins was for the second year in a row a guest of honor at the annual banquet of The Fossils, held in 1922 at the Fossils' favorite meeting place, Pontin's restaurant. Heins provided an extended report in the *American Amateur* for June 1922. He particularly noted his exchange of remarks with oldtimer J. Edson Briggs:

I was glad to meet Mr. Edson J. Briggs of Washington again, as clipper as ever. Many Fossils flit through my mind as having passed here and there a question or a comment to me. The tenor of which were: "How is A.J. today?" "Stick to it." "Don't let office grabbers and old uns run the Association that was meant for youth." "Those of a latter day than ours have a right to meet the same as we, but not to crowd out the kids, for these made A.J. great in the past and can do it again in the future." Well, I'm fighting to that end, and these has-beens who are trying to lick candy of what in their own youth they couldn't get, ought to take a tumble to themselves.

Page 218 of Heins's *American Amateur* for June 1922 has a stray note that does not seem to continue any article:

. . . and that's counting all the "ringers" you managed to push in for yourself. They also defeated Houtain as Executive Judge had they really been counted. But what about this "Mister" Houtain, the "surprise candidate," who only was elected, as he sneered at me, by one vote, either of which was given by my mother and father, and who now is hanging on to his office like grim death, although before his election he promised every one at the convention, that of course decency would demand, when the President became his wife he would of course resign. Catch this faithbreaker giving up anything that has once come into his clutches if it is to his advantage.

Heins refers here to fact that George Julian Houtain received just one vote more than the minimum required for election as executive judge at the July 1921 convention. (Houtain and ex-President Moitoret were elected on the first ballot; it took three ballots to choose Laurie A. Sawyer as the third executive judge. By the time the controversies over the January 1922 *National Amateur* arose, Moitoret had resigned and been replaced by James F. Morton, Jr.) If Houtain had made a promise to resign as executive judge if he married president MacLaughlin, he certainly did not choose to honor it after he married her on August 30, 1921.

Recruiting has always been an important activity for the amateur journalism hobby and doubtless the Houtains wished to have a successful record of recruiting during the 1921-22 official year. The listing of new members printed on p. 46 of the *National Amateur* for March 1922 shows William Dowdell in the lead with 11 recruits, followed by E. Dorothy Houtain with 10, R. J. Jeffreys with 9, A. F. Moitoret with 8, William Labovitz with 7, Rowan White with 5, Gladys Fraze with 5, H. E. Martin with 3, B. B. Jones with 2, E. F. Suhre with 2, W. A. Cook with 2, Leston M. Ayres with 2, C. W. Smith with 2, and eleven other members with 1 recruit each, for a total of 79 new members so far in the 1921-22 official year. Some of Heins's other criticisms of the Houtains seem quite trivial and even mean-spirited. Dorothy's acknowledgments of members' birthdays in her presidential messages may not have been the best use of space in the *National Amateur*, but she was certainly within her rights to use her space in this manner.[33] George Houtain certainly expected the entire official board to be "team players" in his wife's administration, to accept criticism from the executive, and to take appropriate actions to remedy perceived problems. Having felt the sting of removal from office under Edith Miniter's administration in 1909, he was doubtless willing to advise his wife to use the same power when it advanced the interests of the administration.[34] Drawing up legal papers against John Milton Heins (just as he did against Mrs. Miniter when he was himself removed from office in 1909) was probably also a mistake, as were attempts to promote *Home Brew* within amateur journalism. The Kroywen dinners and the relentless requests for financial support were all part of the style of the Houtain administration. The Houtains felt free to vent their beliefs even if they sometimes succeeded in offending important contributing members like Sonia H. Greene. Perhaps they sometimes failed to realize that others did not have skins as thick as their own. The pressures exerted on Lovecraft must have been considerable—a United loyalist who took a major National honor but declined any financial contributions to the National association and only carried his membership as a token of inter-associational cooperation. The Heinses must from time to time have perceived Lovecraft as another Houtain catspaw, with his story "The Music of Erich Zann" featured in Dowdell's *National Amateur* for March 1922 and his series "Grewsome Tales" (aka "Herbert West—Reanimator") running in Houtain's *Home Brew*. Despite the earlier dispute between Sonia Greene and Dorothy Houtain, Sonia's *Rainbow* received much favorable notice in Dowdell's *National Amateur*. We will probably never know the whole story of the exchanges between Lovecraft and the Houtains regarding his NAPA laureateship, but it is difficult to believe that the Houtains did not dish out some criticism of Lovecraft's perceived lack of support of the National. For his part, Lovecraft successfully negotiated his relationship with the Houtains. He kept his laureate award and medal. His stories ran in *Home Brew* and the *National Amateur*. Even more honors in the National Amateur Press Association were shortly to come his way.

The New York amateurs led by James F. Morton finally insisted that the hostilities between the Heinses and the Houtains come to an end before they destroyed the association. A peace conference was held on June 15, 1922, under Morton's auspices. All the issues were hashed out among the principals except for four, which were left to a referee, A. M. Adams, to decide. Adams made his decisions the same day. The Proclamation containing a short account of the conference and Adams's rulings was published in the *American Amateur* for June 1922 and is reproduced below:

A PROCLAMATION
TO THE MEMBERS OF THE
NATIONAL AMATEUR PRESS ASSOCIATION:

June 15, 1922

At the instigation of James F. Morton, Jr., and at the urgent request of the local Amateurs, a conference was arranged at which it was agreed by the undersigned, for the general good of the National Amateur Press Association, of Amateur Journalism as a whole and the coming N.A.P.A. convention in New York in particular, that all matters in controversy between and among the parties signatory to this document be and are adjusted to their mutual satisfaction, with the exception of those submitted to A. M. Adams as referee, whose decisions they agree to accept. All matters pertaining to this controversy heretofore submitted to the Executive Judges of the National Press Association are to be withdrawn.

Dorothy E. Houtain   George J. Houtain
John Milton Heins   Charles W. Heins

DECISION RENDERED BY REFEREE.

(1) On the question of whether John Milton Heins resigned or was removed from the office of Official Editor of the National Amateur Press Association; I find that he resigned.

(2) On the question of whether John Milton Heins should be allowed $25 for the January issue of the National Amateur; I find that said John Milton Heins has waived his claim for such payment.

(3) In the matter of the disputed Essay Laureate award; I find that the award of a judge, once announced, is unassailable, and that Howard Lovecraft is therefore entitled to Honorable Mention.

(4) Decision on all other matters discussed at the conference was waived by all parties concerned.

June 15, 1922   A. M. Adams, Referee

It would be interesting to find out if any remaining issues from the disputes were reviewed at the New York convention in 1922 but I have not had access to the convention minutes in the *National Amateur* for September 1922. However, Spencer's *History of Amateur Journalism* (p. 70) records that William J. Dowdell was the only candidate for president in 1922, receiving 66 of 81 total votes (and all of the proxy votes but 7). In the fall of 1922, however, Dowdell left his wife Lucie and decamped with a chorus girl. He resigned as NAPA President on November 27, 1922. James F. Morton suggested Lovecraft as the right choice to bring harmony to the divided association, and the executive judges tendered the presidency to him, which he accepted on November 30, 1922. He inherited a competent board of officers from Dowdell, with Harry E. Martin of Cleveland as official editor. Many members were shocked to find a United loyalist at the helm of the older National association but overall Lovecraft enjoyed a stable seven months in office. Spencer (p. 70) wrote of his term:

> President Lovecraft, excelled by no President in intellectual power, laid great stress upon the literary side of amateur journalism, and sought diligently to arouse a spirit of honest, intelligent criticism of the work of author and editor. In this he was greatly aided by Ex-President Cole, a member of the Bureau of Critics. Recruiting was not largely carried on, but the general tone of the whole institution was changed for the better. President Lovecraft's position is well realized by the perusal of this extract from his farewell message: "Our primary purpose, if we are to claim a place of unique merit in the world, must be to promote artistic self-expression for its own sake. I believe every effort should be made to keep the National to its proper goal of aesthetic and intellectual encouragement."

Edward H. Cole tried to convince Lovecraft to accept a full term as NAPA president, but he declined. He was succeeded by Hazel Pratt Adams (wife of A. M. Adams) for the 1923–24 term. He did accept election as an executive judge for the 1923–24 term. This was the first time he held office as NAPA executive judge. He held this office a second time in 1935–36, after his 1933–35 service as chair of the bureau of critics.

John Milton Heins did not accept the verdict of the conference of June 15, 1922 gracefully. In the *American Amateur* for June 1922, he wrote under the title "Bokays and Brikbatz":

This issue is a conglomeration of, "To be continued on page so and so" two important omissions and even one article "killed" at its head. I must even forego the scoop of the year and bury my final triumph and grand surprise at the Convention,—all because some Amateurs including my father, decided that the differences and wrongs inflicted on me were to be adjusted. I am not retracting nor betraying the friends who believe in me. I am merely agreeing in the Proclamation printed elsewhere, to rest the matter and not create unpleasantness during the convention. Even if I am a boy I can maintain my rights in the future as I have in the past, and my former adversaries can make the most of that, if that will give them any comfort.

John Milton Heins's own high school years were looming as his controversies with the Houtain administration in 1921–22 ended. He dropped his separate membership in NAPA after September 1924.

Sometime after the close of their 1921–22 administration, the Houtains moved from Brooklyn to Staten Island, where they remained for some years. George Julian maintained some contact with local amateurs as an "elder statesman." He was the first to inform Rheinhart Kleiner of the marriage of Lovecraft and Sonia H. Greene in March 1924. George Julian eventually qualified for the bar, as one might have guessed from his propensity to have legal papers drawn up. In the thirties he worked in real estate and insurance in Albany, New York. However, it was in counseling and career guidance that he finally found his niche. He qualified for the ministry and was pastor of a church in a fashionable Dedham suburb of Boston when he died suddenly at the age of sixty on August 21, 1945. His last major appearance in amateur journalism was as toastmaster at the banquet at Boston's NAPA convention in July 1944. He had been slated to perform the same function at UAPA's fiftieth anniversary banquet in Philadelphia on September 2, 1945, but died before he could fulfill that role. His old adversary Charles W. Heins had to serve in his stead. Heins wrote of Houtain in the *Phoenix* for November 1945 (p. 309):

> Houtain apart of politics and friendships, was the hale-well-met type, whose infectious laugh and bubbling over good nature and eloquence was the eclat to any gathering. His loss to our cause, while irreplaceable still remains a treasured monument of a meteoric and successful career watched from its early start, and an inspiration to many of us.

After the death of her husband, E. Dorothy Houtain had nothing to do with amateur journalists. She asked to be removed from the rolls of the National Amateur Press Association and resumed her maiden name of Elsie Grant. Born in Greenwood, Massachusetts, on June 2, 1889, she died in Saco, Maine, in November 1980, in her ninety-second year. Houtain's son J. Swain Houtain by his first wife Ethel Houtain followed him into the ministry and was pastor of the Methodist church in Chews, New Jersey, at the time of his father's death. J. Swain Houtain died at the age of seventy-eight in Keene,

New Hampshire, on March 9, 1995. His mother Ethel Houtain (born May 7, 1886) had died in Ocean Grove, New Jersey, in October 1967.

Charles W. Heins died at his home in Ridgefield Park, New Jersey, in October 1968, in his ninety-third year. The United Amateur Press Alumni Association and its official organ, the *Phoenix,* were the great loves of his later years. Some veterans of the amateur journalism hobby like William H. Groveman still remember him well. Of his son John Milton Heins I have been able to discover nothing more. That he was an assertive young man is not to be doubted—one of the most famous stories about him concerns his nearly being turned away from NAPA's 1919 Newark convention hotel by a desk clerk who did not believe one so young could be a registrant for the convention. Whether his father Charles W. Heins—an old amateur press warrior in his own right—might have steered his son in a more conciliatory direction is one of those never-to-be-answered "what ifs." As it was, John Milton Heins left amateur press rolls as early as 1924 and was doubtless engaged with getting on with high school and his own life. One Social Security Death Index decedent who might fit with the known facts concerning John Milton Heins is John Heins, born April 27, 1908, who died in July 1973 in Staten Island, New York.

William J. Dowdell's personal and business lives eventually settled down. He was working for the Cincinnati *Enquirer* when he served as a genial host for NAPA's 1938 convention. He eventually became the editor of an English-language newspaper in Italy and died in Rome in 1953 at the age of fifty-five.

Since my own sources have leaned so heavily toward the Heins camp, perhaps the best way to conclude this monograph is to quote Truman Spencer's appraisal of the E. Dorothy Houtain administration (p. 70):

Elise Dorothy Grant, a native of Greenwood, Mass., entered amateur journalism when 17 years of age. She became prominent in the affairs of the local Boston organization, the famous Hub Amateur Journalists Club, and was for a time Editor of its official organ the *Quill.* She edited the *National Tribune,* and won the editorial laureateship in 1922. The contest for presidential honors at the Boston convention of 1921 was between her and Miss Edna Hyde of New York, editor of *Inspiration,* a talented author, who had won the poet laureateship in 1919, and in the judge's opinion would have won it again in 1920 but for the constitutional provision that no person could hold the title two successive years. Miss Hyde, formerly known as Miss Von der Heide, was Official Editor in 1914. After a keenly fought campaign Miss Hyde was defeated. The new President, the third woman to hold the office and the second to be elected to the position,[35] soon after her election, on August 30, married George J. Houtain, who a few years before had served two terms as President. Her administration was a rather stormy one, but on the whole successful, and at its close she was presented with a loving cup in recognition of her work. One of her difficulties was over the official organ. Young John Heins, as we have seen, was elected Second Vice-President at Newark [1919]. He was made

First Vice-President the next year at Cleveland [1920]. He did well in office, and at Boston [1921] was elected Official Editor. Thirteen years old, he was by far the youngest amateur ever to hold the office. He started out well and showed much ability in the editorial chair, but he was a boy, and evidently wanted to have his own way. He became involved in a controversy with the President, was threatened with removal, and resigned after issuing two numbers of the *National Amateur*.[36] William Dowdell of Cleveland, Ohio was appointed in his place.

Another reminiscent sketch of Dorothy Houtain and her administration appeared years later in the *National Amateur* for December 1978:

E. Dorothy McLaughlin was elected NAPA President at 33, after as distasteful a campaign of personalities as the National has ever seen. The 1921 political campaign was well under way even in January: Official Editor Outwater declined to run, planning marriage; Hub Club members sponsored their Dotty McLaughlin for President; and Ohio amateurs and *Tryout* shouted for Edna Hyde. But with Houtain, Morton, the Heins's and local amateurs pushing the steamroller, Dorothy was elected at Boston 98–47 in singularly heavy balloting.

Born 1889 in Greenwood, Mass., Elsie Dorothy Grant's mother had been a compositor, her father a printing plant manager. At 17, she had entered an office where Laura Sawyer was her immediate superior, and through this contact learned of A.J. Joining the Hub Club, she eventually held most offices including president.

She attended the 1912 NAPA Boston convention, but did not join until 1916. From 1916–21 she held the Librarian honorarium, and in 1918 was elected Executive Judge.

Editor of the *Hub Club Quill* 1918–19, and editor of several other papers, she started *The National Tribute* in 1916 and put out ten issues, winning editorial laureate for the five issues during her presidential term.

Clever, energetic, and with magnetic personality, she wrote penetrating comments on amateur social and political matters, and was an outspoken critic of Moitoret both before and after his election as President. (Early in the 1920 campaign she proposed Harrington and Outwater over Moitoret and Dowdell.)

In 1921 she was transferred by her employer to New York, where she joined both Blue Pencil and Gotham clubs and was introduced to the city by their members.

Her administration was a rather tempestuous one. Young John Milton Heins had been elected Official Editor 69–68 over Bill Dowdell. After difficulties with the unmanageable 14-year-old Editor (whom she had helped elect) Heins was removed and Dowdell appointed. The association gaped at *two* January 1922 official organs!

She worked hard at recruiting (20 recruits 1920–21, and 10 while President) and stimulating interest and publication of papers. In August she and George Julian Houtain were married, both for the second time. (They had no children.)

Dorothy also attended 1919, '21, '22 and '37 New York and Boston conventions. In 1926 the Houtains visited English amateurs during a three-month trip abroad. She did some professional writing for newspaper and trade journals, and included ceramics, dogs, and linoleum block printing (on cloth) among her hobbies.

After eight years in Albany, where George sold insurance and embarked on his ministerial work, the Houtains drifted back to Boston. They had turned over their amateur papers to Ralph Babcock in 1934. Following George's death in 1945 Dorothy reverted to her maiden name and requested that she be removed from membership.

Looking over some of the numbers of the *National Tribute* published by Dorothy MacLaughlin does provide some perspective on "her side of the story." She had addressed the Hub Club's A.J. Conference in Boston on February 22, 1921, on the subject of her presidential candidacy, and, newly arrived in New York, she quoted from these remarks under the title "Plank Down" in her May 1921 number:

> As a matter of fact I would not enjoy being a Queen and sitting on a throne to be gazed at. I think I'd like better to be the kind of a Queen who stayed in the kitchen and made tarts and had poetry written about her. I'd like to keep the throne nicely dusted and polished but as for sitting on it—well, I like the busy workroom and the satisfaction of doing things rather than the applause one gets for either the posing or the work. Therefore I need not make promises.
>
> A political platform, like all other platforms, is constructed with planks. In order that it may be strong, firm and able to bear the weight of a heavy year we must make a careful selection of material and be certain that it is substantial.
>
> The first and most important plank in my platform is "plank down." If elected to the Presidency of the National Amateur Press Association, that is going to be my policy from beginning to end and I am not going to ask of anybody what I am not ready to do myself. I want every member to plank down good hard work for the cause. Be active, publish papers, write. I want every officer to live up to his obligations. I believe that they should be solemnly sworn to fulfil the duties of their offices.
>
> Politics as politics is to be condemned. Politics as a means of betterment is commendable. For myself, I will work for the National in a clean, straightforward manner, perform the duties as outlined in the constitution and work in every way for the best interests of the National Amateur Press Association.
>
> What more can be said, except to ask for your confidence and the opportunity to do these things.

In the same number, she endorsed John Milton Heins as her candidate for Official Editor, and called his laureateship medals fund "a praiseworthy stimulant." The August 1921 number was devoted to the 1921 Boston convention and pictured the editor and George Julian Houtain on the beach at

Nantasket on its inside front cover. George Julian Houtain's account of the Houtains' trip to Albany, Buffalo, and Cleveland in the October 1921 number contained these words concerning their professional venture *Home Brew*:

> Naturally our thoughts and talk drifted around to our hobby Amateur Journalism and the National Amateur Press Association. Out of a clear sky it came— Dorothy's lament that it was positively wasteful that some of the very exceptional talent of our members should not find professional recognition; that it had long been her ambition to be of real service to her fellow members and start them on a lucrative and recognized career; that she would like to issue a professional publication and be responsible for their introduction to the field of professional letters; if there was only some stepping stone which she could give them to tide them over from amateur to professional. Under the spell of her enthusiasm, we decided upon the publication of a professional monthly of 64 pages and over, 5½ × 7½ and christened it HOME BREW [logo] and determined that its policy would be for America and the Home first and to disrobe the hypocrite and expose pretense.

Writing under the title "The Courage of Silence" in the December 1921 number, President Houtain reflected on *ad hominem* accusations and had words of wisdom for UAPA loyalist Howard Lovecraft as well:

> Last year the "National Tribute" was not slow to censure those of its editor's presidential supporters who launched a campaign of slander and abuse against her opponent [Edna Hyde]. Tribute very emphatically holds to its opinion of last year, that one's private life is his own and that there is enough in the amateur record of everyone on which to base opinions. Amateur Journalism has always been more or less a world apart. In it are those who in other spheres may be of the upper crust or of the lower strata, who may have broad or puritanical ideas, who may be Catholic, Protestant, Jew, or Infidel, who may be Republican, Democrat, Socialist or anything else, but in amateur journalism, the great leveller, there is no such thing. It makes no difference in Amateur Journalism just so long as you are an Amateur Journalist, and keep extraneous matters where they belong. Our concentration on this one thing makes us belittle things outside our own particular interests. We are not ashamed of this, if we were we would be different. In my opinion, therefore, Edna Hyde, against whom the campaign was launched, rose to great heights in not recognizing, in any way, those who tried to belittle her. Nobody thinks any the less of her than they did before they read what was said about her. The only effect was to make us think less of those who wrote such things. Amateurs need only defend their amateur records, and those who refuse to answer other attacks, who have the courage of silence, should be commended for their strength.
>
> Howard P. Lovecraft may well say, in criticizing the National Association, that we do not spend enough time on literary attainment and too much time in digging up other peoples' skeletons and trying to bring them to life. We have just as good writers in our own association as there are in any other, but

some of them do not direct their efforts in the right channels. This does not mean that politics and contenders for office should be ignored, they have a deserving place in our annals. Only keep politics free from vulgarities and above the level of ward heeler methods. If one feels sufficiently slandered or libelled he can resort to the police courts to rebuke his villifiers. Amateur Journalism should not be the back-yard for the washing of dirty linen.

In the same number, President Houtain wrote under the heading "Home Brew":

For the very few who may be shocked at the appearance of a professional paper from our sanctum named "Home Brew," I want to explain that its entire contents will not be devoted to the elimination of the 18th amendment. We will take pleasure in knocking certain blue law advocates as we think they should be knocked, but we trust that there will be nothing between its covers to offend any who may care to imbibe with us. The fact that it does emanate from our sanctum gives it its name. It is a home product and roots for the home in many different ways. Like tea, it cheers but not inebriates.

In her February 1922 number, President Houtain contemplated the campaign for NAPA office for the 1922-23 term and announced her own firm refusal of a second term in "A Houtain Proposed for a Fourth Term":

Speaking of politics, I almost forgot that I had been proposed for a second term. I was quite overwhelmed, especially as it came from the camp of last year's dear enemies. I know that the man who Mr. Fingulin hailed at the Labor Day banquet as "the man who gave the Presidency of the National to his wife as a wedding present," could put her there again, but much as I love the National, I have given it one year of my life, the best I had to give, when I could well have occupied it to much material advantage to myself. I stuck against some odds, but shall be glad to hand it over to a better man next July.

She noted the appointment of Bill Dowdell as Official Editor to replace "John Heins, removed," and had the following comments about the "Kroywen Club":

Is it possible that there is anybody who does not recognize that Kroywen is New York spelled backward! To show that HOME BREW is a good advertising medium the secretary has received four letters from its readers asking about the club and wanting to join. We have found the Greenwich Village Inn and the Lobster Trappe to be unsatisfactory, and the next dinner will be held at The Green Witch, a place which has been tried by several connoisseurs and pronounced the best dinner in New York for the $1.25. Edward V. Riis gave us a delightful talk last month about his newspaper experiences, especially that on the Ford Peace Ship, and the next dinner will be honored by the presence of Mr. Samuel C. Elby, who will talk on "Amateur Writing and

Personality." There will be present also a character reader, so that all those who have not a clear conscience, take warning and stay away.

Favorable reviews of *Home Brew* from *Broadway Brevities* and the *New York Evening Globe* were quoted, along with the following editorial comments:

> This is possibly the first time any amateur journalists, while actively engaged in the work of the hobby, have ever so pretentiously entered the professional field. Those amateurs who had contributions in the February number had an audience of ten thousand actual copies printed and distributed. Those who appear in the March number will have a circulation of 25,000.
>
> To such amateur journalists who had subscribed for HOME BREW, sending in their $2.50, we extend our thanks. There will be no further copies mailed to the members of the association—except by request—accompanied by remittance.

A greater access to primary source materials would undoubtedly permit a more unbiased account of the controversies of 1921-22 than I have provided. Certainly, there remain some topics for research. The laureateships that Lovecraft won over his 1914-37 career in amateur journalism are a topic deserving research. He did not seek honors, but nevertheless he won some. A book the length of Joshi's biography could doubtless be written on the subject of Lovecraft's involvement in the amateur journalism hobby by an author with access to the necessary primary research material. Alas, by now this is all written material, since all the contemporaries of Lovecraft in the amateur journalism hobby, including his recruit Victor E. Bacon (1905-1997), have died. Lovecraft knew how to modulate his participation in the hobby. His first love was criticism and literary improvement. He did not mind literary controversies, of which he had his fair share, but he always eschewed politics, and he did not particularly enjoy the administrative tasks of his terms as president and executive judge. But he served loyally. Even when the laureate controversies of 1921-22 threatened to touch him personally, he succeeded in navigating the treacherous waters. He kept on good terms with the Houtains and did not allow the controversy over the essay laureate award deter the pursuit of his romance with Sonia H. Greene. Perhaps wisely, the two of them elected to bypass NAPA's New York City convention in July 1922.[37] On December 5, 1922, Lovecraft experienced his epiphany in Marblehead, Massachusetts. In the succeeding year, he would find in *Weird Tales* a new professional market for his stories, far superior to Houtain's *Home Brew*. Some critics might say that he and his wife allowed the old Hoffman-Daas faction of the United to wither on the vine after they were returned to office in 1923-24 and 1924-25, but in truth interest the hobby across all the associations was at a low ebb in the mid- and late-1920s. For example, only four persons attended the National's 1928 convention in Niagara Falls, New York. Nevertheless, Vincent B. Haggerty was elected president and conducted a successful administration (1928-29). Even if the old Hoffman-Daas United was defunct, the National was on a rebound, and Lovecraft attended the 1930 convention in Boston at the invitation of Edward H. Cole. Denys Peter Myers (1884-1972) and Ethel Johnston-Myers (1882-1971) honored Cole and Lovecraft with a dinner at their home in Cambridge, Massachusetts. Edith Miniter was unable to attend the 1930 Boston convention because of poor health, but Lovecraft did get to visit her one last time on a personal trip to Wilbraham, Massachusetts, in 1928. Lovecraft might have attended NAPA's 1933 New York convention, but he and his aunt Annie Gamwell had moved to a new home at 66 College Street in Providence in May 1933. Almost immediately after the move, Annie broke her ankle in a fall on the stairs and Lovecraft had to spend most of the spring and summer as nursemaid. Nevertheless, at Cole's urging, he served NAPA well on the bureau of critics in 1931-35, the last two years as chairman, by appointment of president Harold Segal. His final honor was a second term as executive judge in 1935-36. The controversies between Edwin Hadley Smith and Ralph Babcock during the administration of president Hyman Bradofsky (1935-36) gave the executive judges a workout, but Lovecraft was glad to serve as an arbiter of the disputes and a conciliator of the disputants. He knew how to modulate his feelings, and how to enjoy the amateur journalism hobby without becoming embroiled in its politics. Could he have kept the Hoffman-Daas United going had he been less devoted to literary improvement and more committed to organizational development and recruiting? We do not know. For the long run, he certainly did well to follow his own priorities.

Did Lovecraft preserve the silver medal that John Milton Heins worked so hard to give him despite his own reluctance to accept the award? The record sayeth not. Yet another mystery for the intrepid Lovecraft researcher. A pamphlet reprinting the honorable mention essay and depicting the medal that it received would doubtless be of considerable interest to Lovecraft's reading public. Both the man and his work transcended the petty feuds of the amateur journalism hobby. Nevertheless, he remained grateful to the hobby that had rescued him from the life of a recluse. From amateur journalism, he learned to modulate his feelings and to interact appropriately with individuals with very different goals and personalities. He did his share of yeoman's work for the hobby—one thinks especially of his labors for the critical bureaux and of his laborious toil as an executive judge in 1935-36—but he also knew how to stay out of feuds and how to prosper while they raged. To the extent possible, he tried to be a conciliator—a leadership skill that the Houtains and Heins & Son never really mastered. When provoked by hobby opponents Ida C. Haughton, he could issue sharp reprises, but his normative *modus operandi* was to debate the issues and forego the personalities. In this manner, he benefited both the amateur journalism hobby and his own advancement in life.

That he was a reluctant laureate award recipient amidst the political toils in 1921 was doubtless the case; but nevertheless he received (and doubtless deserved) the handsome award. It is possible that his accommodation with the Houtains and with *Home Brew* proved of assistance when he became a professional author in his own right in *Weird Tales* and had to cope with Farnsworth Wright's erratic acceptance policies. Out of the political toils of amateur journalism in 1921–22 came a wiser man, better able to cope with the challenges he would have to face during the remainder of his life.

Notes

1. Two separate editions of the *National Amateur* (44, no. 3) were produced with the date of January 1922—one by John Milton Heins, who had resigned as official editor on 19 December 1921, and one by his replacement William J. Dowdell. (See below for details.) I presume this letter comes from the "unofficial" January 1922 number produced by Heins. Heins had Lovecraft's honorable mention essay set in type at the time he resigned the official editorship, and I presume that his January 1922 *National Amateur* includes Lovecraft's essay. It is possible that the letter appeared in both the Heins and the Dowdell January 1922 numbers, since Heins complained that Dowdell stole most of his contributed matter. I have not been able to examine either January 1922 number in the preparation of this essay. Currently, NAPA laureates cover chronological years and are awarded at the convention held the next following July. I do not know if the same rules applied during the Anthony F. Moitoret (1920–21) and E. Dorothy Houtain (1921–22) administrations. If so, Lovecraft's honorable mention essay (awarded in July 1921) would have to have been published during the calendar year 1920.

2. As noted below, my broken file of the *National Amateur* indicates that Lovecraft rejoined after the July 1920 convention and maintained his membership continuously thereafter. However, the possibility remains that he resigned prior to writing his acknowledgment letter to Heins and decided to re-apply shortly thereafter. As Heins himself related (see below), NAPA President E. Dorothy Houtain had a dispute with Sonia H. Greene in the fall of 1921, which nearly led Mrs. Greene to relinquish her NAPA membership. Perhaps Lovecraft contemplated resignation from NAPA in sympathy with Mrs. Greene's position.

3. *Collected Essays*, ed. S. T. Joshi (New York: Hippocampus Press, 2004–06), 1.304.

4. The thirteen-year-old son of veteran amateur Charles W. Heins (1875–1968) had been elected official editor for the 1921–22 year at NAPA's Boston convention (attended by Lovecraft) in July 1921, after serving as second vice president under President W. Paul Cook (1919–20) and as first vice president under President Anthony F. Moitoret (1920–21). Heins resigned his position on 19 December 1921, and NAPA President E. Dorothy Houtain appointed William J. Dowdell (the losing candidate for official editor at the July 1921 convention) to replace him.

5. One result of the dispute was Lovecraft's poetic satire "Medusa: A Portrait," first published in Charles W. Smith's *Tryout* for December 1921.

6. Howard R. Conover was elected president, Edward T. Mazurewicz first vice president, Stella V. Kellerman second vice president, Alma B. Sanger secretary-treasurer and Edward Delbert Jones chairman of the department of public criticism. None of these individuals was allied with Lovecraft's "literary" faction.

7. The definitive account of happenings in the Hoffman-Daas United faction during these years may be found in S. T. Joshi, *H. P. Lovecraft: A Life* (West Warwick, RI: Necronomicon Press, 1996), pp. 259-61.

8. *Letters to Rheinhart Kleiner*, ed. S. T. Joshi and David E. Schultz (New York: Hippocampus Press, 2005), pp. 120-21.

9. A reference to Harry E. Martin, elected president for the 1917–18 at NAPA's New York convention in July 1917. He succeeded George Julian Houtain, who served two successive terms as NAPA president in 1915-16 and 1916-17.

10. Frank Graeme Davis (1881-1938) originally joined NAPA in 1901 and proclaimed his primary affiliation with that association in a manifesto in the final (winter 1904-05) issue of *El Gasedil*. He commenced publication of the *Lingerer* in 1910 and was sharply critical of the rival UAPA in its second and third issues dated winter and summer 1917; Lovecraft replied in his article "A Reply to *The Lingerer*" in *Tryout* for June 1917. Davis was elected official editor for the 1917-18 term at NAPA's New York convention in July 1917. He was elected president for the 1918-19 term at NAPA's Chicago convention in July 1918. Davis recollected his and Lovecraft's mutual agreement "to be good" in his late publication *A Letter from the Lingerer* (September 1937).

11. Joshi, *op. cit.* (pp. 196-97) cites *Epgephi* for September 1920 for information that Lovecraft got a "quiet room to himself" and that the household was "chaperoned" by Michael Oscar White and a Mrs. Thompson. It was the first time since 1901 that Lovecraft had slept away from home—454 Angell Street until 1904 and 598 Angell Street thereafter. While Sonia H. Greene (1883-1972) and Winifred V. Jackson (1876-1959) were certainly the women closest to Lovecraft in amateur journalism, it seems a pity that we know so little about other early female associates like Alice Hamlet. The Social Security Death Index contains two individuals bearing the name Alice Hamlet: one, born on 25 April 1897, who died in Enosburg Falls, Vermont, in April 1978; and a second, born on 2 February 1889, who died in Sheridan, New York, in December 1984. Both of these individuals had SSNs issued in Massachusetts. I do not know which of them was Lovecraft's friend; it is possible that neither of them was, if in fact Lovecraft's friend later married and died bearing a different surname.

12. Miniter and her mother Jennie E. T. Dowe (1840-1919) had lived at 17 Akron Street in Dorchester from 1906 until 1918, when they took up residence with Charles and Laura Sawyer and their family at 20 Webster Street in Allston.

13. He stayed overnight at the home of Miss Little. Chaperon arrangements not known. There is a Myrta Little, born 17 April 1886, died August 1979, in Austin,

Texas, in the Social Security Death Index. I do not know whether she can be identified with the Myrta A. Little who lived in Hampstead, New Hampshire, in 1921.

14. *Letters to Rheinhart Kleiner*, p. 197.

15. The Rocky Mount convention was probably the high point for the Hoffman-Daas UAPA faction. It is a pity that Lovecraft was never able to attend a UAPA convention, especially Rocky Mount in 1915.

16. Houtain never forgave Hyde her resignation of the official editor's slot, least of all when she was again a candidate for the presidency in 1921, running against E. Dorothy MacLaughlin. Note Houtain's articles in the *American Amateur*: "An Open Letter" (April 1921) and "Replying to Mr. Baber" (June 1921). In the second article he wrote: "It is the truth, Miss Hyde knows it is the truth, practically every member attending the Brooklyn 1915 convention knows it is the truth that when Edna Hyde was defeated for President she was offered the Official Editorship, on condition that she would faithfully serve out the year. She promised and she, herself, won't deny this, and as a result of that promise she was elected. Nor will Miss Hyde deny, because it is the truth, that on August 13th (six weeks after her election and two weeks before the *National Amateur* should be mailed) she resigned as Official Editor and THAT SHE RESIGNED WITHOUT ANY PRELIMINARY WARNING OR INTIMATION OF ANY KIND WHATSOEVER. Miss Hyde, I am sure, will further acknowledge that there existed the most pleasant relationship between us after her election and up to the time of her resignation and that her resignation was not because of any differences we had, because we had none."

17. *Collected Essays*, 1.277.

18. As Sonia H. Greene noted in the *Rainbow* for May 1922, Professor McDonald also resigned simultaneously from the Hoffman-Daas UAPA.

19. The job of the Proxy Committee was to rule on the validity of the proxy ballots submitted for the election (i.e., the votes of those association members not present in person at the convention). A voter had to be both a member in good standing and to meet activity requirements for voting.

20. Contributors were asked to pay $1.50 per page to cover the costs of printing and mailing.

21. I particularly regret not having had access to the rival Heins and Dowdell numbers of the *National Amateur* for January 1922 and the April 1922 number of MacLaughlin's *National Tribune*.

22. Many other issues concerning the admission of members (i.e., credentials) and the counting of proxy ballots—too numerous even to summarize here—were also discussed by the convention.

23. Lovecraft had earlier contributed a poem to the first issue of Anne V. Tillery's *Pinfeather*, dated November 1914. In 1936, he did extensive work on Mrs. Renshaw's book *Well Bred Speech*. Most of Lovecraft's work was omitted from the published book.

24. Lovecraft, Miss Hamlet, and others had attended a reading by Lord Dunsany at the Copley Plaza Hotel in Boston in November 1919. In appreciation, Miss Hamlet

subsequently gave Lord Dunsany an original holograph letter written by Abraham Lincoln. Perhaps Lord Dunsany sent the cable to thank Miss Hamlet for the gift.

25. Lovecraft and Houtain had both sung at a Boston amateur gathering in 1920. Refer to *Letters to Rheinhart Kleiner*, pp. 212-15, for the quotations in this paragraph from Lovecraft's letter to Kleiner dated 30 August 1921—the very day of the Houtain wedding.

26. *Letters to Rheinhart Kleiner*, p. 215.

27. This article bore the subtitle: "No. 1.—Dealing with the Lovecraft Matter, and the Exposure of the Inside of a 'Fake Trial' by the National Executive Judges."

28. Heins must have actually completed the printing and mailing in December 1921, since Anthony F. Moitoret wrote to acknowledge the receipt of his copy as early as 2 January 1922. The Houtains did not receive their copy of Heins's *National Amateur* for January 1922 until mid-January.

29. Note that Heins is explicit here that he produced and mailed the controversial January 1922 issue of the *National Amateur* including Lovecraft's "honorable mention" essay. The first three numbers of the 44th volume of the *National Amateur* were dated September 1921, November 1921, and January 1922. There were actually two third numbers dated January 1922—one produced by John Milton Heins and one produced by William J. Dowdell.

30. Dowdell had erroneously printed the addresses of Charles W. Heins and John Milton Heins as Ridgefield Park, N.Y., instead of Ridgefield Park, N.J., in the *National Amateur* for January 1922.

31. President Houtain removed secretary Martin from office for inactivity on 7 January 1922, and appointed Wesley H. Porter to replace him.

32. The proofreading for Dowdell's numbers of the *National Amateur* was poorer than one might hope for, even in an amateur magazine. The actual title of this report as printed is "REPORT OF EXECUTIVE JONES."

33. Oldtime amateur journalist Edward F. Daas also loved to note members' birthdays in his journals in UAPA in the 1950s.

34. That secretary Martin had been slow to respond and that Scout representative White had financial issues to resolve were doubtless true, but the Houtains probably misjudged the situation in removing them. The constitution had a strong activity requirement for officers, but historically failure to meet publishing requirements was often overlooked albeit criticized.

35. Jennie Irene (Maloney) Kendall (later Mrs. John Plaisir) succeeded her husband Frank as NAPA president when he died in office in 1913. Edith Miniter had been elected president for the 1909-10 term.

36. Note that Spencer declines to consider Heins's January 1922 number an official number.

37. As far as is known, Houtain did not proceed to publish the staged photograph of Lovecraft and Greene that he had taken the year before.

Lovecraft's "He"

Lovecraft's story "He" was composed by the author in Scott Park in Elizabeth, New Jersey, on Tuesday, August 11, 1925 (*SL* 2.23).[1] The first professional publication was in *Weird Tales* for September 1926. A twelve-page typescript of the story dated August 11, 1925 is held in the Lovecraft Collection of the John Hay Library of Brown University.[2] "He" is perhaps best known for the author's autobiographical description of his own disillusionment with New York City, which is encapsulated in the first five paragraphs of the story. Lovecraft begins with his encounter with the mysterious stranger: "I saw him on a sleepless night when I was walking desperately to save my soul and my vision" (*D* 266). But he launches immediately into his own disillusionment with the city:

> My coming to New York had been a mistake; for whereas I had looked for poignant wonder and inspiration I had found instead only a sense of horror and oppression which threatened to master, paralyse, and annihilate me. (*D* 266)

"If you want to know what I think of New York," he later wrote to his friend Donald Wandrei, "read 'He'" (*SL* 2.101). Indeed, Lovecraft had to travel to the colonial surroundings of Elizabeth (which he always referred to by its ancient name, Elizabethtown) to summon up sufficient composure to put his feelings onto paper. Whether, as Winfield Townley Scott attributed to Samuel Loveman,[3] Lovecraft carried a "phial of poison" with him during this period, it is certain that the year 1925 represented the nadir of his life to date.

He had eloped to New York City with Sonia H. Greene in March 1924, married at St. Paul's Church in Manhattan, and settled into his wife's apartment at 259 Parkside in Brooklyn. The Lovecrafts subsequently acquired a lot for a future residence in Yonkers, New York (de Camp 202). After he married, Lovecraft spent most of the rest of the year (1924) in the fruitless and demoralizing quest for regular employment—the author found, not surprisingly, that no suitable employers would consider a thirty-four-year-old without a prior history of gainful employment. Lovecraft found consolation with his literary friends of the Kalem Club, but in the fall of 1924 his wife was hospitalized for gastric and nervous complaints (*SL* 1.359–60).

On the last day of 1924, Sonia Lovecraft departed to pursue employment prospects in the Midwest. Lovecraft was left alone in a one-room apartment with alcove at 169 Clinton Street, near the "Red Hook" district in Brooklyn. For a time—through May 1925—his friend, bookseller George Willard Kirk, also kept an apartment in the same building (*SL* 2.116). Driven to near distraction by the sights and smells of the daytime streets of the metropolis, he sought consolation in all-night explorations in search of colonial survivals. Hart Crane recorded one such expedition in a letter to his mother on September 14, 1924:

> Miss Sonia Green and her piping-voiced husband, Howard Lovecraft (the man who visited Sam in Cleveland one summer when Galpin was also there) kept Sam traipsing around the slums and wharf streets until four this morning looking for Colonial specimens of architecture, and until Sam tells me he groaned with fatigue and begged for the subway! (Crane 187)

Of the members of the Kalem Club, perhaps Arthur Leeds was Lovecraft's most enthusiastic companion on his all-night explorations. But by mid-year even the companionship of the Kalems was beginning to wear on Lovecraft. He sought solitude on the streets or in his apartment. His neighbor was a Syrian who played strange musical instruments (SL 2.116). To cap a year of disasters, nearly his entire wardrobe, and other property, were stolen while he slept in his apartment on May 24, 1925 (SL 2.10-11). Amidst this disillusionment and despair, Lovecraft escaped to Elizabeth to give literary expression to his feelings on August 11, 1925. Apart from the poignant expression of his own disillusionment and despair which occurs in the first five paragraphs of the story, however, "He" has received little notice. In its most barebones rendition, the plot involves the preternatural survival of a Greenwich squire who poisoned the Indians who formerly occupied the site of his ancestral manse:

> "These Indians shewed choler when the place was built, and were plaguy pestilent in asking to visit the grounds at the full of the moon. For years they stole over the wall each month when they could, and by stealth performed sartain acts. Then, in '68 [1768], the new squire catched them at their doings, and stood still at what he saw. Thereafter he bargained with them and exchanged the free access of his grounds for the exact inwardness of what they did; larning that their grandfathers got part of their custom from red ancestors and part from an old Dutchman in the time of the States-General. And pox on him, I'm afeared the squire must have served them monstrous bad rum whether or not by intent—for a week after he larnt the secret he was the only man living that knew it." (D 272-73)

The squire encounters the narrator "at about two one cloudy August morning" (D 268) and offers the advantage of his superior knowledge of the antiquarian survivals of the city. Beginning in "a series of detached courtyards" (D 268), the explorers "squeezed through interstices, tiptoed through corridors, clambered over brick walls, and once crawled on hands and knees through a low, arched passage of stone whose immense length and tortuous twistings effaced at last every hint of geographical location I had managed to preserve" (D 269). As they proceed, the uncanny sense of archaic survival increases, epitomized in the narrator's summary of the gradual change in the street lighting from oil lamps to colonial lanterns.

Finally, they pass through a "horrible unlighted court" (D 269) and come to an alley lit only by colonial lanterns:

> This alley led steeply uphill—more steeply than I had thought possible in this part of New York—and the upper end was blocked squarely by the ivy-clad wall of a private estate, beyond which I could see a pale cupola, and the tops of trees waving against a vague lightness in the sky. In this wall was a small low-arched gate of nail-studded black oak, which the man proceeded to unlock with a ponderous key. (D 269-70)

Of course, it is the early Georgian estate of the squire, who leads the narrator, "faint from a reek of infinite mustiness which welled out to meet us" (D 270), to his panelled library, described in such loving detail by the author that one wonders whether his description was based on an actual Georgian library he may have visited. Then, enjoining his guest to quiet, the squire opens the yellow silk curtains of the library and uses the necromantic arts learned from the original Indian settlers to reveal the surroundings as they were before settlement by the whites and in the palmy days of colonial Greenwich. "Good God!" the narrator whispers. "Can you do that for any time?" . . . "Can you—dare you—go far?" (D 273). "Far?" replies the squire. "What I have seen would blast ye to a mad statue of stone! Back, back—forward, forward—look, ye puling lack-wit!" (D 273).

Here the squire reveals to the narrator the hellish city of the far future:

> For full three seconds I could glimpse that pandaemoniac sight, and in those seconds I saw a vista which will ever afterward torment me in dreams. I saw the heavens verminous with strange flying things, and beneath them a hellish black city of giant stone terraces with impious pyramids flung savagely to the moon, and devil-lights burning from unnumbered windows. And swarming loathsomely on aerial galleries I saw the yellow, squint-eyed people of that city, robed horribly in orange and red, and dancing insanely to the pounding of fevered kettle-drums, the clatter of obscene croatala, and the maniacal moaning of muted horns whose ceaseless dirges rose and fell undulantly like the waves of an unhallowed ocean of bitumen. (D 273-74)

The narrator screams, and in fear and rage the squire totters even as the sound of the moccasin-clad Indian ghosts' ascending the stairs can be heard beyond the locked library door:

> The full moon—damn ye—ye . . . ye yelping dog—ye called 'em, and they've come for me! Moccasined feet—dead men—Gad sink ye, ye red devils, but I poisoned no rum o' yours—han't I kept your pox-rotted magic safe?—ye swilled yourselves sick, curse ye, and ye must needs blame the squire—let go, you! Unhand that latch—I've naught for ye here— (D 274)

The denouement proceeds swiftly. The tottering squire pulls down the yellow silk curtains and the library is flooded with the green light of the full moon. As he seeks to attack the narrator, the squire shrivels and blackens until only until his glaring eyes remain. The library door is shattered by the dead Indians' tomahawks and there enters into the room "a colossal, shapeless influx of inky substance starred with shining, malevolent eyes" (*D* 275). The shapeless thing envelops the squire and recedes through the doorway and down the stairs by which it came.

Almost immediately, the floor gives way, and the narrator falls to the first floor, only to see the shapeless thing vanish down the cellar stairs. Now the floor of the first story itself begins to give, and after hearing the crash of the cupola to the ground, the narrator escapes through a window to the grounds of the estate. The narrator scales the wall of the estate but cannot find the steep alley by which he came. Soon, the view of the surrounding walls, windows, and gambrel roofs is hidden by an enshrouding mist. The walltop urn to which the narrator has been clinging itself begins to tremble, and the narrator falls into unconsciousness. The narrator is discovered unconscious, at the end of a trail of blood, "at the entrance of a little black court off Perry Street" (*D* 276). The story ends on a lyrical note:

> I never sought to return to those tenebrous labyrinths, nor would I direct any sane man thither if I could. Of who or what that ancient creature was, I have no idea; but I repeat that the city is dead and full of unsuspected horrors. Whither he has gone, I do not know; but I have gone home to the pure New England lanes up which fragrant sea-winds sweep at evening. (*D* 276)

And of course that is exactly what the author himself did, within a year of the composition of "He." Lovecraft returned to his native Providence on April 17, 1926, to begin perhaps the most fertile creative period of his life.

Unfortunately, the grim story of his New York disillusionment did not survive in the favor of Lovecraft or of his critics. Writing to Frank Belknap Long less than six years after he composed the story, Lovecraft described "He" as "mawkish drivel ... worse than 'Red Hook'" (*SL* 3.296). Most subsequent commentators have dismissed "He" as a conventional tale of ghostly revenge. While the story did make the cut for the first Arkham House collection of Lovecraft's work, *The Outsider and Others*, in 1939, it was relegated to the third volume of Lovecraft's collected stories, *Dagon and Other Macabre Tales* (1965; reprinted with texts revised by S. T. Joshi, 1986) when Lovecraft's fiction was reprinted by Arkham House in 1963–65.

Notwithstanding its lacklustre fate, "He" remains an important story in the Lovecraft oeuvre. It effectively serves as a bridge between (i) the early horror tales like "The Picture in the House" (1920), "The Music of Erich Zann" (1921), "The Rats in the Walls" (1923), "The Festival" (1923), and "The

Shunned House" (1924) and (ii) the mature work of Lovecraft's final years in Providence. "He" is bracketed in Lovecraft's literary work by the considerably more garish New York City tale "The Horror at Red Hook" (August 1-2, 1925) and the spare New England tale of physical horror "In the Vault" (September 18, 1925). "Cool Air," another grim tale of physical horror and the last Lovecraft chose to set in New York City, followed in March 1926. By mid-April, he had returned to Providence and was ready to write such things as "The Call of Cthulhu," "Pickman's Model," "The Silver Key," and his remarkable novels *The Dream-Quest of Unknown Kadath* and *The Case of Charles Dexter Ward*, all of which he completed within a year of his return to Providence.

In what sense, then, may "He" be considered a "bridge" between the earlier and later work?

The preternatural survival of the squire's colonial world, and the squire's necromantic ability to summon up visions of past and future, prefigure Lovecraft's central concerns with the fourth dimension, concerns that preoccupy so much of his later work. The hellish vision of far-future New York unveiled by the squire prefigures the mysteries of the far future and the far past to be unveiled in later work like *At the Mountains of Madness* and "The Shadow out of Time." Early stories like "The Terrible Old Man" (1920) and "The Picture in the House" (1920) reveal Lovecraft's early preoccupation with the theme of preternatural survival. In "The Lurking Fear" (1922) and "The Rats in the Walls" (1923) entire hidden races of degenerates survive to wreak havoc in the modern-day world. In "He," however, Lovecraft returned to the unease created by an individual interloper:

> He spoke to me without invitation, noting my mood and glances as I studied certain knockered doorways above iron-railed steps, the pallid glow of traceried transoms feebly lighting my face. His own face was in shadow, and he wore a wide-brimmed hat which somehow blended perfectly with the out-of-date cloak he affected; but I was subtly disquieted even before he addressed me. His form was very slight, thin almost to cadaverousness; and his voice proved phenomenally soft and hollow, though not particularly deep. . . . As he spoke, I caught a glimpse of his face in the yellow beam from a solitary attic window. It was a noble, even a handsome, elderly countenance; and bore the marks of a lineage and refinement unusual for the age and place. Yet some quality about it disturbed me almost as much as its features pleased me— perhaps it was too white, or too expressionless, or too much out of keeping with the locality, to make me feel easy or comfortable. Nevertheless I followed him; for in those dreary days my quest for antique beauty and mystery was all that I had to keep my soul alive, and I reckoned it a rare favour of Fate to fall in with one whose kindred seekings seemed to have penetrated so much farther than mine. (D 268–69)

The squire leads the narrator through tangles of courtyards and narrow passages "without needless words" (*D* 269); and it is only when the narrator is seated in the squire's library that he has a chance to observe his host more closely:

> Without his hat he took on an aspect of extreme age which was scarcely visible before, and I wondered if this unperceived mark of singular longevity were not one of the sources of my original disquiet. When he spoke at length, his soft, hollow, and carefully muffled voice not infrequently quavered; and now and then I had great difficulty in following him as I listened with a thrill of amazement and half-disavowed alarm which grew each instant. (*D* 270)

Only when the squire beckons the narrator to view the visions beyond his silk-draped library window does the narrator encounter the squire in the flesh:

> My host now took my hand to draw me to one of the two windows on the long side of the malodorous room, and at the first touch of his ungloved fingers I turned cold. His flesh, though dry and firm, was of the quality of ice; and I almost shrank away from his pulling. But again I thought of the emptiness and horror of reality, and boldly prepared to follow whithersoever I might be led. (*D* 272)

Finally, in anger and fear caused by the narrator's scream, the squire pulls down the library drapes, admitting the light of the full moon, and commences his own unnatural dissolution:

> In those greenish beams the candles paled, and a new semblance of decay spread over the musk-reeking room with its wormy panelling, sagging floor, battered mantel, rickety furniture, and ragged draperies. It spread over the old man, too, whether from the same source or because of his fear and vehemence, and I saw him shrivel and blacken as he lurched near and strove to rend me with vulturine talons. Only his eyes stayed whole, and they glared with a propulsive, dilated incandescence which grew as the face around them charred and dwindled. (*D* 274–75)

In this remarkable passage it becomes apparent that not only the squire but also his entire milieu are interlopers in the narrator's world; indeed, both share an almost simultaneous demise after the arrival of the vengeful Indian ghosts. One might interpret Lovecraft's "He" much as Lovecraft interpreted Poe's "The Fall of the House of Usher": for, just as Roderick Usher and his sister shared a common soul with their house, so the milieu of the squire, his estate, and its surroundings constitute one unified impenetration of the narrator's New York.

Virtually all of Lovecraft's horror fiction from the 1920-25 period concerns itself, in one way or another, with archaic incursions into the modern world. In "He," a hidden, haunted New York of past and of future overlays and impenetrates the actual New York of the narrator. Of the early horror fiction, "He" most powerfully expresses the motif of the "conquest" of the fourth dimension that so preoccupies the later work.

That the theme of dislocation of time and the impenetration of the present by the lost past could hold personal terror for author is shown by the recurrence of this theme in his dreams. One of the most notable of these dreams was related by Lovecraft to his friend Clark Ashton Smith:

> Only last night I had another dream—of going back to 598 Angell Street after infinite years. The neighbourhood was deserted and grass-grown, and the houses were half-falling to pieces. The key on my ring fitted the mouldering door of 598, and I stepped in amidst the dust of centuries. Everything was as it was around 1910—pictures, furniture, books, etc., all in a state of extreme decay. Even objects which have been with me constantly in all later homes were there in their old positions, sharing in the general dissolution and dust-burial. I felt an extreme terror—and when footsteps sounded draggingly from the direction of my room I turned and fled in panic. I would not admit to myself what it was I feared to confront . . . but my fear also had the effect of making me shut my eyes as I raced past the mouldy, nitre-encrusted mirror in the hall. Out into the street I ran—and I noted that none of the ruins were of buildings newer than about 1910. I had covered about half a block—of continuous ruins, with nothing but ruins ahead—when I awaked shivering. At the last moment my great fear seemed to be of passing my birthplace and early home—the beloved 454 Angell Street—toward which I was headed. (SL 4.327)

Certainly, "He" is far from a merely conventional story of ghostly revenge. Maurice Lévy has written of Lovecraft's houses as the nexus between the daylight worlds of everyday life and the hidden worlds that lie above and beneath it:

> The dwelling is a fantastic place par excellence, insofar as it demarcates and isolates the malefic region in a particularly adequate way. It materializes the mythical threshold that makes possible the necessary transgressions and justifies the inevitable retribution: the horror it inspires is primordial and brings up in each individual the most archaic layers of racial memory. The same irrepressible anguish seizes all the characters the moment they cross the forbidden portico, knowing confusedly that they are performing the irremediable and are binding themselves irreversibly. Being the meeting place of the here and the beyond, all the houses are in a way fateful. Lovecraft cannot bring the abnormal to his hero except within the interior of these tragic walls, which enclose, contain, and up to a point dam up the irrational. (Lévy 38)

One would have to go far to realize an archaic survival more powerful than the Georgian estate that figures as the locus of "He." "A reek of infinite mustiness . . . the fruit of unwholesome centuries of decay" (D 270) wells out to greet the narrator even as he enters. The Georgian architecture and furnishings of the house are described in loving detail by the author: the small-paned windows, the candelabrum of twelve sconces, the doorway pediments, the Doric cornice, the Chippendale table, the lyre-back chair in which the squire seats himself, even the eighteenth-century costume in which the squire himself is dressed.

The powerfully realized Indian ghost—in which the reader can surely see the fruits of Lovecraft's reading of Machen and of M. R. James—is a cut above the overly literal conceptions of Lovecraft's later fiction. The real point of the tale, however, is not the squire's crime and the Indians' revenge—very real as each of them are—but the survival and impenetration of this entire scenario of horror into the "deadness" of modern New York. "To my ancestor," the squire says to the narrator,

> there appeared to reside some very remarkable qualities in the will of mankind; qualities having a little-suspected dominance not only over the acts of one's self and of others, but over every variety of force and substance in Nature, and over many elements and dimensions deemed more universal than Nature herself. May I say that he flouted the sanctity of things as great as space and time, and that he put to strange uses the rites of sartain half-breed red Indians once encamped upon this hill? (*D* 271)

Few of the horror stories written by Lovecraft during the 1920-25 period have as powerfully realized a locus as the Georgian mansion in "He." Certainly, the ancestral restorations of "The Moon-Bog" (1921) and "The Rats in the Walls" (1923) are far inferior in their realization. The hauntingly powerful crumbling of the Georgian mansion, commencing almost instantly upon the seizure of the squire by the Indian ghosts, is nearly unmatched in power in Lovecraft's fiction. Surely, he had come a long way since the blood dripping from the ceiling in "The Picture in the House." The mansion falls into its cellar while the narrator barely escapes, and then the urn to which he clings on the wall of the estate crumbles even as he surveys the surroundings of the mansion in confusion.

The description of the final fall of the Georgian mansion in "He" is so vivid and haunting that one wonders why it has not figured prominently in the early cinematic adaptations of Lovecraft's work. Effective realization of the Indian ghost would doubtless pose problems, but the chromatic possibilities of the yellow silken draperies and the greenish moonlight plus the overall atmosphere of wavering unreality ought to interest the auteur. The "Nightmare on Elm Street" movies—marred so badly by the emergence of Freddy Krueger as a camp figure—struggle in their dream sequences toward something with a fraction of the power of Lovecraft's conceptualization of the terrible mansion in "He."

The steep, lantern-lit alley by which the narrator and the squire ascend to the Georgian mansion—and which the narrator cannot afterward locate from his vantage point on the wall—is surely an after-echo of the powerfully conceived Rue d'Auseil in "The Music of Erich Zann," the story of another locus where the cosmic and the everyday worlds meet and probably the only prior one of Lovecraft's stories that exceeds "He" in merit. Like the alley in "He," it is incredibly steep and cannot afterward be found on maps of the city. Both conceptions are probably after-echoes of Lovecraft's early exposure to the precipitously steep streets of colonial houses that ascend College Hill in his native Providence. The grade is so steep on Meeting Street that the street must be broken with a flight of steps; and similarly, the cobbled stretch of Bowen Street opposite the Sullivan Dorr mansion becomes too steep, ultimately, for vehicular traffic, and a mere pathway ascends from Pratt Street to Congdon Street alongside Prospect Terrace, where Lovecraft loved to overlook the city. If the world of past and future that impenetrates the world of today is both above and below that world, it only conforms to reason that the ascent or descent thereto must be steep—just as in popular Christian belief purgatory was conceived as a mountain of ascending circles of decreasing torment and increasing hope and hell as an underground world comprised of descending circles of increasing and eternal misery. In Lovecraft's later fiction, contemporary human beings must descend below the surface of the earth to discover the earthly remains of the distant past and the distant future in *At the Mountains of Madness* and "The Shadow out of Time."

"He" transcends the conventional tale of ghostly revenge. The story of revenge is present but is actually only a frame for the more important happenings of the story—namely, the squire's defeat of time and the penetration of his ancient world into the world of Lovecraft's New York City, 1925. Few of the earlier and few of the later stories join present and past more effectively than in the nexus of the haunted Georgian mansion in "He."

Finally, "He" contains among the most powerful revelations of Lovecraft's own soul in his horror fiction. The opening paragraphs that describe the narrator's disillusionment with New York City are among the most powerful autobiographical writing in Lovecraft's work, and writers on Lovecraft have cited them over and over. When the narrator meets the squire "at about two one cloudy August morning" in "a series of detached courtyards . . . now accessible only through the unlighted hallways of intervening buildings" (D 268), one is hauntingly sure that the narrator is Lovecraft himself on one of the night-long walks that he took to escape the horror and desolation he felt amidst the teeming daylight world of New York City. One can almost hear Sam Loveman begging for the subway, or Art Leeds sharing with Lovecraft the joy of discovery of an obscure courtyard of early nineteenth-century survivals. Clifford M. Eddy, Jr. and Lovecraft had engaged in similar expeditions in the slums that bordered on downtown Providence in the early 1920s (SL 1.269-72, 278-79). More subtly, one can detect Lovecraft's pain at the failure of his marriage and his growing isolation and unhappiness in New York City. He writes of the narrator's choice of Bohemian Greenwich Village as his place of residence:

> Then, on a sleepless night's walk, I met the man. It was in a grotesque hidden courtyard of the Greenwich section, for there in my ignorance I had settled, having heard of the place as the natural home of poets and artists. The archaic lanes and houses and unexpected bits of square and court had indeed delighted me, and when I found the poets and artists to be loud-voiced pre-tenders whose quaintness is tinsel and whose lives are a denial of all that pure beauty which is poetry and art, I stayed on for the love of these venerable things. (D 267–68)

One must remember that Lovecraft intended that his marriage and settle-ment in New York City form the basis for the foundation of a family that he hoped that his aunts Lillian D. Clark and Annie E. Gamwell would eventually join. L. Sprague de Camp's narration of how the Lovecrafts acquired a lot in Yonkers, New York, in the expectation of building a family home is a poignant expression of the hopes of the bride and the groom (de Camp 202). These dreams were shattered by the reality that Lovecraft was no more employable in conventional employment in New York City than he was in Providence, just as the dreams of Lovecraft's own parents were shattered by the illness of his fa-ther Winfield Scott Lovecraft (SL 1.33). No wonder Lovecraft, whom his wife remembered as "entirely adequate sexually" as a husband (de Camp 194), was offended by the casual mores of the Greenwich bohemians of his day. While the friendship of the Kalem Club members helped Lovecraft survive the failure of his marriage, they could not relieve his essential misery and isolation in New York City after its failure. All this is poignantly, if subtly, expressed in "He." No friend of the Kalem Club reading the story in the September 1926 *Weird Tales* could have doubted that Lovecraft was writing of himself, or failed to re-joice that the author, like his narrator, succeeded in returning to his New Eng-land home.

Lovecraft's narrator spares no words in his final verdict on the metropolis:

> So instead of the poems I had hoped for, there came only a shuddering blankness and ineffable loneliness; and I saw at last a fearful truth which no one had ever dared to breath before—the unwhisperable secret of secrets—the fact that this city of stone and stridor is not a sentient perpetuation of Old New York as London is of Old London and Paris of Old Paris, but that it is in fact quite dead, its sprawling body imperfectly embalmed and infested with queer animate things which have nothing to do with it as it was in life. (D 267)

While "He" is not marred by the same rabid racism as "The Horror at Red Hook," written only a few days previously, it is perhaps an even more final verdict on the metropolis, epitomized by the terrible vision of the far-future city summoned up by the squire. One can only hope that Lovecraft was mistaken and that a human thread of continuity still binds the great city with the rest of the nation. For Lovecraft, when he later visited his friends of the Kalem Club in the city, it remained the "Pest Zone." One wishes, indeed, that one knew more of Lovecraft's night-long explorations of the city, in and out of the company of his friends. Perhaps his reference to "Perry Street" at the end of "He" is a clue that will enable future researchers to flesh out some of his inspiration.[4]

A broad thinker may regret that Lovecraft did not find more to like in New York City. He pronounced the city dead, and "He" is in a sense the death certificate he wrote to formalize his verdict. More certainly than in any other fictional work from his pen, the author is the narrator, wandering the desolate streets of the city to relieve his misery and loneliness. Underlying what can be read as a conventional story of ghostly revenge lies the hope and subsequent disillusionment that resulted in the issuance of the author's verdict and one of the most fantastic and grippingly realized of the scenarios he concocted to alter the laws of nature to make mingling of past, present, and future a fictional reality. The squire's musty Georgian mansion—realized with such care and fidelity—crumbles almost instantaneously. Its approaches are occult and are not rediscoverable even if we wished to do so. Such gateways to the hidden world of the subconscious are difficult to find in fiction—and it is hoped a loyal coterie of readers will continue to speak for this story. "He" deserves a more prominent place in the history and criticism of Lovecraft's oeuvre; and perhaps this essay will make a small contribution toward its reaching that goal.

Notes

1. Lovecraft first visited Elizabeth on 29 August 1924, after seeing an article on the town in the *New York Post*, and apparently revisited the town on 11 October 1924. At Bridge Street and Elizabeth Avenue he saw the 1735 Andrew Joline house, which reminded him of the Babbitt House at 135 Benefit Street in Providence, and served as partial inspiration for his story "The Shunned House" (*SL* 1.357).

2. Lovecraft records (*SL* 2.23) that he wrote "He" in pencil in a dime composition book he had purchased. This autograph manuscript does not appear to survive.

3. My copy of *Marginalia* (Sauk City, WI: Arkham House, 1944), once owned by Benjamin Crocker Clough (1888–1975), Professor of Classics in Brown University, who reviewed the book for the *Providence Journal* (18 January 1945), contains on p. 323 opposite Scott's attribution of the story of the "phial of poison" to Samuel Loveman (1887–1976) the following handwritten annotation by Clough: "So he [Loveman] told me and I WTS [Winfield Townley Scott]. 'Phial' I'm not sure of."

4. In *H. P. Lovecraft: A Life*, S. T. Joshi provides a detailed account (p. 372) of the *New York Evening Post* article (29 August 1924) of a "lost lane" off Perry Street that inspired

Lovecraft's exploration of the area. Citing Elaine Schechter's *Perry Street–Then and Now* (New York, 1972), Joshi describes a mansion that stood in the block bordered by Perry, Charles, Bleeker, and West Fourth streets from its erection between 1726 and 1744 and its demolition in 1865. Joshi opines: "Lovecraft almost certainly knew the history of the area, and he has deftly incorporated into his tale."

Works Cited

Crane, Hart. *The Letters of Hart Crane*. Edited by Brom Weber. New York: Hermitage House, 1952.

de Camp, L. Sprague. *Lovecraft: A Biography*. Garden City, NY: Doubleday, 1975.

Joshi, S. T. *H. P. Lovecraft: A Life*. West Warwick, RI: Necronomicon Press, 1996.

Lévy, Maurice. *Lovecraft: A Study in the Fantastic*. Detroit: Wayne State University Press, 1988. Translated by S. T. Joshi from Lévy, *Lovecraft ou du fantastique* (Paris: Christian Bourgois Editeur, 1972; rpt. 1985).

"The Silver Key" and Lovecraft's Childhood

Dedicated to David E. Schultz

My style in both prose and verse was basically the same at 11 or 12 as it is now (although of course my handling of ideas and images was then ludicrously immature)—and my continuous memory of those far-off days is so keen that I can still enter into all their thoughts and feelings. It takes no effort at all especially when I am out in certain woods and fields which have not changed a bit since my boyhood—for me to imagine that all the years since 1902 or 1903 are a dream . . . . . . that I am still 12 years old, and that when I go home it will be through the quieter, more village-like streets of those days—with horses and wagons, and little varicoloured street cars with open platforms, and with my old home at 454 Angell St. still waiting at the end of the vista—with my mother, grandfather, black cat, and other departed companions alive and unchanged. (*SL* 4.233)

Like many persons who find only moderate degrees of fulfillment in adult experience, Howard Phillips Lovecraft always harked back to his childhood as an almost magical experience. After an infancy spent in suburban Boston, Lovecraft grew up in his birthplace, the privileged home of his maternal grandfather Whipple V. Phillips (1833–1904) on the East Side of Providence, R.I.. His descriptions of that spacious home, extending even to the colors of the wall coverings (*SL* 2.165), are almost lyrical. To the east were the open fields and the banks of the Seekonk River where Lovecraft constructed small altars to his favorites among the gods and goddesses of Greek mythology. Later in life, he wrote his friend Frank Belknap Long, Jr. that he never knew what it was like to play in a crowded city street (*SL* 3.317).

The declining fortunes of Whipple V. Phillips forced the sale of the family home shortly after his death in the early spring of 1904. His young grandson was doubly heartbroken, first by the loss of the only father figure he had ever known and then by the loss of the home in which he had grown up. Within weeks, Whipple Phillips's executor Clarke Howard Johnson (1851–1930) had disposed of the property for the benefit of the estate and Lovecraft and his mother removed to a cramped flat at 598 Angell Street where they remained together for the troubled years of Lovecraft's adolescence and young adulthood. Shockingly, Lovecraft wrote to J. Vernon Shea that he considered drowning himself in the Barrington River during the summer following his grandfather's death—perhaps the first notable instance of suicidal ideation in a life marked by repeated battles against depression (*SL* 4.26, 357–58). Fortunately, Lovecraft's family had the wisdom to enroll him in Hope Street High

School for the 1904–05 term (he had been tutored since leaving Slater Avenue Primary School in 1902) and the beckoning of new fields of intellectual endeavor reawakened his interest in life. At Hope Street High School Lovecraft achieved a moderately respectable academic record, but in 1908–09 he suffered a major breakdown that forced his withdrawal and cancelled his academic prospects. Only amateur journalism eventually rescued him from the hermitage of 598 Angell Street and its dim prospects for any kind of normal adult life. Little wonder that Lovecraft looked back on his happy childhood years at 454 Angell Street as an almost magical experience.

No story reflects the magic of Lovecraft's childhood with clarity as crystalline as "The Silver Key" (1926). The exact date of its composition does not seem to be assignable based upon as-yet published correspondence or the surviving manuscripts, but I believe that it must have been composed very shortly after the one-day pilgrimage to ancestral sites in Foster, R.I., that Lovecraft and his younger aunt Mrs. Gamwell undertook in October 1926 (thoroughly described in Lovecraft's letter of October 26, 1926, to Frank Belknap Long, Jr., *SL* 2.81–89). Despite his great prowess as a bicyclist during the years 1908–13, Lovecraft had visited Foster only twice previously: in 1896, when he and his mother spent two weeks at the farmhouse of his great-uncle James W. Phillips (1830–1901) (elder brother of Whipple V. Phillips) on Johnson Road, and in 1908, when they returned for a single-day visit (*SL* 2.81).

I believe that something magical and something important for the course of Lovecraft's development occurred during that first visit to Foster in August 1896. I do not know exactly what it was, but I hope to offer some hints in the course of this reading of "The Silver Key." In the course of the explication, I will also draw upon the sequel "Through the Gates of the Silver Key" (1932–33), which eventuated when Lovecraft agreed to collaborate with his friend E. Hoffmann Price (1898–1988) on a new Randolph Carter adventure that the latter had sent to him in draft. Lovecraft found the work of reconciling Price's fast-paced narrative with his own deep identification with the Randolph Carter character extremely difficult and ended by rewriting the story entire (*SL* 4.349). Some of Price's original concepts may be found preserved in section V of the narrative. In truth, however, "Through the Gates of the Silver Key" was not an artistic success, and Robert H. Barlow rightly advised August Derleth that it should not be included in the premiere collection of Lovecraft's work. (Derleth ultimately chose to include "Through the Gates of the Silver Key" in *The Outsider and Others*.) The sequel is nevertheless worthy of consideration for the additional light it can shed on the circumstances of the 1896 Foster visit and its impact on Lovecraft's development.

Some readers will quickly object that "The Silver Key" clearly places the ancestral Carter home in Arkham, Massachusetts, the centerpiece of Lovecraft's Miskatonic Country and a far cry from Foster if there ever was one.

The sequel "Through the Gates of the Silver Key" fixes the date of Randolph Carter's return to the ancient Carter homestead and subsequent disappearance as October 7, 1928 (MM 422). "The Silver Key" itself waxes poetic in describing Carter's approach to his ancestral homestead:

> In the brooding fire of autumn Carter took the old remembered way past graceful lines of rolling hill and stone-walled meadow, distant vale and hanging woodland, curving road and nestling farmstead, and the crystal windings of the Miskatonic, crossed here and there by rustic bridges of wood or stone. At one bend he saw the group of giant elms among which an ancestor had oddly vanished a century and a half before, and shuddered as the wind blew through them. Then there was the crumbling farmhouse of old Goody Fowler the witch, with its little evil windows and great roof sloping nearly to the ground on the north side. He speeded up his car as he passed it, and did not slacken till he had mounted the hill where his mother and her fathers before her were born, and where the old white house still looked proudly across the road at the breathlessly lovely panorama of rocky slope and verdant valley, with the distant spires of Kingsport on the horizon, and hints of the archaic, dream-laden sea in the farthest background.
>
> Then came the steeper slope that held the old Carter place he had not seen in over forty years. Afternoon was far gone when he reached the foot, and at the bend half way up he paused to scan the outspread countryside golden and glorified in the slanting floods of magic poured out by a western sun. All the strangeness and expectancy of his recent dreams seemed present in this hushed and unearthly landscape, and he thought of the unknown solitudes of other planets as his eyes traced out the velvet and deserted lawns shining undulant between their tumbled walls, the clumps of faery forest setting off far lines of purple hills beyond hills, and the spectral wooded valley dipping down in shadow to dank hollows where trickling waters crooned and gurgled among swollen and distorted roots. (MM 415)

Returning to the ancestral Carter homestead with the ancient silver key and mysterious manuscript he found among his family papers, Carter finds everything mysteriously restored to its 1883 aspect; the homestead itself, reduced to a cellar hole by 1928, restored to its prior aspect, his deceased relatives still living, and the Congregational steeple on Central Hill in Kingsport, long demolished to make way for a hospital, rising in all its glory. When he visits the mysterious Snake Den where his ancestor Edmund Carter, a refugee from the 1692 Salem witch persecutions, was reputed to have worked his sorceries, Randolph Carter encounters the Keeper of the Gateway and is transported from the human ken. The sequel, "Through the Gates of the Silver Key," makes explicit that Carter was transported into the body of the sorcerer Zkauba on the planet Yaddith in a distant galaxy whence he returns after countless ages to the planet earth of 1930 to seek the key to the recovery of his human aspect in the guise of the Swami Chandraputra. Lovecraft's instincts regarding the sequel were correct; it would have been better to end the narrative, as he did in "The Silver Key" itself, with Carter's mysterious transmutation back in time and subsequent disappearance. But "Through the Gates of the Silver Key," despite its artistic failure, is nevertheless valuable for the additional insights which it can shed on Lovecraft's conceptions.

How then can I argue that a story set so clearly in Lovecraft's beloved Arkham owes much of its background to a remote Rhode Island region that Lovecraft apparently visited only four times in his life (1896, 1908, 1926, and 1929, when he and Mrs. Gamwell returned for another excursion [see *SL* 3.15–20, 25])? First of all, it must be noted that Lovecraft delighted in intermingling his fictional settings. There are indeed no precise identifications for such fictional settings as Arkham, Dunwich, Innsmouth, and Kingsport, even though Salem, Wilbraham-Monson-Hampden, Newburyport, and Marblehead may have been their respective principal contributing sources. Arkham's Miskatonic University clearly had its origin in Providence's Brown University. (Salem had no university during Lovecraft's lifetime.) The literature has demonstrated copiously the difficulty of fixing any exact location for Arkham. The fact is that Lovecraft deliberately utilized inconsistencies relating to his fictional settings to heighten their imaginative appeal. So there is no general argument to disprove that he interjected Foster elements into his Arkham environment. I will argue from both the descriptions of the Carter homestead and the family names that occur in "The Silver Key" and its sequel that Lovecraft's early and late perceptions of Foster were a strong contributing factor to the fictional environment he created in these, and possibly other, stories.

The James W. Phillips farmhouse where Lovecraft stayed for two weeks in 1926 is usually referred to as the "Place-Phillips farm" and is enumerated as #270 in the survey of Foster historic buildings in *Foster, Rhode Island: Statewide Historical Preservation Report P-F-1* [HPCR] (63). The handsome one-and-a-half-story farmhouse was probably erected shortly after 1826 by Abraham Place (1800–1852), the uncle of James W. Phillips's wife Jane Ann Place (1829–1900). Abraham Place married Nabby Rathbun (1794–1851), the sister of Lovecraft's great-grandmothers Sarah (Sally) Rathbun (1787–1868) (m. Stephen Place, Jr.) and Robie Rathbun (1797–1848) (m. Jeremiah Phillips); but the couple had no children. In 1853, James W. Phillips married Jane Ann Place and they probably came into possession of the Place-Phillips farm shortly thereafter. The setback ell and porch were probably added to the home by James W. Phillips during the early part of his tenure. James W. Phillips and his wife occupied the home through the end of the century; of their five children, only two, Walter Herbert Phillips (1854–1924) and Jeremiah Wheaton Phillips (1863–1902), survived to maturity.

This beautiful property, nestled among the rocky hills of Foster, faces east on Johnson Road. Along with Daniel W. Lorraine and Marc A. Michaud, I had the privilege of inspecting the premises while they were for sale during 1990. The beautifully symmetrical Johnson Road façade of the main structure includes a centrally placed door with attractive sidelights with two twelve-paned windows located on either side. Inside the house, the ground floor is dominated by a parlor on the east [Johnson Road] side and a kitchen on the west side. The smaller rooms on the ground floor were probably used as bed-rooms, and it is likely that the second half story provided children's sleeping quarters. The west windows enjoy a beautiful country view, and a small well-kept lawn gradually blends into fields as the land rises. To the west of the house are several twentieth-century outbuildings as well as an abandoned black granite quarry that was worked by the Rock of Ages Company of Barre, Vermont, in the late 1960s or early 1970s. To the north, a small orchard separates the house from a rocky knoll whose summit offers an impressive view of the outspread countryside.

East of the house, a beautiful gurgling brook crosses Johnson Road, to join the Moosup River to the west. Well set back from the opposite side of the road, on rising land, stands an older Place homestead, the Benejah Place farm, enu-merated as #269 in the *Historical Preservation Commission Report* (p. 63). The original structure was erected by Benejah Place (1742–1815), the grandfather of Abraham, about 1760 and altered considerably over the years. It was subse-quently occupied by Benejah's grandson Job Wilcox Place (1795–1879) and his wife Asenath Pierce (1793–1881), who married in 1818 and had children Moses Place (1819–1822), Aaron B. Place (1822–1892), Jane Ann Place (1829–1900), and Henry Lester Place (1839–1902). Henry Lester Place is still shown as the owner of the property in the 1895 Everts and Richards map of Foster, but he died in Providence in 1902.

Along a fenceline immediately south of the Benejah Place farm stands the Place-Phillips cemetery (Foster Historical Cemetery #86), where are buried James W. Phillips, his wife Jane Ann Place, and all their children except Jeremiah Wheaton Phillips. Also buried in this ancient, neglected cemetery are Jane Ann Place's parents, Job Wilcox Place and Asenath Pierce, her early-deceased brother Moses Place, her uncle Abraham Place, her aunt Nabby (Rathbun) Place, and her grandparents John Place (1763–1846) and Lydia (Wilcox) Place (1773–1856). It is quite possible that the small, neglected cemetery contains other, older Place burials as well. It would surely be a natu-ral resting place for Benejah Place and his wife Mary (Perkins) Place (1741–1829). Benejah's parents Enoch Place (1704–1789) and Hannah (Wilcox) Place (ca. 1710–1802), who first settled in Foster in 1751, probably rest under fieldstones close to their original homestead.

When Lovecraft and Mrs. Gamwell visited Foster in October 1926, they were first received in the hamlet of Moosup Valley by Nabby Emogene (Tyler) Kennedy (1854–1945), a remote relative who had attended school with Lovecraft's elder aunt Mrs. Clark. Mrs. Kennedy and her husband Alvero A. Kennedy (1853–1936), the son of Rev. George W. Kennedy, then occupied the so-called Tyler Tavern Stand (HPCR #239, p. 64), which the Historical Preservation Commission Report dates to c. 1780. (Lovecraft indicated that "some" dated this house as early as 1728 [SL 2.83]; in any case, it was largely rebuilt following the 1815 gale.) From the hamlet of Moosup Valley, Lovecraft and Mrs. Gamwell worked their way eastward past the former home of Otis and Reusha Foster ("Aunt Rushy") to the intersection of Moosup Valley and Johnson Roads, which marked the focus of the Place family settlement in Foster. When the 1820 federal census was taken, Stephen Place, Samuel Place, Christopher Place, Peleg Place, Stephen Place 2d, Newman Place, and Hazard Place all resided in this immediate area. By the 1830s the ranks of the Place family in Foster were beginning to thin as younger families left for better opportunities in New York and the western states. By the time of the 1900 federal census, Aaron B. Place's son Job D. Place (1858–1905) was the only descendant of the original settler Enoch Place still farming in Foster.

When Lovecraft and Mrs. Gamwell visited the Phillips-Place farm in October 1926, it was occupied by Nabby (Tyler) Kennedy's daughter Bertha T. (Kennedy) Bennis (1893–1974) and her husband Ellis B. Bennis (1890–1976), whom Lovecraft jokingly referred to as his "333d cousin Bennis" (SL 2.87). (Actually, both Ellis B. Bennis and his wife Bertha T. Kennedy were fourth cousins of Lovecraft through common descent from Enoch Place and his wife Hannah (Wilcox) Place, progenitors of the Place clan in Foster.) After graciously allowing Lovecraft and Mrs. Gamwell to view the Phillips-Place farmhouse both inside and out, Mr. Bennis drove his two visitors to the hamlet of Greene, across the Coventry, R.I., line, so that they could visit with old associates of Lovecraft's maternal grandfather Whipple V. Phillips, who had made his first fortune in the environs and lost it to a speculator named Hugog c. 1869, before removing to Providence c. 1874.

Lovecraft's beautiful description of the Phillips-Place farm in 1926 is marred only by his resentment of the new Finnish settlers who then occupied the Benejah Place farm across the road:

> We now proceeded to the old James Phillips place, scene of my 1896 visit, and here again I was astonisht by the beauty of the landskip. The antient white house nestles against a side hill whose picturesque rocks and greenery almost overhang the north gable end, while across the road is a delicious combination of hill and vale—hill to the left, with the Job Place estate and its burying ground at the top, (James Phillips, having married Job Place's daughter Jane, lies there) and to the right the exquisite "lower meadow" with its musical winding brook. The only flaw in the picture is a recent social-ethnic one—for FINNS, eternally confound 'em, have bought the old Job Place house! This Finnish plague has afflicted North Foster for a decade, but has hardly se-

cured a real foothold in Moosup Valley, only two families marring the otherwise solid colonialism. They are seldom seen or heard—but it does make me crawl to think of those bovine peasants in the house where my great-uncle's wife was born—and tramping about an antient Place graveyard! Maybe a *hand* will reach up thro' the rocky mould some day. . . . (SL 2.86)

His description of the interior of the Phillips-Place farm is briefer but more to the point:

The house pleas'd me as much as it did in 1896, and I envy'd afresh the rag carpets and the wealth of colonial furniture. The Dyckman cottage in New York will illustrate the atmosphere of the place better than anything else in your benighted metropolitan reach—allowing of course for the difference betwixt Dutch and New-England designs. I was permitted to revisit the corner room where I slept thirty years ago, and where I used to see the green side hill thro' the archaick small-paned windows as I awoke in the dewy dawn. Certainly, I was drawn back to the ancestral sources more vividly than at any other time I can recall; and have since thought about little else! I am infus'd and saturated with the vital forces of my inherited being, and rebaptis'd in the mood, atmosphere, and personality of sturdy New-England forbears. A pox on thy taowns and decadent notions—one sight of the mossy walls and white gables of true agrestick America, and pure heredity can flout 'em all! (SL 2.87)

It seems without question that this heightened sense of ancestral identity led Lovecraft to pen "The Silver Key" shortly after his October 1926 Foster visit. Therein he wrote of modern decadents who rejected the heritage of their culture-stream:

Warped and bigoted with preconceived illusions of justice, freedom, and consistency, they cast off the old lore and the old ways with the old beliefs; nor ever stopped to think that that lore and those ways were the sole makers of their present thoughts and judgments, and the sole guides and standards in a meaningless universe without fixed aims or stable points of reference. (MM 411)

While visiting Moosup Valley in October 1926, Lovecraft carefully transcribed the epitaphs of his great-great-grandfather Stephen Place, Sr. (1736–1817) (son of Enoch and brother of Benejah) and his wife Martha (Perkins) Place (1747–1822) (a first cousin of Benejah's wife Mary) and noted their religious conventionality (SL 2.86):

[Stephen Place, Sr.:]
The dust must to the dust return,
And dearest friends must part and mourn;
The gospel faith alone can give
A cheering hope, the dead shall live.

[Martha (Perkins) Place:]
Hail, sweet repose, now shall I rest,
No more with sickness be distress'd;
Here from all sorrows find release,
My soul shall dwell in endless peace.

Note how he writes of the religious conventionality of Randolph Carter's ancestors in "The Silver Key":

> In the first days of his bondage he had turned to the gentle churchly faith endeared to him by the naive trust of his fathers, for thence stretched mystic avenues which seemed to promise escape from life. Only on closer view did he mark the starved fancy and beauty, the stale and prosy triteness, and the owlish gravity and grotesque claims of solid truth which reigned boresomely and overwhelmingly among most of its professors; or feel to the full the awkwardness with which it sought to keep alive as literal fact the outgrown fears and guesses of a primal race confronting the unknown. (MM 410)

Lovecraft's maternal grandparents Whipple V. Phillips and Robie Alzada Place (1827–1896) had been early associated with Rev. George W. Kennedy (1824–1900) in his work at the Rice City Christian Church. Although they resided across the Coventry line in Greene, Whipple V. Phillips and his wife probably continued to worship with Rev. Kennedy after he assumed the pastorship of the Moosup Valley Church in 1868. Although Whipple V. Phillips and his family removed to Providence c. 1874, his wife and daughters did not join the First Baptist Church there until 1883, and Whipple V. Phillips and his only son Edwin E. Phillips (1864–1918), both active masons, apparently never joined. Perhaps Whipple V. Phillips and his son elected to keep their membership in the Moosup Valley Church despite their removal to Providence.

Whipple V. Phillips's brother James W. Phillips was serving as secretary of the Moosup Valley Church under Rev. Kennedy in 1890 (see Bayles 2.635). Lovecraft and his mother undoubtedly had the experience of attending church in Moosup Valley with James W. Phillips and Jane Ann (Place) Phillips during their two-week stay in August 1896. The regular attendance of Lovecraft's own immediate family at the First Baptist Church in Providence seems to have lapsed during the illness of his maternal grandmother Robie Alzada (Place) Phillips in 1895. Robie Phillips died of enteritis, catarrhal fever, and nervous exhaustion, aged sixty-eight years, at the family home in Providence on January 26, 1896, plunging the household into mourning and giving the young Lovecraft, aged only five and a half years, his first taste of Victorian funeral customs. The body of Robie Phillips was probably embalmed by a mortician and then returned, encoffined, to rest in the parlor at 454 Angell Street for visitation by friends and relatives. After a memorial ser-

vice, a few close friends and relatives probably returned to the home to ac-
company the body to Swan Point Cemetery for burial. The Phillips sisters
wore full mourning for months after their mother's death, and Lovecraft attempted to relieve the gloom by pinning small scraps of bright cloth to their
dresses, necessitating inspections before they left their home for the limited
social activities allowed during their period of mourning.

The death of her mother and the continuing decline of her father's economic affairs must have represented severe blows to Lovecraft's mother, Sarah
Susan (Phillips) Lovecraft. Having married Winfield Scott Lovecraft in Boston
on June 12, 1889, Sarah Susan had enjoyed a normal married life for less
than four years when her husband was committed as a paretic to Butler Hospital in Providence on April 25, 1893, after breaking down on a business trip
to Chicago. Her husband lived more than five years at Butler Hospital, not
expiring until July 19, 1898, aged forty-four years nine months, but by 1895–
96 it was apparent that his condition was terminal. Deprived of the normal
gratifications of married life in her prime, Sarah Susan had only her son and
her family home to fall back on. Perceived by family attorney Albert A. Baker
(1862–1959) as a "weak sister," Sarah Susan may have become dysfunctional
as a parent in the wake of the death of her mother and the continued decline
of her husband. At this time, Howard Phillips Lovecraft was Whipple V. Phillips's only grandchild; a second grandchild, Phillips Gamwell (1898–1916),
the son of Edward F. and Annie (Phillips) Gamwell, was not born until two
years later. Despite the comfort he undoubtedly derived from his young
grandson's presence, Whipple V. Phillips probably decided that two weeks in
the country with his brother James W. Phillips and sister-in-law Jane Ann
(Place) Phillips would do the boy and his mother good in the wake of the grief
that preoccupied the 454 Angell Street household in 1896. In addition,
Whipple probably knew that the two weeks' room and board for his daughter
and grandson would be welcomed by his elder brother and sister-in-law, who
were increasingly unable to cope with the demands of farming. By the 1890s,
receiving summer boarders from the city had become a cottage industry of its
own in Foster, whose decline as an agricultural center would only be stemmed
by the infusion of Finnish settlers in the twentieth century.

In "The Silver Key" Randolph Carter revisits the ancient Carter homestead
outside of Arkham on October 7, 1928, and is mysteriously transmuted back
into the world of forty-five years before, October 7, 1883, when he was a nine-
year-old boy. His uncle Chris and aunt Martha and their aged hired man Benijah Corey are all mysteriously restored to life just as Carter is restored to his
boyhood. As he approaches the home of his ancestors, Carter's wonder increases:

> Something made him feel that motors did not belong in the realm he was
> seeking, so he left his car at the edge of the forest, and putting the great key in his

coat pocket walked on up the hill. Woods now engulfed him utterly, though he knew the house was on a high knoll that cleared the trees except to the north. He wondered how it would look, for it had been left vacant and untended through his neglect since the death of his strange great-uncle Christopher thirty years before. In his boyhood he had revelled through long visits there, and had found weird marvels in woods beyond the orchard. (MM 415–16)

Carter is startled to hear the voice of old Benijah Corey, Uncle Christopher's and Aunt Martha's hired man, summoning him to dinner. Lovecraft recapitulated Randolph Carter's feelings concerning the transmutation of October 7, 1928, in "Through the Gates of the Silver Key":

> Then in the deepening twilight he had heard a voice out of the past. Old Benijah Corey, his great-uncle's hired man. Had not old Benijah been dead for thirty years? Thirty years before when? What was time? Where had he been? Why was it strange that Benijah should be calling him on this seventh of October, 1883? Was he not out later than Aunt Martha had told him to stay? What was this key in his blouse pocket, where his little telescope—given him by his father on his ninth birthday two months before [probably intended as August 20, 1883]—ought to be? Had he found it in the attic at home? Would it unlock the mystic pylon which his sharp eye had traced amidst the jagged rocks at the back of that inner cave behind the Snake-Den on the hill? That was the place they always coupled with old Edmund Carter the wizard. People wouldn't go there, and nobody but him had ever noticed or squirmed through the root-choked fissure to that great black inner chamber with the pylon. Whose hands had carved that hint of a pylon out of the living rock? Old Wizard Edmund's—or others that he had conjured up and commanded? That evening little Randolph ate supper with Uncle Chris and Aunt Martha in the old gambrel-roofed farmhouse. (MM 428–29)

"The Silver Key" tells the story of the return of the truant in more detail:

> So Randolph Carter was marched up the road where wondering stars glimmered through high autumn bows. And dogs barked as the yellow light of small-paned windows shone out at the farther turn, and the Pleiades twinkled across the open knoll where a great gambrel roof stood black against the dim west. Aunt Martha was in the doorway, and did not scold too hard when Benijah shoved the truant in. She knew Uncle Chris well enough to expect such things of the Carter blood. Randolph did not shew his key, but ate his supper in silence and protested only when bedtime came. He sometimes dreamed better when awake, and he wanted to use that key.
>
> In the morning Randolph was up early, and would have run off to the upper timber-lot if Uncle Chris had not caught him and forced him into his chair by the breakfast table. He looked impatiently around the low-pitched room with the rag carpet and exposed beams and corner-posts, and smiled only when the orchard boughs scratched at the leaded panes of the rear win-

dow. The trees and the hills were close to him, and formed the gates of that timeless realm which was his true country. (MM 417–18)

Now, the Phillips-Place farmhouse has no gambrel roof but it is situated on a gentle hill sloping toward the west. The orchard trees on the knoll to the immediate north still approach the rear of the house closely and may have been more numerous nearly a century ago. The northwest bedroom with its small window panes looks out on the orchard knoll and may have been the very one where Lovecraft slept during his visit in 1896. The house still shows its exposed beams and corner-posts and the kitchen with its wide floor-boards seems to differ very little from the room where the young Lovecraft break-fasted early during his 1896 visit. But for me it is the rag carpets of the Carter homestead (MM 417) and of the Phillips-Place farmhouse (SL 2.87) that clinch the identification of the latter as a principal source for the former. In addition, the general setting of the Phillips-Place farmhouse, which Lovecraft describes as "a delicious combination of hill and vale" (SL 2.86), is mirrored by his description of the setting of the ancestral Carter homestead (MM 415–16). "The exquisite 'lower meadow' with its musical winding brook" of the Phillips-Place farmhouse (SL 2. 86) is mirrored by "the spectral wooded valley dipping down in shadow to dank hollows where trickling waters crooned and gurgled among swollen and distorted roots" of the Carter homestead (MM 415). When Carter sets out in search of his quest after being waylaid by his Uncle Christopher for breakfast the morning following his transmutation back to 1883, the description of his passage again mirrors the geography of the Phillips-Place farmhouse and its environs:

> Then, when he was free, he felt in his blouse pocket for the key; and being reassured, skipped off across the orchard to the rise beyond, where the wooded hill climbed again to heights above even the treeless knoll. The floor of the forest was mossy and mysterious, and great lichened rocks rose vaguely here and there in the dim light like Druid monoliths among the swollen and twisted trunks of a sacred grove. Once in his ascent Randolph crossed a rush-ing stream whose falls a little way off sang runic incantations to the lurking fauns and aegipans and dryads. (MM 418)

In addition, Lovecraft's description of the approach to the ruined hill-top Carter homestead and "the old white house . . . where his mother and her fathers before her were born" (MM 415) is surely grounded in part upon the Place-Battey homestead on Moosup Valley Road (HPCR #234), which Love-craft and Mrs. Gamwell passed on their way to the James W. Phillips home-stead in 1926. Lovecraft's mother Sarah Susan Phillips, grandmother Robie Alzada (Place) Phillips, and great-grandfather Stephen Place, Jr. (1783–1849) were all born in this house, originally erected by his great-great-grandfather Stephen Place, Sr. The house remained in the family until the death of Sarah

(Sally) (Rathbun) Place, the widow of Stephen Place, Jr. Lovecraft cherished a crayon drawing of the house made by his mother and hung it on his study wall. When Lovecraft and Mrs. Gamwell revisited Foster in 1929, they had the joy of seeing the interior of the Place-Battey house. If Lovecraft had had the economic wherewithal to become a rural "squire," one does not doubt that he would have chosen the ancestral Place-Battey house, still lovely today, as his residence, and it is not surprising that he chose to weave a brief reference to it into his description of the ruined Carter homestead and its environs.

But the supporting evidence for the 1926 Foster visit as a principal source for the setting of "The Silver Key" does not end with the Phillips-Place farmhouse itself. Carter actually disappears from the human ken the morning following his transmutation back in time to October 7, 1883, in a hidden, ill-reputed cave called the "Snake Den," associated with the unsavory doings of his witch-ancestor Edmund Carter, a refugee from the Salem persecutions of 1692. Carter discovers a secret inner, hidden chamber with a pylon that shows hints of non-natural formation. "The Silver Key" describes Carter's approach:

> Then he came to the strange cave in the forest slope, the dreaded "snake-den" which country folk shunned, and away from which Benijah had warned him again and again. It was deep; far deeper than anyone but Randolph suspected, for the boy had found a fissure in the farthermost black corner that led to a loftier grotto beyond—a haunting sepulchral place whose granite walls held a curious illusion of conscious artifice. On this occasion he crawled in as usual, lighting his way with matches filched from the sitting room match-safe, and edging through the final crevice with an eagerness hard to explain even to himself. He could not tell why he approached the farther wall so confidently, or why he instinctively drew forth the great silver key as he did so. But on he went, and when he danced back to the house that night he offered no excuses for his lateness, nor heeded in the least the reproofs he gained for ignoring the noontide dinner-horn altogether. (MM 418)

The sequel "Through the Gates of the Silver Key" tells of Randolph Carter's encounter with the "Snake-Den" in a similar fashion:

> Next morning he was up early, and out through the twisted-boughed apple orchard to the upper timber-lot where the mouth of the Snake-Den lurked black and forbidding amongst grotesque, overnourished oaks. A nameless expectancy was upon him, and he did not even notice the loss of his handkerchief as he fumbled in his blouse pocket to see if the queer Silver Key was safe. He crawled through the dark orifice with tense, adventurous assurance, lighting his way with matches taken from the sitting-room. In another moment he had wriggled through the root-choked fissure at the farther end, and was in the vast, unknown inner grotto whose ultimate rock wall seemed half like a monstrous and consciously shapen pylon. Before that dank, dripping

wall he stood silent and awestruck, lighting one match after another as he gazed. Was that stony bulge above the keystone of the imagined arch really a gigantic sculptured hand? Then he drew forth the Silver Key, and made motions and intonations whose source he could only dimly remember. Was anything forgotten? He knew only that he wished to cross the barrier to the untrammelled land of his dreams and the gulfs where all dimensions dissolve in the absolute. (MM 429)

The Snake-Den reappears in the sequel when Carter, upon return from his sojourn in the body of the wizard Zkauba on Yaddith, secretes the metal capsule in which he has traversed the dimensions in the Snake-Den after landing in the lower meadow below the old Carter place. He also changes into his human disguise within the Snake-Den before beginning his quest for the R'lyehian parchment that holds the key to recovery of his true human identity. When the medication that suppresses his Zkauba facet is exhausted, he secretes the capsule in a new hiding place to bar his rival identity from attempting a return to Yaddith (MM 451).

Would that Lovecraft had been able to construct a more satisfactory denouement for the saga of Randolph Carter and the Silver Key than may be found in "Through the Gates of the Silver Key"; the regrettable truth is that he felt himself bound by Price's conception of Carter as an extra-dimensional traveller and struggled mightily to conform the Carter/Zkauba concept with the basic intent of his original story "The Silver Key." The sequel does provide fascinating sidelights to the original narrative and has some effective moments of its own, including Carter's final disappearance into Etienne-Laurent de Marigny's [i.e., Price's] mysterious coffin-shaped clock—a device that provided partial inspiration for the novel-length adventures of Titus Crow written by England's Brian Lumley.

The sequel does provide a number of useful echoes concerning the "Snake-Den" setting of the transformation narrative:

Detectives from Boston said that the fallen timbers of the old Carter place seemed oddly disturbed, and somebody found a handkerchief on the rock-ridged, sinisterly wooded slope behind the ruins near the dreaded cave called the "Snake-Den". It was then that the country legends about the Snake-Den gained a new vitality. Farmers whispered of the blasphemous uses to which old Edmund Carter the wizard had put that horrible grotto, and added later tales about the fondness which Randolph Carter himself had had for it when a boy. In Carter's boyhood the venerable gambrel-roofed homestead was still standing and tenanted by his great-uncle Christopher. He had visited there often, and had talked singularly about the Snake-Den. People remembered what he had said about a deep fissure and an unknown inner cave beyond, and speculated on the change he had shewn after spending one whole memorable day in the cavern when he was nine. That was in October, too—and ever after that he had seemed to have an uncanny knack at prophesying future events. (MM 423)

The detectives are not able to make much of Carter's disappearance from the world of October 7, 1928. "The Silver Key" itself relates the results of their investigations quite succinctly:

> Half way up Elm Mountain, on the way to the ruins of the old Carter place, they found his motor set carefully by the roadside; and in it was a box of fragrant wood with carvings that frightened the countrymen who stumbled on it. The box held only a queer parchment whose characters no linguist or palaeographer has been able to decipher or identify. Rain had long effaced any possible footprints, though Boston investigators had something to say about evidences of disturbances among the fallen timbers of the Carter place. It was, they averred, as though someone had groped about the ruins at no distant period. A common white handkerchief found among forest rocks on the hillside beyond cannot be identified as belonging to the missing man. (MM 419)

As is characteristic of its retellings of the basic narrative of "The Silver Key," the sequel adds new shadings and details:

> Later on people found the car at the side of an old, grass-grown road in the hills behind crumbling Arkham—the hills where Carter's forbears had once dwelt, and where the ruined cellar of the great Carter homestead still gaped to the sky. It was in a grove of tall elms near by that another of the Carters had mysteriously vanished in 1781, and not far away was the half-rotted cottage where Goody Fowler the witch had brewed her ominous potions still earlier. The region had been settled in 1692 by fugitives from the witchcraft trials in Salem, and even now it bore a name for vaguely ominous things scarcely to be envisaged. Edmund Carter had fled from the shadow of Gallows Hill just in time, and the tales of his sorceries were many. Now, it seemed, his lone descendant had gone somewhere to join him. . . .
>
> It had rained late in the night that Carter vanished, and no one was quite able to trace his footprints from the car. Inside the Snake-Den all was amorphous liquid mud owing to copious seepage. Only the ignorant rustics whispered about the prints they thought they spied where the great elms overhang the road, and on the sinister hillside near the Snake-Den, where the handkerchief was found. Who could pay attention to whispers that spoke of stubby little tracks like those which Randolph Carter's square-toed boots made when he was a small boy? It was as crazy a notion as that other whisper—that the tracks of old Benijah Corey's peculiar heel-less boots had met the stubby little tracks in the road. Old Benijah had been the Carters' hired man when Randolph was young—but he had died thirty years ago. (MM 422–23)

I believe it is very possible that Lovecraft derived the "Snake Den" locale used in "The Silver Key" and its sequel from his 1896 visit to Foster as well. Rhode Island is rich in natural rock outcroppings resulting from glacial action in distant ages, and Foster is particularly rich in such formations. Snakes are naturally attracted to outcroppings and ledges on account of the natural warmth they tend to retain, and therefore many such formations acquired local repute as "snake dens." The Snake Den Management Area in Johnston, R.I., is probably the most notable place name in the state, taking its name from this popular label, although one might also take notice of Snake Hill and Snake Hill Road in Glocester, R.I. However, I believe the place name "snake den" was used locally for rock ledges, outcroppings, and caves wherever snakes might be found in abundance.

One such notable formation is the so-called John Harrington Cave depicted on p. 70 of *Foster: A Bicentennial Celebration 1781–1981* (1981). According to information provided to me by Margery I. Matthews of Foster, this cave is located on the Harrington Johnson farm on Johnson Road about one mile north of the Place-Phillips farm. It acquired its name from John Harrington, one of Foster's earliest eighteenth-century settlers, who is reputed to have used the cave for shelter. Modern research, however, supports the claim of John Harrington as the first white settler in Foster; there is a Harrington deed as early as 1714, and family tradition maintains that John Harrington first settled in Foster a decade earlier. *Foster: A Bicentennial Celebration 1781–1981* writes as follows of John Herendon or Harrington:

> The first settler in the southwest part of Foster, and according to the opinion of some, the earliest to establish himself in the town was Mr. John Herendon, or Herenton, who came from Smithfield. He chose a pleasant spot on the eastern bank of the Moosup River to build his house. It was erected a mile south of Bennett's hill, on the farm now improved by Mr. E. Johnson, and the rock which formed the side of the house, where the chimney stood, is pointed out, with the five stairs upon it. According to tradition, he was very fond of hunting and fishing, and he selected his home in the then wilderness in a spot highly favorable for the gratification of his tastes. The precise period of his arrival is not known. In the Scituate records, of which Foster formed a part until 1781, there are deeds of gift of land by him, dated June 8, 1729, to his sons, John, Josiah, and Stephen Herenton, mentioned as his first, second and fifth sons, and designed "for their comfortable settlement in the world." The lands are called the Westquanoid, or Westquanaug purchase. An association for this purchase was formed June 8, 1678, but there are two deeds of sale of an earlier date, namely, May 8, 1662, and September 23, 1662. Mr. William Vaughan, his friends and associates, the purchasers in one, and Zachariah Rhodes and Robert Westcott, in the other. The land is marked as being on the west line of Providence. But little had been accomplished in settling this purchase in 1724 . . . though Mr. Herenton may have occupied his lands as early as 1700.

The photograph on p. 70 of this volume depicts Whipple V. Phillips's close friend Clarke Howard Johnson and two ladies seated in front of the large rock formation containing John Harrington's cave. If it is the same rock formation about which Rev. Beaman wrote in connection with Mr. Harrington's dwelling place, it may be noted that man-made workings, including steps carved in the stone (presumably carved to enable ascent to the second story of Mr. Harrington's home), probably abound. Mr. Harrington's predilection for hunting and fishing suggests a preference for wild surroundings, and what more natural than that he should have built his first residence in the partial shelter of a large rock outcropping? What better place than a natural cave occurring in this formation for secure storage and the like?

What a perfectly wonderful place, nearly two hundred years later, for a six-year-old boy to go about exploring on vacation from the pressures of his home in the Providence metropolis! Having discovered the Harrington cave for himself, what more natural than that the boy should take matches from his great-uncle's match-safe to light the way for further exploration, or that he should so lose himself in his explorations as to neglect the midday dinner-horn and return only in time for the evening meal? By 1900, James W. Phillips and his wife Jane Ann (Place) Phillips had living in their household a twenty-two-year-old farm laborer named Olney Paine, and perhaps he was already present by the time Lovecraft visited in 1896. While he could hardly qualify as a model for the aged Benijah Corey, he could easily have been set out in search of the absent boy when the sun began to set without his appearance.

The Moosup River was named for a local Indian chief, and all of Rhode Island may be said to be rich in native American lore. I have, however, not to date been able to ascertain any Indian legends specifically associated with the locality of Foster. Both Beaman and Tyler in their histories relate many colorful stories of the early white residents of the locality. Most accounts date the first permanent white settlement early enough to include late refugees from the persecutions of the Massachusetts theocracy. John Harrington or Herendon, who reputedly came from Smithfield as early as 1700, would have been a very early settler indeed if he came so early. James Savage, in his *Genealogical Dictionary of the First Settlers of New England* (1860-62), notes an Edward Harraden or Harrendine in Ipswich, Mass., in 1651 and in Gloucester, Mass., in 1658 and—in favor of Lovecraft's inference that the settlers of Foster may have included refugees from the Salem witch persecution—a Dr. Harraden recorded in Salem in 1689.

Further scraps that may possibly support a "Salem refugee" origin for some of the early Foster settlers are two local place names that Bayles records in his *History of Providence County* (627): Witch Hollow and Witch Rocks. These place names cannot be found on modern maps or in Henry Gannett's *A Geographic Dictionary of Rhode Island* (1894), but Foster local historian Margery I. Matthews wrote me that she was familiar with a Witch Hill in the north part of the town and with a Witch Hollow—not near Moosup Valley—whose connected legend she did not recall. She was not familiar with the "Witch Rocks" place name as cited by Bayles. One need only tour Foster briefly however to envisage the wild environment upon which the earliest settlers intruded. Beasts and Indians were everyday threats in seventeenth-century New England, and this situation continued into the early decades of the eighteenth century, especially in sparsely settled localities. Little wonder that the first settlers should have sought safety under some of the massive outcroppings or that they should have found the outcroppings and boulders haunting by moonlight. The Foster "witch" place names cited by Bayles and Matthews may reflect legends of Indian medicine men and conjurers or legends of white outcasts who sought welcome refuge in the wilderness. The story of John Harrington suggests that the first settlers of Foster were a hearty breed whose wives may not have readily suffered persecution and discrimination after they became widows. Some such seeking shelter in a shanty by rocks might readily have given rise to the "witch" place names cited by Bayles and Matthews.

On his way to his own ancestral homestead in Arkham, Carter passes "the crumbling farmhouse of old Goody Fowler the witch, with its little evil windows and great roof sloping nearly to the ground on the north side" (MM 415). In the sequel, the narrator remarks that "It was in a grove of tall elms near by that another of the Carters had mysteriously vanished in 1781, and not far away was the half-rotted cottage where Goody Fowler the witch had brewed her ominous potions still earlier" (MM 422).

The name of Goody Fowler Lovecraft probably took from the Capt. Samuel Fowler House (1809) in Danvers, Mass. (166 High Street at Liberty), which he visited in the spring of 1923 (SL 1.218-21). The house was then owned by the Society for the Preservation of New England Antiquities, which had permitted Capt. Fowler's aged granddaughters to remain as caretakers after the purchase of the property. Lovecraft was much impressed with the granddaughters as specimens of decayed New England gentility. From the Capt. Fowler House, he walked out to the famous Rebecca Nurse house, where widow Nurse, one of the victims of the Salem witchcraft persecution, had resided in 1692. Lovecraft probably based his description of Goody Fowler's decaying residence on his impressions of the Nurse house outside Danvers:

> Beyond a low crest a thick group of spectral boughs bespoke some kind of grove or orchard—and in the midst of this group I suddenly decry'd the rising outline of a massive and ancient chimney. Presently, as I advanced, I saw the top of a grey, drear, sloping roof—sinister in the distant setting of bleak hillside and leafless grove, and unmistakably belonging to the haunted edifice I sought. Another turn—a gradual ascent and I beheld in full view the sprawling, tree-shadow'd house which had for nearly three hundred years brooded over those hills and held such secrets as men may only guess. Like all old farmhouses of the region, the Nurse cottage faces the warm south and slopes

low toward the north. It fronts on an ancient garden, where in their season gay blossoms flaunt themselves against the grim, nail-studded door and the vertical sundial above it. That sundial was long concealed by the overlaid clapboards of gothick generations, but came to light when the house was restored to original form by the memorial society which owns it. Everything about the place is ancient even to the tiny-paned lattice windows which open outward on hinges. The atmosphere of witchcraft days broods heavily upon that low hilltop. (SL 1.221-22)

Lovecraft's viewing of the Rebecca Nurse house in 1923 helped him formulate an archetype of the sinister, decayed seventeenth-century hillside New England farmhouse, with its low-slanting hillside roof and small-paned windows, an archetype he continued to use in his fiction and poetry. In the sonnet "The Howler," Goody Watkins is reputed to have lived in "the vine-hung cottage by the great rock slope" (AT 69). Writing to August Derleth on September 2, 1931, he explained some of the emotions that the ancient New England rural landscapes he knew so well engendered in him:

> All rural and architectural beauty have acquired for me a symbolic value, with bearings on my own personal past and on the vividly envisaged past of my family and race-stock. Certain collocations of scenic or architectural details have the most powerful imaginable effect on my emotions—evoking curious combinations of poignant images derived from reading, pictures, and experience. Old farmhouses and orchards move me about as profoundly as any one kind of thing I know—though general rural landscapes are also supremely potent. They give me a vague, elusive sense of half-remembering something of great and favourable significance—just as city spires and domes against a sunset, or the twinkling lights of a violet city twilight seen from neighbouring heights, always inspires a vaguely stimulating sense of adventurous expectancy. (SL 3.405)

Writing five weeks later to Elizabeth Toldridge on October 9, 1931, he explained the darker element that the connection of many New England antiquities with the Puritan oligarchy interjected into his imaginings:

> As for New England as a seat of *weirdness*—a little historic reflection will show why it is more naturally redolent of the bizarre & the sinister than any other part of America. It was here that the most gloomy-minded of all the colonists settled; & here that the dark moods & cryptic hills pressed closest. An abnormal Puritan psychology led to all kinds of repression, furtiveness, & grotesque hidden crime, while the long winters & backwoods isolation fostered monstrous secrets which never came to light. To me there is nothing more fraught with mystery & terror than a remote Massachusetts farmhouse against a lonely hill. Where else could an outbreak like the Salem witchcraft have occurred? Rhode Island does not share these tendencies—its history & settlement being different from those of other parts of New England—but just

across the line in the old Bay State the macabre broods at its strongest (*SL* 3.423)

Lovecraft's own fullest explication of his views on the Salem witchcraft persecution probably occurs in his letter to Robert E. Howard dated October 4, 1930 (*SL* 3.174-84). While he was skeptical that a formal coven existed at Salem, he nevertheless believed that Rev. George Burroughs and others may have been involved in witch-cult practices. "Most of the people hanged," he opined to Howard, "were probably innocent, yet I do think there was a concrete, sordid background not present in any other New England witchcraft case" (*SL* 3.183). He commented in the same letter on the sequelae of the Salem persecutions:

> Puritan witch-belief by no means ended with Salem, although there were no more executions. Rumours and whispers directed against eccentric characters were common all through the 18th and into the 19th century, and are hardly extinct today in decadent Western Massachusetts. I know an old lady [Edith May (Dowe) Miniter (1867–1934)] in Wilbraham whose grandmother, about a century ago, was said to be able to raise a wind by muttering at the sky. Nothing of all of this, however, reached Rhode-Island. With our colonists witchcraft was a remote thing—at most, a whimsical thing to joke about or scare children with. Whatever real belief existed here, was confined to Indians and negroes. No witchcraft trial ever took place within our boundaries. . . . (*SL* 3.183)

Lovecraft's final comments regarding the relative absence of witch-belief in Rhode Island are certainly significant. He would certainly have been unlikely, in his writing, to attempt to set a witchcraft story in Rhode Island. The Bay State, where the Puritan oligarchy exercised its most oppressive sway, would have been his natural choice for any such narrative. On the other hand, the use of witch legend in "The Silver Key" and its sequel clearly does not cripple the thesis that the Phillips-Place farmhouse and its environs contributed to the setting of these stories. Lovecraft acknowledges that witch legends were current among the Indians and Negroes of his native state and that, as might be expected, stories of New England witchcraft were used to entertain and to frighten. The obscure witch-related place names that one finds in Foster make it clear that that part of the country was not without its believers and its storytellers. The dark, brooding woods, the looming rock outcroppings and boulders in the moonlight, the call of wild animals, and the constant Indian threat helped form an environment in which any solitary eccentric could be accused of alliance with the infernal powers.

Echoes of Lovecraft's sensitivity to the darker aspects of the New England landscape can be found throughout his work. Note the following early entry in his *Commonplace Book*: "Blind fear of a certain woodland hollow where streams writhe among crooked roots, & where on a buried altar horrible sacrifices have occur'd—Phosphorescence of dead trees. Ground bubbles" (MW 93). A later *Commonplace Book* entry which Lovecraft dated to 1925 even uses one of the witch-related place names found in Foster:

> Witches' Hollow novel? Man hired as teacher in private school misses road on first trip—encounters dark hollow with unnaturally swollen trees & small cottage (light in window?). Reaches school & hears that boys are forbidden to visit hollow. One boy is strange—teacher sees him visit hollow—odd doings—mysterious disappearance or hideous fate. (MW 97)

Perhaps this *Commonplace Book* entry was based upon a story told to Lovecraft by his grandfather Whipple V. Phillips, who taught in the local schools in Foster early in his career. Lovecraft wrote about his grandfather's storytelling abilities in his extremely self-revelatory letter to J. Vernon Shea dated February 4, 1934:

> I never heard oral weird tales except from my grandfather—who, observing my tastes in reading, used to devise all sorts of impromptu original yarns about black woods, unfathomed caves, winged horrors (like the "night-gaunts" of my dreams, about which I used to tell him), old witches with sinister cauldrons, & "deep, low, moaning sounds." He obviously drew most of his imagery from the early gothic romances—Radcliffe, Lewis, Maturin, &c.—which he seemed to like better than Poe or other later fantaisistes. He was the only other person I knew—young or old—who cared for macabre & horrific fiction. (SL 4.354)

Among Lovecraft's stories, "The Tomb" (1917) is clearly an early predecessor of "The Silver Key" and shares many structural and thematic similarities. Jervas Dudley is unnaturally fascinated by the ancient hillside tomb of the Hydes (surely a name Lovecraft took from Robert Louis Stevenson); and before he is removed to the asylum he, at least, believes that he has caroused with the Hydes in their long-vanished mansion on the hilltop. The strong New England stories of the 1920s that W. Paul Cook so admired—culminating with *The Case of Charles Dexter Ward* and "The Dunwich Horror"—share many common themes with "The Silver Key" and its sequel. Despite his flirtation with the scientific romance in the 1930s, the theme of dark, hidden ancestral influence in the New England landscape was still haunting Lovecraft at the end of his life as his friend Ernest A. Edkins recalled:

> Just before his death Lovecraft spoke to me of an ambitious project reserved for some period of greater leisure, a sort of dynastic chronicle in fictional form, dealing with the hereditary mysteries and destinies of generations of an ancient New England family, tainted and cursed down the diminishing generations with some grewsome variant of lycanthropy. It was to be his magnum opus, embodying the results of his profound researches in the occult legends of that grim and secret country which he knew so well, but apparently the outline was

just beginning to crystallize in his mind, and I doubt if he left even a rough draft of his plan. (Edkins 94-95)

I believe that Edkins's recollection gives the genesis of the novel that Lovecraft would have attempted had he survived another decade. *The Case of Charles Dexter Ward* and "The Shadow over Innsmouth"—along with various ones of the New England horror stories—might be regarded as preparatory exercises for the novel Lovecraft knew he had to write in order to be published in book form and to make his first break with the stranglehold of original pulp publication. Lovecraft admired Herbert S. Gorman's *A Place Called Dagon* (1927), which treated of a still-surviving colony of Salem witchcraft refugees. Perhaps Gorman's work laid the seed in his mind that might have developed into the novel that would have freed him at last from the pulp conventionalities that marred earlier dynastic chronicles like "The Lurking Fear" and "The Rats in the Walls." Lovecraft's early death, regrettably, cut off any possibility that his readers would ever enjoy the work he contemplated in correspondence with his friend Edkins.

As a final observation on the witchcraft themes in "The Silver Key" and its sequel, it may be noted that the family name of Uncle Christopher's hired man, old Benijah Corey, is that of two of the most prominent victims of the Salem witch persecution. Giles Corey, a brutal and feared man, was pressed to death in Salem on September 19, 1692, aged about seventy-five years, after refusing to plead to the charges against him. (He thereby saved his estate for his daughters.) His third wife Martha Corey was hanged as a witch in Salem three days later, on September 22,. Corey, who lived in what is now the town of Peabody, Mass., was survived by daughters Deliverance, Margaret, and Elizabeth. Perhaps Lovecraft sought to raise a suspicion among knowledgeable readers that Benijah Corey was a descendant of the Salem witchcraft victims Giles and Martha Corey. There was also a Corey connection with Lovecraft's immediate family. James W. Phillips's oldest son Walter Herbert Phillips married Emma J. Corey (1861-1954) and had by her a daughter Vivian Evangeline Phillips (1884-1963) and a son Elston Corey Phillips (1890-1977). Emma J. (Corey) Phillips descended from William Corey (d. 1682) of Portsmouth, R.I., not Giles Corey.

Unnaturally long life was a recurring theme in Lovecraft's fiction from his juvenile story "The Alchemist" (1908) onward; "The Terrible Old Man" (1920) and "The Picture in the House" (1920) are notable examples of this theme preceding the echoes of it that can be detected in "The Silver Key." Lovecraft wrote of the longevity of his own ancestors: "I might add that longevity is very rare. Most of us tend to shuffle off around seventy, though the Place strain is long-lived (my elder aunt [Mrs. Clark] looks like the Places, and I therefore have high hopes of her long survival despite her poor health)" (SL 3.366).

Indeed, Lovecraft's Place strain was markedly long-lived. One need only look at the generations back of James W. Phillips's wife Jane Ann Place for an example: Job Wilcox Place (1795-1879) and his wife Asenath (Pierce) Place (1793-1881); John Place (1763-1846) and his wife Lydia (Wilcox) Place (1773-1856); Benejah Place (1742-1815) and his wife Mary (Perkins) Place (1741-1829); Enoch Place (1704-1789) and his wife Hannah (Wilcox) Place (c. 1710-1802). In this long list of ancestors, Benejah Place is the only person who died before his eightieth birthday. Portraits of Job Wilcox Place and Asenath (Pierce) Place, who lived to celebrate their sixtieth wedding anniversary in 1878, would have formed natural adornments for the parlor in the home of their daughter Jane Ann (Place) Phillips and her husband James W. Phillips, the home visited by Lovecraft and his mother in 1896. One wonders if a stern-looking portrait of Asenath (Pierce) Place may have influenced Lovecraft's choice of names in his depiction of Asenath Waite in "The Thing on the Doorstep." He was certainly capable of associating grim imagery with his Place ancestry, as when he fantasized about a hoary hand's emerging from the ancient, neglected Place-Phillips cemetery where his ancestors rested and grasping the heel of one of the Finnish newcomers who had purchased the Job Place homestead by 1926 (SL 2.86).

Apart from the geographic and historical data that support the Phillips-Place farmhouse and its surroundings as a fertile source of Lovecraft's inspiration for "The Silver Key" and its sequel, there is also a body of genealogical information relating to the names he chose to use for the characters in these stories. Lovecraft was an ingenious inventor of authentic-sounding New England names: George Gammell Angell, Edward Pickman Derby, Nahum Gardner, Obed Marsh, Frank H. Pabodie, Nathaniel Wingate Peaslee, Richard Upton Pickman, Asenath Waite, Wilbur Whateley, and Elihu Whipple among many equally appropriate choices. But "The Silver Key" and its sequel enjoy a unique position among all of Lovecraft's fiction in that they employ directly names of his own ancestors and collateral relatives, especially from his Place line.

The connection with the Place line is not immediately apparent to the casual reader of "The Silver Key" and its sequel. Most of the principal characters seem to be named Carter: the protagonist Randolph Carter (1874-1928?), his grandfather —— Carter, his great-uncle Christopher Carter, and Christopher Carter's wife Martha Carter. The identification of Carter's colleagues Harley Warren and Etienne-Laurent de Marigny with friends Samuel Loveman (1887-1976) and E. Hoffmann Price (1898-1988), respectively, will be apparent to readers familiar with Lovecraft's biography. Randolph Carter's servant Parks and Christopher Carter's hired man Benijah Corey and housekeeper Hannah —— seem to be relatively minor figures. Finally, there is Carter's apoplectic old cousin Ernest B. Aspinwall, Esq. (1864-1932), of Chicago, who challenges Carter/Swami Chandraputra at the estate conference held in New Orleans in 1932, with fatal results when Carter's Zkauba entity is revealed to him. The association with Lovecraft's Place family lines may not seem immediately apparent, but a close analysis will reveal that the author deftly wove some of the facts of his ancestry into the tapestry of these tales.

To begin with Randolph Carter himself, it is clear from the narrative that he is to be identified with the authorial voice, although Lovecraft has chosen to remove him a half a generation back in time from his own birth date of August 20, 1890, to Carter's assigned birth date of August 20, 1874 (MM 422, 428). As is well known to students of his correspondence, Lovecraft loved to call himself "Grandpa" even before attaining his thirty-fifth birthday. So his setting Randolph Carter back half a generation fell naturally in line with his own predilection for aging his own person. Note the double blind of the interjection of Ward Phillips, "an elderly eccentric of Providence, Rhode Island, who had enjoyed a long and close correspondence with Carter" (MM 424) as a minor voice supporting the position of Etienne-Laurent de Marigny and Swami Chandraputra/Carter concerning the settlement of the Carter estate in the sequel. Lovecraft narrates of this Ward Phillips that he had a

> still more elaborate theory, and believed that Carter had not returned to boyhood, but achieved a further liberation, roving at will through the prismatic vistas of boyhood dream. After a strange vision this man published a tale of Carter's vanishing, in which he hinted that the lost one now reigned as king on the opal throne of Ilek-Vad, that fabulous town of turrets atop the hollow cliffs of glass overlooking the twilight sea wherein the bearded and finny Gnorri build their singular labyrinths. (MM 424)

Perhaps Lovecraft was not content with aging his principal fictional voice in "The Silver Key" by a mere sixteen years. He describes Phillips as "this old man" (MM 424) and paints of him the compact portrait: "Phillips, the Providence mystic, was lean, grey, long-nosed, clean-shaven, and stoop-shouldered" (MM 425). A description he might very well have given of himself in correspondence—although the lean frame and clean-shaven face were sources of pride and cultural identification rather than of any self-denigration or artificial aging. From the description of Ward Phillips as "an old man" at the time of the 1932 conference, one presumes that he was at least the contemporary of Carter's elderly cousin Ernest B. Aspinwall, Esq., and therefore born ten years or more before Carter—and nearly a full generation before Lovecraft himself.

Apart from a predilection for a more mature authorial voice, why did Lovecraft choose to date Randolph Carter's birth back to August 20, 1874, and his experience in the Snake-Den to October 7, 1883? For narrative purposes, he could surely as well have dated Carter's birth to August 20, 1890, and his experience in the Snake-Den to October 7, 1896. The 1928–32 section of the narrative of the original story and the sequel would have flowed as well had Carter been transmuted from October 7, 1928, to October 7, 1896—

a span of thirty-two years or a whole generation. The author can only hazard the guess the Lovecraft may also have had a bias toward disguising his authorial voice. Randolph Carter and Ward Phillips are clearly the characters in these stories most identifiable with that voice. Yet their stated ages were probably designed to confound those of Lovecraft's friends and correspondents who knew that he himself was born in Providence on August 20, 1890. Lovecraft's New England reserve is always present, to one degree or another, both in his fiction and in his letters.

In "The Silver Key," the third-person narrator identifies Randolph Carter's deceased grandfather and deceased great-uncle Christopher Carter as the only relatives "who understood his mental life" (MM 412). At the time of the 1928 narration, Randolph Carter's mother and grandfather had both been deceased for "a quarter of a century" (MM 413), accurate enough as respects Lovecraft's own maternal grandfather Whipple V. Phillips but a very material misstatement of facts with respect to his mother Sarah Susan (Phillips) Lovecraft (1857–1921). Curiously, Randolph Carter's father is mentioned only once, in the sequel, as having presented Carter with a telescope on his ninth birthday in 1883 (MM 428). Effectively, Lovecraft assigns both of Carter's parents to early oblivion in "The Silver Key" and its sequel. Perhaps this was as close as he was willing to get to an identification of Carter's parental situation with his own.

Carter's grandfather appears to him in a dream early in the narration of "The Silver Key" but then fades from the narrative in favor of more remote relations:

> Then one night his grandfather reminded him of a key. The grey old scholar, as vivid as in life, spoke long and earnestly of their ancient line, and of the strange visions of the delicate and sensitive men who composed it. He spoke of the flame-eyed Crusader who learnt wild secrets of the Saracens that held him captive; and of the first Sir Randolph Carter who studied magic when Elizabeth was queen. He spoke, too, of that Edmund Carter who had just escaped hanging in the Salem witchcraft, and who had placed in an antique box a great silver key handed down from his ancestors. Before Carter awakened, the gentle visitant had told him where to find that box; that carved oak box of archaic wonder whose grotesque lid no hand had raised for two centuries. (MM 413–14)

It is, however, not Carter's beloved grandfather but his "strange great-uncle Christopher" (MM 416) who figures as the principal family player in the 1883 segment of the narrative of "The Silver Key" and its sequel. Relating to the same key of which his grandfather had told him a dream, Lovecraft narrates: "Uncle Chris had told him something odd once about an old unopened box with a key in it, but Aunt Martha had stopped the story abruptly, saying it was no kind of thing to tell a child whose head was already too full of queer fancies" (MM 417).

Of the young Carter's truancy on that miraculous day and night of October 7, 1883, the narrator relates that Aunt Martha "knew Uncle Chris well enough to expect such things of the Carter blood" (MM 417). Both Uncle Chris (MM 416) and his hired man Benijah Corey (MM 428) had died thirty years before the 1928 portion of the narrative. The narrator of the 1928 events remarks with wonder that old Benijah Corey would have been "well over a hundred" had he been alive in that year, pointing toward a date of birth of c. 1825 for the hired man. Clearly, there is some subsidiary identification of great-uncle Christopher Carter with Lovecraft's own great-uncle James W. Phillips (1830–1901), whose actual lifespan fits well with that assigned to Christopher Carter.

By the mid-1880s James W. Phillips and Jane Ann (Place) Phillips were alone on their Foster farm and already in their mid-fifties. By the time of the 1900 federal census they had twenty-two-year-old Olney Paine as their hired man; Jane Ann (Place) Phillips died on the farm in August of that year and her husband the following February, at the home of his elder son Walter Herbert Phillips in Providence. The burning of the 1890 census in the 1920s deprives us of a view of the James W. Phillips household in that year; perhaps it is not impossible that an older man, perhaps even someone born as early as 1825 or thereabouts, was helping on the farm at that time. Widowers or single men who had worked as farmers would often board with married couples and labor for their keep. It was not unusual for elderly men to be so engaged into their seventies and even their eighties, for these active men grew so accustomed to physical labor that they often preferred to continue to work until they were physically no longer able.

The sparse surviving correspondence of Whipple V. Phillips shows him to have been a man of cultivation and good humor, and we may assume that James W. Phillips, while perhaps more conventionally religious than his younger brother, shared these traits. Both were active as Masons and both may well have enjoyed telling stories. It is really difficult to say much more with regard to the identification of Carter's grandfather with Lovecraft's maternal grandfather Whipple V. Phillips and of his great-uncle Christopher with Lovecraft's great-uncle James W. Phillips. It is difficult to think of either as readily conforming to the descriptors of "delicate and sensitive" that the narrator applies to Carter's ancestor in "The Silver Key" (MM 413). Both Whipple V. Phillips and his elder brother James W. Phillips came from a poor family; orphaned in 1848 by the deaths of both of their parents, they saw the family farm and all their possessions except the clothes on their backs sold out from under them to extinguish their father's debts the following year. Two sisters, Susan Esther Phillips (1827–1851) and Abbie E. Phillips

(1839–1873), also survived Jeremiah E. Phillips and his wife Robie (Rathbun) Phillips to be provided for. A belief in hard work and pride in ancestry probably distinguished both Whipple V. Phillips and his brother James W. Phillips. The cultural traditions they instilled in Howard Phillips Lovecraft remained with him throughout his lifetime. Whatever his intellectual and artistic sympathies with the decadents might be, in his own life he lived out the patterns and traditions set by his ancestors.

Whipple V. Phillips suffered a cerebral hemorrhage in the office of Alderman Grey at the Providence City Hall on March 27, 1904, and was taken to his home at 454 Angell Street, where he died the following day. Lovecraft referred to his illness as "a shock," a term commonly used for a cerebrovascular impairment like a stroke. Late portraits of Whipple V. Phillips with his mutton-chop whiskers (perhaps patterned on those of Rhode Island hero Gen. Ambrose Burnside) seem to depict a man whom today's psychologists might classify as "type A." The love and attachment that Lovecraft felt for his maternal grandfather was modulated, after the latter's death, by the feelings of pain and loss that his young grandson experienced. Perhaps some of this resentment passed into "The Silver Key" and its sequel in the shadowy presence of Carter's gentle grandfather and noisy presence of Carter's cousin Ernest B. Aspinwall, Esq. (1864–1932) of Chicago, who represents the Carter relatives at the estate conference held by executor Etienne-Laurent de Marigny in New Orleans in 1932. Lovecraft describes Aspinwall as "a man ten years Carter's senior, but keen as a youth in forensic battles" (MM 424). He interrupts the narrative of Swami Chandraputra from time to time with brash interjections demanding that the conference return to common-sense matters. Describing Aspinwall's first such interjection, the narrator relates that "Mr. Aspinwall grew doubly apoplectic-looking as he sputtered" (MM 427). When Chandraputra finally produces the silver key itself as proof of the veracity of his narrative, Aspinwall vilifies him as "a nigger" and accuses him of murdering his cousin Randolph Carter (MM 454). When Aspinwall comes to the conclusion that Chandraputra is actually in disguise, Carter acknowledges his identity with the admission: "Uncle Chris had told him something odd once about an old unopened box with a key in it, but Aunt Martha had stopped the story abruptly, saying it was no kind of thing to tell a child whose head was already too full of queer fancies" (MM 417). But Aspinwall proceeds to seize the mask in his "apoplectic fist" and falls down dead with a "frightful gurgling cry" when Zkauba is revealed underneath (MM 456).

Unhappiness certainly reared its ugly head in the privileged world of 454 Angell Street during the decade (1893–1904) Lovecraft and his mother resided there. John McInnis has raised the problematic issue of the dwelling place of the Lovecraft family during Winfield S. Lovecraft's final descent into madness in 1892–93 and has offered the thesis that the family resided in the home of Sarah Susan's parents at 454 Angell Street in Providence during this critical period. Certainly, the illness of Winfield S. Lovecraft cast a dark shadow over the entire family for most of the decade. Until her husband died, Sarah Susan chose to be listed in the Providence City Directories as Miss Winfield S. Lovecraft; perhaps Howard was even presented to strangers as a nephew during this period.

One senses that the family lost a gentle, steadying influence with the death of Robie Alzada (Place) Phillips after a long struggle in January 1896. Annie Phillips married Edward F. Gamwell in 1897 and Lillie Phillips married Franklin C. Clark in 1902, leaving Whipple V. Phillips alone with his daughter Sarah Susan and his grandson Howard Phillips Lovecraft in the large house at 454 Angell Street, where the domestic servants had been reduced from five in 1890 to one in 1900 because of economic difficulties. Whipple Phillips had survived several reversals of his western business interests including the bursting of the Owyhee Land and Irrigation Company's Bruneau River dam in the spring floods of 1890 (the dam was rebuilt by 1893), but the renewed washing out of the company's irrigation ditch only weeks before his death in the spring of 1904 was probably a final blow. One senses that Mr. Phillips may very well have been having a heated discussion with Alderman Grey over some business or political matter when his fatal shock occurred. Maybe Lovecraft tells us obliquely, through the unfavorable portrait of Ernest B. Aspinwall in "Through the Gates of the Silver Key," that more sensitivity and love would have added much to the privileged household of 454 Angell Street. We shall never know, for the author's discretion has left these doors closed before us, with no key to unlock them.

It may be noted briefly that Whipple V. Phillips had a business partner named Lafayette Aspinwall—not mentioned in Lovecraft's *Selected Letters*—during the period (1877–79) he was promoting Lincoln's patent fringing machine, in connection with which he visited the Paris Exposition in 1878. Whether Lovecraft knew of this business partner and used his name for the gruff lawyer of "The Silver Key" and its sequel is unknown to me. If Whipple V. Phillips and this business partner had an unfriendly parting—as sometimes occurs with the best of partners—perhaps Lovecraft deliberately chose to use the Aspinwall name for an unlovable character. Another possibility is that Lovecraft may have modelled Aspinwall, in part, on his grandfather's executor and business partner, attorney Clarke Howard Johnson (1851–1930), who had to sell most of Whipple V. Phillips's holdings to honor his debts and bequests. Lovecraft and his mother may possibly have felt resentment against Johnson because of the loss of their home, but in the reduced circumstances of the family it was apparent that the home could not be retained to house Lovecraft and his mother only. Daughters Lillie (Phillips) Clark and Annie (Phillips) Gamwell were entitled to their own equal shares of the estate.

One final consideration concerning roughly contemporary echoes in "The Silver Key" and its sequel is the question of why Lovecraft chose a date of October 7, 1883—rather than a date of 1896—for the central events of his narrative. The protectiveness he also exercised with regard to his authorial voice is certainly one explanation; by dating Carter's mysterious transformation in the Snake Den to a period nearly seven years before his own birth, he effectively rebuffed biographical inquiries and surmises that might have occurred had he chosen to date the same event to 1896, the year of his own first visit to Foster. Another very curious consideration, however, is that the climactic events in Lovecraft's masterful story "The Colour out of Space," written not long after "The Silver Key," are dated nearly simultaneously. The meteor descends on the Nahum Gardner farm near Arkham in June 1882, and by the summer of 1883 the family is descending into madness. The terrible denouement of the story occurs in October 1883, nearly simultaneously with Randolph Carter's strange transformation in the Snake Den on Elm Mountain outside of Arkham.

Clearly, Lovecraft deliberately chose to date the climactic occurrences of these two important stories nearly simultaneously. Why he chose to do so and what significance the October 1883 date may have actually had for his immediate family remains a difficult question. John McInnis has interpreted "The Colour out of Space" as a veiled narrative of the hidden poisons that sapped the strength of the Phillips and Lovecraft families, but has offered little if any explanation for the chronological sequence of events in the story. By contrast, in 1896 the only thing that happens in Lovecraft's fiction appears to be the principal events of "The Picture in the House," in which a genealogical researcher seeking data along the Miskatonic Valley, driven indoors by November rain, encounters an aged hermit who has prolonged his life unnaturally through cannibalism.

I have failed to identify any family trauma dating to October 1883 that might explain Lovecraft's use of this month for the crucial events of both "The Silver Key" and "The Colour out of Space." Asaph and Esther Phillips's last surviving child, Waite (Phillips) Fry (1791–1883), the widow of Richard Fry, died full of years on September 21, 1883. She had been excluded from her father's 1828 will, but this may indicate nothing more than that she and her husband enjoyed relative prosperity compared to her siblings. Lucy (Fry) Phillips, sister of Richard Fry and widow of Waite (Phillips) Fry's eldest brother Benoni Phillips (1788–1850), died at the Providence home of her son Harley F. Phillips on June 17, 1884, also aged in her nineties. On the Place side of the family, old Job Wilcox Place, the father of James W. Phillips's wife Jane Ann Place, passed away on April 1, 1879, in his eighty-fourth year. His widow, Asenath (Pierce) Place, was still living, old and paralyzed, on the Benejah Place farm with her youngest son Henry Lester Place and his family when the 1880 federal census was enumerated, but she died the following summer, on August 20, 1881, in her eighty-seventh year. Thus it may be offered that some of the last representatives of the Phillips and Place generations before Whipple V. Phillips and his brother James W. Phillips passed away in the early 1880s.

Perhaps these deaths symbolized, for Lovecraft, the loss of simpler, more independent modes of existence to the onslaughts and demands of an increasingly complex, mechanized age. But it is a weak identification. The following rather obscure entry in Lovecraft's *Commonplace Book* (which I date to 1928) may indicate that I have indeed missed some far more significant loss that deeply affected the fortunes of the Phillips family in the 1870s and 1880s: "Certain kind of deep-toned stately music of the style of the 1870's or 1880's recalls certain visions of that period—gas-litten parlours of the dead, moonlight on old floors, decaying business streets with gas lamps, &c—under terrible circumstances" (MW 99). That Lovecraft did associate the parlor of his boyhood home of 454 Angell Street with Victorian funeral customs may be seen from the comment which he made about the motion picture *The World Changes* in his February 4, 1934, letter to J. Vernon Shea: "The parlor where the funeral was held [in the motion picture] might have been taken out of 454 Angell Street" (SL 4.363). If some deep, personal tragedy affected the fortunes of Whipple V. Phillips and his family in the 1870s and 1880s, I have not been able to identify it.

It may be that Lovecraft is simply shifting dates on his readers again. The event that had the most shattering impact on the Lovecraft family's fortunes was surely the commitment of Winfield S. Lovecraft to Butler Hospital on April 25, 1893. If indeed both "The Silver Key" and "The Colour out of Space" contain echoes of this family tragedy, Lovecraft may simply have decided upon a ten-year chronological shift to protect his authorial voice. It is curious to note that Winfield S. Lovecraft's Butler Hospital medical record dates the onset of noticeable symptoms to a period one year before his commitment; similarly, in "The Colour out of Space," the germination period from the time the meteor strikes earth on Nahum Gardner's farm to the final tragedy that destroys his family is only slightly more than a year June 1882–October 1883).

If one were to insist that all the chronological shifts in "The Silver Key" be parallel, Randolph Carter's August 20, 1874, birthdate establishes a sixteen-year displacement that would move the fictional October 7, 1883, to October 7, 1899, a year in which nothing much notable is known of Lovecraft's fortunes save for the appointment of Albert A. Baker as his guardian and the summer that he and his mother spent in Westminster, Mass. The fact is, however, that the ever-reserved Lovecraft would by natural instinct have avoided any such simple schema that might have led to the undesired revelation of his authorial voice. One must be content to detect shadows and echoes of the authorial voice in Lovecraft's fiction; for the design of the author was to make his readers experience his own feelings without any undue familiarity with them. One ought never to underestimate Lovecraft's New England reserve: it is ever-present in his life and in his writings.

Lovecraft's choice of the name Carter for his protagonist is interesting in and of itself. John Carter (1745–1814), the famed Providence printer and publisher, descended from a distinguished old Virginia line. His youngest daughter Elizabeth Ann Carter married Walter Raleigh Danforth (1787–1861), a Providence attorney, publisher, and antiquarian, who was first cousin to Edward T. Clark (1816–1849), father of Lovecraft's uncle Dr. Franklin Chase Clark (1847–1915). From Dr. Clark Lovecraft inherited both a first edition of Cotton Mather's *Magnalia Christi Americana* (1702) and an early edition of Samuel Johnson's *Dictionary* that had belonged to Walter Raleigh Danforth. Lovecraft told the story of this connection by marriage in his letter to Elizabeth Toldridge dated June 10, 1929 (*SL* 2.352–53). Danforth, who served as Mayor of Providence in 1853–54, was a noted antiquarian in his own right whose "Reminiscences of Providence," edited by Clarkson A. Collins, III, were published serially in *Rhode Island History* beginning in 1951. I do not know exactly how Walter Raleigh Danforth and Edward T. Clark were related. Danforth was the son of Job Danforth and Sarah Coy. Clark was the son of Henry Finney Clark (1790–1820) and Alice Taylor (1789–1883). It may be that Lovecraft did not intend to imply strict first cousinship by using the phrase "own cousin." In any case, he doubtless found the patrician background of the Carter family of Providence an attractive association for his character Randolph Carter. "This transportation of a Virginia line to New England always affected my fancy strongly—hence my frequently recurrent fictional character 'Randolph Carter,'" he wrote to his correspondent Miss Toldridge. Crawford Carter Allen (1861–1917), grandson of Walter Raleigh Danforth and Elizabeth Ann Carter, was a close friend of Dr. and Mrs. Clark and his widow Maude d'Arc Carsi, daughter of a Roman count, still visited Mrs. Clark as a widow.

A remarkable final aspect of the Foster identifications that may be found in "The Silver Key" and its sequel involve the names of several of the principal characters: Great-Uncle Christopher Carter, his wife Great-Aunt Martha Carter, their hired man Benijah Corey, and their housekeeper Hannah. All these names are in fact names found among Lovecraft's Place family ancestors in Foster. The only hint of most of these identifications that occurs in Lovecraft's *Selected Letters* is his description of his 1926 host [Ellis B.] Bennis as "a distant kinsman (whose mother was Christopher Place's daughter)" (*SL* 2.86–87). Ellis B. Bennis's wife was Bertha T. Kennedy, the daughter of Alvero A. Kennedy and Nabby (Tyler) Kennedy. When Lovecraft and Mrs. Gamwell visited Foster in 1926, Ellis and Bertha (Kennedy) Bennis were living in the

James W. Phillips farmhouse. Mrs. Bennis's mother, Nabby (Tyler) Kennedy, who was then living with her husband Alvero A. Kennedy at the Tyler Tavern Stand in Moosup Valley, first greeted Lovecraft and Mrs. Gamwell in the morning, and then daughter Bertha (Kennedy) Bennis and her husband Ellis B. Bennis were their hosts for the afternoon. After graciously allowing Lovecraft and Mrs. Gamwell to inspect the interior of the James W. Phillips farmhouse, Mr. Bennis drove the pair across the Coventry, R.I., line to Greene so that they could visit with Squire G. Wood and other old business associates of Whipple V. Phillips.

Most interesting for Lovecraft's choice of character names of "The Silver Key" and its sequel is Ellis B. Bennis's descent from Rufus and Abigail Place. (Rufus was a son of the original settler Enoch and a brother of Stephen, Sr. and Benejah.) Rufus's and Abigail's son Christopher Place (1780–1855) stayed in Foster all his life and married Betsey Kennedy (1787–1855), the daughter of Alexander Kennedy (1745–1826). Christopher and Betsey had a son, Christopher Perry Place (1820–1897) who married Nancy Blanchard (1824–1911) in 1855. They had only one child, a daughter Jennie Foster Place (1859–1948), who married James M. Bennis (1851–1912) in 1876. Ellis B. Bennis was one of their family of six children. Lovecraft and his mother may well have visited the Place-Bennis farm on Moosup Valley Road during their Foster visit of 1896. Both Christopher Perry Place and his wife Nancy (Blanchard) Place were still living in 1896; thus, Lovecraft may well have met a living Christopher Place during his 1896 visit.

Neither of the Christopher Places in the ancestry of Lovecraft's 1926 host Ellis B. Bennis had a wife named Martha. However, the careful delver into the sources of Lovecraft's fiction must always be ready to accept shifts that deflect the knowledgeable from a too-ready revelation of the authorial voice. The name Martha is nevertheless quite common among the Place women of Foster. The most prominent among Lovecraft's ancestors was certainly Martha Perkins, the wife of his great-great-grandfather Stephen Place, Sr. However, numerous other instances among the Place family of the given name Martha could be cited.

The given names of Uncle Christopher's and Aunt Martha's hired man Benijah Corey and housekeeper Hannah —— may also be found among the Place family of Foster. Most notably, Benejah Place was the younger brother of Lovecraft's great-great-grandfather Stephen Place, Sr. James W. Phillips's wife Jane Ann Place was the great-granddaughter of Benejah Place and his wife Mary (Perkins) Place. The name Hannah may also be found in the Place family in Hannah Wilcox (c. 1710–1802), the wife of Enoch Place (1704–1789), the progenitor of the Foster branch of the family, and in Hannah Cole, the wife of Enoch Place's father Thomas Place (1663–1727) of North Kingstown, R.I. Many more occurrences of the name Hannah might be found among the Foster Place family and their descendants.

A mind like that of Lovecraft's Ernest B. Aspinwall, Esq. might offer the challenge that "The Silver Key" and its sequel are so clearly the fanciful constructions of the author's imagination that such dim and questionable echoes of the author's actual impressions that the reader may detect in their texts are really of little if any value. Mr. Aspinwall would undoubtedly urge the reader to enjoy these stories as fantasies and not to trouble his mind with the actual impressions and emotions of the author that may have contributed to their writing. No doubt, "The Silver Key" and its sequel may be enjoyed on this level—as pure fantasy. Surely, "The Silver Key" can stand on its own as a well-crafted little fantasy, and the sequel can struggle along as a none-too-successful explication of the original story in terms of an extra-dimensional identity replacement theme with science fictional trappings. I contend, however, that there is so much of Lovecraft's own personal experience buried in these two stories—much of it clearly explicable from coincidences in name and place references—that the neglect of the factors contributing to his authorial voice deprives the stories of much of the significance they might otherwise have for the knowledgeable reader.

In conclusion: while "The Silver Key" and its sequel are set in Lovecraft's Arkham, Massachusetts, milieu, the James W. Phillips homestead and its immediate surroundings were strong contributing factors in the author's inspiration.

Lovecraft and his mother visited the home of his great-uncle James W. Phillips for two weeks in August 1896, at the time of his sixth birthday. He and his mother were probably sent to the country to escape the tensions in his grandfather's household following the death of his grandmother Robie Alzada (Place) Phillips.

Perhaps for the first time in his life, the boy Lovecraft had the ability during his Foster vacation of 1896 to structure his own days as he pleased, apart from the regimen of daily meals and bedtime. Much of his later love of nature and of the New England countryside was probably formed by the quiet beauty he encountered on and around his great uncle's farm.

He discovered the John Harrington Cave during his vacation and learned the local stories concerning its original inhabitant. Perhaps he also heard local legends concerning the witch place names in Foster. On one notable occasion he filched matches from the match-safe in his great uncle's parlor and spent the entire day exploring the cave. He probably had to be fetched by his great-uncle's hired man (perhaps in 1896 still an older man) as the darkness fell and his great-aunt became concerned about his safety. He contrasted the wonder and beauty of his wild, free days in the Foster countryside with the drab restrictions of the sabbath day and enforced attendance with his great-uncle and great-aunt at the Moosup Valley Church and undoubtedly preferred the free-dom of the rest of the week to the restrictions of the sabbath day.

He learned a bit about his family origins from his great-aunt and great-uncle—as much as a six-year-old might readily absorb. When he returned to Foster with Mrs. Gamwell in 1926, the familiar sights of this wonderful youthful period of liberation stoked a flame in his soul that resulted in won-derful expression in "The Silver Key." The mature man added to the sum-ming up of his boyhood dreams and adventures his own adult knowledge of the cultural history that underlay the milieu.

He returned to Providence with a renewed love for the open fields to the east of his home and the wild, ravined banks of the Seekonk River. The great period of his discovery of ancient mythology and the *Arabian Nights* largely overlapped with his wonderful experience in Foster. It is probably no coinci-dence that his first fictional efforts date from the same year as his Foster vaca-tion. He wrote his correspondent J. Vernon Shea that his non-extant first story "The Noble Eavesdropper" concerned a mysterious conversation over-heard *in a cave*. The surviving stories he wrote as a teenager—"The Beast in the Cave" (1905) and "The Alchemist" (1908)—both involve underground pas-sages and chambers.

As the realization of his failure to make a normal adjustment to adulthood became inescapable during the years 1908–13, the bicycle provided Love-craft's mode of escape from the tension-filled confines of the flat he shared with his mother at 598 Angell Street in Providence. The love of the quiet, sometimes mysterious New England landscape and the deep identification with the cultural history of the region that saw its birth in the sensitive six-year-old set free to roam on his great-uncle's farm in Foster was confirmed and strengthened by the young man who set out on his bicycle for solace amidst the beauties of the countryside. He overcame the urge to drown his sorrows in the Barrington River and after false starts realized his destiny in the creation of literary works that might enable his readers, albeit briefly, to identify with the emotions he felt in his New England surroundings.

Somehow, Lovecraft was convinced that the bicycle was no longer a suit-able exploration mechanism when he was a young man in his twenties. The old Great Meadow Country Club was breaking up as its members entered into adult life. Perhaps Lovecraft himself was forced into an unsuccessful ex-periment with a clerkship in a business office at this time. The reception he found in amateur journalism beginning in 1914 saved him from total isola-tion during the difficult years of his third decade. When his disastrous do-mestic situation was finally resolved with the hospitalization of his mother in 1919, Lovecraft bloomed as never before and while, regrettably, he did not resume the use of his bicycle, his stamina as a walker put him back in touch with the natural wonders he had first experienced so strongly as a boy in Foster during the later summer–early autumn of 1896.

The personal background for "The Silver Key" was so rich that even the careful shifts and disguises that Lovecraft interposed between himself and the reader fail to operate with complete success for the informed reader. The conclusion is inescapable that the James W. Phillips farmhouse is the setting for "The Silver Key" and Lovecraft and his ancestors the principal characters of the story. These identifications are surely not complete, nor were they so intended by the author, but they so enrich the narrative that their exclusion impoverishes the author's creation. In the last analysis, Lovecraft's letters inform the knowledgeable reader of the facts of his inspiration for these stories. The letters and the fiction, taken as a whole, produce a sum greater than either of the parts. "The Silver Key" is a noble story of what it means to experience the beauty of this world in the human context. The strongest emotions that Lovecraft experienced, as a boy and as a man, are encapsulated in what might seem to be a brief, inconsequential fantasy to the casual reader. The inescapable conclusion is that Lovecraft is clearly one of those rare authors whose work continues to yield new levels of understanding and appreciation with each reading.

What can one say in closing of the characters and the locale of "The Silver Key"? These people lived! That farmhouse was! That boy was in the landscape! And Lovecraft has brought it all alive for his readers in "The Silver Key." Wherever and whenever dreamers read this story, they can touch all the beauty of this place, all the humanity of these lives. What better dream, what richer heritage.

> I never knew what it was to play on a city street; for from the age of three my mother always took me walking in the fields & ravines, & along the high wooded riverbank, (the latter still unchanged, thanks to the Met. Park System). I knew the old New England country as well as if I had been a farmer's boy; for I paused long at all the ancient white farmsteads (some still remaining, tho' ingulph'd by new urban streets) at every season of the year, & learned intimately every sight & sound & smell of the archaick, hereditary life—the mystical wonder of spring & the upland ploughing & the budded orchard boughs & the fragrance of new earth; (God, I can whiff it now!)—the apple-blossoms of May tapping at old attic windows—the dreamy buzz of summer, with the droning hives, the mottled kine splashing in valley brooks, & the supernal luxuriance of green ingulphing all the world & half stealing away one's senses in a languor of enchanted sweetness; the haying—the creaking wain & teeming loft, the swish of the scythe & the barking of distant dogs, the flashing pitchforks & sweating farmers; the weird golden light of autumn over leagues of order'd sheaves stack'd in the meadows, glint of fire in—small-paned windows—barnyards stacked with orange pumpkins & varicoloured fruits & melons—harvest home—Ceres—Pomona—Vertumnus—*sunt la-*

chrymae rerum—tinted leaves—crystal well water—crowing roosters—the great round Harvest Moon over the rows of sheaves; & silent, terrible winter with its deadening white blanket & hushed farmyard, or its bare brown earth & curious smells of matted leaves—& the fires inside antient cottages, throwing a red glow on low ceilings & lighting up carved Georgian mantels & panelling, & wide-planked, polisht floors with rag carpet rugs—& the sleek, friendly cats gliding from the kitchen to the living-room & back again, & the homely speech of the rural cotter & his buxom family . . . (SL 3.317–18)

Works Cited

Bayles, Richard M. *History of Providence County.* 2 vols. New York: W. W. Preston, 1891.

Edkins, Ernest A. "Idiosyncracies of H. P. L." In *Lovecraft Remembered,* ed. Peter Cannon. Sauk City, WI: Arkham House, 1998. 93–96.

Foster Bicentennial Committee. *Foster: A Bicentennial Celebration 1781–1981.* Foster, RI: Foster Bicentennial Committee, 1981.

Gannett, Henry. *A Geographic Dictionary of Rhode Island.* 1894. In *A Geographic Dictionary of Connecticut and Rhode Island.* Baltimore, MD: Genealogical Publishing Co., 1978.

Gorman, Herman S. *The Place Called Dagon.* New York: Doubleday, Doran, 1927.

McInnis, John. "An Autobiographical Study of 'The Colour out of Space.'" *Books at Brown* 38–39 (1991–92): 67–100.

———. "'The Call of Cthulhu': An Analysis." *Fantasy Commentator* 7 (Fall 1992): 268–81.

———. "Father Images in Lovecraft's 'Hypnos.'" *Fantasy Commentator* 7 (Fall 1992): 41–48.

Rhode Island. Historical Preservation Commission. *Foster, Rhode Island: Statewide Preservation Report P-F-1.* Providence, RI: RIHPC, June 1982.

Savage, James. *Genealogical Dictionary of the First Settlers of New England.* 1860–62. 4 vols. Baltimore, MD: Genealogical Publishing Co., 1986.

I wish to acknowledge the kind assistance provided by Margery I. Matthews on questions relating to the history and geography of Foster, R.I. However, the opinions stated in this article are solely my own responsibility. I note with sadness that the James W. Phillips house on Johnson Road was burned to the ground in April 2004. The owner has rebuilt on the property.

The Dream-Quest of Unknown Kadath

I first read H. P. Lovecraft in Herbert Wise and Phyllis Fraser's Random House anthology *Great Tales of Terror and the Supernatural*. The volume, which I still have, had been a wartime gift to my parents from my maternal grandmother. I don't think it had been much read, for I think I remember finding it on the top shelf of a clothes closet in our home. I can vividly recall my fascination with the two Lovecraft tales—"The Rats in the Walls" and "The Dunwich Horror"—that concluded the volume. The credits for the Lovecraft stories and the brief biographical notice of the author held promises of further discoveries.

During that summer of 1964, when I was sixteen years old, I had formed the habit of making a monthly expedition by bus to the main public library in Cincinnati, Ohio. I was a voracious reader during this period—perhaps more so than I have ever been since—and the main public library offered a variety of selection that I could not find in the local branches. Many subjects that still fascinate me I first explored on the shelves of this library.

It was in the main public library in Cincinnati, that I first held a book by H. P. Lovecraft—*At the Mountains of Madness and Other Novels*—in my hands. I seem to recall that it was on the new acquisitions shelf and therefore available only for seven-day loan. However, I discovered that books borrowed from the main public library could be returned to the local branch, and made the hour-long bus trip home with a volume by H. P. Lovecraft in the small suitcase I used to transport books during my monthly expeditions.

I spent a solid week with *At the Mountains of Madness and Other Novels*—and I seem to recall returning it with considerable reluctance. Of the three longer works by Lovecraft printed in the volume, *The Dream-Quest of Unknown Kadath* fascinated me the most—I seem to recall that I read it through twice during that week. Certainly, the framing of *Kadath* by the other Randolph Carter stories in *At the Mountains of Madness and Other Novels* enhanced its impact, but I think it was the fact that this picaresque adventure took place in an artificially constructed dreamland that fascinated me the most. On re-reading *Kadath* in 1989 in preparation for writing this essay, I can appreciate why some writers like Lovecraft's biographer L. Sprague de Camp have regarded *Kadath* as a juvenile work. There is a fairy-tale quality to many of Lovecraft's inventions in this short novel—the resplendent cities, the curious creatures, the felines who leap in one bound from dreamland to the hidden side of the moon. Peter Cannon and Donald Burleson, among Lovecraft's critics, however, have pointed out that *Kadath* is not without moments of stark horror.

Carter's terrifying visit to the sinister monastery of Leng, the climactic battle between the ghoul army and moon-beasts, and the first vision of the Cyclopean castle of the gods on Kadath impressed me as vividly twenty-five years later as they did upon my first reading in 1964.

At the Mountains of Madness and Other Novels and in particular Kadath opened so many new worlds to me. The listing of other volumes of work by Lovecraft on the dust-jacket of the book was a temptation I could not long resist—although I made the mistake of placing my first order for Arkham House books through a department store book department, whose jobber took months to fill my order. (I later learned that jobbers sometimes gave orders for Arkham House books poor service because of the firm's "short discount" policies.) I seem to recall that my initial order consisted of The Dunwich Horror, Dreams and Fancies, and Collected Poems. My long wait was not without reward, however. The Dunwich Horror opened to me the world of Lovecraft's major writings. Dreams and Fancies remains one of my favorite Lovecraft volumes, undoubtedly because of my fascination with Lovecraft's dream-based fiction. When Collected Poems finally arrived, I was delighted to note that the volume was signed by the illustrator, Frank Utpatel. When, years later, I finally acquired a copy of The Shadow over Innsmouth as printed by Bill Crawford and illustrated by Frank Utpatel, I wished I could have had the volume similarly signed, but the illustrator was already deceased.

Kadath opened for me a world whose fascination has not dimmed in the twenty-five years since I first read the works of H. P. Lovecraft. Within a few months, I discovered that John M. Kidd & Sons, a local bookseller, would give far quicker service on orders for Arkham House books than the department store. By 1965, I was buying books directly from Arkham House and volumes like Dagon and Other Macabre Tales and the first volume of Selected Letters arrived in my mailbox in their familiar Arkham House cartons virtually upon publication. (Let us hope that Arkham House never decides to rent a postage meter: those mailing labels with the Arkham colophon, framed by ample strips of small-denomination stamps, have become almost as much a tradition as Arkham House books themselves.) I found Arkham House service incredibly prompt—books generally arrived in my mailbox in Cincinnati, Ohio, within a week of my sending my order to Sauk City. A generous minority of books ordered directly from Arkham House arrived in the form of signed copies; I am still particularly proud of my signed copies of The Mask of Cthulhu and The Trail of Cthulhu as memories of my own humble association with August Derleth and his publishing firm. I gradually came to realize that it was August himself, with very little outside help, who made the firm operate as efficiently as it did. The next two summers, during which I read through the Arkham House backlist, were a delight. Soon I had a small Arkham House collection of my own.

The Arkham House books led to many other discoveries. "Supernatural Horror in Literature," as printed in *Dagon*, served as my guide to the entire field of supernatural fiction. I can remember discovering with delight the fantasies of Lord Dunsany in the original Luce editions in the Cincinnati public library. I also tried to read more about H. P. Lovecraft and his work. Colin Wilson's book *The Strength to Dream* led me not only to a better appreciation of Lovecraft but also to the work of J. R. R. Tolkien. I can remember being as powerfully affected by Tolkien's *Lord of the Rings* trilogy as I was by *Kadath*; in fact, I can recall making Tolkien's work the subject of an essay required by one of the colleges to which I applied. Surely, I will never re-read the "Lord of the Rings" trilogy—not because I would not enjoy a re-reading, but because I simply lack the time. But the pleasure I found in re-reading *Kadath* tells me that I would experience similar pleasure in re-reading the "Lord of the Rings." Obviously, both are quest books and they both have a similar lesson to teach.

Those golden summers of 1964–65 soon passed. My family moved away from Cincinnati, where I had lived all my life to date, and I stayed with relatives in order to complete high school in 1966. Like Lovecraft, I was lonely and sheltered as a youth, and the transition from home to college was miserable for me. Again, my life was helped immeasurably by a library—this time, the university library at Northwestern, where I elected to go to school. (Come to think of it, I think I wrote my Tolkien essay for the Northwestern application.) Many the happy hours I spent at the university library! In the rare books room, I discovered many of the early Arkham House books I had not been able to read before. The collection included things like *The Shunned House* (which I'd just missed buying from Arkham House for $17.50, to my everlasting regret) and a file of Walter J. Coates's magazine *Driftwind*, in which I delighted. Dealers like Gerry de la Ree, Steve Takacs, and Ken Krueger helped me make small additions to my own collection of supernatural fiction and Arkham House books. I can still remember scraping together fifteen dollars to buy a copy of Hodgson's *The House on the Borderland and Other Novels* from Gerry in the late sixties. I enjoyed buying from Ken Krueger his Shroud Press publications, particularly his separate edition of *The Dream-Quest of Unknown Kadath*. (It is curious to note that of the three longest works by Lovecraft, *At the Mountains of Madness* has yet to receive separate publication, a defect to be remedied by a 1990 illustrated deluxe edition from the press of Donald M. Grant. I would love to see Grant follow up with similar illustrated editions of *Kadath* and *Ward*.)

Twenty-five years later, I am grateful that I made my first acquaintance with the work of H. P. Lovecraft as an adolescent. Perhaps that is why the after-glow of the first reading has lasted so long and stayed so warm. Frankly, I had been reluctant to re-read the Lovecraft fiction when the new Joshi editions came out from Arkham House, but my experience with *Kadath* tells me only one thing—GO AHEAD!

Scholars much better than I have written on *Kadath*; I have tried to re-read some of this material in preparation for this essay, but my copy of S. T. Joshi's essay on *Kadath* (*Crypt of Cthulhu*, No. 5) is currently inaccessible, stored among my old mailings of the Esoteric Order of Dagon Amateur Press Association. *Kadath* has so many vivid images and ties together so many bits and pieces of Lovecraft's imaginative life; for myself, I find it still an incredibly rich work. A casual reading of Lovecraft's *Commonplace Book* will show any reader how many themes and ideas Lovecraft tied together in *Kadath*. The reader needs to realize that "Pickman's Model" does not complete the saga of Richard Upton Pickman; nor "Celephaïs," that of the dreamer Kuranes; nor "The Cats of Ulthar," that of the feline inhabitants of dreamland; nor "The Statement of Randolph Carter," the fabulous adventures of Lovecraft's alter-ego. The reader will miss the full development of Lovecraft's dream-world if he or she never reads *Kadath*. *Kadath* also has many after-echoes in Lovecraft's work, particularly in the *Fungi from Yuggoth* sonnet cycle. Together with the *Commonplace Book* and the *Fungi from Yuggoth*, *Kadath* contains in my opinion some of the purest and most direct reflections of H. P. Lovecraft's dream-life. There is something purposefully literary about the later Arkham cycle, and without denigrating the greater power of the Arkham tales I can say for myself that I more fully appreciate Lovecraft's imaginative genius in *Kadath*. Objectively, I know that "The Colour out of Space" is a far more important and mature literary work, but nevertheless I experience Lovecraft's imaginative genius more directly in reading my old favorite *Kadath*.

Kadath, the reader should realize, represented a homecoming for Lovecraft. Rescued from near-disaster in New York City the previous spring, he spent the early winter of 1926-27 on the composition of *Kadath*, finishing his work on January 22, 1927. Almost immediately thereafter, he launched into the composition of his longest fictional work, *The Case of Charles Dexter Ward*, a very different kind of paean to his native place, in the form of a gothic horror story set in Providence. What wonderful flights of imagination the pen of H. P. Lovecraft transcribed during the wee hours of the morning in his cramped room at 10 Barnes Street during that winter of 1926-27! What a creative stimulus it must have been to be back in his native place, with his dear aunt Lillian resting sound and secure on the floor below. (Despite Lovecraft's hatred for Providence's winters, we should probably be grateful in that much of his lasting creative work was done while he was largely confined to home during the cold winter months.)

In some ways, I like to think of H. P. Lovecraft as I think of Emily Dickinson, as giving birth to works of genius in the midst of worldly neglect. But then perhaps the secure bosom of home gives birth to more works of human genius than we know. For Lovecraft, *Kadath* and *Ward* (followed shortly by his scholarly accomplishment in "Supernatural Horror in Literature") were in many ways a homecoming. That *Kadath* and *Ward* languished in manuscript during Lovecraft's lifetime and were only rescued by R. H. Barlow and published by Arkham House following the author's death must certainly be a cause for regret. Had Lovecraft taken the time to revise and transcribe *Ward*, he might well have achieved a published novel by the beginning of his last decade of life; how this might have altered his literary career and subsequent recognition will never be known. That *Kadath* and *Ward* escaped destruction, however, is enough to be grateful for. While August Derleth and Donald Wandrei certainly deserve the lion's share of the credit for Lovecraft's posthumous literary recognition, the key role of young Robert Barlow in arranging for the preservation of his literary papers is too easily forgotten. Generations of students of Lovecraft and his work will continue to owe much to Barlow.

This essay is a homecoming celebration for its author—perhaps a very minor echo of the great creative burst that was Lovecraft's homecoming celebration in 1926-27. Those golden summers of 1964-65, when I first read H. P. Lovecraft, Clark Ashton Smith, Robert E. Howard, Lord Dunsany, Arthur Machen, Algernon Blackwood, and many others discussed in Lovecraft's "Supernatural Horror in Literature" can never be recaptured. The secure haven of that home in which I spent the best years of my youth passed away as early as 1966. Many of the most important persons in my life from those years are long deceased. But I have found that the delight of what I learned to love in youth fades only very slowly if at all. While re-reading *Kadath* in 1989 may not have been an event as magical for me as my original reading of it in 1964, the delight remains. Some adult readers of *Kadath* complain of weariness—but adventures never weary the eager child. Perhaps I benefited by re-reading *Kadath* while I was tired and preoccupied with other matters; I could only read small segments at a time and I was able to savor each episode for its own particular magic. How wonderful, once again to visit Inganok, Celephaïs, Dylath-Leen, and Sarkomand! How fearful to read again of Leng's forbidden monastery and cyclopean Kadath itself! How delightsome to remake the acquaintance of the felines of Lovecraft's dream-world and to watch them defeat the untrustworthy zoogs! How much more reserved was my reacquaintance with the race of the ghouls, but no less my delight in their hard-won victory over the moon-beasts that haunt the dream-world! Surely no one could be unimpressed with the fearful night-gaunts, whose winged faceless horror is such that only the nightmares of a child could originate. If indeed gugs and ghasts and bholes no longer fascinate me as they did upon first reading, I suppose I must admit I am growing old.

Lovecraft's dream-world, as epitomized in *Kadath*, however, will never age. By rescuing Lovecraft's manuscript of *Kadath* from the dust-bin, Barlow and

Arkham House have secured immortality for Lovecraft's dream-world. Using the treasure of the original manuscript in Brown University's John Hay Library, S. T. Joshi has given us a new text, free of the errors of the old. In a word, *Kadath* is secure for many new generations of young dreamers. I hope they will find it as fascinating as I did. It opened a whole world of literary discovery and delight for me. It also taught me that the simple things of home are of quintessential importance in a human context, both in the waking and dream worlds, whatever the importance of human affairs on a cosmic scale. I shall not accuse Lovecraft of telling his story for the sake of a moral; the simple truth is that *Kadath*, like "Lord of the Rings" and *Pilgrim's Progress*, is a fiction that integrates high moral and literary standards in one work. The title of Colin Wilson's powerful book, *The Strength to Dream*, is very apt here; for it requires both moral and physical strength to liberate oneself from day-to-day cares in order to dream. Lovecraft's work has always strengthened that capacity in me. Re-reading *Kadath* after twenty-five years was, for me, and imaginative homecoming to those golden summers of 1964–65 when I first discovered the work of H. P. Lovecraft. Hopefully, the reading of *Kadath* will continue to be a magical experience for young readers who encounter it. For readers in middle age who find *Kadath* tiresome, I recommend the experience of reading the story episode by episode to an audience of early teens. I venture to say they will not be bored. (In my mind, *Kadath* is too strong for younger children.) In the grips of middle age myself, there is little I can do to commend the delights of Lovecraft's dream-world to younger readers. Perhaps someday one of our movie moguls will decide to attempt the translation of Lovecraft's dream-world into film through the magic of animation and special effects. Certainly, this would tempt thousands of young readers to read the novel itself. Based on recent adaptations of Lovecraft's work for film, I am dubious that a filmed *Kadath* would do much good for the appreciation of Lovecraft's dreamland quest novel. Would the battle of the night-gaunts and ghouls against the moonbeasts and their lackeys be turned into a bloody gore-fest? All that I can say with virtual certainty from my own experience is that *Kadath* will continue to appeal to its youthful readers, who will find in its narratives if not the most polished reflection of H. P. Lovecraft's imaginative genius, perhaps the most direct. Some works, like *Kadath*, may in fact benefit by surviving only in early draft, directly as they flowed from the pens of their creators.

Lovecraft's Unknown Friend:
Dudley Charles Newton

L ovecraft rejoiced to return to Providence in April 1926 after the failure of his marital experiment in New York. However, there is no question that his domestic circumstances, both in terms of budget and living space, were constrained after his return to Providence. He and his collection of several thousand books had to fit into a single room at 10 Barnes Street, the same building where his elder aunt Lillie Clark (1856-1932) had a room. He had to pay for rent and other living expenses from his modest draw on the capital left by his grandfather Whipple V. Phillips and whatever additional money he could earn by professional writing and revision. In addition, he had to continue to discuss the future of his marriage with Sonia Lovecraft. By March 1929, he gave Sonia to understand that their divorce had been finalized. Given the difficult domestic circumstances of the years after his return to Providence, it is not surprising that Lovecraft seized the opportunity for more recreational travel when it arose. Above all, he sought the welcoming warmth of the American South, where he spent extended stays in Florida in 1931, 1934, and 1935, and traveled as far west as New Orleans in 1932. Charleston, South Carolina, with its rich colonial charm, was undoubtedly his favorite southern city, but the near-tropical warmth of Florida assured its place among his favorite destinations.

Two of Lovecraft's Florida hosts are well known to his readers: Rev. Henry S. Whitehead (1882-1932) of Dunedin, his primary host in 1931, and Robert H. Barlow (1918-1951) of Cassia, his primary host in 1934 and 1935. Despite the extended stays he spent with Whitehead in Dunedin and Barlow in Cassia, St. Augustine remained Lovecraft's favorite Florida destination. Stephen J. Jordan provides an ample discussion of Lovecraft's stays in Florida in his article "Lovecraft in Florida" in *Lovecraft Studies* 42-43. On all three trips, Lovecraft spent significant time in St. Augustine. In 1931, he stayed with Whitehead in Dunedin between May 21 and June 16, but he was in St. Augustine both before (May 7-21) and after (June 16-21) his stay in Dunedin. After each of his extended visits with Barlow and his family in Cassia in 1934 and 1935, Lovecraft spent about a week in St. Augustine: from June 21 to 28 in 1934 and from August 18 to 26 in 1935. Altogether, Lovecraft spent over a month in St. Augustine during his three visits to Florida.

We know—but just barely—that his St. Augustine host in 1931 was one Dudley Charles Newton, who found Lovecraft a room at his own residence, the Hotel Rio Vista on Bay Street, for the bargain rate of $4.00 per week. There is no mention of Dudley Newton in Lovecraft's *Selected Letters*, but Jordan cites an unpublished letter to Lillie Clark (June 10–11, 1931) that mentioned that "my friend Newton" had found lodging for him. In his biography of Lovecraft, S. T. Joshi speculated that Newton may have been "an elderly amateur acquaintance" (p. 509), but I have found no reference to an amateur of that name in publications of the era. So, we are moved to ask, who was Dudley Charles Newton and how did he come to be a friend of H. P. Lovecraft?

Newton does not pop up and then disappear, for he spent all the rest of his life in St. Augustine. A veteran St. Augustine librarian recalled for researcher R. Alain Everts Newton's heavy patronage of the local library. Newton died in St. Augustine on October 10, 1954, aged ninety years. He had made prior arrangements for removal and burial in New York, and the informant for his death certificate was funeral director P. E. Garcia of 20 Cordova Street in St. Augustine. Newton's body was to be removed to New York City for burial by New York Burial Service. Garcia stated that Newton had lived in St. Augustine for twenty-five years—probably an approximate figure. Garcia did not know Newton's marital status or the names of Newton's parents, but could state that Newton had been born on August 4, 1864, in New York City. Newton's residence at the time of his death was Gilmer Nursing Home at 189 San Marco Avenue in St. Augustine. His usual occupation was retired clothing buyer.

With the computerization of federal census and other vital records, hardly any person who lived in the United States in the latter part of the nineteenth century or the twentieth century has disappeared without a trace. We can find "traces" of Dudley Charles Newton's life in the federal census and other vital records. Probably the most informative "hit" occurs in the 1880 U.S. federal census, which recorded the household of Charles I. Newton in Manhattan, New York City (ward 8, district 126). Head of household Charles I. Newton, a white male aged forty-five, was born in New York of English-born parents. He worked as a bookbinder. His wife, Eleanor, a white female aged thirty-eight, kept house, and was born in Ireland or Irish-born parents. Their sons Dudley, aged sixteen, and William, aged eleven, were both in school.

I do not find another really good "hit" for Dudley Charles Newton until the 1910 federal census, where I find him, a single white male aged forty-five, as a lodger at 109 West 54th Street in Manhattan (ward 22). Probably the most significant fact concerning Newton in the 1910 census is his occupation: salesman in the wholesale millinery business. I have not succeeded in finding Newton in the 1870, 1900, or 1920 federal censuses. In the 1930 census, he is recorded as a lodger in the boarding house of John H. and Lula C. Dean in Panama City, Bay County, Florida. Ancestry transcribes his age in the 1930 census as fifty-two, but it looks to me like it might be sixty-two in the census image. In any case, the age is understated, since Newton would celebrate his sixty-sixth birthday on August 4, 1930. In both the 1910 and 1930 census records, Newton's marital status is recorded as single (never married).

Turning to other resources, I found Newton listed as a buyer for Scully Brothers & Company in Trow's 1917 New York City Directory, with his home in Georgetown, Connecticut. Scully Brothers & Company, Inc., is listed in the same directory as a dealer in millinery goods, with offices at 417 Fifth Avenue, room 1101. In Trow's 1918 New York City Directory, Newton is still listed as a buyer for Scully Brothers, but his home address has changed from Georgetown, Connecticut, to 109 West 54th Street, the same address he had in the 1910 federal census. I do not find Newton in New York City directories before 1917 or after 1918.

Three Port of New York records apparently refer to our Dudley Newton. In 1903, Dudley Newton, a thirty-nine year-old salesman and an American citizen, sailed on the *S. S. Philadelphia*, departing Southampton, England, on August 22, 1903, and arriving in New York City on August 29, 1903. Then, in 1911, Dudley Newton, an American citizen aged forty-six, departed from Antwerp on the *S. S. Kroonland* July 8, 1911, bound for New York City. Finally, Dudley Newton, a single male aged fifty-five, born 1865 in New York City, sailed on the *S. S. Fort Hamilton*, departing Bermuda on March 13, 1920, and arriving in New York City on March 15, 1920. The 1920 record gives Newton's residence as Banbury, Connecticut (a mistranscription for "Danbury").

Two letters from Dudley Newton to H. P. Lovecraft survive in the Lovecraft Collection at Brown University. I am deeply indebted to Chris G. Karr for taking the time to transcribe these two letters for me during his own research trip to Providence in 2008. The first letter, dated September 15, 1930, is handwritten on the letterhead of Jordan & Selleck of Bridgeport, Connecticut. Newton regrets having to omit a visit to Providence after he had to terminate his stay in Maine early, but anticipates that he may visit Boston soon, and asks Lovecraft to recommend "a moderate price hotel" in Providence. He expresses gratitude for Lovecraft's opinion of Poe and states that his recent reading has included a new biography of Benjamin Franklin. In conclusion, he writes: "Excuse this letter—it's so hot that my hand sticks to the paper and my typewriter is locked up in my bunk. Mr. Selleck is an old friend and I use his office & paper."

Newton wrote to Lovecraft again from Bridgeport on November 2, 1930. He promises to send Lovecraft two examples of the productions of a "paper book club." He has found them all of interest, although of "varying excellence." The only title to attain popular attention so far has been *The Bridge of San Luis Rey*. Lovecraft has evidently written to Newton of a recent professional story sale, for Newton remarks: "Well, if you sell many mor [sic] stories at the price you tell I am afraid you will be going to Charleston in your yacht—or something of that sort—I wish I could reel off any stories that anyone would be willing to pay real money for." He continues: "As yet I have no plans for the Winter apt. to do something new—and perhaps we may meet—who knows? all plans are more or less a matter of ways and means—if Margaret Fuller had been left a large fortune in hr youth—and this happened to some—her life would have been quite another story—always glad to hear from you." Margaret Fuller (1810-1850) was an American critic in Boston and New York. She traveled to Europe and married the Marquis of Ossoli in 1847. She and her husband and child were lost in a shipwreck off Fire Island, New York, in 1850.

So end the "tracks" of Dudley Charles Newton that I have so far discovered. I commend to future researchers the references to Connecticut localities—to Georgetown in Trow's 1917 New York City Directory, to Danbury in the 1920 Port of New York record, and to Bridgeport in the 1930 correspondence with Lovecraft. Finding Newton in either the 1900 or the 1920 federal census might also reveal new information concerning him. It is important to keep him distinct from the Newport, Rhode Island, architect Dudley Newton (1845-1907). By 1920, the son and grandson of the Rhode Island architect, Dudley II (b. 1880) and Dudley III (b. 1906) were living in Berkeley, California; by 1930, Dudley II was in Sacramento. I am not aware of any relationship between Lovecraft's friend Dudley Charles Newton and the similarly-named Rhode Island architect.

I think the most important facts so far discovered about Dudley Charles Newton are his occupation—salesman or buyer in the clothing industry, more specifically (at least in 1910-18) the wholesale millinery business—and his love of literature. (Perhaps Newton's 1911 trip to Holland and Belgium concerned the acquisition of lace for the millinery business.) Both of these facets of Dudley Charles Newton might have brought him into friendship with H. P. Lovecraft. The business of Lovecraft's wife Sonia Haft (Greene) Lovecraft was retail millinery, and if wholesaler Dudley Charles Newton went out of his way to assist Sonia Lovecraft in her business endeavors, he might well have won the friendship of her husband as well. We tend to forget that the Lovecrafts started their married life with some conventional aspirations, and even acquired a house lot in Yonkers, New York. If Lovecraft and Newton found that they had a common interest in literature, that might only have cemented their friendship. If Lovecraft did meet Newton through Sonia, his reticence concerning his friendship with Newton is consistent with his reticence concerning his marriage.

Perhaps it was dual invitations from Henry Whitehead and Dudley Newton that finally influenced Lovecraft to "take the plunge" for a Florida trip in 1931. As single men, these hosts may have reinforced for Lovecraft the belief that there could be meaningful life after the failure of his marriage. Certainly, Lovecraft flourished in the near-tropical warmth of Florida. "O Fortunate

Floridian!" he would address his later Florida host, the youthful Robert H. Barlow. Of the Florida hosts, Whitehead was a few years older than Lovecraft, while Barlow was young enough to be Lovecraft's son and Newton old enough to be Lovecraft's father. Perhaps the only reasonable conclusion is that Lovecraft was willing to form friendships with congenial persons, and especially males, of all ages. We should be particularly grateful to all three of Lovecraft's Florida hosts—for the reinvigorating warmth and pleasure of his extended Florida stays undoubtedly helped to relieve the stress of his constrained domestic circumstances in Providence. While the more commodious accommodations which he enjoyed at 66 College Street with his aunt Annie Gamwell (1866–1941) from May 1933 forward doubtless played their own part in boosting the author's spirits and relieving his frayed nerves, I believe the long, relaxed, and congenial stays with his three Florida hosts were also essential elements of his artistic and psychic survival in the 1930s, in the face of declining health and fortune.

I only wish we knew more of Lovecraft's host in St. Augustine—Dudley Charles Newton. I suspect that the destruction of Sonia Lovecraft's file of letters from her husband eliminated our richest possible source of information concerning Newton, but perhaps the ongoing digitalization of information will eventually enrich our knowledge. New knowledge can come from unexpected places. Perhaps there are resources relating to the millinery business in early twentieth-century New York City that will eventually yield useful information concerning Newton and his relationship with the Lovecrafts.

Works Cited

Jordan, Stephen J. "Lovecraft in Florida." *Lovecraft Studies* Nos. 42–43 (Autumn 2001): 32–45.

Joshi, S. T. *H. P. Lovecraft: A Life.* West Warwick, RI: Necronomicon Press, 1996.

Lovecraft, H. P. *O Fortunate Floridian: H. P. Lovecraft's Letters to R. H. Barlow.* Ed. S. T. Joshi and David E. Schultz. Tampa: University of Tampa Press, 2007.

Special thanks to Chris G. Karr, for research assistance at the John Hay Library.

R. H. Barlow

From this tree
No further fruit.
Search the boughs, look where the ant looks.
Only as cold-veined snakes knotting on the mud,
Daggering their bird heads at a shadow,
Will they respond.
A fire has bounded past
And the bark is scorched.
                    —"From This Tree," from *View from a Hill* (EG 180).

Like a fire bounding past, Robert Hayward Barlow lived among us in the brief years between 1918 and 1951. To a subclass of us whom we may for convenience name "Lovecraftians," he is known as the dreamy youth who became at nineteen H. P. Lovecraft's literary executor. He thereafter journeyed to California, became interested in México, and died there in 1951. To another subclass, he was an artist and a poet. He wrote several collections of innovative and faintly tragic verse. He was earlier involved in the world of pulp fiction of the 1930s, and afterwards became an expert in Mexican anthropology and history. He died by his own hand in 1951. To yet another subclass, he was a profound student of the native races of México—their culture, language, and history. He had formerly been a writer and an artist, with obscure connections to a pulp writer named Lovecraft.

Since R. H. Barlow was such a constellation of different things to different people, it occurred to me one day—when I perchance found an article about him in a Mexican magazine—that a tying-together of the threads might prove of interest to some of the persons who knew him through one or the other of his different activities. I should admit from the start that my bias was that of a Lovecraftian, for those who may find too much attention given to Barlow's teenage years. Perhaps some of the people who knew Barlow in one capacity or another will find the unfamiliar aspects of his life merely boring and inconsequential. To me the different aspects of his life—as an associate of Lovecraft's, as an artist and a poet, and as a scholar—were all one tapestry woven by a man of unusual perception and ability.

The materials that have been published about Barlow are scant. Undoubtedly, the most important statements have come from Clare Mooser, Ignacio Bernal, George T. Smisor, and Barlow himself—which is not in any way to reflect upon others who wrote about him.

I wish to thank E. Wayne Barlow, George T. Smisor, and Roy A. Squires for their permission to reprint certain materials. Thanks are also due to the staff of the Special Collections at the John Hay Library of Brown University for their assistance in examining certain materials of the Lovecraft collection relating to Barlow, particularly the letters which Lovecraft sent to Barlow from 1931 to 1937. Needless to say, the opinions expressed in this paper are my own. There are also undoubtedly many errors and inaccuracies in matters of fact, for which I would appreciate receiving corrections.

1. The Moon Pool

Robert Hayward Barlow, or R. H. Barlow, as he preferred to sign his name, was born on May 18, 1918, in Leavenworth, Kansas, the son of Lieutenant Colonel Everett D. Barlow and Mrs. Bernice Barlow. Of Barlow's ancestry I know very little. At one point he became interested in genealogy through Lovecraft and did some research on the family tree, finding a connection making himself a distant cousin of Lovecraft, and another relating him to the famous divine Warren Sloan Barlow (1820-1889). He failed to make any connection with the more famous colonial writer Joel Barlow (1754-1812). LTC Barlow was a career military officer, and it is possible that his branch of the family had a military tradition; there are quite a few Barlows in a register of U.S. Army officers which ends in the year 1903. LTC Barlow's duties kept the family moving from post to post around the country. In the years he corresponded with Lovecraft alone, Barlow wrote from such diverse places as Leavenworth; Kansas City; Cassia, Florida; Fort Benning, Georgia; Washington, D.C.; and Daytona Beach. Kansas seems to have been considered the family home, however, and Barlow gravitated back several times during his lifetime. We know very little of Barlow's youth; he is mentioned in several places as having been a bright, introverted, and sensitive child, not much suited to the life of a military family. He was probably driven to reading for companionship because of his family's frequent moves. At any rate, he seems to have made the acquaintance of fantasy and macabre fiction quite early, and by the time he wrote Lovecraft in the spring of 1931 he was probably a steady reader of *Weird Tales* and associated magazines. The early thirties seem to have been the years of greatest flourishing of weird/fantastic fiction magazines, and they certainly must have provided a magnificent pastime for a lonely thirteen-year-old boy moving about the country with his father and mother. Wrote Barlow in *Marginalia*: "I had no friends nor studies except in a sphere bound together by the U.S. Mails and the magazines of fantastic stories for which Lovecraft wrote" (WG, 358). One imagines that Barlow wrote to Lovecraft through *Weird Tales*, since the first "fan" magazines were just being born at the time Barlow began his correspondence with Lovecraft, and it is unlikely that the migratory Barlow had heard of them. Later, these magazines, swollen to something like twenty-five in number by 1935–36, brought dozens of new correspondents to Lovecraft, most of them youths fascinated by fantastic fiction or trying to break into the field.

Lovecraft's reply indicates that Barlow's initial letter was a polite request for information about earlier Lovecraft stories. Lovecraft dutifully listed his published stories, adding a customary deprecation of his works. Very soon manuscripts of Lovecraft's stories were making their way to Barlow's home in Kansas City. Gradually a working relationship developed whereby Barlow would provide typewritten copies of Lovecraft's tales in return for the possession of the original manuscripts. This relationship between author and collector did not take full bloom until Barlow's Florida period (1934–36), but it is easy to see that Barlow was beginning to mold his fantasy collection, and indeed his whole life, around Lovecraft's personality and works. Lovecraft led most of his young correspondents through his favorite writers in the literature of the macabre—Poe, Machen, Blackwood, and others—and there can be little doubt that he did the same for Barlow. Barlow evinced a strong interest in collecting the fine literature and the ephemera of the fantasy genre. One imagines that he had read several of the popular books of the 1920s and 1930s concerning book lore, for he early appreciated the value of manuscripts, first editions, and the like. While he maintained his mental balance against the worse excesses of bibliomania, Barlow rapidly brought together one of the finest and most distinctive fantasy collections in history. His consistent interest in the preservation of important materials in the genre was probably one of the reasons Lovecraft chose him as executor over others of his correspondents who were more preoccupied with other matters.

The early correspondence is essentially one between teacher and pupil. One of Barlow's earliest enthusiasms was for collecting copies of old back issues of *Weird Tales*, and, while encouraging him in his search for rare back numbers, Lovecraft also directed his correspondent to the standard literature of the genre. The letters Lovecraft sent gradually become longer and longer as the correspondence develops rapidly toward more of a dialogue than an instruction. Unfortunately, only the Lovecraft portion of the correspondence is on file at the John Hay Library at Brown; while other correspondences exist in their entirety, we have only one side of the Lovecraft-Barlow correspondence, thus depriving us of some insights into the developing interests and personality of young Barlow. It is likely that Lovecraft discarded the early letters from Barlow; later on, he speaks of keeping a file of some of Barlow's artwork and stories, which may have included some of the later letters; in any case, the whole of "Barloviana," as it was dubbed, returned to Barlow as Lovecraft's literary executor; the bulk of the material may still reside with his heirs.[1]

Although we are thus deprived of an important insight, it is evident that Barlow's intellectual development during the years of the Lovecraft correspondence was rapid. Very soon, he was making his own attempts at macabre fiction and artwork. Lovecraft undoubtedly found his usual careful revision and criticism a congenial task, since Barlow wrote by preference in Lovecraft's own favorite genre. A series of nine early fantasies saw print in the *Fantasy Fan* between October 1933 and February 1935 under the title "Annals of the Jinns." Like most of the early pieces, the "Annals" have a Dunsanian ring. Undoubtedly, the earliest pieces were somewhat clumsy and crude, but by 1935 or so it is clear that Lovecraft was very serious in his praise. At about the same time, Barlovian art and fiction was beginning to make the rounds in manuscript among the growing number of Lovecraft's associates. By 1935, discussions of writing or artwork as a career were occupying the attention of Lovecraft and his young correspondent.

But we have skipped a little ahead of the chronological sequence of events. In 1933, both Lovecraft and Barlow took up their roots and moved. Lovecraft's aunt, Mrs. Lillian D. Clark, had died in July 1932, and in May 1933 he and his surviving aunt, Mrs. Annie E. Phillips Gamwell, moved to the famous residence at 66 College Street. Somewhat earlier, the Barlow family had pulled up its roots in Kansas City and moved to central Florida. Although Barlow spent a brief period in Washington, D.C., in 1934 seeking treatment for his eyes, Florida was to be his home until mid-1936. And a felicitous residence for his association with Lovecraft it was indeed. Lovecraft had visited the author Henry St. Clair Whitehead (1882–1932) at his home in Dunedin, Florida, in 1931, and had even penetrated as far south as the Keys. Only finances prevented a hop across the Caribbean to Cuba. He returned to his native New England with a deep love for the balmy climate and Spanish antiquities of Florida. Indeed, the entire Southland was Lovecraft's special preserve, and he made another extensive jaunt through the area in 1932, this time reaching as far as New Orleans. Charleston, South Carolina, with its numerous examples of colonial architecture, was probably his second-favorite city in America, after Providence. Thus, the stage was set for the two fruitful visits that Lovecraft made to his young friend during the summers of 1934 and 1935.

Perhaps only a small minority of Lovecraft's correspondents ever saw him in person, and these visits, each extended more than a month at the insistence of the Barlow family, were certainly crucial in cementing the relationship of friendship and trust which led to the naming of Barlow as Lovecraft's literary executor. The initial invitation was extended by the Barlow family in the spring of 1934, and although Lovecraft was unable to make an immediate decision because of financial uncertainties, the afternoon of May 2, 1934, found him arriving by Greyhound Bus in De Land, the closest city of any size to the Barlow home. Barlow left a moving portrait of the visit in his article "The Wind That Is in the Grass," written for the Lovecraft collection *Marginalia,* and in the notes that were ultimately published in *Some Notes on H. P. Lovecraft* (1959) and reprinted in *The Dark Brotherhood and Other Pieces* (1966). The Barlows lived on the main highway from Eustis to De Land, three miles from their nearest neighbors. The nearest town was tiny Cassia. The morning of Lovecraft's visit, Barlow drove eighteen miles into De Land in the old family Ford to procure needed furniture for the guest room, which occupied the second story of the Barlow home along with his own room and a sleeping porch. He promptly returned to De Land to greet Lovecraft upon his arrival by Greyhound.

They seem to have fallen to discussing their common literary interests almost immediately. Barlow wrote: "Life was all literary then; that is, all I cared to accept as life" (WG, 358). The discussion was apparently omnivorous, ranging from the great masters of the fantasy genre to obscure pieces in the pulps that Barlow had so meticulously collected. Again Barlow: "Our talk was full of off-hand references to ghouls and vaults of horror on the surfaces of strange stars, and Lovecraft wove an atmosphere of ominous illusion about any chance sound by the roadside as we walked with my three cats" (WG, 359). There were also boat rides on the small lake on the Barlow property, a notoriously unsuccessful Lovecraftian attempt at berry-picking, and long sessions spent on joint composition and verses. Manuscripts on file in the John Hay Library make it certain that the parody "The Battle That Ended the Century," which burst upon the fantasy world from a Washington, D.C., address in May, 1934, emerged from Barlow's and Lovecraft's hands. In a file marked "joint parodies," there is a fragmentary first draft with annotations in Barlow's hand (one leaf, typewritten); a complete second draft with revisions in Lovecraft's hand (four leaves, typewritten, dated circa May 20, 1934, by Barlow), and three mimeographed copies evidently prepared for circulation (two leaves each, stapled).[2] It seems evident that the parody was forwarded to Washington, D.C., where it was remailed by some acquaintance of Lovecraft's or Barlow's. Such a parody seems to be precisely the sort of pleasant pastime that might have suggested itself to a young man totally absorbed in the world of fantasy fiction and its authors. There were also rhyming bouts; in one case, the object was apparently to compose poetry to fit a given rhyme scheme, leading to the following delightful efforts, dated May 23, 1934:

Beyond Zimbabwe

The drums of the jungle in ecstasy boom,
And summon the chosen to torture and doom;
The quivering throngs wait expectant and sad,
While the shrieks of the priest echo drunkenly mad,
Round the altars are tributes of barley and cream,
And the acolytes stagger in opiate dream.
It is thus that the Shadow grows mighty and whole,
As it feeds on the body and sucks at the soul.

The White Elephant

Dim in the past from primal chaos rose
That form with mottled cloak and scaly hose
Who bade the lesser ghouls, to earn their bread
Perform dread rites, and echo what he said.
They bred the leprous trees and poison flower
And pressed dim aeons into one black hour.
Wherefore we pray, as pious pagans must,
To the white beast he shaped from fungous dust.

There were also undoubted some serious attention given to young Barlow's poetry and prose, and the tale "'Till A' the Seas'" may date from about this time, although personally I would date it a little later, perhaps 1935. Barlow was also at this time beginning to appear in various of the small fantasy-oriented amateur magazines that were springing up. A complete record of his appearances in the *Fantasy Fan* is in the bibliography; he may well have appeared in other magazines, including *Fantasy Magazine*. His first biography in print was no doubt the short notice of him given by F. Lee Baldwin in the July 1934 issue of the *Fantasy Fan*:

> R. H. Barlow is a very talented youth. He is a pianist, painter, sculptor in clay, landscape gardener, and book collector. He has completed a clay bas-relief of Cthulhu and a statuette of Ganesa, the Hindoo Elephant God. One of his favorite bindings for his books is snake skin. He shoots many snakes around his home in Florida and tans the skin. (Baldwin, July 1934)

In the August 1934 issue, Barlow wrote to youthful editor Charles D. Hornig to tell him that he was doing a good job except for "wasting space on that ass Barlow in Baldwin's column." Lovecraft may have introduced Barlow to the amateur press associations (specifically the National Amateur Press Association [NAPA]) at the same time. It was my impression from reading Lovecraft's letters to Barlow that Barlow did not begin NAPA activity until about 1935 or so, but a note by F. Lee Baldwin in the September 1934 *Fantasy Fan* states that Barlow won a NAPA laureate award in 1933.

Lovecraft remained in Florida for considerably more than a month, taking tours in the Barlow Ford to see what Barlow later termed the "faintly fraudulent Hispanic character of Florida" (WG, 359). Trips took them to De León Springs, where Barlow notes with his characteristic wit "an Eighteenth Century Spanish windmill exists in an advanced state of restoration" (WG, 359), to the ruins of an abandoned monastery at New Smyrna; and to St. Augustine, where Lovecraft was genuinely enthralled by the authentic Hispanic atmosphere of the old town. Again Barlow: "On a more adventurous *Ausflug* we visited the Chapel of Nuestra Señora de la Leche, and a mosquito-cursed graveyard full of tombs of young people who died of plague a hundred years before" (WG, 359). And so on for a month and more into the summer the visit continued, Lovecraft and Barlow exploring their common interests and in general passing the time to their mutual satisfaction, with discussions and outings during the afternoon and evening, and long writing sessions by Lovecraft at night. The visit, which cemented their friendship on a face-to-face basis, ended on June 21, 1934.

The next two years were years of increasingly cordial and lengthy correspondence. During this period Barlow gradually came to the decision to expand his activities from collecting and reading to publishing. By this time, he had one of the most extensive collections of fantasy books and periodicals of his day, so distinguished as to be written up in one of the small amateur magazines. This vast horde of material, including duplicate and even triplicate copies of some of the pulps of his day, Barlow kept in a closet that he dubbed Yoh-Vombis, from Clark Ashton Smith's mordant tale of caverns of horror on Mars. Wrote Barlow:

> Lovecraft said to me at a later moment of annoyance that he loved literature, and that I loved books, in which there was some truth. The curator of Yoh-Vombis at that time considered bibliophily a serious occupation, filing autographs of Wells and Verne with those of popular magazine writers, and searching for old *Weird Tales* along with out-of-print Cabell. It was indeed this bibliophily which led me to write to Lovecraft first, in 1931, when I was just thirteen. (WG, 358)

I have remarked that before Barlow, whose formal education had ended by the time the family moved to Florida, must have acquainted himself with book lore from some of the books on the subject that were popular in the 1920s and 1930s. (His fondness for the words biblio-this and biblio-that makes me wonder whether he was familiar with Holbrook Jackson's *The Anatomy of Bibliomania* [Scribner's, 1930], which deals at length with these phenomena. Barlow also possessed a stamp reading "R. H. Barlow: Bibliomaniac," which appears on some of his early papers in the Lovecraft collection.) He also somehow picked up the art of bookbinding, at which he became a skilled craftsman. In any case, by 1935 Barlow was a collector and bookman of some sophistication, perfectly cognizant of the value of manuscripts, proofs, presentation copies, and the like. Several bibliographic notes in the *Fantasy Fan* (March and May 1934) reflect his interests.

Without doubt, his most important role was as the retainer of Lovecraft's original manuscripts. By 1935 the relationship whereby Barlow provided typewritten copies of Lovecraft's works in return for possession of the original manuscripts had been finalized. Most of Lovecraft's holograph manuscripts before 1931 were destroyed as soon as the work appeared in print, including the manuscripts of most of the great stories of the late 1920s like "The Colour out of Space." Of these manuscripts, Lovecraft told Barlow that only the manuscripts of "The Shunned House" and perhaps of "The Rats in the Walls" survived (WG, 361). A few of the manuscripts of very early stories—including "The Doom That Came to Sarnath," "The Transition of Juan Romero," "The Quest of Iranon," "The Other Gods," and "The Strange High House in the Mist"—were given as gifts to Barlow. After 1931, the situation changed drastically with Barlow serving as an eager scribe to the willing Lovecraft, probably quite happy to be relieved of what he considered to be one of the most onerous tasks of authorship. To Barlow's diligence in requesting Lovecraftian material for transcription we owe not only the survival of a good many of Lovecraft's manuscripts but also very likely the survival of a number of the major works. As is well known, Lovecraft became quite discouraged about his writing in the 1930s, principally as a result of editorial rejections, and he destroyed one draft of "The Shadow out of Time" and threatened to do the same with the second. Barlow persuaded Lovecraft to allow him to put the manuscript into typewritten form; later the story was marketed by a friend and is today held to be perhaps Lovecraft's finest work. *The Case of Charles Dexter Ward* (1927) and *The Dream-Quest of Unknown Kadath* (1926-27) would also likely have actually perished had not Barlow coaxed the manuscripts out of a dubious Lovecraft in 1934.[3]

Barlow began transcription of these novels, but I do not know whether the work was complete until after Lovecraft's death. All the manuscripts that Barlow received from Lovecraft were deposited with the John Hay Library in the years immediately following Lovecraft's death (1937-42), with the single exception of the manuscript of "The Shadow out of Time," which Barlow retained.[4] Because of Barlow's diligence, the Library now has a near-complete collection of Lovecraft's important manuscripts of the 1930s. Two later manuscripts—"The Thing on the Doorstep" and "The Haunter of the Dark"—did go to other Lovecraft associates (Duane Rimel and Donald Wollheim, respectively), Lovecraft remarking that he did not think a monopoly proper if his manuscripts ever did become valuable. Duane Rimel later donated the manuscript of "The Thing on the Doorstep" to the Lovecraft Collection, while the manuscript of "The Haunter of the Dark" apparently remains in private hands.

Barlow's collecting zeal soon began to blossom in other directions. He transformed many of his books and magazines into handsome hardbound volumes. I have seen his bound volume of the *Fantasy Fan* in the Lovecraft Collection at Brown University: with its marbled boards and half-leather spine with gold lettering it is the equal of many fine professional bindings I have seen. For Lovecraft he bound several volumes of *Weird Tales* and a copy of Lovecraft's 1928 book *The Shunned House* for presentation on the occasion of Lovecraft's second visit to Cassia in June 1935. A more significant development of his "bibliophily," however, was the urge to find a press of his own and to publish. As early as 1932, following Henry St. Clair Whitehead's death on November 23 of that year, Barlow proposed issuing a memorial volume of letters that Whitehead sent to his friends, or "Caneviniana." This apparently actually proceeded to the editing stage, but Barlow was apparently still too inexperienced to undertake the task of publication. That the project did hang around for a long while is indicated by F. Lee Baldwin's note in the April 1934 *Fantasy Fan* announcing a forthcoming 35-copy edition of fifty of Whitehead's letters from Barlow; however, in the press of other activities, this never reached even a trial printing.[5]

The urge to publish seems to have remained with Barlow, and he was particularly impressed with the fine volumes issued by W. Paul Cook's Recluse Press, which he obtained through Lovecraft. By 1935 he was more ready to undertake the task of publishing, and he began discussions with Lovecraft concerning the foundation of a small private press after the model of Cook's enterprise. Somehow, Barlow managed to round up a printing press and type, and after some discussion he settled upon the typically Floridian name of the "Dragon-Fly Press" for his endeavor. Its colophon was the image of a dragon-fly. The first production of the new press was a slim volume of fantastic poems by Lovecraft's close friend Frank Belknap Long entitled *The Goblin Tower*. An inscription on a proof sheet of one of the poems makes it likely that Lovecraft assisted in the printing during his visit to Cassia in the summer of 1935 (Squires, 3). *The Goblin Tower* was issued in a one hundred-copy edition in the fall of 1935, coming as a surprise to Long, who had not known when the volume would be issued.

Despite a lack of tangible response, Barlow remained enthusiastic about publishing. He proposed such a welter of projects that Lovecraft had to advise him more than once to limit himself to one project at a time. "Caneviniana" was still in the background; and at one time Barlow apparently had manuscript for collections of poems by Clark Ashton Smith (to be entitled *Incantations*) and by Elizabeth Toldridge, an elderly friend of Lovecraft's whom Barlow had met during his residence in Washington, D.C., in 1934. None of these books ever advanced to the stage of even a trial printing, so far as I know.[6] One project that did progress at least to the proof stage was a proposed edition of Lovecraft's *Fungi from Yuggoth*. Lovecraft had been sending Barlow samples of his poetry for some time and was somewhat dismayed when he learned that Barlow was proposing to issue some of his verse from the Dragon-Fly Press. However, when Barlow proved insistent, Lovecraft proposed that the poems be divided into two small volumes—one to consist of the *Fungi*, the other of Lovecraft's selection of his other poems.[7] Around Christmas 1935, Lovecraft was distressed to hear from the grapevine that a volume of his work had appeared from the Dragon-Fly Press without his express review of the contents—perhaps he feared an unwanted resurrection of some of his old amateur poems—but was pleased to receive a few days later a small booklet containing his Dunsanian fantasy "The Cats of Ulthar," a booklet that actually constituted Barlow's Christmas card, and of which forty-two copies were distributed to friends. The printing of the *Fung from Yuggoth* itself never progressed beyond the proof stage, for mid-1936 brought the removal of Barlow to Kansas City, with the consequent disruption of his collecting and publishing efforts. A good deal of the original Yoh-Vombis remained in Florida at the family home, and was still there at the time of Barlow's death in 1951.

The year 1936 indeed contains some significant developments in the Barlow-Lovecraft relationship, but I have glossed too quickly over the development of their correspondence in treating of publishing and collecting matters. The year 1935 found Barlow submitting a steady stream of fiction and artwork for Lovecraft's criticism. More often than not, Lovecraft provided a full and detailed revision of the fiction. Among the fantasies Barlow may have composed at about this time I have found the names "A Dim-Remembered Story," "Memory and a Dream," "The Bright Valley," "The Root Gatherers," and "The Night Ocean." At the same time, Barlow seems to have become more active in NAPA affairs; with Lovecraft's encouragement, he issued two numbers of an amateur paper entitled the *Dragon-Fly* for NAPA under the presidency of Hyman Bradofsky. Of other material by Barlow that may have appeared in the papers issued by members of NAPA, I am ignorant. Several of Barlow's stories appeared in the *Californian,* edited by Bradofsky himself. The two issues of the *Dragon-Fly,* dated October 15, 1935, and May 15, 1936, contained material by J. Vernon Shea, Jr., Clark Ashton Smith, Ernest Edkins, August Derleth, E. B. Kuntz, Elizabeth Toldridge, and Barlow. Lovecraft inevitably felt less able to offer criticism of Barlow's artwork, but that he esteemed it highly can be seen from the fact that "Barlovian" art shortly began making the rounds of Lovecraft's correspondents. Lovecraft himself was pleased to accept as gifts various drawings depicting the weird beasties from his tales.

At the same time, Barlow's literary work continued to develop. He must have continued to appear in the science fiction-fantasy "fan" magazines after the folding of the *Fantasy Fan* in February 1935, but I have not been able to find much of his work in the scattered issues of these magazines which I have had available to me. A continuation of the "Annals of the Jinns" was announced in the July 1936 *Phantagraph*, edited by Donald A. Wollheim of New York City; this continuation began with the August 1936 issue. In the November 1936 *Phantagraph* occurs another of the mini-biographies of Barlow, this one written by Wollheim:

> R. H. Barlow, who visited your correspondent a month ago, tells of two Lovecraft novels which he has in manuscript which have never been typed out or submitted. Their titles are *The Case of Charles Dexter Ward* and *The Dream-*

Quest of Unknown Kadath. Barlow, who owns a press, occasionally puts out a NAPA publication or a book, is looking for an old Washington hand press so that he can hope for some especially fine work.

"The Bright Valley"—"a weird tale of a fabled promised land, haunted by a death that made gods of its victims"—was announced in the September 1936 issue of the *Planeteer,* edited by James Blish and William H. Miller, but it never appeared. Nevertheless, it is clear that Barlow continued to contribute actively to fandom. In fact, Barlow retained at least a loose connection with fandom for several years following Lovecraft's death, despite giving up most of his collecting activities.

In August 1937, with the financial assistance of Lovecraft's friend and fellow amateur Ernest A. Edkins, Barlow issued from Leavenworth, Kansas, one hundred copies of an amateur magazine entitled *Leaves.* A massive production for its day, the first issue of *Leaves* contained eighty pages of closely typed fiction and poetry. The quality of the material included is indicative of Barlow's developing literary judgment: "The Story of Princess Zulkais and the Prince Kalilah," an unfinished episode from William Beckford's *Vathek,* in the translation by Sir Frank T. Marzials; a "Conclusion to the Story of the Princess Zulkais and the Prince Kalilah," by Clark Ashton Smith; "With a Set of Rattlesnake Rattles," by Robert E. Howard; "Cats and Dogs," by Lewis Theobald, Jr. [i.e., H. P. Lovecraft]; "Dead Houses," by Edith Miniter; "The Beautiful City," by Frank Belknap Long; "The People of the Pit," by A. Merritt; "The Panelled Room," by August Derleth; "The Twilight of Time" (later retitled "The Red Brain"), "On the Threshold of Eternity," and "A Legend of Yesterday," by Donald Wandrei; and verses by H. P. Lovecraft, Elizabeth Toldridge, Clark Ashton Smith, and Arthur Goodenough. Barlow himself wrote a perceptive if opinionated defense of imaginative fiction. A second issue of *Leaves* followed from Lakeport, California, in 1938, and probably marks the definitive end of Barlow's activity within fandom as editor and publisher.

The world of the small fantasy magazines and their followers was an important one for Lovecraft and his young friend Barlow. The springing up of these magazines in the mid-1930s brought Lovecraft many new correspondents and made his name more well-known than it otherwise would have been. By January 3, 1937, Lovecraft could write Barlow that he had some 97 correspondents on his list, a good number of them brought in through these magazines. By 1936, however, Barlow's interests had definitely begun to broaden beyond this tiny microcosm of a world, to the delight of his mentor Lovecraft. By 1936 Barlow was attempting to write a full-scale novel. Politics and current affairs began to obtrude upon the Lovecraft-Barlow correspondence. Lovecraft's last letter to Barlow, dated January 27, 1937, is principally a long discussion of Lovecraft's views on the future of the capitalistic system. Social and private mores inevitably came up for discussion, with Lovecraft outlining the unconventional reasons for his conservative, traditionalist stand. Indeed, in his final recorded estimate of Lovecraft, Barlow speaks not so much of Lovecraft's prowess as an author but of "a man who had the courage to ignore the Machine Age and its leveling-out-to-rubble of life's rich irregularities, who had the courage to study and think and converse and write, in accordance with the deeper traditions of a more orderly age" (WG, 362).

At about this time, in mid-1936, the long-standing illness of Barlow's father forced a breakup of the family, the father remaining in Florida and Barlow and his mother journeying home to Kansas City. It was inevitably a time of strain and discomfort for Barlow, marking a definite end to the halcyon days in the shaded world of the Moon-Pool, as he and Lovecraft had dubbed the small lake on the Barlow property in Florida. In connection with the removal to Kansas City, Barlow made a swing northward, including a month-long stay with Lovecraft in Providence in August 1936. The principal recorded event of the visit was a versifying session held by Lovecraft, Barlow, and Adolphe de Castro in St. John's Churchyard, a Providence landmark frequented by Edgar Allan Poe during his courtship of the Providence poet Sarah Helen Whitman in 1847 and 1848. At the suggestion of Barlow, each of the three companions composed a rhymed acrostic poem on the name of EDGAR ALLAN POE. De Castro's poem was sent apace to Farnsworth Wright of *Weird Tales*, where it saw publication in the May 1937 issue, taking precedence over Barlow's and Lovecraft's poems, which saw publication in the March–April 1937 *Science-Fantasy Correspondent*, edited by Corwin F. Stickney. The only other notice I have seen of the 1936 visit occurs in Adolphe de Castro's letter of August 12, 1936, to Lovecraft, containing his revisions of the poems of August 7 (which were not adopted) and the following remarks:

> Au reste, I have to thank you for a liberal education and sore pedals. But it was fun. And the greatest fun was dear young Barlow. Bob actually desires to be old, not knowing what treasure he owns in his youth and brains and his overindulgence in imagination, and good memory of what he reads.[8]

In any case, the visit must have been a happy moment for Lovecraft and his young associate. De Castro's complaint of "sore pedals" leads one to imagine that there were several long treks through the by-ways of Providence and the nearby countryside.

Upon his arrival in Kansas City, Barlow began studies at the Art Institute there. It was probably his first formal classwork in a number of years, apart from a short art course he took at the Corcoran Gallery while in Washington, D.C., temporarily in late 1934. Barlow's interest in art had been growing for some time, as evinced by the growing circulation of his works among the Lovecraft Circle in 1934–36. By 1936, he seems to have decided upon art as his career. His course work at the Kansas City Art Institute included instruction under the famous painter and muralist Thomas Hart Benton (1889–1975). Lovecraft of course sent his well-wishes, but there is also a note of regret that the happy Florida days were ended. Lovecraft was always intimidated by the vastness of the Midwest, and although he planned eventually to make a swing through the area to see his many friends there (including August Derleth, a correspondent since 1926), such an extended trip was never possible during his lifetime.

2. The Sorceror Departs

In the spring of 1937, with Barlow in the midst of his studies at the Kansas City Art Institute, came the unexpected blow. A telegram from Mrs. Gamwell on March 12 told of Lovecraft's entrance into the hospital, and a letter that arrived a few days later told of Lovecraft's grave illness and his entrance into the Jane Brown wing of Rhode Island Hospital on March 10. On March 15 came the telegram informing Barlow of Lovecraft's death early that morning ("Last Days of H. P. Lovecraft"). Barlow was also informed that he had been named to take charge of Lovecraft's papers. Within a day or two he boarded a bus for the long ride to Providence; he arrived shortly after Mrs. Gamwell and Edward H. Cole had laid Howard to rest in Swan Point Cemetery on March 18. The first of the Barlow tributes titled "H.P.L." must date from these emotion-wrought days:

> There is engrained in us the twisted myth
> Which, using as symbol the change from worm to wings
> Or slain year's birth ensuing eager springs,
> Makes parables to silence weeping with.
> Since it distracts the empty hand of grief,
> I set the scentless blossom in my soil
> And seek to mend with slow uneager toil
> The ravaged plot, the broken stem and leaf.
> And I know I shall not fail, though wandering far
> To see the gulf which bounds my yesterday.
> Since Sorrow's word must hastily be drowned. . . .
> They prate of Somewhere, call you highly crowned
> With Christian wreaths throughout eternal day.
> You, who are crowned with Death's tremendous star!
>
> (EG 153)

Since Mrs. Gamwell wished to be alone following the loss of her nephew, Barlow took a room at the YMCA, about a fifteen- or twenty-minute walk from 66 College Street. During the day, still undoubtedly stunned by his loss, Barlow undertook the arrangement and disposition of Lovecraft's papers. Mrs. Gamwell showed him the letter she had found among Howard's papers naming Barlow as literary executor and giving him "first choice of all my

books and manuscripts" (Lovecraft, "Instructions in Case of Decease," 71).
The remaining instructions regarding specific books to be returned or be-
queathed Barlow fulfilled to the last detail. Various Lovecraft associates inherited individual books, and Lovecraft's large collection of amateur papers went
by his direction to the collection of amateur papers in the Benjamin Franklin
Memorial Library in Philadelphia.[9]

The decision seems to have been made at this point to deposit the bulk of
Lovecraft's correspondence and manuscripts in the John Hay Library of Brown
University, only a stone's throw from Lovecraft's home at 66 College Street.
Professor S. Foster Damon of the English Department and members of the Library staff collaborated with Barlow in the removal of the bulk of the Lovecraft
papers to the Library. Barlow packed for shipment to Kansas City some of the
Lovecraft materials he had not yet copied, Lovecraft's magazine files, and some
150 books from Lovecraft's library of several thousand. And then by April 2 he
was gone, headed back to Kansas City. With Mrs. Gamwell he thereafter exchanged several friendly letters, mostly concerned with arranging various minor matters appertaining to Lovecraft's literary estate. The correspondence
ended in 1940. Mrs. Gamwell maintained the house and Howard's possessions until her death in January 1941. The bulk of Lovecraft's library was
thereafter sold by Mrs. Gamwell's executor to Mr. H. Douglas Dana of Dana's
Old Corner Bookshop of Providence, R.I. Some of the books were purchased
by the Brown University Library, although most were scattered.

Upon his return to Kansas City, Barlow seems to have launched into a determined preparation of Lovecraft's remaining manuscripts for publication.
Deposits of Lovecraft material which Barlow and other Lovecraft associates
had finished transcribing continued to flow to the John Hay Library from
1937 to 1942. By October 1942, Barlow was completely cleaned out of Lovecraft manuscripts, with the exception of "The Shadow out of Time." He was
also diligent about seeing that Lovecraft's file of *Weird Tales* reached the Library. This file he had stored in various places in San Francisco prior to his
beginning his studies in Berkeley in 1941. A determined effort located all of
Lovecraft's file except the issues for 1923–25—the only Lovecraft materials
Barlow ever permanently misplaced, to the best of my knowledge. The other
issues, covering 1925 to 1937, were shipped to the Library in February and
March of 1942. Barlow promised to make up the missing issues from his own
collection, then in storage in Florida. Small shipments in April 1943 and
June 1946 completed the file from v. 2 no. 1 to v. 30 n. 3. Barlow eventually
supplied the library with microfilm of the scarce first volume (comprising the
first six issues). Barlow's last correspondence with the Library took place in
1946, in two letters dated June 1 and June 30 from his home in Azcapotzalco,
México. He proposed to send the Library the entirety of his remaining fantasy
collection including the 150 or so books he selected from Lovecraft's library

at the time of Lovecraft's death and the vast holdings of Yoh-Vombis stored in Florida—in return for a printing press and type for a Náhuatl newspaper he was at the time undertaking in México. By the time the Library had investigated the feasibility of Barlow's proposal, Barlow had apparently obtained a printing press and type elsewhere, and no further correspondence ensued.

At the time of his death in 1951, Barlow had with him in México perhaps 75 of the 150 books he removed from Lovecraft's library in 1937, his correspondence from Lovecraft, and no doubt a number of his copies of Lovecraft's manuscripts and a few associational items. The rest of his fantasy collection remained in storage at the family home in Florida, where his mother had apparently returned after Bob's college days in California. George T. Smisor, of whom more later, was named Barlow's literary executor; he took possession of the materials in México and no doubt contacted Mrs. Barlow with regard to the collection in Florida. In a letter of January 23, 1951, Mr. Smisor offered the entire collection to the John Hay Library; but again no arrangement was completed.

Barlow's other Lovecraftian activities for the years 1937–51 are rapidly summarized. The arrangement whereby the Lovecraft manuscripts were deposited in the John Hay Library, formalized by Barlow's note of March 3, 1939, gave the Library possession following his death. Barlow collaborated fully with August Derleth and Donald Wandrei in supplying material for the Arkham House editions of Lovecraft's works. Barlow seems to have always maintained a great respect for his early mentor, and regretted in print at least once that he did not have enough time to write a thorough evaluation. The tributes titled "H.P.L." continued through 1940 and the beginning of Barlow's association with Hart's activist group. There are other scattered poems of tribute dating as late as March 15, 1947. A number of unpublished Barlow manuscripts reportedly are in possession of Arkham House (Mooser).[10]

April 1937 found Barlow back in Kansas City. I do not know whether he continued his studies at the Art Institute for long after his return to Kansas City. Of all the phases of Barlow's career, the least has been written about his artistic endeavors. Of Barlow's art work, I have seen only a painting presented to Lovecraft on May 3, 1934, which is held in the Lovecraft Collection at Brown. The painting depicts a squatting monster (with snout and tentacles) glaring into the night on a moon-litten blue-green plain. There is a genuine touch of the macabre, but the piece is on the whole rather primitive, no doubt representing one of Barlow's earliest ventures into the genre. Other examples of Barlow's work undoubtedly reside in private hands. In 1969 Roy A. Squires offered for sale a bound notebook containing some 130 Barlow drawings—some Aztec-Mayan but most of them his conceptions of Lovecraftian monsters. The fine bookbinding that was done by Barlow also attests to his eventual prowess as an artist. Yet these interests were not to hold Barlow's central attention for long. He seems to have had a strong drive to attain intellectual and personal maturity through a career, and evidently eventually concluded that his prowess in art could not support such ambitions. Summer 1937 found him in Leavenworth; by winter 1937–38 he was back in Kansas City, apparently still pursuing his studies. A trip taken to México in the summer of 1938 seems definitely to have marked the end of his artistic studies.

During this period, Barlow seems to have been still very much involved in Lovecraftian activity, much of which has been detailed above. *Leaves* appeared in 1937 and 1938. During the period 1937–42 Barlow actively collaborated with Arkham House in assembling the material for the Lovecraft omnibuses. The very last Lovecraftian material he personally edited was the manuscript of Lovecraft's *Commonplace Book,* which was printed along with several other Lovecraft documents in May and June of 1938 by the Futile Press of Lakeport, California. The same press had brought out Clark Ashton Smith's *Nero and Other Poems* in 1937 and printed Clyde Beck's *Hammer and Tongs*—the first volume of science fiction criticism—in the same year it issued *The Commonplace Book.* November 1939 marked the publication of the first Arkham House volume of Lovecraft's work—only four years after the humble *Cats of Ulthar.* A new phase of Lovecraft's posthumous rise to fame was begun thereby, a phase in which Barlow was hardly to participate except as a trustee of manuscripts.

Indeed, a break with the past was apparent almost immediately after Lovecraft's death. Within months, Barlow had ceased to buy the pulps that he once lovingly collected for Yoh-Vombis. In fact, he had been railing against the low quality of the pulps for some years, and made quite a strong attack in the first issue of *Leaves,* but the cessation of collecting activity definitely heralds a significant break with the past. I doubt whether he ever again bothered to collect material in the fantasy genre, save perhaps for the initial volumes from Arkham House that August Derleth sent to him. Writing to the John Hay Library on June 30, 1946, Barlow said: "For my part, I'd prefer you to have everything, books, mss., drawings & even correspondence—the whole collection I assembled with such pains and enthusiasm, unconsciously building it around Lovecraft's personality & leaving it almost at once on his death."

3. The Activist Poet

His principal connection with the world of fantasy literature broken, Barlow seems to have turned to serious literature. While he had still been corresponding with Lovecraft, he had begun a serious novel; in 1936, as noted before, the Lovecraft-Barlow correspondence turned more and more to serious political and social questions. Summer 1938 marks a brief visit to México, heralding his developing interest in that ancient land. On September 7, 1938, he wrote to Professor S. Foster Damon of Brown: ". . . I have come to México, wound up with typhus, and am shortly returning to work this winter with a small press—thereby augmenting the output of printed verse in America yet a little more." The press to which he referred was the selfsame Futile Press of Lakeport, California, which had issued *The Commonplace Book* in May and June of 1938. Although there appears to be no book of verse bearing the Futile Press imprint for the period Barlow worked there in the winter of 1938-39, it is likely he helped Groo Beck, one of the partners in the Futile Press, with the printing of a posthumous collection of the poems of George Sterling (1869-1926), entitled *After Sunset*, issued by John Howell in San Francisco in 1939. Barlow himself wrote a brief introductory note for the book.[11]

Spring 1939 found Barlow residing in San Francisco, ready to begin what was to prove one of the most fruitful and significant periods of his life—as a poet. He had previously written some macabre poetry in a traditional vein—including the Edgar Allan Poe acrostic poem "St. John's Churchyard," and a memorial sonnet "R.E.H.," the latter of which appeared in the October 1936 *Weird Tales* (the only appearance of Barlow's fiction or verse in that magazine, as far as I have been able to determine from the Day and Cockcroft indices). In 1939, however, Barlow came into contact with the "Activist" group of poets led by Lawrence Hart in the San Francisco Bay area. The Activist group was founded by Hart in San Francisco in 1936 and included among its original members Rosalie Moore, Jeanne McGahey, Robert Horan, and Amelia Machatyre. One of the central tenets of Hart's group seems to have been the rejection of traditional poetic modes of expression. Hart, in essays he wrote for *Ideas of Order in Experimental Poetry* and the May 1951 issue of *Poetry: A Magazine of Verse*, outlines the thesis that emotion can be evinced more strongly by the subjective meanings of words than by their objective meanings. The Activists attempted to construct poetry almost exclusively through the connotative meaning of phrases, cutting out long passages of explanatory linkages long considered obligatory. The totality of the emotional impact of the poem would thus be imparted through a succession of connected connotative phrases, rather than by a simple narration. And the Activists did hit upon colorful and unusual phrases to use in their poetry—in fact, the phrases were meant to possess interest in their own right. Hart speaks of many face-to-face sessions at which the poets of his group worked out acceptable phrases, using examples that Hart had dug out of traditional poetry.

It was all undoubtedly a very new experience for Barlow. Apart from the close association with the other poets of the group, the rules of the game must have forced him into consideration of facts about his own life and personality which had never in his brief life before come to the surface. As he wrote in his brief piece in *Ideas of Order in Experimental Poetry*, "Lovecraft taught me to say what I had in mind; Hart underlined that expression was strongest when put in retina and esophagus-twitching words" (IO, 19). His poetry, he said in the article, was primarily visual in origin, arising usually from a scene he felt the desire "to paint in words," or perhaps occasionally from the sound of a spoken phrase or from a dream. From there, wrote Barlow, he would think about the painting he wanted to paint until some small meaning, some possible experience connected with the painting, came to mind; whereupon he would try to relate the experience to the picture through the connotative phrases of Hart's poetry. "All sorts of devilishnesses and indirect ways of saying things occur to me," he wrote (IO, 19), and it is veritably so, for his phrases are often pregnant with unexpected color and suggestion: "golden bladders of fish igniting the sea" ("The City," *EG* 194); "butterflies hook metal feet in vases" ("The City," *EG* 194); "the armored ants of pain exploring the marrow" ("First Year: Sebastian," *EG* 185); ". . . your ribs, that breathing box / filled with the jewels of air which feed the flood / of tumbling jewels and rubies of your blood" ("'Que Quieres? ¿Mis Costillas?'", *EG* 187); "a claw delicately holding air" ("On a Feather Poncho," *EG* 182); "the soft spider of his brain / weaves rapid angles" ("Date Uncertain," *EG* 175); "arabic of a tunnel written underground" ("blotted a beetle," *EG* 184); "a marshalling of bony mud" ("Fifth Year: Viktoria," *EG* 186); "the bees in your nostrils twitching their wings" ("Explanation to M.," *EG* 178); "the varnished bamboo green as a bug's underneath" ("We Kept On Reading 'Tuesday,'" *EG* 190); "where night is wedged between tulips on a hill" ("Framed Potent," *EG* 193). And if the images are brilliant at times, the weaving of a group of them into meaningful poetry is often more so. As Lawrence Hart observes, not all the poems are uniformly successful; sometimes the "devilishness" of his phrases seems to have taken too strong a hold on the poet, producing at times a near-Carrollian nonsense; witness the phrases "two velvet lobsters confer on the spelling of Babylon" ("Framed Portent," *EG* 193) and "the read-letter day Saint, Nathaniel Froghorn, base and viol" (in *Ideas of Order in Experimental Poetry*). There is also the delightful

Table Set for Sea-Slime

Clams claw their pots shut,
Sublimate their doors,
Slot their lophophores
On floors and floors
Of pearls and sycamores
At fours, and half past fours.

The small submerged fowl,
The gill-hung owl,
The crawling towel,
Locks up its drawers;
Surprising us spoons pulled out on floors,
Clams slain their clocks shut, button up their wars

At fours, and half past fours. (*EG* 185)

Entertaining as these phrases may be, the true core of Barlow's poetry lies in the "little meanings" that his most successful images provoke when woven into a unit as a poem. As Hart observes, while Barlow was an utterly up-to-date and innovative poet, his vision of the world was still a romantic, backward-looking one—with an aura of felt but inexpressible tragedy. His heavy use of Aztec and Mayan images reflected not only his preoccupying intellectual interests but also his love of lost peoples and times—and the consequent enigma of adjustment in the Machine Age. Recall his estimate of Lovecraft's greatness not as a creator of weird tales, however skilled Lovecraft may have been at the art, but as a man who lived a life of meaning in the increasingly meaningless age. There are often references to long-lost peoples and more meaningful ways of life:

> We have a word of their language—it means "god" (or, possibly, "devil")
> And a paper bagful of potsherds we think they made.
> These pieces of dishes are petals
> From one of the many flowers which here and there on the moun-
>   tains of Time,
> In summers, of a different sun and winters of a different rain,
> Have unfolded beyond the reach of our gathering.
> ("Tepuzteca, Tepehua," EG 183-84)

Sometimes there is also a wry skepticism about the importance of life:

The School Where Nobody Learns What

> Oh, only to be buried in Babylon,
> And you'll see what I mean.
> Seize a moment to lament,
> There is scarcely time even for that.

> Fill the little slate and call it done,
> You needn't come back tomorrow.

> The janitor is anxious to shelve Johnny Ape's Botany book
> With Jennifer Pterodactyl's. (*EG* 176)

That many of Barlow's poems are essentially "black," I think few will disagree; for the constant hints of the ineffable tragedy of the human condition I know no other close parallel than Kafka. There is a series of five poems written during the years of the Second World War in which Barlow, unlike other poets who have been seduced by visions of martial glory, clearly perceives the unholiness of the whole carnage:

First Year: Sebastian

If only once
Arrows have strained between hemp
   And bark,
And blood gone salt behind sewn lips,
Fifty vertical granite spires on the Norman coast
Or five hundred domes in Cairo and Sophia overscrawled with gold
   writing,
Could not sanctify the earth,
   Her seeds would be blackened.

If only once
Eyes had beheld the desperate rolling of eyes
—And not in a fever men cure; but in a
   fever where cure is forbidden—
Had beheld the armored ants of pain exploring the marrow,
All the chrysanthemum-heavy mist,
Green-and-salmon,
Of the endless dynasty of Sung
Could not cover the spotted soil of the world,
Not the towers of New York with their knives of light upheld.
But this!
What fruit do you anticipate in the orchard of your arrows,
O likewise young soldiers? (*EG* 185)

The final poem of this series, "Viktoria," is almost macabre in its evocation of the desperation of military victory. There are also more personal poems of dark complexion:

We Kept on Reading "Tuesday"

The collapsing garden, the varnished bamboo green as a bug's un-
   derneath,
The chopped tassel of the banana,
Purple rotting to scarlet on one seceding leaf—
Ants like thoughts working within a wound,
Burying glass mummies in capsules,
All was suddenly shadowed from the west.

Over so soon! There is no time
To write Harriet, or unclutter the calender
Of days invalid, whose folly is no longer optional,
The sun, too long on the vine, drops down.
Column pines support (like Chichen's walls)

> The parrot-colored lintel of the night.
> Fish eyes heaped up in a shell;
> The skeleton-jointed stars hold the world. (*EG* 190)

It would be wrong, however, to leave the impression of unrelieved darkness and gloom; there are indeed genuine instances of humor in Barlow's poetry, albeit sometimes "black" humor:

> Let us acknowledge we are tomcats mummified in alabaster vases
> With powdered stuff, nutmeg and bay leaves, flavoring the sockets of
> our eyes—
>
> ("Rainy Day Pastime," *EG* 195)

> One who did not
> Quarrel with the abbot over the right spot to plant parsnips
> Was certain to be transformed in the chronicle Brother Paul
> Was writing into an example of virtue.
>
> ("Of the Names of the Zapotec Kings," *EG* 192)

> They have condemned her flesh for settlements of worms,
> Who also have livers and lymph, and in a sense can be said to live,
> As indeed, one could say of Grandma.
>
> ("Mourning Song," *EG* 193)

Occasionally a note of whimsy asserts itself:

> Day is black if you like; I am convinced
> This bougainvilla
> Weighs more than those iron-livered hills.
>
> ("Respect Not the Leaf," [*AB*; as "[Untitled]" in *EG* 195)

Altogether, there are perhaps some 50 or 60 mature poems by Barlow that have seen publication; taken as a unit, they are an indelible personal relation of life by a man of obvious talent and perception.

Barlow remained closely associated with the Activists until he took up permanent residence in México in 1943. Rosalie Moore (1910–2000) left probably the most personal account of Barlow's development as a poet in her brief memoir in *Accent on Barlow: A Commemorative Anthology*, published by Lawrence Hart in 1962. One cannot do better than to quote her memoir in full; anything less would be a mere paraphrase of her words:

> With his scholarly bearing, large spectacled eyes, and precise manners, strict as a beetle, Robert Barlow was often such a person that you did not want, in his presence, to do anything that was not accurate, use the vague word, or keep any of your pretensions toward conventional falseness.

He also had a forbearance which allowed you time for making the right re-lation, and a great deal of warmth and sympathy which furnished a sort of climate in helping you to find it.

Sometimes, like the rest of us, he simply made mistakes of judgment, or burbled inaccuracies, and because they were stumbles or errors (and anyone with his brilliance of range was bound to make them) he would barely forgive himself; then, after a while, do so—although not until he had pounded unfor-givably on some bar, told an unpleasant anecdote, or executed some other saleable tantrum in self-revenge.

I have seen Robert Barlow also commit himself to the most joyfully aban-doned behavior, launch into a speech or a wild dance like a short Dionysus; yet in some way this was done as a matter of policy, forgiving himself in ad-vance.

This was the character of the man who wrote these poems, as we knew him in the Activist Group. If you could say only one thing about him, you would say he was a gentleman and a sort of pedant. But if you were allowed to say two, you would say that he was a breaker of forms. Actually, it was deeper than that. Barlow was an essentialist, and if he couldn't get to the center of a thing, he broke it.

However, Barlow did seem to gain an ability to evaluate the whole process during his Activist period, and to realize that feeling the censure of one's in-accuracies was all a part of the learning process. As he began to work with more skill in poetry, his confidence grew; and he stopped throwing the puni-tive tantrum which had been so hard to put up with. He changed from the unpredictable and difficult colleague, making an accurate personal alignment which lasted as long as we knew him.

Obviously, the transition from solitary bibliophile-fantasiste to poet was not an easy one for Barlow. Yet it was inevitably a step in his personal devel-opment—a step that enlarged the horizons of his life. Although the majority of his work as a poet was done in the period 1939-43, he remained a capable poet to the end of his days. In 1942, while he was an undergraduate at Berke-ley, his poems won both the Emily Chamberlain Cook Prize and the Ina Coolbrith Memorial Prize. Roy Squires relates that the Cook award "included an honorarium [of $65]—and the obligation to publish! For Barlow to have paid a commercial printer would have made his 'prize' a net financial loss." Barlow's friend George T. Smisor came to the rescue and printed a small booklet of Barlow's poems, entitled *Poems for a Competition*, without charge. In 1947 Barlow himself supervised the private publication of some of his best poems in *View from a Hill*. His work appeared in *Poetry, Saturday Review, Quar-terly Review of Literature*, the *Berkeley Journal, Circle, Contour*, and *Number*. Law-rence Hart included an article about Barlow and several of his poems in the May 1951 issue of *Poetry: A Magazine of Verse*, which was devoted to the Activ-ist group and was issued only a few months after Barlow's death. In 1962,

Hart published *Accent on Barlow: A Commemorative Anthology,* containing 39 of Barlow's poems (40 counting "From This Tree," which was used as the dedication) and others by various members of the activist group. (Also included was Barlow's translation of E. Ortiz de Montellano's macabre play *The Sombrerón.*) Of course it would be overstating the case to say that Barlow earned fame as a poet; his reputation is a minor one, and the number of people familiar with his poetry probably does not exceed the number of people familiar with him as the curator of Yoh-Vombis and the director of the Dragon-Fly Press. Yet one feels that these poems marked a distinct achievement for Barlow, albeit unrecognized by any large number of people.

4. Of the Names of the Zapotec Kings

The last phase of Barlow's life marks a significant departure: as a student of Mexican antiquities, he finally earned the distinction to which his genius was entitled, only to be cut off by his tragic suicide on January 1, 1951. To begin the story of Barlow's career in Mexican anthropology and history, one must again turn back the clock, this time to 1939 and San Francisco. That Barlow remained unsatisfied with his literary efforts is clear. Of course, every creative artist remains unsatisfied with his work, but with Barlow the discontent took other directions. The years of his literary and artistic efforts were those immediately following the Great Depression, and Barlow evidently felt a strong obligation to find some activity which he might adopt as a career. Ignacio Bernal observed that Barlow acquired from his father a strong sense of the dignity and necessity of work, in spite of his dislike of the military life which LTC Barlow had chosen. Barlow seems eventually to have concluded that his artistic and literary efforts could never serve as a career. Indeed, the candor which his work as a poet of the Activist school forced upon him seems to have been somewhat uncongenial: Barlow was always a very private man, and while he no doubt recognized the validity of poetic expression, he doubtless found such expression difficult. His tendency was always toward the cryptic and the concrete and away from the baring of his own emotions—although some of the poems do contain what one imagines must be quite a bit of his own inner feelings. Nor would an ordinary job in the outside world do. Barlow wrote (IO, 16) that he had always had difficulty dealing with ordinary business people in the everyday affairs of life. The beginning of his association with the Activists in 1939 found him still quite unsure of what he wanted to do with his life. A while later, he was classified 4F for U.S. military service, freeing him from that obligation.

According to George Smisor, it was Barbara Meyer, a leader of the National Youth Administration, who first understood Barlow's problems and suggested that he study anthropology and make scholarship in the field—an activity congenial to him from his publishing and bibliophile days—his life's work. Wrote Smisor: "She even suggested Mexican anthropology, introduced him to leading California professors in this field, and encouraged him to pursue such courses at the local junior college" (Smisor, 97-102). Barlow's attraction to Mayer's suggestion seems readily understandable. His love for archaic races and lost languages is clear from such early pieces as the "Annals of the Jinns." Clare Mooser, in her excellent article on Barlow in the *Mexico Quarterly Review,* makes what I think is the correct suggestion that Barlow identified the native peoples of México with Lovecraft's Old Ones or perhaps with the numerous "lost races" of fantasy fiction in general. Lovecraft had even adopted Mexican gods for use in the Cthulhu Mythos in a few stories—including "The Curse of Yig" and "The Mound," written in collaboration with Zealia Bishop. Many other pulp writers of the 1930s, including E. Hoffmann Price, Otis A. Kline, and H. Warner Munn, wrote stories with an Hispanic background—in most of which the Spaniard was depicted as the conventional evil and sensual villain, as witnessed in Munn's story "The Wheel" (*Weird Tales,* May 1933). Indeed, Barlow's sympathies in his research and writing seems to have been with the native peoples in the struggle to maintain their culture against the Spanish influx, although it would be ridiculous to attribute this sympathy to any pulp fiction he might have read in his youth, knowing his later contempt for the pulps in general. His respect for Hispanic culture was genuine, and any taking of sides was always within the bounds of professional scholarship. His fascination with the native peoples of México is clearly indicated in a number of his poems, including "Mourning Song," earlier quoted in part.

In any case, in 1939 or 1940 he began study at the Polytechnic Institute in San Francisco with the objective of learning the prerequisites for his chosen career. In the summer of 1940 he was registered at the National University Summer School in México City, studying Náhuatl, the ancient Indian language of the Valley of México, under the famous scholar Wigberto Jiménez Moreno. It was during this summer that he first met George Smisor, who was also taking Jiménez Moreno's Náhuatl course. The course met at 8 o'clock in the chilly Mexican morning, and as Barlow and Smisor later recalled: ". . . we forgot the cold drafts in our classroom in our enthusiasm to learn a half-legendary and difficult language from an eminent scholar" (Barlow & Smisor, ix-xi). Smisor wrote in his later obituary of Barlow that

> During that summer I often went to Barlow's apartment to study Náhuatl with him. This studying together gave me the opportunity to see Barlow's keen, nimble, and retentive mind at work. He had an intellectual driving force that never seemed to relax, that picked me up and carried me along with it, as it likewise did later many others. He had a facility of expression that brought life to long-dead happenings. This happy facility was a carry-over from

his years of reading and writing fantasy fiction and poetry. But there was nothing fantastic in this carry-over. He now insisted on accuracy of fact with brilliance of expression. At last he had discovered the career that appealed to him. He once said to me that summer, "This is the first time in my life I knew what I wanted to be. I'm going to devote myself to Mexican anthropology."

Even at this early date, Barlow and Smisor seem to have contemplated bringing into print some of the important unpublished source materials which they came into contact with in their studies of Náhuatl. This association was later to prove quite fruitful for scholarship in the field.

Returning to the States in the fall of 1940, Barlow completed a year at the Polytechnic Institute and then returned to México for the 1941 summer session. During this summer he also worked in the Mexican libraries with George Smisor, who photographed more than 16,000 pages of documents in the course of his work. Then in the fall of 1941 Barlow went with Smisor and his wife to Berkeley, where he began serious work in the department of anthropology under Dr. Alfred L. Kroeber. By 1942 Barlow was deep into research on México's native peoples; in a letter of February 25, 1942, addressed to Professor S. Foster Damon of Brown University *re* Lovecraftian matters, Barlow complained of the press of academic affairs, comparing himself with the ivory-tower academe suffering from "agoraphobia," or fear of open spaces. The same year saw his first scholarly articles, published in *American Notes and Queries,* and his attainment of the B.A. degree—the last degree that he ever bothered to obtain, although he did work equivalent to several Ph.D. dissertations. Frequent trips to México to consult rare documents and hunt for undiscovered material continued. Barlow shortly joined the faculty of the department of anthropology as a research assistant. Support from Berkeley continued through 1943, at the end of which year he seems to have become a permanent resident of México. Much of his later work was also supported by grants. He held a grant from the Rockefeller Foundation in 1944–45 and on April 14, 1945, was named a Guggenheim Fellow for the first of two consecutive years. In the last year of his life, he was an associate of the Carnegie Institute's Division of Historical Research, which supported his investigations into the Mayan culture in the Yucatan. While these grants allowed him the time for the immense amount of scholarly work he accomplished in his decade of activity (still known as the "Barlow decade"), he was also busy as a teacher, giving courses at the Universidad Nacional, the Escuela Nacional de Antropología e Historia, the Colegio de México, and México City College (later renamed the University of the Americas). Among the courses he taught were the ancient history of México, introduction to Mexican anthropology, modern Náhuatl, códices, source materials in ancient Mexican history, and bibliography. He also lectured to scholarly societies and worked temporarily at libraries like the Benjamin Franklin in México City. In 1948 he was named chairman of the department of anthropology at México City College, a post he held until his death. Although he seems to have been able to earn the independent living he desired, money was by no means ever plentiful. His house at 27 Santander, Azcapotzalco, D. F., acquired in 1945 or 1946, had to be mortgaged before his death, as he could not make ends meet.

For a non-expert to write of Barlow's career in Mexican anthropology is to experience as great an embarrassment as did Barlow when he was writing his memoir "The Wind That Is in the Grass" for the collection *Marginalia*, on July 9, 1944:

> Old respect and affection, all apart from his caliber as a personality, demand a very careful evaluation of Lovecraft, but there is no time. The fact that there is no time, which is no one's fault, seems full of disrespectful meaning.
>
> The publisher suggests I write "at least a little piece" for this volume, which must be printed at once, and though ten years have passed and Tlatelolco Xalliyacac in the rain of the cool summer night, with the *cargadores* asleep in the doors of saloons and *La Virgen de la Macarena* being played on someone's radio is in no way like the Florida countryside where Lovecraft visited me, I shall try to evoke that former landscape and the two vanished people who moved in it. (WG, 356)

It is equally impossible for one acquainted with Barlow mainly through the Lovecraftian connection to write an adequate appraisal of his scholarly work. Yet one feels that at least something should be included for the sake of accuracy and balance. Ignacio Bernal's obituary of Barlow in the *Boletín Bibliográfico de Antropología Americana* contains the fullest appraisal of Barlow's scholarly work, and the bibliographies published in the same periodical offer a guide to the more than 150 articles, books, and sets of notes that were published during his lifetime. The articles by Clare Mooser and George Smisor also include much useful information; I have of course relied heavily upon all of them.

One of Barlow's first projects, undertaken in collaboration with Smisor, was to bring into print at least a representative sample of the Indian códices that remained scattered in various libraries in and out of México. Wrote Barlow and Smisor in the preface to their publication *Nombre de Dios, Durango: Two Documents in Náhuatl Concerning Its Foundation:*

> It is not generally realized how voluminous the native literatures dominated by Náhuatl are, nor indeed how much these languages live today, in the face of four centuries' combat with Spanish. At the first, Náhuatl came close to being the official language of New Spain. . . . It is audacious to opine upon her [México's] colonial history without the constant consciousness of her submerged and slowly assimilating natives, who speak to us through such texts. If two hundred volumes of them were brought out, one might feel a little safer.

Barlow and Smisor never did achieve such a vast issuance of native materials, but an excellent beginning was made with *Nombre de Dios, Durango*, a small book containing two documents concerning the foundation of the town of Nombre de Dios in Durango. The book was brought out in an edition of 130 copies in 1943 by Barlow and Smisor under the imprint of the "House of Tlaloc," taken from the name of the "sometimes beneficent god of rain who makes vegetation prosper."[12] Smisor, who had been a printing teacher in the Sacramento City Schools, no doubt arranged for the issuance of the publication, which was distributed from his Sacramento address; he also made the English translation from the Spanish and Náhuatl text (1845) of the Indian lawyer Chimalpopoco Galicia, copied by him from the earlier Indian texts of the sixteenth century. Barlow did the accompanying map and footnotes, although he was in every sense a full collaborator in the publication. The book was a handsome and unorthodox one—with the text in Náhuatl, Spanish, and English given on each pair of facing pages. The documents were chosen from among those the great Mexican bibliophile and sometime politician José Fernando Ramírez left to the Archivo General de la Nación in México City.[13] Prior to the twentieth century, the great bulk of material that had been published in Náhuatl consisted of utilitarian grammars and religious texts, and Barlow and Smisor chose the documents as representative of the numerous more interesting historical texts that remained unprinted. The book enjoyed a good reception and encouraged Barlow and Smisor in undertaking the more ambitious project of issuing a scholarly journal that would have as its principal purpose the publication of such texts. They chose the name *Tlalocan*, meaning "Tlaloc's kingdom or domain," for their new journal, and, fortunate in their acquaintance, drew the prominent scholars Rafael García Granados, Wigberto Jiménez Moreno, Federico Gómez de Orozco, Paul Radin, and Carl Sauer as editorial advisors. Introducing the new journal to a war-torn world, Barlow and Smisor wrote in the first issue of *Tlalocan*:

> To begin a journal at this time dedicated not to aeronautics nor to the restitution of the Holy Roman Empire is not an easy task, but it is one worth while. Civilized people are fighting for fewer clichés than anyone has ever fought for, in the long run, and one of their goals is to open again the jailed universities and publishing houses of Europe and Asia; but in the manning of the guns to do this and the chemical factories has depopulated many of their own seminars and print shops. Yet what they do with the wrecked world afterward depends on what they know. A new scholarly journal is not, therefore, a thing inexplicable by the times, however distant its theme may appear to be.
>
> *Tlalocan* is called a journal of source materials on the native cultures of México. By México, however, we mean the whole area formerly embraced by New Spain, without any desire to offend patriots of neighboring states sliced off. By source materials, we mean primarily unpublished materials from ar-

chives, the thousands of folios lying safely (and sometimes not so safely) in libraries and private collections throughout the world, untouched by those who prefer to solve México's past by a citation of Clavijero. But source materials may mean also bibliographies and indexes to manuscripts or published materials, and we do not rule out the reprinting of source and fugitive items, which may briefly have been circulated before. Aside from documents, such things as *Bilderhandschriften*—the ambiguously named "códices"—and other such pictorial records, whether carved on rock or bone or hammered in gold, are eligible.

What we are after are materials which will contribute to an understanding and appreciation of the Indian peoples who have been so often libeled, grotesquely romanticized, or ignored by even their own ashamed descendants. Agreeing with Garciá Izcabalceta, we say: "Cada día echa mayores raíces en mi ánimo la convicción de que mas se sirve a nuestra historia . . . con publicar documentos inéditos o muy raros, que con escribir obras originales, casi nunca exentas de deficiencias y de errores."

Thus the materials we present may be texts in native languages, sometimes of purely linguistic, sometimes of mythologico-historical interest, or they may be descriptions of wicked dances buried in the formula of a proceso. They may be drawings off a vase. *Tlalocan* does not intend to become a vehicle for the publication of contemporary ethnographic or archaeological reports, for there already exist numerous journals in these fields. Nor will it feature studies based upon groups of documents, unless these discussions are of documents *Tlalocan* has pulished. Notes, queries, and reviews of occasional books or journals, with no pretense to completeness, will also appear in its pages. . . .

A first volume appeared in 1943–44, printed, distributed, and co-edited by Smisor. In its pages occurred many of Barlow's early articles—mostly texts he edited—and a multitude of scholarly notes and queries. Along with the footnotes in *Nombre de Dios, Durango*, these notes by Barlow in *Tlalocan* give a genuine flavor of his interests and erudition. "Barlow is a born historian," his teacher Dr. Kroeber is reported to have said once (quoted in Bernal). One of his interests, along with the customs and languages of the peoples he investigated, was the minutiae of their history. The following account of Moctezuma's dissolute sister, reproduced without footnotes from *Tlalocan*, 1, no. 1, pp. 73–75, gives a flavor of his penchant for this sort of detail:

> Among the historical data unlocked by Charles E. Dibble's edition of the *Códice en Cruz* is the only picture of the once-celebrated adulteress who was Queen of Texcoco in the late Fifteenth Century. Dibble quotes the 1498 entry from the *Anales de Cuauhtitlan* in his identification of the drawing, and the story from Ixtlilxochitl, but overlooks further details in Pomar, Chimalpahin, and the *Epistolario de Nueva Espana*, which enable us to restore the whole incident a little more critically.

222 THE UNKNOWN LOVECRAFT

Chalchiuhnenetzin was one of the sisters of the Younger Moctezuma. She was the one of the sisters to attain note, with the doubtful exception of the one who is said to have married the Zapotec cacique of Tehuantepec. Two other sisters whose names are not recorded married the caciques of Tecamachalco and Ocuilan, in eastern Puebla and southern México State, respectively; but they are shadows, while Chalchiuhnenetzin remains a definite personality.

Axayacatl, conqueror of Tlaltelolco and Toluca, had many wives and many children besides Moctezuma II. "The 18th child was a princess who was asked for by the king of Acolhuacan-Texcoco," Nezahualpilli, we are told. And other source speaks of Nezahualpiltzintli and "his legitimate wife," daughter of Axayacatzin, king of México.

A descendant of the Texcocan kings gives us the amplest version. Chalchiuhnenetzin was one of a number of noble maidens sent to the king of Texcoco, Nezahualpilli, for the latter's purpose of sorting them over, selecting a "legitimate wife," and keeping the rest for concubines. She being the daughter of his powerful western ally, the king saw fit to choose her. Since she was very young, the king put her away in a palace with idle hands and far too many servants. Being "astute and diabolical" and doubtless very bored, she began to have affairs with all the young men she fancied, afterwards killing them in remorse. She is said to have kept artisans busy making and adorning statues of them which she kept in her quarters—perhaps a garbled version of some funerary rite. These statues became very numerous, and the king asked her what they meant. She put him off by calling them her gods. Knowing the superstitious nature of his neighbor the Mexican king, and being a man of the world, he seems to have accepted this explanation.

Three of her lovers she had not slain, either because she was still diverted by them or because of their importance. One—which one is not stated—ruled the town of Tizayocán. This lack of efficiency on her part proved her undoing. One of the lovers was noticed by the king wearing a jewel he himself had given to the "astute" woman, and his suspicions were aroused. Going to her quarters at night, the king was told his lady was asleep, but pushed his way in and found only a wooden figure of her reclining on the couch. (Fatal predilection of hers!) Much afflicted, he called his guards, and soon routed out the missing wench performing certain questionable dances with all three of her lovers.

The matter was given to the judges—who can hardly have had much choice—and they found her and all her servants, artisans, jewelers, undertakers, and other helpers guilty. Persons of rank were condemned to strangulation, the traditional punishment for high-ranking citizens. This was carried out publicly, with full knowledge of her Mexican relatives. The *tlatoani* of México and Tlacopan attended the executions. Indeed, the former "came to kill her," says one account. All the neighboring princes who could be quartered in the town were invited, and they were required to bring along any young daughters who might profit by the example. Chalchiuhnenetzin and her three lovers were strangled, the others killed somehow, and their bodies burned with all the collection of statues. Some may even have been burned alive. The adulterous ashes were gathered in a great jar made especially for the purpose, and thrown into a gorge near the Temple of Adulterers. The archaeologists may seek it there.

A large number of people certainly perished in this affair. Two thousand, according to our chief informant; another lowers this to four hundred, both men and women, adding that "among these were very important persons."

The goods of the offenders were seized, and their houses razed. The ruins were conspicuous years after the Spanish conquest although these events took place in 1498, as we see confirmed in the *Códice en Cruz.*

Although "legitimate wife" Chalchiuhnenetzin left no blood in the veins of the Texcocan rulers, her status as a Queen must have contributed to the fratricidal strife prevailing when the Spaniards arrived. Her successor, Tlacoyehuatzin, became the mother of eleven princes (we are told), among them the pair Cortes found disputing the interrupted succession.

In 1945, on Barlow's recommendation, his collaborator George Smisor was appointed as Head of the Microfilm Laboratory, U.S. Archives, at the Benjamin Franklin Library in México City; in the press of his new duties, Smisor was no longer able to collaborate, leaving Barlow with the sole task of editing, printing, and distributing *Tlalocan.* Money was scarce and the survival of the journal must have been touch and go for some time, but Barlow finally managed to get out the first issue of the second volume in 1945, through the generosity of the Instituto Nacional de Antropología e Historia. A moving portrait of Barlow's plight and his scholarly vision can be seen in the editorial he wrote for this issue:

> Volume two of *Tlalocan* is begun herewith, at a changed address and lorn of one of its parents. Whether this and future volumes can be completed, depends wholly on whether or not the journal be favored with some subsidy, for the modern *Tlalocan* is not as opulent as the old. This number has been made possible only because the Institute Nacional de Antropología e Historia generously purchased a number of copies. Even this type of support was refused by another institution because *Tlalocan* is "not published by an institution," but most improperly "by the individual." The emergency help provided by the INAH is appreciated, but *Tlalocan* (unlike various political organs) cannot live in terms of perpetual crisis and alarum. Money is needed for printing and photo-engraving—perhaps even the routine hackwork of ruffling through a few old documents at hand, of scrawling of a haphazard copy, of slapping a few hasty and ill-considered notes onto this and glancing vaguely in on the printer from time to time should be recompensed—though it would be grotesque to propose that any special ability is needed for the production of such a journal as *Tlalocan*, or that it requires more than a few odd moments of the editor's endless lotus-filled leisure.

It is rather too bad, though. We were just beginning to feel a little like Francesco Petrarch amid the mouldy monastery books of Fourteenth Century Ghent or Verona. We were just toying with the idea of devoting a whole issue to documents about Don Pedro de Moctezuma Tlacahuepantzin Youalliehocatzin—principal heir of Moctezuma, and tippling lord of Tula. A body of Maya songs was troubling our conscience. We had hoped to straighten out the fate of that astonishing corpus, the Boturini Collection, what with one and another new document and a little long-distance exploration of the libraries of the world. Certain Tarascan pastorals had come to our attention. In fine *Tlalocan* was hearing and heeding Time's winged chariot, and planning its tasks as the latter-day heir of many great men and libraries. Siguenza and Boturini (we fancied), the Colegios of San Gregorio and Santa Cruz; Ramirez and del Paso; the former University and a hundred other persons and institutions had very considerably been engaged for some three or four or five centuries in the sole task of heaping up códices and chronicles and informes; in copying these and losing them and discovering them again, just for *Tlalocan*. They formed (we imagined) a fair staff of contributors for a journal which is too young to die.[14]

Fortunately, an able and sympathetic printer, Alan Farson of Cuernavaca, was found, and Barlow managed to complete the second volume of *Tlalocan* at the rate of one issue per year from 1945 to 1948. Papers from scholars continued to appear in abundance, and it is clear that *Tlalocan* had an enthusiastic if small audience. In addition to the duties of the editorship, Barlow continued his scholarly output; at this time he did a good deal of work with his friend and fellow Náhuatl scholar Byron McAfee. In 1949, with the first issue of the third volume, the San Jacinto Museum of History Association took over sponsorship of *Tlalocan*, through the efforts of George A. Hill. This undoubtedly left Barlow with more time to devote to his scholarly work. Upon Barlow's death, Ignacio Bernal and Fernando Horcasitas Pimentel undertook the continuation of *Tlalocan*. Smisor's obituary of Barlow appeared in v. 3 no. 2 (1952), and a few papers by Barlow appeared posthumously in this and the next two issues. After v. 3 no. 3 the support of the Museum Association appears to have lapsed, and Horcasitas concluded the series with a final issue in 1957.[15] Although this marked the end of the House of Tlaloc, the papers and notes that appeared in *Tlalocan* remain standard reference works for researchers in Mexican antiquities. *Tlalocan* was undoubtedly one of the major aspects of Barlow's scholarship, produced with more effort and personal sacrifice than he probably cared to admit.

Barlow's specialty was the native peoples of the Valley of México, those peoples once ruled by what is commonly called the Aztec Empire, but for which Barlow preferred the term Culhua-Mexica. However, his interest in the native peoples, languages, and history of México was omnivorous. One of his principal works was *The Extent of the Empire of the Culhua-Mexica*, researched at the Bancroft Library from March to December 1943, under the aegis of the grant he received from Berkeley. The study, a magnificently detailed piece of scholarship that set out to determine precisely which areas were subject or tributary to the Empire of the Culhua-Mexica, was revised periodically until May 27, 1946; it finally emerged from the University of California Press on March 25, 1949. Among the other works that Ignacio Bernal mentions as Barlow's most significant are "The Period of Tribute Collection in Mocte-zuma's Empire," "Materiales para una cronologia del imperio de los Mexica-nos," and "La fundacion de la Triple Alianza." Nor is this but a very partial list of Barlow's work: in connection with his teaching, he produced a number of sets of mimeographed course notes, including notes for a course in Náhuatl given while he was at México City College. Today, nearly every schol-arly work dealing with the native cultures of México, and especially with the Aztecs and Náhuatl language, is replete with references to Barlow's works. His ability to gain a rapid competence in any area he set out to investigate was al-most phenomenal. He had a fluent speaking knowledge of Náhuatl, an ac-complishment rare even among Mexican scholars. In the last year of his life, he began to investigate the Mayan culture and language, and after a very brief period of book study and a trip to the Yucatan he returned with a good, if imprecise, knowledge of Mayan. In preparation for a trip to Europe in 1948 to investigate códices in Paris and London, he provided himself with a work-ing knowledge of French in but a few days. So intense was his love of the na-tive languages that he often spoke Náhuatl instead of Spanish with those of his associates who also had mastery of the tongue.

Contrary to the impression one might form from what I have related pre-viously, Barlow did not achieve his tremendous erudition from books and códices alone. Although the native texts were his chief scholarly interest, he also did field work among the Mexican Indians—observing their culture and language and gathering examples of their myths and legends. An expedition to western Guerrero in the spring of 1944 brought him into contact with the remains of the mysterious Tepuzteco, or Copper People, about whom he penned the moving poem "Mourning Song." Again in the poem "Stela of a Maya Penitent" we see his love of the Indian cultures:

> While the Jaguar clambered down the night and the Turtle clam-
>   bered up,
> What silver honey did you browse in at the pace of trees budding,
> In your world that never heard of Caesar? (AB)

Barlow's concern for the Indian did not stop at the conquest, but carried over strongly to the Indians of his own time. In 1945 he was appointed by the Mexican government as director of the literacy campaign among the Indians of Morelos. Finding that the Indians had virtually nothing to read in Náhuatl,

Barlow set up a print shop at his Azcapotzalco home and printed some thirty-four issues of *Mexihkayotl,* a small newspaper in Náhuatl. His principal collaborator in this endeavor was the Náhuatl scholar Miguel Barrios E. Barlow also brought Indians from remote corners of the republic to his Azcapotzalco home to be educated in their native tongues while working for him in the house and the print shop. In time, Barlow became a sort of minor folk hero among the Indians of his region. Of course, he continued his own investigations of the Indians—their culture, language, myths, and history. A fitting tribute to his work was penned by his secretary, Lieutenant Antonio E. Casteñada, in a letter sent to George Smisor following Barlow's death:

> Vivió entre nosotros saboreando nuestros idiomas con dulzura, y amó tanto al Indio mexicanos que convivía con él a gusto pleno; pero al mismo tiempo que saboreada sus idiomas, sus platillos y sus costumbres, lo estimulaba hacia el progreso que había de redimirlo de las condiciones en que vive. . . . Yo me considero altamente privilegiado por haber estado al servicio de ese genio en ciencia y en bondad. Mi agradecimiento como Mexicano hacia él será imperecedero, porqué en verdad genios extranjeros como él que dedicó en cuerpo y alma a todo lo mexicano, son muy raros en mi país.[16]

5. Tragedy

There remains precious little to tell of Barlow's life. In 1948 came the appointment as chairman of the department of anthropology at México City College. At the time México City College was a raw, young institution, but had drawn the heady intellectual adornment of scholars such as Pablo Martinez del Rio, Ignacio Bernal, Wigberto Jimenez Moreno, Pedro Armillas, Fernando Horcasitas Pimentel, Luis Weckmann, Justino Fernandez, Pedro Bosch Guimpera, José Gaos, and Edmundo O'Gorman. The same year found Barlow studying Mexican manuscripts in Paris and London libraries, at the very peak of his scholarly career and output. His last year—1950—saw his rapidly developing investigation into the Maya and the foundation of a second journal in the field of Mexican anthropology, entitled *Mesoamerican Notes.* Barlow handset the first two issues of *Mesoamerican Notes* and printed them two sheets at a time on his press at Azcapotzalco. Some 350 copies of the first issue and 500 of the second were produced (Paddock). The journal had much the same flavor and content as *Tlalocan,* with perhaps a somewhat wider range of subject matter, including in the second issue Fernando Horcasitas Pimentel's series of descriptions of "La Llorona," the Mexican mother condemned for the murder of her children. *Mesoamerican Notes* has been continued by the department of anthropology at the University of the Americas, where John Paddock is the present editor [at the time of the writing in the early 1970s]. By this time, the strain of overwork was beginning to tell, and in the summer of 1950 Barlow was given leave of absence because of health. Perhaps in an effort to regain his spirits, Barlow planned a series of costume parties for his Azcapotzalco home—in which guests were to come attired as Aztec gods—but only one such party ever took place. A growing disillusionment with his life and career seems to have added to his nervous agitation. Clare Mooser states that he was badly mistreated by some of the Indians who stayed at his house toward the last.

In any case, following an uncharacteristically fashionable New Year's Eve party, Barlow locked himself in the bedroom of his Azcapotzalco home on the afternoon of January 1, 1951, leaving a note on the door in Maya reading "Do not disturb me, I wish to sleep a long time," or something to that effect. Inside, he penned an eighteen-page letter in Spanish to Dr. Pablo Martinez del Rio, one of his few close friends, and then killed himself by taking twenty-six tablets of Seconal. Reading his message, the Mayans living at his house at the time did not disturb him, and his body was found on January 2, 1951. The letter written to Martinez del Rio, speaking of insomnia and other personal problems, was subsequently burned. Barlow's body was cremated and the ashes buried in the Desierto de Leones with only Martinez del Rio in attendance. Martinez del Rio was named executor and took charge of Barlow's papers. The bulk of the unpublished scholarly papers were classified by anthropologists Charles Wicke and Fernando Horcasitas Pimentel and now reside in the Archivo Barlow of the University of the Americas; a few may still be in the custody of the family of the late Dr. Pablo Martinez del Rio. Barlow's literary papers, books, and magazines were entrusted by Martinez del Rio to Barlow's old friend and collaborator George T. Smisor, then still working at the Benjamin Franklin Library in México City, since he was the only person in México very familiar with Barlow's literary work. A word has been said previously about the provenance of these collections.

The personal reasons for Barlow's suicide are hardly a fit subject for many words; any real knowledge of the immediate causes of his death went to the grave with the late Martinez del Rio. Shy and introverted, Barlow undoubtedly suffered from some social maladjustments; these may have complicated and worsened his nervous collapse in 1950. Clare Mooser states that Barlow was almost invariably ill at ease at social functions; his idea of a series of costume parties in 1950 hints of an attempt to break loose from his essential loneliness and solitude and to resurrect the kind of social relationships he had while he was a member of the Activist circle of poets. In the end, the "personal problems" that Barlow mentioned in his suicide letter form only part of what must have been some greater disillusionment.

In her paper, Clare Mooser sees Barlow as a sort of Mexican T. E. Lawrence, an exile from his own land, a lover of another race and culture, a man who burnt out his life with feverish activity before the physical end came. Of these theses I am of a mind to object only to the last—Barlow's suicide seems to me to have been much more probably the result of a deep spiritual malaise than of overwork and strain. Lawrence Hart perhaps makes a closer approximation to the truth when he states in his brief memoir that "Barlow fled from every success he ever had" (Hart, 1951, 115). Indeed, at various times during his life, Barlow seems to have been mortally dubious of the worth of his own activities—in spite of the fact that he excelled in almost everything he tried. That he was an idealist who lived for his visions seems clear; whenever these visions slipped somewhat out of focus in making some sort of adjustment, Barlow seems to have experienced a crisis.

Probably the happiest period of his life was his decade of intense scholarly devotion to the antiquities of México, a decade in which the goals of his life were well in focus. Undoubtedly, the period of his mature relationship with Lovecraft was another period of fulfillment and happiness. While the urgent necessity to do something "worthwhile" was certainly not the reason for Barlow's succession of careers, the notion—which must have been impressed quite strongly upon him by the Great Depression—was always a factor. Deeper, perhaps, was the necessity to get at the "real" concerns of life. Barlow, like his mentor Lovecraft, was no believer in the Christian God, and thus had to make his own accommodation with life—and its succession of grief, happiness, failure, achievement. Like many another sensitive person, Barlow simply chose to reject everyday life for the core of his existence and to exist in terms of his intellect—first in the world of wonder and beauty constructed by Lovecraft; then in the wider realms of art, literature, and poetry; and finally in the magnificent world of scholarship. That he came to question each of these worlds in succession reflects more nearly his chronic intellectual activity and self-evaluation than any deep-seated morbidity and maladjustment.

One can imagine the occasional qualms he must have felt about the vast indifference with which the world at large received the fruits of his genius. When a friend once remarked that he was overtiring himself, Barlow burst into tears: "After I am dead, which will be soon, who is going to work on this codex? It may be two hundred years before anyone looks at it again!" (Mooser). His achievements were nearly all single-handed, accomplished with the help of a very few friends and collaborators. That he came to doubt the worth of his scholarly life in personal terms is believable; that he literally burned out his interest in scholarship by overwork, less so. After all, this scholarship was the relish and lasting achievement of his whole life. Rather, I would suppose, the mortal doubt, the ever-recurring self-examination in personal terms, interposed and perhaps coupled with the strain of overwork and personal problems, snapped the cord of meaning and continuity that had sustained him in his great achievement of 1939-51. While the poems of his Mexican years, printed in *View frow a Hill* under the heading "Frescoes of

Priests and Beans," are predominantly redolent of his fascination with the ancient peoples of México, the dark element of doubt as to the validity of life itself shows up consistently in his poetry in general. Clare Mooser chooses the poem "New Directions" as an example of this type of darkness in Barlow's poetry; it is a fine choice. Also redolent of darkness were the poems that Barlow wrote about the World War. Another which seems especially grim in its impatience with life and its foreboding of death is

A Escoger

Strophe:
Manifestly you cannot sit
Forever in this draughty antechamber
And your host off drunk in another universe,
But the question is, which door?
They are all so nicely hung
With the same every coloured curtain
That the first or the third or the fourth
Seems adequate,
Save for a suggestion of mice
Or whispering, or bones not too well cured
Or other flowers behind them.

Antistrophe:
Whichever you choose will lead
To no amazing golden berries
Or rain of music, or flares
Of ports across the hills to the sea,
Whichever you choose, and you may not delay forever,
Given on a black garden where gargoyles have gone mad
From the starlight.

Strophe:
Whichever you choose will be wrong
But what else can you do with a life? (EG 189)

And so, at the age of thirty-two, Robert Barlow decided that January 1st of so many years ago to pass through the gate. What of Sterling and Howard and Bierce?—indeed, of the Tepuzteco?—they had all passed through. Lovecraft had spoken of it, darkly. But Barlow found at last the world no longer an adequate waiting place, no longer a place suitable for the environment and pursuit of his dreams; he took the step through the gate. Many people of many places thus lost a friend in spirit, and a ripple went through the worlds in which he had created. Though Robert Barlow chose to break the last and most brilliant of the lives he carved out for himself, the reliquiae of his few brief years of genius will live on—for those who knew him through Lovecraft, for those who knew him as a poet, for those who knew him through his love of México and her native peoples:

Having done what was mine to do,
Like the snow falling,
Having fingered the earth, the fern, the soft skeleton of the twig,
And having slid the latch of every wasp-visited gate,
I claim to know these fields.
* * *
If I trace out again any path,
My orbit will be not more unexplained than the suns,
My curving trend then that of the long-named planets.

—"View from a Hill" (*EG* 188)

Acknowledgments

Special Thanks to Marcos Legaria for reviewing the Spanish names and phrases in this article.

Notes

1. George T. Smisor microfilmed all the literary papers and correspondence that Barlow had with him in Mexico at the time of his death. The Barlow family has a collection of material consisting mostly of letters of Barlow to various members of his family. Both collections include examples of Barlow's drawings. Both have been copied for the collection of material that I deposited at the John Hay Library.

2. There exist at least four other Lovecraft-Barlow collaborations in the files of the Hay Library. One is a single sheet entitled "Bout Rimés" and contains the two parodies reproduced herein; it is filed among Lovecraft's poems. Another is a manuscript of three leaves entirely in Barlow's hand entitled "Collapsing Cosmoses: A Fragment," as by "Hammond Eggleston." I doubt Lovecraft had much of a role in this interplanetary farce. The fourth manuscript is Lovecraft's revision of Barlow's "'Till A' the Seas," published in the *Californian*, the *Arkham Collector*, and *The Horror in the Museum and Other Revisions*; it is perhaps typical of the early pieces Lovecraft revised and criticized for Barlow. The fifth and last collaboration in the files is a fragmentary essay on national defense by Barlow's father, with indications that some suggestions for it were made by Lovecraft. Such an essay appears in the *Californian* under the byline of LTC Barlow. Of the parodies, "The Battle That Ended the Century" was published in *Something about Cats* (1949).

3. In 1940, when the second Arkham House Lovecraft volume was starting to be organized, Barlow, then living in San Francisco, found his copies of *The Case of Charles Dexter Ward* and *The Dream-Quest of Unknown Kadath* inaccessible in Kansas City. He thereupon borrowed the original manuscript versions, which had been deposited earlier in the John Hay Library, returning them to the Library in late 1941. Perhaps this is the origin of stories that the text of these two novels was temporarily "lost." Barlow was scrupulous in his care of Lovecraft materials insofar as I have been able to deter-

mine. The only significant materials that were ever permanently removed after having been deposited in the John Hay Library were the letters that Robert Ervin Howard (1906–1936) wrote to Lovecraft, which were deposited in March 1937 and removed later in the same year to go to Dr. I. M. Howard (1871–1944), who wished to deposit them in the memorial collection of his son's materials in the library of Howard Payne College in Brownwood, Texas. For some reason, Dr. Howard shortly thereafter removed all the Howard materials from Howard Payne College; shortly before his death in Ranger, Texas, on 12 November 1944, Dr. Howard sent some of the papers to E. Hoffmann Price, who had originally been named Howard's literary executor. Through a series of loans, the Howard letters to Lovecraft were eventually lost. They are believed to have been in the possession of Francis T. Laney (1916–1958), the editor of the Lovecraftian journal the *Acolyte* (1942–46), at one time. Laney was one of the few Lovecraftians I know to have corresponded with Barlow after 1938, aside from August Derleth of Arkham House. About 1944 Barlow sent Laney several packets of Lovecraft material (no doubt typewritten copies) for possible use in the *Acolyte*. [After these lines were written, Glenn Lord, administrator of the estate of Robert E. Howard, succeeded in locating the Howard letters to Lovecraft, some of which have appeared in Howard's *Selected Letters* published by Necronomicon Press. The location of Lovecraft's letters to Howard is still unknown to me, but Messrs. Derleth and Wandrei did borrow them from Dr. Howard during the latter's lifetime and extracts have appeared in Lovecraft's *Selected Letters*.

4. Years later, the estate of one of Barlow's students donated the autograph manuscript of "The Shadow out of Time" to the Lovecraft Collection at Brown University.

5. Barlow seems to have had a strong admiration for Whitehead, who also became a lover of foreign culture. His admirable biography of Whitehead, which appeared in the collection *Jumbee and Other Uncanny Tales* (1944), perhaps atoned for his inability to issue *Caneviniana*. Barlow did type some of the Whitehead letters onto stencils, and these were eventually reproduced and circulated through the Fantasy Amateur Press Association by Paul Freehafer in 1942.

6. Barlow did receive letters and manuscripts from Robert Ervin Howard before Howard's suicide in 1936. After Howard's death, he proposed publishing a memorial collection of poetry. After Barlow's association with the brothers Beck of the Futile Press in Lakeport, California, he collaborated with Groo Beck, one of the brothers, in the printing of George Sterling's *After Sunset* in San Francisco in 1939. Although the book bore the imprint of bookseller John Howell, Barlow and Beck considered it the first publication of their "Druid Press." No books were ever actually published by the Druid Press, but Barlow and Beck kept the Howard poems under consideration for some time. At the request of Dr. Howard, Barlow microfilmed the poems he was interested in seeing in book form and returned the original manuscripts to Dr. Howard's agent, Otis A. Kline, in February 1940. This microfilming was a happy circumstance, since many of these poems are known only in the form of the microfilm copy. On 1 April 1941, Dr. Howard wrote to Kline to ask him to withdraw the

offer to the Druid Press. Barlow deposited the microfilm of the Howard papers at the Bancroft Library, University of California at Berkeley.

7. Lovecraft's list for the proposed contents of this collection was published in *Lovecraft Studies* Nos. 22/23 (Fall 1990): 68.

8. Adolphe de Castro, letter to H. P. Lovecraft, 12 August 1936 (ms., John Hay Library).

9. These amateur papers have now been moved to the Special Collections Department of the University of Wisconsin at Madison (Library of Amateur Journalism Collection).

10. Peter Ruber of Arkham House located these manuscripts and made them available for study.

11. In a letter to August Derleth dated 3 June 1938 (ms., State Historical Society of Wisconsin), Barlow wrote: "I am living on Telegraph Hill with Groo Beck; we are printing a collection of new George Sterling poetry which I compiled and edited from manuscript sources."

12. *Tlalocan* 1, No. 1 (1943): 1.

13. Ramirez must have been a bibliophile after Barlow's heart, since many of the documents he collected proved to be quite useful in Barlow's own research. Barlow himself seems to have lost most of the collector's urge by this time; the following amusing note occurs in a letter to Professor S. Foster Damon regarding the deposit of the Lovecraft-Barlow file of *Weird Tales* in the Lovecraft Collection at Brown: "Later on, when the fact gets around that you have these rare and sacred issues, you'll have to keep an eye on any young devotees who may consult them and have a pocketful of razor-blades, like the German scholars in the Archivo General in Mexico, who are always snipping out documents for their own files! I know the bibliophile, as opposed to the scholar, too well." Interestingly enough, Barlow obtained microfilm copy of one of Ramirez's books from the John Carter Brown Library at Brown University. Barlow was a great devotee of microfilm, to which he was introduced by Professor Damon. Some of the materials in the Lovecraft Collection were deposited in the form of microfilm.

14. *Tlalocan* 2, No. 1 (1945): 2.

15. *Tlalocan* has been revived in the past few years by Fernando Horcasitas.

16. Quoted in George T. Smisor, "R. H. Barlow and *Tlalocan*." "He lived among us, savoring our languages with humility, and loved the Mexican Indian to such an extent that he lived alongside of them with complete pleasure, but at the same time that he was relishing their languages, their food, and their customs, he urged them toward the progress that would set them free from the conditions in which they live. I consider myself highly privileged to have been in the service of that genius in science and goodness. My gratitude as a Mexican toward him will prove imperishable, because in truth foreigners like him who dedicate himself in body and soul to everything that was Mexican, are extremely rare." (Translation by Donald Sidney-Fryer.)

Bibliography

Accent on Barlow: A Commemorative Anthology. Ed. Lawrence Hart. San Jose, CA: Privately printed, 1962. [Abbreviated in the text as *AB*.]

"The Barlow Tributes." In H. P. Lovecraft and Divers Hands, *The Shuttered Room and Other Pieces*, ed. August Derleth. Sauk City, WI: Arkham House, 1959.

Eyes of the God: The Weird Fiction and Poetry of R. H. Barlow. Edited by S. T. Joshi, Douglas A. Anderson, and David E. Schultz. New York: Hippocampus press, 2002.

"Introduction" (with George T. Smisor). In *Nombre de Dios Durango.* Sacramento, CA: House of Tlaloc, 1943. ix-xi.

Letter. *Fantasy Fan* 1, No. 12 (August 1934): 178.

O Fortunate Floridian: H. P. Lovecraft's Letters to R. H. Barlow. Edited by S. T. Joshi and David E. Schultz. University of Tampa Press. 2007.

Poems for a Competition. Sacramento, CA: The Fugitive Press, 1942. [Abbreviated in the text as *PC*.]

A View from a Hill. Azcapotzalco, D.F.: Privately printed, 1947. [Abbreviated in the text as *VH*.]

"The Wind That Is in the Grass" (1944). In *Lovecraft Remembered*, ed. Peter Cannon. Sauk City, WI: Arkham House, 1998. [Abbreviated in the text as *WG*.]

Secondary

Baldwin, F. Lee. "Within the Circle." *Fantasy Fan* 1, No. 11 (July 1934): 164.

——. "Side Glances." *Fantasy Fan* 2, No. 1 (September 1934): 13–14.

Bernal, Ignacio. "Robert H. Barlow." *Boletin Bibliografico de Antropologia* 13, No. 1 (1950): 301–4.

Hart, Lawrence. "A Note on R. H. Barlow." *Poetry* 78, No. 2 (May 1951): 115.

Hart, Lawrence, ed. *Ideas of Order in Experimental Poetry.* San Francisco: George Leite, 1945. [Abbreviated in the text as *IO*.]

Jordan, Stephen J., "H. P. Lovecraft in Florida," *Lovecraft Studies* No. 42–43, pp. 32–45.

"The Last Days of H. P. Lovecraft: Four Documents." *Lovecraft Studies* No. 28 (Spring 1993): 36.

Lovecraft, H. P. "Instructions in Case of Decease." *Lovecraft Studies* No. 11 (Fall 1985): 71–73.

Monjarás-Ruiz, Jesús, Elena Limón Rios et al., *Obras de Robert H. Barlow,* vols. 1-7, México City and Puebla: Instituto Nacional de Antropológica e Historia (INAH) e Universidad de las Americas (UDLA), 1987-1999.

Monjarás-Ruiz, Jesús, and Elena Limón Rios, *La Obra Historico-Antropologica de R. H. Barlow*, México City and Puebla: Instituto Nacional de Antropológica e Historia (INAH) e Universidad de las Americas (UDLA), 2005.

Mooser, Clare. "A Study of Robert Barlow: The T. E. Lawrence of México." *México Quarterly Review* 3, No. 2 (1968): 5–12.

Paddock, John. "Preface." *Mesoamerican Notes* Nos. 7/8 (México City: Department of Anthropology, University of the Americas, 1966): vii.

Smisor, George T. "R. H. Barlow and 'Tlalocan.'" *Tlalocan* 3, No. 2 (1952): 97–102.

Roy A. Squires, *Catalog II: Clark Ashton Smith, H. P. Lovecraft, R. H. Barlow*. Glendale, CA: Squires, n.d. [1969].

Wollheim, Donald A. "Phantascope." *Phantagraph* 2 (November 1936): 3.

Robert H. Barlow as H. P. Lovecraft's Literary Executor: An Appreciation

The question has often been asked: How did it come to pass that Robert H. Barlow, a youth who had not yet attained his nineteenth birthday at the time of the death of H. P. Lovecraft on March 15, 1937, was designated by the twentieth-century American master of supernatural fiction to manage his literary affairs after his death? Frankly speaking, the question was asked by many friends and correspondents of Lovecraft of maturer years and longer standing. August Derleth and Donald Wandrei, who in the days immediately following Lovecraft's death determined that they would see the work of their mentor preserved in hardcovers, pondered the question of the eighteen-year-old "literary executor" (as Lovecraft's "Instructions in Case of Decease" had described his duties) long and hard. Lovecraft's longstanding amateur friend, W. Paul Cook, when he read the news, undoubtedly had difficulty believing his eyes.

Cook, who single-handedly persuaded Lovecraft to return to the writing of supernatural fiction in 1917, published several of Lovecraft's stories in his own amateur magazines and capped the achievement with the publication of Lovecraft's extended essay "Supernatural Horror in Literature" in the *Recluse* in 1927. Cook, a printer by trade, did yeoman's work for amateur journalism; and by the late 1920s he was issuing under his Recluse Press imprint handsome books that were noted by the book-collecting world at large. Under the Recluse Press imprint, he published works by Frank Belknap Long, Donald Wandrei, Samuel Loveman, John Ravenor Bullen, and others in the Lovecraft Circle. By 1928, Lovecraft's novelette *The Shunned House* was complete in an edition of 300 copies in unbound sheets; but then disaster struck. Cook's wife passed away, he lost his printer's job in Athol, Massachusetts, and his personal problems overcame him. A removal to the Midwest to reside with fellow amateur Paul J. Campbell and his wife removed Cook from the possibility of the frequent visits with Lovecraft that he had previously enjoyed. In 1934/35, based upon the recommendation of Lovecraft, he had shipped to Barlow from his sister's home in New Hampshire the remainder of the unbound sheets of *The Shunned House,* in the hope that Barlow would be able to bind and distribute the book. Alas, the break-up of the Barlow household in Florida in 1936 prevented the achievement of this goal, and Barlow managed to bind and distribute a bare half-dozen copies. *The Shunned House* again went into storage, and Cook was disillusioned. (The remainder of the edition was finally transferred to Arkham House, either by Barlow himself or by his mother following his death in 1951. In 1961, Arkham House bound and of-fered for sale 100 copies out of the original edition.)

Even worse, after Barlow had taken charge of Lovecraft's literary papers, he proceeded in the summer of 1937 to issue from Leavenworth, Kansas, the first number of a literary magazine, *Leaves*, whose contents he and Lovecraft had planned together during the balmy Florida days. Among the material chosen for the first issue was Edith Miniter's sketch "Dead Houses," which many ama-teurs, including Cook, considered the finest example of the late amateur au-thor's New England regional work. (Mrs. Miniter, who had died in 1934, published one book, *Our Natupski Neighbors*, with Henry Holt in 1916.) Cook had long planned "Dead Houses" as the centerpiece for a Miniter memorial volume that he envisioned as a posthumous tribute and for which Lovecraft himself had written an extended appreciation. (This latter, together with a considerable amount of the other material originally intended for the Miniter Memorial, eventually appeared in Hyman Bradofsky's handsomely printed magazine the *Californian*, the premier amateur journal of its day.) *Leaves* was neatly produced by mimeograph, with the financial assistance of longtime amateur Ernest A. Edkins, but this did not assuage Cook's rage at Barlow for "stealing" this item originally intended for the Miniter memorial volume. Lovecraft himself considered Barlow "unreliable," as he fumed about him in correspondence.

How indeed did such a young and inexperienced literary executor come to be chosen by Lovecraft? Had Lovecraft died before his marriage in 1924, there is no question that Cook would have been responsible for whatever modest posthumous recognition the Providence writer might have achieved. Had death taken the author during the period of his marriage to Sonia Greene, there is little question that Sonia would have played a primary role in the management of his posthumous literary affairs. After the author's return to Providence in 1926, there is little question that Cook, who visited him while he was still unpacking at 10 Barnes Street, would have played a predominant role in the event of his untimely death, especially after the Lovecraft marriage finally came apart in 1928 and Lovecraft in 1929 gave his wife to understand that the marriage had ended. (Lovecraft, at Sonia's insistence, had sued for divorce in the Rhode Island courts on the grounds of abandonment; but, as Cook and a few other intimate friends knew, Lovecraft could not bring him-self to sign the final divorce decree, protesting that a "gentleman" did not di-vorce his wife without good cause.) But then Cook's personal tragedies, of which Lovecraft was well aware, reduced their relationship to a very infre-quent correspondence.

During the 1930s, other friends and correspondents came forward to as-sist Lovecraft in the promotion of his literary efforts. Lovecraft himself hated typing, and numerous friends and correspondents assisted him with putting his manuscripts into typescript over the years. Some revision clients were even known to pay off debts in this manner. By this time, rejections by *Weird Tales* and by book publishers to whom he had submitted his stories had reduced Lovecraft to a very low opinion of his literary work, for it appeared he could neither satisfy the demands of Farnsworth Wright for more "action" nor meet the requirements of the book editors for more sophistication. Actually, I believe that the primary impediment to the book publication of Lovecraft's work was not lack of sophistication, but the lack of a full-length novel, which publishers then and now have always preferred to story collections. Had Lovecraft prepared *The Case of Charles Dexter Ward* for publication following its completion in 1927, instead of allowing it to remain in manuscript in his files until Barlow coaxed it out of him for typing in 1934, I believe that Lovecraft would probably have seen this work professionally published. The success of a novel-length work would in turn have paved the way for publication of a story collection. But it was not to be. Such was Lovecraft's discouragement that his friend Donald Wandrei submitted "The Shadow out of Time" to *Astounding Stories* on his own initiative in 1936; the result, in conjunction with agent Julius Schwartz's earlier selling of *At the Mountains of Madness* to the same magazine, was Lovecraft's largest single literary check, $595, which relieved an economic situation so pinched that the author was not able to take one of his customary summer jaunts southward in that year. Regrettably, Lovecraft himself always had a tendency to regard Farnsworth Wright's judgment as final; perhaps he feared to alienate the one market he had developed through the placement of work elsewhere. Wright had been displeased by the appearances of "The Colour out of Space" in *Amazing Stories* in 1927 and of "Cool Air" in *Tales of Magic and Mystery* in 1928.

After Lovecraft's death, August Derleth's efforts to persuade publishers, including his own, to undertake a collection were unsuccessful, so that he and Donald Wandrei finally decided to publish the first collection, entitled *The Outsider and Others*, on their own under the Arkham House imprint in November 1939. The honor of placing a published book in Lovecraft's hands fell to the young amateur printer, William L. Crawford, who delivered *The Shadow over Innsmouth* to Lovecraft under his Visionary Press imprint during the final months of Lovecraft's life, in November 1936. (Barlow did bind a half-dozen copies of the edition of *The Shunned House* earlier that year, including one copy in leather that he presented to the author himself, but this hardly counts as publication. Before *The Shadow over Innsmouth* had come only chapbooks and brochures. Hence the rarity of Lovecraft's signature on his published works. I would guess that perhaps a dozen, at the outside, of the unbound sheets of *The Shunned House,* and of the small edition of *The Shadow over Innsmouth,* were ever inscribed by Lovecraft. (Collectors considering major purchases should look for inscriptions, rather than mere autographs, and for established provenances linking the material to the original recipient.) During Lovecraft's final years, Julius Schwartz, editor and agent, also undertook to market Lovecraft's stories. There was obviously no deficiency of friends and correspondents willing to help to the best of their ability. Why then Barlow as literary executor?

I think the final answer must be the closeness of Lovecraft's personal relationship with Barlow. Barlow began in the spring of 1931, as did many correspondents of Lovecraft, by writing to him through *Weird Tales* to ask where he might find his older stories. At the time of their first correspondence, Barlow, an army brat, was living with his parents at Fort Benning, Georgia, and Lovecraft was visiting with his friend Henry S. Whitehead at Dunedin on the Gulf Coast of Florida. Because of his family's frequent moves, Barlow had had little formal schooling, but in the world of *Weird Tales* and the science fiction pulp magazines the brilliant youth found a fascinating preoccupation. At first, the correspondence of Lovecraft and Barlow was a modest one, with Lovecraft educating his young friend in the highlights of supernatural literature. About 1932, Barlow's father, a career army officer, retired on disability and established a homestead eighteen miles outside DeLand, Florida, near a hamlet called Cassia. Here was to be forged the close personal association of Lovecraft with young Barlow. In 1934, in connection with his annual southern jaunt, Lovecraft accepted the invitation of the Barlow family to visit. Barlow himself has recorded their memorable meeting as Lovecraft stepped from the bus in DeLand on May 2, 1934, in his *Marginalia* memoir, "The Wind That Is in the Grass," which is still basic reading for anyone who wishes to understand what Lovecraft and Barlow meant to each other. Soon the two were huddled deep in literary discussions, broken by occasional walks and jaunts further afield and by the insistence of young Barlow's parents that he retire at something like a reasonable hour.

In 1935, Lovecraft paid an even more extended visit to the Barlow household, staying several months. Not only did Lovecraft and Barlow plan and discuss literary work during this period, they also printed Frank Belknap Long's slim poetry collection *The Goblin Tower* on Barlow's press in the shed across the small lake that lay on the Barlow property. (Lovecraft and Barlow dubbed this lake "The Moon Pool" and the closet that housed Barlow's book and magazine collection "The Vaults of Yoh-Vombis," after the Clark Ashton Smith story.) Should you be so fortunate as to acquire a copy of this scarce book today, you very probably have in your hands a piece of presswork on which Lovecraft himself labored.

During these visits, Barlow's role as the principal trustee of Lovecraft's literary manuscripts was solidified. In return for assistance in preparing typescript, Lovecraft agreed to entrust his original manuscripts to Barlow. (Previously, he had destroyed most of his holographs upon publication of the material involved.) The manuscripts of *The Case of Charles Dexter Ward* and *The Dream-Quest of Unknown Kadath* came to Barlow for transcription, a task completed only after Lovecraft's death. In return for a "neatly typed" copy, Lovecraft presented his original *Commonplace Book* to Barlow. The *Commonplace Book* became the one significant Lovecraft work that Barlow personally supervised in publication, at the Becks' Futile Press during the summer of 1938. Two issues of the small amateur magazine the *Dragon-Fly* were printed by Barlow for the National Amateur Press Association, with contributions by many of the Lovecraft Circle; in addition, Lovecraft and Barlow plotted out the contents of a literary magazine, *Leaves*, whose first issue, as noted, appeared from Barlow's home in Leavenworth, Kansas, in 1937, and whose second and final issue appeared from the Becks' home in Lakeport, California, in 1938. *Leaves* was head and shoulders above most of the amateur magazines of the day in content and production; because of its rarity, it forms, together with Francis T. Laney's famed magazine the *Acolyte* (1942–46), a duo of early Lovecraftian publications that should certainly someday be reproduced in facsimile for collectors and students.

Lovecraft and Barlow were to meet face-to-face two more times, after Lovecraft departed for Providence to face accumulated stacks of mail in August 1935. At Christmastide, 1935, Barlow joined the members of the fabled Kalem Club for what had become their traditional holiday reunion in New York City. Lovecraft himself would customarily have Christmas dinner with Mrs. Gamwell at the boarding house across the rear garden at 66 College Street, and then depart by train or bus for the holiday reunion in New York. The 1935 reunion was the first opportunity for many of the Lovecraft Circle to meet Barlow face-to-face; and while Barlow took a lot of good-natured ribbing about his newly grown moustache and his demand for hotel accommodation with private bath, Frank Belknap Long and others of the Circle recognized his brilliance and promise. Barlow surprised not only Belknap with *The Goblin Tower*, but also Lovecraft with a 42-copy edition of his early tale "The Cats of Ulthar." Lovecraft and Barlow had been planning and debating the contents for a collection of Lovecraft's poetry for some time, and Lovecraft, upon hearing the rumor of a Barlovian surprise, feared that his poetry had been published prematurely, but, happily, such was not the case. Ultimately, two separate volumes of poetry were agreed upon: *Fungi from Yuggoth* and a collection of other poems. The former reached the stage of proof prints, some of which survive, but, like many of the other projects of the Dragon-Fly Press, was left incomplete when Barlow's parents separated in the summer of 1936 and Barlow and his mother returned to Kansas. The second issue of the *Dragon-Fly* was the last completed publication of Barlow's press. Other items that died a-borning were collections of poetry by Clark Ashton Smith (to be titled *Incantations*) and by Elizabeth Toldridge and a collection of letters by Henry S. Whitehead (to be titled *Caneviniana*). Paul

Freehafer ultimately published in the Fantasy Amateur Press Association a small gathering of the Whitehead letters for which Barlow had prepared the stencils. In 1944, Barlow contributed an excellent memoir of Whitehead to the first Arkham House collection of his fiction, *Jumbee and Other Uncanny Tales.* For some time, Barlow had also negotiated with the Wandrei brothers for a collection of Donald's poetry and Howard's art, but the negotiations were not successful.

The split-up of the Barlow household in Florida in the summer of 1936 also occasioned Barlow's final visit with Lovecraft, this time in Lovecraft's native Providence, where Barlow visited from July 28 through September 1. He stayed at the selfsame boarding house across the rear garden at 66 College Street where Lovecraft and his aunt were accustomed to take their Christmas dinner; and so there was no barrier to extended discussions and planning sessions. Busy at the time with his revision of Anne Tillery Renshaw's *Well-Bred Speech,* Lovecraft complained in correspondence about the demands placed upon his time by his young visitor. Barlow the bibliophile naturally had to visit all of the local bookshops, and one of the proprietors, Mary V . Dana, recorded her memories of Lovecraft's and Barlow's visit for Grant and Hadley's *Rhode Island on Lovecraft* (1945). Lovecraft and Barlow also made the rounds of the local museums. On August 15, they visited Newport (undoubtedly taking the ferry from Providence) and on August 20, Lovecraft's forty-sixth birthday, the last he would ever celebrate, they visited Salem and Marblehead in the company of another young member of the Lovecraft Circle, Kenneth Sterling, who had lived for a time in Providence the previous year. It has not been recorded for history, but one hopes very much that the day was concluded with a suitably festive birthday celebration, with ice cream, cake, and coffee loaded with sugar—all foods that Lovecraft especially adored.

Earlier, on August 7, old Adolphe De Castro, the onetime collaborator of Bierce, had joined Lovecraft and Barlow to pen acrostic poems on the name of EDGAR ALLAN POE whilst visiting St. John's Churchyard in Providence, just below the Sarah Helen Whitman home on Benefit Street where Poe came a-courting in 1848. De Castro stayed for a visit of five days, during which Lovecraft showed both his young and his old visitors a good bit of colonial Providence, to the extent that de Castro complained of "sore pedals."

Later, Lovecraft showed Barlow the ins and outs of genealogical research at the library of the Rhode Island Historical Society abutting the Brown University front campus on Waterman Street; here they established that they were indeed sixth cousins, descending in common from one John Rathbone or Rathbun, born 1658. (Through the good graces of E. Hoffmann Price, Barlow was to meet another close friend and distant relative of Lovecraft: James Ferdinand Morton, Jr., the curator of the Paterson, New Jersey, municipal museum, in California in 1939.) At the Historical Society library Lovecraft also showed Barlow the portrait of a long-deceased Rhode Island relative[1] who was the spitting image of Lovecraft himself. Finally, another scene in another bus station, this time in Providence. On September 1, Lovecraft bade farewell for the last time to his young friend, probably not without relief in terms of the time and energy expended upon the visit, but not yet knowing, at least consciously, that it would be their last meeting. After stopping to see C. L. Moore and her mother in Indianapolis, Barlow returned to Kansas City, where he enrolled in classes in the Art Institute.

During the fall of 1936, Mrs. Gamwell, Lovecraft's aunt, with whom he had shared the second floor flat at 66 College Street since May 1933, was shocked to discover an envelope marked "Instructions in Case of Decease" in a desk containing Lovecraft's personal papers. Whether she questioned her nephew on this subject at the time is unknown, but the fears of the seventy-year-old aunt soon were tragically fulfilled. In December 1936 and January 1937 Lovecraft's intestinal "grippe" was worse than usual, and by February 1937 he was a very ill man indeed. In actual fact, he was dying of cancer of the intestine, although a final diagnosis was not made until the time of his hospitalization in March. From Providence, telegrams went out to Lovecraft's closest associates, including Barlow, advising them of his serious illness.

Finally, on March 15, a telegram advised of Lovecraft's death that morning. Almost immediately, Barlow boarded the bus for the long ride to Providence, where he arrived several days after Lovecraft's funeral on March 18. So as not to disturb Mrs. Gamwell in her grief, which was severe, since she herself had lost her only son at the age of eighteen in 1916 and had never expected to lose her nephew Howard, Barlow stayed at the YMCA in downtown Providence on Broad Street, a fifteen- or twenty-minute walk from 66 College Street. There, during the days, he sorted and classified Lovecraft's literary papers. Authorized by Lovecraft's "Instructions" to make the first selection from Lovecraft's books and magazines, he chose about 150 volumes, including the copy of *The Shunned House* that he himself had bound for the author and Lovecraft's file of *Weird Tales*. Since Mrs. Gamwell wished to retain Lovecraft's holograph instructions, Barlow asked her to copy this document for him in her own hand; this copy, together with Lovecraft's original envelope, came to reside in the John Hay Library through Barlow. On the twenty-sixth, he and Mrs. Gamwell signed a contract formalizing his management of Lovecraft's posthumous literary affairs, in return for a commission of three percent upon any sales.

During these same days, contact was made with John Hay librarian S. Foster Damon of Brown University. The John Hay Library, built in 1905 on the northwest corner of Prospect and College Streets, was the next-door neighbor of Lovecraft's final home at 66 College Street. (The latter was removed in the 1950s to 65 Prospect Street and has for many years been the home of John C.

A. Watkins, retired chairman of the Providence Journal Company; the original site of Lovecraft's final home is now the site of Brown University's List Gallery.) Damon and several others of the Brown English faculty, including Bob Kenny, knew of Lovecraft, but the acceptance of the papers of such an obscure writer was certainly a risky bet at the time. Impressed, perhaps, with the brilliance of young Barlow, Damon made the right decision and accepted the Lovecraft papers on deposit at Brown. In a card to Damon dated 1939, Barlow expressed his intention that the papers become the property of Brown University following his death.

During the period 1937–42, of which more anon, Barlow sent to Brown all the remaining material Lovecraft had given him during his lifetime, with the sole exceptions of his personal letters from Lovecraft and the notebook in which Lovecraft had written his second draft of "The Shadow out of Time." The letter file came to Brown University after Barlow's death in 1951; the autograph manuscript of "The Shadow out of Time" arrived there many years later, donated by the estate of one of Barlow's Mexican students. The *Weird Tales* file came back to Brown University, as did the bits and pieces of Lovecraft's papers that Barlow had removed from 66 College Street to Kansas City after Lovecraft's death. While Brown University's Lovecraft Collection has grown considerably from Barlow's original deposits, these still form the basic core of the John Hay collection. Few authors who died as obscure as Lovecraft have enjoyed the benefit of a comparable preservation of their manuscripts and literary papers. Through Barlow himself, the files of Lovecraft's letters to Lillian D. Clark, his elder aunt who had died in 1932, and to Elizabeth Toldridge, an elderly retired government employee with whom Lovecraft had corresponded copiously for many years, both came to the Brown University Collection; and through the generosity of Barlow's mother and his own literary executor George T. Smisor, Barlow's own letters from Lovecraft reached the John Hay Library in 1951.

By the mid-'forties, Barlow had become a permanent resident in México, engaged in full time research on México's native races and their languages; his correspondence with the library and involvement in Lovecraftian affairs by necessity became less. During this period, he planned and carried out with the assistance of Miguel Barrios E. the publication of a newspaper in the native Náhuatl language; the title was *Mexihkayotl* and some thirty-four issues appeared during this period. While seeking a printing press, in 1946, Barlow proposed to the John Hay librarian, Christine D. Hathaway, that Brown University trade him a printing press and type for the full remainder of his fantasy collection in México and Florida. Before the arrangement could be fully investigated, however, Barlow apparently secured a press elsewhere. Nothing further developed.

By the late forties, a Brown University graduate student, James Warren Thomas, made application to consult the Lovecraft papers still owned by Barlow, which permission Barlow granted. When August Derleth found the resultant Thomas thesis too unbalanced to permit publication in full, Barlow reluctantly consented to his judgment, while counselling that permission should not be denied simply because the portrayal of Lovecraft was in part unflattering. Derleth, for his part, felt that Thomas placed too much of the blame for the failure of Lovecraft's marriage on Lovecraft himself, and was fearful that the full publication of Lovecraft's racial remarks in letters to his aunt Lillian D. Clark might be harmful to his reputation. The Thomas matter was virtually the last Lovecraftian matter to come to Barlow's attention before his untimely death.

In 1948 he travelled to Europe to study codices and manuscripts in libraries there; in 1950, he was preoccupied with the publication, by hand-press, of a new journal, *Mesoamerican Notes* (which was continued after his death by the University of the Americas) and with gaining a command of the Mayan language. Strained by overwork and threatened by aspects of his personal life, he committed suicide in his Azcapotzalco, D.F., home on January 1, 1951. At the time of his death, he was some months short of his thirty-third birthday, but had already accomplished as much in his own scholarly field as many scholars do in a full lifetime. The *Boeltin Bibliografico de Antropologia Americana* (1947, 1950) contains bibliographies of Barlow's scholarly work in his chosen field. In addition to *Mesoamerican Notes*, he was editor of the scholarly journal *Tlalocan*, initially in collaboration with his friend George T. Smisor.

While understanding the disappointment of older friends, particularly Cook, one might wonder what was the real difficulty with the choice of Barlow as Lovecraft's literary executor. His unsettled circumstances following the death of Lovecraft were probably a considerable part of the perceived difficulty. Some of the summer of 1937 he spent back in Florida; then, in 1937-38, he continued classes at the Kansas City Art Institute, where Thomas Hart Benton was one of his teachers. During the summer of 1938, he paid his first visit to México, contracting a serious case of typhus, and he spent the winter of 1938-39 with the Beck family in Lakeport, California (whence he issued the second and final issue of *Leaves*) and in the San Francisco area, where he assisted Groo Beck, one of the three brothers, in the preparation of George Sterling's *After Sunset*, published by John Howell in 1939 with a prefatory note by Barlow. In 1939-40 he entered junior college in San Francisco and in 1941-42, the University of California at Berkeley, where he became a student of Alfred Kroeber in the anthropology department. During part of this period, Barlow's mother, Bernice, came to California to live with her son.

Barlow kept up a few Lovecraftian associations in California. As remarked above, he met James Ferdinand Morton, Jr., on a jaunt with E. Hoffmann

Price in 1939. He knew several of the early Los Angeles area fans, including Paul Freehafer. He contributed small bits and pieces of Lovecraftiana to Francis T. Laney and Larry B. Farsaci for their amateur journals the *Acolyte* and *Golden Atom*. By 1943, however, he was spending most of his time in México, initially working at microfilming source documents with his friend and associate George T. Smisor. After 1942, his Lovecraftian contacts were few and far between. Not that Barlow forgot about Lovecraft. He carefully preserved his own letters from Lovecraft in his home in México. For many years, the anniversary of Lovecraft's death called forth a poetic tribute from Barlow; a number of these were published by August Derleth in *The Shuttered Room* (1959). In 1939–40 Barlow had become associated with the "Activist" school of poets led by Lawrence Hart in the San Francisco Bay area, and his later tributes bear the hallmark of the stark word-images of the Activist school. Barlow published two slim sheaves of poetry during his lifetime, *Poems for a Competition* (Sacramento, 1942) and *View from a Hill* (Azcapotzalco, 1947). After his death, Lawrence Hart published *Accent on Barlow: A Commemorative Anthology* (San Jose, 1962).

The frustrations incident upon Barlow's unsettled circumstances reached a boiling point in 1938. August Derleth and Donald Wandrei were still trying to market Lovecraft's work to the New York publishing houses, when during the summer of 1938 *The Commonplace Book* emerged in an edition of about seventy-five copies from the Futile Press of the brothers Beck. Barlow had provided manuscript for this project and seen it through press and made a token royalty payment of ten dollars to Mrs. Gamwell. Derleth and Wandrei, I believe, became concerned that scattershot projects by the young Barlow, then visiting México, could subvert their efforts to secure professional publication for Lovecraft's work.

Sometime later that year Derleth and Wandrei visited Providence and expressed their concerns to Mrs. Gamwell. She referred them to Albert A. Baker, the lawyer who had handled Lovecraft's estate, and shortly thereafter there went out to Barlow from Baker a letter demanding that he return all the manuscripts and supernatural books and magazines that he had removed from College Street and that he surrender the management of Lovecraft's literary affairs to Derleth and Wandrei. (This entire matter was discussed extensively by George T. Wetzel in his essay "Lovecraft's Literary Executor," which originally appeared in Scott Connors's *Continuity* [1976] and was reprinted just shortly before Wetzel's death in 1983 in *The Lovecraft Scholar,* a collection of his work edited by Sam Gafford and John Buettner and published under the imprint of the Hobgoblin Press.) On October 12, 1938, Barlow wrote a dignified reply to Baker, in which he cited Lovecraft's "Instructions in Case of Decease" in defense of his actions but expressed in addition willingness to cooperate with Derleth and Wandrei in the publication of Lovecraft's work, while at the same time waiving the three percent commission upon which he had agreed with Mrs. Gamwell.

Albert Baker was taken aback by Barlow's letter, having apparently been unaware of the "Instructions in Case of Decease" at the time he wrote. As executor, Baker expressed his willingness to let matters continue to stand as they did so long as Barlow agreed to continue to cooperate with Derleth and Wandrei in the publication of Lovecraft's work on behalf of Mrs. Gamwell. He expressed confidence that all parties to the erstwhile dispute seemed well-disposed to Mrs. Gamwell, and expressed his opinion that she continued to deserve their goodwill and support. As executor, he withdrew his demand that Barlow return the books, magazines, and manuscripts that he had removed from 66 College Street. Of course, the primary concern of Baker, as executor, was to preserve any substantial financial benefit that Lovecraft's literary work might produce for Mrs. Gamwell. Lovecraft's own estate had been proved at less than $500, consisting almost entirely of the mortgage on a quarry operated by the DeMagistris family in Providence. (This property, which Lovecraft probably inherited from Whipple Phillips, was the object of visits by Lovecraft and James Ferdinand Morton, Jr., in quest of mineral specimens during several visits of the latter to Providence.) At Mrs. Gamwell's death in 1941, she left an estate of about $10,000, evenly divided between her friend Edna W. Lewis and her cousin Ethel P. Morrish. (Her 1940 will left the royalties from *The Outsider and Others* to Derleth and Wandrei.) However, as the last survivor of Whipple Phillips's children and grandchildren her funds were slim, and at the time of Baker's correspondence with Barlow in 1938 even Lovecraft's modest funeral expenses were still unpaid.

While Wetzel criticizes Baker for not making a more definitive resolution of the question of Lovecraft's posthumous literary affairs, one must remember that he was dealing with an estate that was already very poor, whose prospects hardly seemed to justify further contractual arrangements and expense. It is possible, also, that Baker may have been aware of Lovecraft's failure to complete his divorce of Sonia Greene, although I do not consider this likely. (Another attorney, Ralph M. Greenlaw, had handled Lovecraft's divorce suit in 1929.) Having reached an accommodation between the disputing parties that seemed to produce the maximum benefit for his client Mrs. Gamwell, Baker undoubtedly considered his duties discharged. Wetzel makes an ample discussion of the legal considerations, and the matter may yet be determined by a court of law if the descendants of Mrs. Gamwell's cousin Ethel P. Morrish should proceed with an action to establish ownership of at least one-half of the Lovecraft literary estate in the Rhode Island courts. Baker had had a long association with the Lovecraft family, having been Winfield S. Lovecraft's guardian during his incompetency (1893–98) and H. P. Lovecraft's guardian during his minority (1893–1911) and then executor following his death. I believe his reminiscences were used at least in part by Winfield T. Scott in his essay "His Own Most Fantastic Creation" in *Marginalia*. When Baker died in 1959, he was at age ninety-seven the oldest practicing attorney in Rhode Island. He had had a fairly prominent career, being city attorney for Providence during the period when he was guardian for Lovecraft and his father.

The emotional effects of this temporary debacle were overcome only with time. Barlow's hurt can be measured from part of his reply to Baker:

> I am sorry that Mrs. Gamwell believes—as you state—that I "rushed her" in fulfilling Howard's instructions. It had been my hope to reach Providence before his death—when I could not, I went to give what small aid I could. As she will tell you, I knew his literary affairs better than anyone else, and it is not without significance that he wished me, and not Mr. Derleth, or Mr. Wandrei, or some other person, to take care of them.
>
> A copy of this letter will reach Mrs. Gamwell—I am moved by the keenest desire to cooperate with her; but in view of the above-mentioned circumstances, not, perhaps, fully known to you, cannot feel obliged to comply with your demands. it is immeasurably depressing to be confronted with such an attitude over the gifts and will of my dead friend.

Hoping to restore, to the extent possible, good feeling, Baker concluded the reply in which he withdrew his earlier demands as follows: "I think that there has been some misunderstanding which could have been avoided if you and I had been so situated that we could have had a personal interview and discussed the matter." Regrettably, Mrs. Gamwell would appear to have remained disturbed the longest of anyone concerned. In correspondence to Barlow in the fall of 1938, she was still agonizing over the correctness of her actions. One hopes that she eventually attained peace of mind regarding her handling of her nephew's property; perhaps one day the file of her correspondence at Arkham House will tell us more. Certainly, the publication of *The Outsider and Others* in November 1939, must have been an event thoroughly pleasing for her, although one wonders how this old-fashioned, determined little New England lady reacted to the dust jacket by Virgil Finlay. Perhaps the Margaret Brundage *Weird Tales* had more than steeled her for the Finlay dust jacket. During 1940, she became ill and spent part of her time in a nursing home; she died of cancer at the end of January 1941, the last of the descendants of Whipple Phillips. I do not believe that Barlow had corresponded with her after 1938; in one of his memorial poems, he expressed lack of knowledge as to the fate of Mrs. Gamwell and of the home at 66 College Street. Presumably, Derleth or another Lovecraft associate finally filled him in.

After 1938, Derleth and Barlow strove to mend their differences. A report of a dispute which surfaced in Robert W. Lowndes's amateur magazine *Le Vombiteur* in 1939 was denied. In his foreword to *Marginalia*, Derleth paid tribute to the assistance of Barlow, whose "generous assistance" with the

Lovecraft papers he described as "unstinting." For his own part, Barlow did help to provide Derleth with the texts he needed and agreed to provide a memoir for *Marginalia* and the introduction for Henry S. Whitehead's *Jumbee and Other Uncanny Tales*. I suspect Barlow was impressed with what he saw in the Arkham House publication of Lovecraft's work in handsome omnibus volumes. After the matter of his removal of the books, magazines, and manuscripts from 66 College Street was resolved, his only difference with Derleth would appear to have been an editorial one, over the inclusion of the collaboration "Through the Gates of the Silver Key" in the first Lovecraft omnibus volume. Generally speaking, Barlow seems during his Mexican years to have considered the Lovecraft literary estate well managed by Arkham House. Whatever the legalities may be, Derleth always described this charge as having devolved fully on Arkham House with the death of Barlow in 1951.

If you wish to understand the relationship of R. H. Barlow and H. P. Lovecraft, by all means seek out a copy of *Marginalia*. Barlow's brief memoir "The Wind That Is in the Grass" tells the story well and movingly. The snapshots that Barlow took of Lovecraft's study in 1937, also reproduced in that book, are a moving tribute to their association. One wishes that the photographs were of much better quality, so that more details of this book-lined study might be revealed. One would love to get a look at the titles on the spines, the mementos and paintings hanging on the walls, and all the rest of the detail that the snapshots only hint of. Had Lovecraft died as well-known as he is today, Clark Ashton Smith's suggestion that 66 College Street be permanently preserved as a museum in his memory might have been realized.

Finally, I would suggest a reading of the Barlow "tributes" as published in *The Shuttered Room*, which is dedicated to Barlow and those other members of the Lovecraft Circle who "have gone to join him in the Great Abyss beyond Kadath in the Cold Waste." There one may read of Barlow's humble breakfast at the Providence YMCA, which he feels Lovecraft would have liked; of an unwelcome homosexual "pass" from a man in the restroom of the "Y" during the same visit; of the as-yet blank inscription on the Phillips monument for Lovecraft and of the wilted flower that Barlow removed from the grave and subsequently lost; of his concern for, and lack of knowledge of Mrs. Gamwell and the fate of the 66 College Street house—all the small, everyday human events that actually pull most strongly on our emotions. In the last analysis, if the truth be told, I believe that Robert H. Barlow became something very close to a son for H. P. Lovecraft. What more natural than that a man should leave the management of his posthumous affairs to his son.

That Barlow had to spread his own wings, to make his own career, was a necessity for a man of his genius. He did so magnificently; tragically, he cut off his own life early, but not before he had provided very well indeed for the literary posterity of his mentor, H. P. Lovecraft. Yielding to the superior opportunities of Messrs. Derleth and Wandrei, he helped facilitate the publication of Lovecraft's work despite earlier differences. Equally important, he saw to it that a permanent base for Lovecraft research was established in the John Hay Library of Brown University. Everyone who has done research there or will do so in the future must be thankful for the foresight and generosity of Robert H. Barlow. It is entirely fitting that when we speak of credit for the growth of Lovecraft's reputation and the publication of his work, we speak first of August Derleth and Donald Wandrei. If we are to be allowed a second breath, however, mention must be made of the role of Robert H. Barlow. The fame of his brief life is secure without any mention of his role in connection with the Lovecraft papers; but the portrait of his life is left incomplete. If these pages have imparted a glimpse of this important aspect of his life, the author will be content.

Notes

1. Commodore Abraham Whipple (1733–1819).

Some Final Thoughts for Readers of This Collection

I am very grateful to S. T. Joshi for making a reality of the idea of a collection of my Lovecraftian essays. Mr. Joshi has done yeoman's work not only in selecting the best of these writings but also in assisting me to improve my writing. I hope the essays collected here will make an interesting and pleasurable reading experience for persons interested in H. P. Lovecraft. (If you dislike Lovecraft and his work, I hope you haven't struggled along to this point!) The focus of my writing on Lovecraft has always been biographical—I do not pretend to be a literary critic. When I first discovered Lovecraft's writings as a teenager, *The Dream Quest of Unknown Kadath* was my favorite among all the wonders that I found in his work. (I can remember reading it several times during the week when I first borrowed *At the Mountains of Madness* on seven-day "new title" loan from the local public library in 1964.) Today, I would probably cite "The Colour out of Space" and "The Music of Erich Zann" as favorite stories, although I also like especially the dark melodrama of "The Shadow over Innsmouth" and "He." Of Lovecraft's stories, I have assayed to write about only *Kadath*, "He," and "The Silver Key."

I have been especially interested in Lovecraft's family background, and "Quae Amamus Tuemur" collected herein tries to summarize the most important progress my collaborators Chris J. Docherty and A. Langley Searles and I have made in this specialized subject area. In my essays on "Lovecraft's Parental Heritage" and "The Silver Key," I have tried to show how Lovecraft's family background touches his work. My readers must judge how well I have succeeded. Both my 1993 Phillips family genealogy and the 2003 monograph that my collaborators and I published on Lovecraft's Devonshire family background are available on film at local LDS family history libraries, for readers who want to pursue these subjects further. Apart from Foster, Rhode Island, other writers have done better work on Lovecraft's New England backgrounds than I.

I particularly recall Bob Marten's magisterial work on the setting of Lovecraft's story "Pickman's Model" in Boston's North End. I wrote in the Esoteric Order of Dagon Amateur Press Association about the relationship of Lovecraft's mother and Louise Imogen Guiney (1861–1920) and about Lovecraft's juvenile clubhouse on Great Meadow Hill, but it was Bob Marten who actually took me to see the Guiney home in Auburndale and the site of the Great Meadow Clubhouse in Rehoboth.

Another specialized interest of mine has been Lovecraft's involvement in the amateur journalism hobby in 1914–37. Since October 2004, I have edited the *Fossil*, the quarterly journal of the history of the amateur journalism hobby. Interested readers can view the text portion of my issues online at thefossils.org. One very small discovery I made concerning the amateur publication of Lovecraft's work was that Wilson Shepherd's edition of *History and Chronology of the Necronomicon*, usually dated to 1938, was actually first circulated in the November 1937 mailing of the American Amateur Press Association. Lovecraft died while the American was still a-borning. His primary activity was in the Hoffman-Daas faction of the United Amateur Press Association (1914-26), and after it faded, in the National Amateur Press Association. He served as president of both of these associations: of the United in 1917-18 (when the poet Elsa Gidlow [1898-1986] was president of the rival United faction) and of the National in 1922-23.

The reader of this collection will naturally want to know a little bit about the author of the essays collected here. I was born in Cincinnati, Ohio, on August 24, 1948—alas! four days after Lovecraft's birthday—the son of Kenneth W. Faig, Sr. (1918-2003) and Edith F. (Kennedy) Faig (1919-1976). I have one sibling, a sister Susan M. (Faig) Schlitz (b. 1952), a former registered nurse who now lives in a Chicago nursing home; she is the widow of Robert L. Schlitz (1952-1995), whom she met and married in a former nursing home. I have a high school diploma (1966) from Greenhills High School in Cincinnati, Ohio, where my proudest achievements were a first place in the Ohio State Achievement Tests in English as a freshman and a third place in Latin as a junior. I have a *magna cum laude* B.A. degree (1970) from Northwestern University in Evanston, Illinois, where I majored in mathematics and minored in physics. I spent two years (1970-72) as a graduate student in mathematics at Brown University in Providence, Rhode Island. Since 1973, I have worked as an actuary (F.S.A., 1978) at North American Company for Life and Health Insurance (1973-87), Allstate Life Insurance Company (1987-89), and PolySystems, Inc. (1989 to date). I married Carol A. Gaber in 1979 and we have two children, Edith (born 1980) and Walter (born 1984). I met Carol at North American Company, where she worked as a programmer. We like to joke that working on insurance policy schedule pages was the origin of our romance. In Illinois, I have lived in Chicago (1973-76), Evanston (1976-89), and Glenview (1989 to date). Outside of my writings on H. P. Lovecraft, I have published several essays on Arthur Machen and professional essays on escheat of life insurance and murderous beneficiaries in the *Journal of Insurance Regulation* (2003).

I first encountered the work of H. P. Lovecraft as a teenager in a copy of Wise and Fraser's *Great Tales of Terror and the Supernatural*, which my maternal grandmother had presented to my parents. It had been stored on an upper shelf in a clothing closet, but I did not allow it to gather much dust after my discovery. I ordered my first few Lovecraft books from a department store book department, but I soon found I could buy books directly from Arkham House, and working my way through the Arkham House backlist was the delight of my high school years. While I was an undergraduate student at Northwestern University, I used the resources of the university library to read many of the works discussed by Lovecraft in "Supernatural Horror in Literature." While I was a graduate student at Brown University, I explored some of the riches of the Lovecraft Collection in the John Hay Library. I was a founding member of the Esoteric Order of Dagon Amateur Press Association in 1973, and also belonged to the Fantasy Amateur Press Association in 1976–91 and to the Necronomicon Amateur Press Association while it was active. Since the late 'nineties, I have also been a member of the mainstream National Amateur Press Association and the American Amateur Press Association, as well as of The Fossils, the alumni association of the amateur journalism hobby. (The last offshoots of the United Amateur Press Association to which Lovecraft belonged withered in the first decade of this century, although they are not beyond the possibility of a revival.) I have been doing micro-editions of Lovecraftiana from my own Moshassuck Press since 1987 and published under that imprint two collections of work by Lovecraft's friend Edith Miniter (1867–1934) and a novel by Lovecraft's uncle Franklin C. Clark (1847–1915). I returned to Providence for the Lovecraft Centennial Symposium sponsored by Brown University in 1990. I do not expect to live to attend the symposium for the centenary of Lovecraft's death in 2037—I would be eighty-nine years old if I survived to that year—but I like to imagine the great strides that will have been made in research concerning Lovecraft and his work by then.

I believe that Lovecraft's work belongs to all his readers. No one school of thought or perspective has a monopoly or even a privileged position. I can recall vividly being on a Lovecraft panel with my friend Robert Weinberg at the World Fantasy Convention in Chicago in 1996. Also on the panel were two young female science fiction writers They had their own story to tell about the influence of Lovecraft's work on their own writing, and while theirs was a perspective very different from my own, I respected their right to present it and was honored to be on a panel with them. While I have tried over the years to expand what we know about H. P. Lovecraft, my work and its perspectives are certainly not for everyone. I dislike gore even when in the able hands of a director like Stuart Gordon, but at the same time I recognize that physical horror plays a significant role in Lovecraft's work. As a very private person, I shrink from being asked about Lovecraft's sexuality, but at the same time I recognize that sexuality plays a strong, if non-explicit, role in his stories. I believe that Lovecraft was a rationalist and an atheist, but I do not reject out of hand suggestions that he may have been an occultist or was subconsciously influenced by occult beings. Lovecraft as philosopher, aesthete, dreamer—all these I must leave to abler hands than my own. Lovecraft's texts belong to all his readers. By 2037, I expect that Lovecraft's *opera omnia* and much, if not all, of the secondary literature concerning the writer and his work will be available in digitized form. While traditional printed material will still have a role to play in scholarship, I like to think that the explosion of digitized knowledge will benefit Lovecraft studies.

For thirty-five years, membership in the E.O.D. amateur press association has been my window on the wider world of Lovecraftian happenings. But the way knowledge is transmitted is changing rapidly. Internet sites like the one maintained by Donovan Loucks (hplovecraft.com) contain a tremendous amount of information about H. P. Lovecraft and his world. Blogs like the one conducted by Chris Perridas (chrisperridas.blogspot.com) often contain an unexpected richness of information—including eBay discoveries like a photograph of Sonia Lovecraft's eighty-fifth birthday celebration and a document containing the address of Sonia's millinery business in Brooklyn. I even find that I still make an occasional discovery in a traditional book. Knowing of my interest in old cemeteries, my daughter Edie presented me with a copy of Douglas Keister's *Stories in Stone: A Field Guide to Cemetery Symbolism and Iconography* (Salt Lake City: Gibbs Smith, 2004). I had always wondered about the particular symbolism of the cross with crown on the central monument of the Phillips lot in Swan Point Cemetery in Providence. Keister's book (p. 113) informs me that the cross with crown is a special symbol of York Rite Masonry—and of course Whipple V. Phillips (1833–1904) and his son Edwin E. Phillips (1864–1918) were both Masons. I hope I will continue to have the joy of making small discoveries like this one. One substantial project I would still like to complete is an annotated edition of Lovecraft's 1926 and 1929 Foster, Rhode Island, travelogues.

A final thank you to S. T. Joshi for making this collection possible. Joshi has been at the forefront of the explosion of knowledge concerning H. P. Lovecraft since his own entry into the field in the mid-1970s. The improved texts of Lovecraft's fiction and poetry that we now enjoy have been the work of S. T. Joshi. He has also been at the forefront of cataloguing and publishing the surviving corpus of Lovecraft's correspondence. He wrote the standard biography of Lovecraft and the standard bibliography of his works. His critical essays on Lovecraft's work have also been of large importance. In a word, he has helped to assure that Lovecraft's future students and readers will enjoy the best possible basis for the extension of knowledge and the formation of opinions. The idea of a Lovecraft symposium in 2390 (five hundredth birth anniversary) or 2890 (one thousandth birth anniversary) fascinates me more than the idea of a symposium for the centenary of his death in 2037. If human civilization manages to survive to 2390 or 2890, I believe that the H. P. Lovecraft worldline 1890–1937 will continue to be studied in those far future years.

The cosmic insignificance of human civilization on this planet was an important aesthetic and philosophical theme in Lovecraft's work. He would tell us that the survival of the human race to 2390 or 2890 or any other specified future year is totally insignificant in the history of the universe from its birth until its death. Lovecraft notwithstanding, his worldline 1890–1937 remains a significant (if arguably measure zero) subset of the worldspace occupied by the human race on this planet (5MM B.C.–?). However we cope with our cosmic insignificance, we may nevertheless hope, as did Lovecraft himself, to find *multum in parvo*. Measure zero sets can be fascinating, complex places for their members. It has been my lifelong belief that H. P. Lovecraft's writings enrich our humanity. They do not teach despair, but rather the perspective of looking at all existence from the perspective of "the fixt mass whose sides the ages are" ("Continuity," *Fungi from Yuggoth* XXXVI). A natural disaster, a pandemic, a cataclysmic episode of human self-predation (e.g., a worldwide nuclear, chemical or biological war)—any of these could spell the end of humanity on this planet. Lovecraft's cosmic perspective does not impoverish, but rather enriches our everyday lives as human beings on this planet.

Printed in the United States
215855BV00003B/9/P